The Palgrave Lacan Series

Jacques Lacan is one of the most important and influential thinkers of the 20th century. The reach of this influence continues to grow as we settle into the 21st century, the resonance of Lacan's thought arguably only beginning now to be properly felt, both in terms of its application to clinical matters and in its application to a range of human activities and interests. The Palgrave Lacan Series is a book series for the best new writing in the Lacanian field, giving voice to the leading writers of a new generation of Lacanian thought. The series will comprise original monographs and thematic, multi-authored collections. The books in the series will explore aspects of Lacan's theory from new perspectives and with original insights. There will be books focused on particular areas of or issues in clinical work. There will be books focused on applying Lacanian theory to areas and issues beyond the clinic, to matters of society, politics, the arts and culture. Each book, whatever its particular concern, will work to expand our understanding of Lacan's theory and its value in the 21st century.

Sinan Richards

Dialectics of Love in Sartre and Lacan

palgrave
macmillan

Sinan Richards
King's College London
London, UK

ISSN 2946-4196 ISSN 2946-420X (electronic)
The Palgrave Lacan Series
ISBN 978-3-031-45797-5 ISBN 978-3-031-45798-2 (eBook)
https://doi.org/10.1007/978-3-031-45798-2

Cover illustration: Luis Diaz Devesa

This Palgrave Macmillan imprint is published by the registered company Springer Nature Switzerland AG.
The registered company address is: Gewerbestrasse 11, 6330 Cham, Switzerland

Paper in this product is recyclable.

Pour ma mère, ma sœur, et mon cœur,

The subject is not master of his thoughts. He is caught in a futile struggle, expressing without any certainty what is nonetheless inexpressible.
F.W.J. Schelling

What I have just written is false. True. Neither true nor false, like everything written about the mad, about men.
Jean-Paul Sartre

Dites n'importe quoi, ça touchera toujours au vrai. *[Say any old rubbish. It will always touch the truth.]*
Jacques Lacan

Preface—*Love: A Pleasing Malady*

Love is a pleasing Malady,
For which my heart no cure can find:
Yet if I could get Remedy,
I'le rather dye than cure my mind.

[*L'amour est un mal agréable,*
Dont mon cœur ne saurait guérir:
Mais quand il serait guérissable,
Il est bien plus doux d'en mourir.]
Scudéry

In the first volume of Madeleine de Scudéry's *Clélie, histoire romaine…* (1654–1660), Scudéry translates and reinterprets a poem fragment by Sappho. Scudéry writes, 'Love is a pleasing Malady/For which my heart no cure can find'. Love, it would seem, is a paradoxical state—a 'pleasing Malady' [*un mal agréable*]. The opening lines of this verse elegantly capture love's oxymoronic characteristics, and yet, somehow for Scudéry, love remains necessary: 'Yet if I could get Remedy/I'le rather dye than cure my mind' (*Clelia* 44). Scudéry's poem captures an emotional and conceptual deadlock that is characteristic of what love offers the subject according to Jacques Lacan, and it describes an impasse that I believe also fascinated Jean-Paul Sartre. Scudéry's words also encapsulate my contention that love in Lacan's ('anti') philosophy is as violent as it is nourishing, as imagined as it is real, and as *necessary as it is impossible*. Love, as it is understood here, is an always already missed task and one whose handling is continually unfinished. Love fulfils a necessary aspect of human subjectivity while simultaneously being a task that forever remains open and incomplete or, as Lacan put it in his 1972 seminar, '*encore*.'

Much like the status of the psychotic subject in Lacan's baroque theoretical project, love requires no cure, for there is nothing to cure. Love is also not a symptom; instead, we could say, it is the *ceaseless hope for the sinthome*. It is the moment the subject is *sent home*. Cast in this way, for Lacan, love is the task of *keeping it together* in the face of an impossible circumstance, a labour of handling our many pathological symptoms in such a way that they never truly bubble up or materialise, and, strictly speaking, keeping sane in this way is the final power of Sartre's *in itself for itself*—or, God herself, as we will see.

For Lacan, the lover's task is necessary—we must insist, even if we know this to be a futile and impossible task.

* *
*

Paris, France
April 2023

Sinan Richards

Acknowledgements

I would like to offer my sincerest thanks and express my gratitude to the *British Academy* for generously funding my research over the last few years. Earlier versions of some of the material included in this book appeared as: '*La Mère dangereuse* Reimagining Scudéry's *Carte de Tendre* with Lacan's Graph of Desire,' *French Studies* 75(2) Oxford: OUP (2021); 'The Logician of Madness: Fanon's Lacan,' *Paragraph* 44(2) Edinburgh: EUP (2021). 'Sartre and Lacan: Reading *Qui Perd Gagne* Alongside *Les Non-Dupes Errent*,' in *Freedom and the Subject of Theory: Essays in Honour of Christina Howells*, eds. Oliver Davis and Colin Davis. Oxford: Legenda (2019); '*Rühre nicht, Bock! denn es brennt*' Slavoj Žižek and Christianity, eds. Sotiris Mitralexis and Dionysios Skliris. London: Routledge (2018).

I would also like to thank my editors at Palgrave, Beth Farrow, Asma Azeezullah, and Nobuko Kamikawa, as well as the following friends: Chiara Ambrosio, Joanne Brueton, Claire Couret, Martin Crowley, Oliver Davis, Louise Delumeau, Agnès Derail, Marie Duic, Patrick ffrench, Derek Hook, Christina Howells, Katherine Ibbett, Kevin Inston, Niall Le Mage, Dasha Lisitsina, Daniel Martini, Philippa Macintyre, Ian Maclachlan, Jo Malt, Jordanna Mancina, Clara Manco, Eric Méchoulan, Calum Neill, Nick Philippe-Desneufbourgs, Marc Porée, Jean-Michel Rabaté, Serene Richards, Judith Still, Nadia Sukhdeo-Goodman, Susan and David Walden.

Contents

1 Introduction—The Necessity of Impossibility 1

2 Ontologically Sick—Sartre's Challenge 15

3 The Decorator Crab—Lacanian Misunderstandings 61

4 A Momentary Folly—The Wish to Be Loved 117

5 *Sent Home*—Lacan's Final Heresy 215

6 Conclusion—Hold Me Tight [*Serre-moi fort*] 259

Bibliography 267

Index 279

Abbreviations

Gilles Deleuze

Critical *Essays Critical and Clinical*
AO *Anti-Oedipus* (co-authored with Felix Guattari)
Islands *Desert Islands and Other Texts (1953–1974)*

Frantz Fanon

Alienation *Alienation and Freedom*

Jacques Lacan

De la psychose *De la psychose paranoïaque dans ses rapports avec la personnalité suivi de Premiers écrits sur la paranoïa*
É *Écrits*
AÉ *Autres écrits*
Scilicet *Scilicet n°6/7*
S0 *L'Homme aux loups*
SI *Freud's Papers on Technique*
SIII *The Psychoses*
SV *The Formations of the Unconscious*
SVI *Desire and Its Interpretation*
SVII *The Ethics of Psychoanalysis*
SVIIa *L'Éthique de la psychanalyse* (transcript)
SVIII *Transference*

SIX	*L'Identification*
SX	*Anxiety*
SXI	*The Four Fundamental Concepts of Psychoanalysis*
SXIV	*La Logique du fantasme*
SXV	*L'Acte psychanalytique*
SXVI	*From an Other to the other*
SXVII	*The Other Side of Psychoanalysis*
SXVIII	*D'un discours qui ne serait pas du semblant*
SXIX	*… or Worse*
SXIXa	*…Ou pire, le savoir du psychanalyste (conférences à Saint-Anne)*
TBW	*Talking to Brick Walls*
SXX	*Encore*
SXXa	*Encore* (transcript)
SXXI	*Les Non-dupes errent*
SXXII	*R.S.I.*
SXXIII	*The Sinthome*
SXXV	*Le Moment de conclure*
Troisième	*La Troisième*
SXXVII	*La Dissolution (séminaire de Caracas)*

Jean-Paul Sartre

TE	*Transcendence of the Ego*
BN	*Being and Nothingness*
EN	*L'Être et le Néant*
EH	*Existentialism is a Humanism*
B	*Baudelaire*
NFE	*Notebooks for an Ethics*

F.W.J. Schelling

Weltalter	*Die Weltalter/Ages of the World* (second draft, 1813)
PR	*Philosophy and Religion*

Madeleine de Scudéry

Clelia	*Clelia, An Excellent New Romance*
Clélie	*Clélie, histoire romaine…*

List of Figures

Fig. 3.1	Saussure's tree schema	90
Fig. 3.2	Lacan's two doors	90
Fig. 3.3	Lacan's formulas of sexuation	96
Fig. 4.1	Lacan's complete graph of desire	118
Fig. 4.2	Lacan's Rudimentary graph of desire	123
Fig. 4.3	Lacan's two doors schema	127
Fig. 4.4	Graph of desire stage 1	128
Fig. 4.5	Rudimentary graph with labelling	129
Fig. 4.6	Intermediary graph of desire	130
Fig. 4.7	Graph of desire with Che Vuoi?	147
Fig. 4.8	Scudéry, M. 1654. La Carte du Pays de Tendre, Clélie (François Chauveau, La Carte du Pays de Tendre (1654), engraving, from Madeleine de Scudéry, Clélie, Histoire romaine. Paris: Courbé. Public domain, via Wikimedia Commons)	154
Fig. 4.9	Sadist's view	206
Fig. 4.10	Sadist as Barred Subject $	207
Fig. 5.1	Borromean Knot (inexact for illustrative purposes)	216
Fig. 5.2	Isolated Symbolic Ring (Borromean Knot)	217

1

Introduction—The Necessity of Impossibility

Sartre's Challenge

> The mad never do anything but realize the human condition in their own way (Sartre).

> Thus, rather than resulting from a contingent fact—the frailties of his organism—madness is the permanent virtuality of a gap opened up in his essence. And far from madness being an "insult" to freedom, madness is freedom's most faithful companion, following its every move like a shadow (Lacan).

Love is an overdetermined concept, and yet it seems that, as subjects, we speak of little else. As Lacan puts it in *Encore*, 'speaking about love, indeed, people have done little else but speak of love in analytic discourse […] to speak of love is in itself a jouissance' (83, translation modified). In a different, but related, discussion Lacan says love 'doesn't stop being written' ['*ne cesse pas de s'écrire*'] (94/86). In concrete terms, it would be imprudent to claim that this book has determinedly clarified anything about the concept of love in formal or even abstract terms, nor should you expect factual or empirical answers from such a work on love. Instead

S. Richards, *Dialectics of Love in Sartre and Lacan*, The Palgrave Lacan Series,
https://doi.org/10.1007/978-3-031-45798-2_1

of answers, various questions have motivated my thinking, for example, was Sartre right to oppose love to freedom? Do subjects need to love in Lacan's psychoanalysis? Is love a metaphysical concept? And, rather than attempt to define something which resists any quantitative explication, I have worked on elucidating an understanding of love that emerges from the many debates in twentieth-century French philosophy and psychoanalysis, focusing predominantly on the period beginning with the publication of Sartre's *Being and Nothingness* in 1943, and ending, somewhat arbitrarily, with Lacan's death in 1981. However, a word of caution, this book is not a study on the inheritance Lacan may or may not owe Sartre, and, though it touches upon these delicate questions, it offers no pretences to exhaustibility. Instead, the task of this book is to understand love as a conceptual failure and impossible dilemma.

Although Sartre (b. 1905) and Lacan (b. 1901) were virtually contemporaries (their respective deaths are also only a year apart 1980 and 1981), for some reason, Sartre and Lacan 'don't look the same age' (Miller 2012: 7). This incongruity between biography and intellectual development is also evident in the way it somehow seems more natural to place the younger Sartre before Lacan when discussing both philosophers together, for example, as Clotilde Leguil does in *Sartre avec Lacan* (2012), or as I have done here. Because, in the twentieth-century history of French philosophy, Lacan only seems to emerge as a philosophical force from 1966 onwards, upon the publication of *Écrits*—even though, by 1966, Lacan's seminars would already have been running for over fourteen years. Lacan, then, emerges with structuralism, while Sartre's philosophical emergence occurred much earlier, notably in the first phase of his philosophical ascendancy, which occurred well before 1950.

'Actually,' the philosopher and critic Jean-Michel Rabaté writes, 'it may come as a surprise that the author who paved the way for Lacan's central concept—the signifier as offering a privileged mode of access to affects—was not Freud or Ferdinand de Saussure but was none other than Jean-Paul Sartre' (Rabaté 2020: 121). As Rabaté explains, Sartre's *Sketch of a Theory of Emotions* (1939) prefigures Lacan's central concern with the signifier and signified. In *Sketch of a Theory of Emotions,* 'Sartre suddenly hits upon a loaded couple of terms, the binary of signifier and signified' (Rabaté 2020: 122). I wholeheartedly agree with Rabaté's conclusions here, not least because Lacan is quite comfortable citing Saussure in his seminars—a relatively uncommon practice for this psychoanalyst (perhaps to throw his auditors off scent regarding the Sartrean heritage of his theory of signification). But, crucially, because, as Rabaté reminds us, 'Sartre highlights the practice of deciphering' (Rabaté 2020: 121). And Rabaté here develops Sartre's idea of deciphering using Sartre's own words: "the behaviour of the subject is in itself what it is (if we call "in itself" what it is *for itself*), but it is possible to decipher it by appropriate techniques, as one deciphers a written language" (Sartre in Rabaté 2020: 121). For Rabaté, then, Sartre not only foreshadows Lacan's concern with signification but also prefigures Lacan's obsession with deciphering codes in the subject's speech. This is a truly remarkable insight, and one which remains one of my central considerations here since, as we will see, the importance of deciphering the written language of the *for itself* is precisely how Lacan will come to understand the translating of the subject's unconscious, essentially adapting this typically Sartrean view of the world.

Undeniably, then, Lacan was an engaged reader of Sartre's philosophy. As Miller explains, 'without putting up much of a fight, Lacan thus adopted to his ends, the finer points of Sartre's thought' (Miller 2012: 9). According to Miller, Lacan even identified and borrowed a concept originally found in Sartre's *Being and Nothingness*. Miller highlights Sartre's final sentence in a note on page 442 of the original French edition, 'the mad never do anything but realize the human condition in their own way' [*un fou ne fait jamais que réaliser à sa manière la condition humaine*] (*BN* 374, translation modified; see also *EN* 442), and, somewhat remarkably, as this book hopes to show, Sartre's seemingly insignificant passing remark in *Being and Nothingness* prophetically reveals the cardinal insight of Lacan's overall psychoanalytic project.[1] As Miller points out, Lacan says in "Presentation on Psychical Causality" published in *Les Temps Modernes* in 1946, before being republished in *Écrits*:

[1] It is unclear from Miller's words if this reference comes directly from Lacan's annotated copy of *Being and Nothingness* or if Miller discovered this connection himself, and although it would be fascinating to investigate this firsthand, "the Lacan archive" has, regretfully, not been made public.

> Thus, rather than resulting from a contingent fact—the frailties of his organism—madness is the permanent virtuality of a gap opened up in his essence. And far from being an "insult" to freedom, madness is freedom's most faithful companion, following its every move like a shadow' (*É* 144/176).

According to Sartre and Lacan, how does 'madness' manifest itself, in its own way, in the human condition? And how does this relate to my understanding of love in Lacan's psychoanalysis? Furthermore, why does Lacan see madness as constituted by a permanent rupture? And why does he see madness as freedom's most loyal companion, perpetually in liberty's shadow? To put it much too crudely, for Lacan, love is a form of madness that is central to human subjectivity, and the 'permanent virtuality of a gap opened up in his essence' is central to understanding love as it relates to human subjectivity. Sartre and Lacan's view that being human is closely related to madness is similar to the argument that F.W.J. Schelling makes in *Die Weltalter* [*The Ages of the World*] (1813); for Schelling, being is something that God *contracts*, and, as we will see, Schelling's fragmentary 1813 text lays some of the groundwork for Lacan's view of human subjectivity as irremediably marked by madness.

For Sartre, as well as for Lacan, love demands ontological and intellectual enquiry. Love is a concept as deserving as the notions of 'freedom' or 'finitude' of philosophical study, and, therefore, I take love to be a philosophical notion akin to 'freedom,' demanding careful examination. Thus, I begin with Sartre who offered a powerful, though to my mind somewhat flawed, theory of love in *Being and Nothingness.* Sartre's main philosophical preoccupation in the first phase of his philosophy, roughly up until the mid-to-late 1940s, was the concept of freedom. As Christina Howells puts it in *Sartre: The Necessity of Freedom* (1988), 'freedom [...] is the pivot of Sartre's writings' (Howells 1988: 1) and Sartre's fascination with the unrooted and unfixed qualities of the subject can be gleaned as early as the publication of Sartre's *The Transcendence of the Ego* published in 1936.

Sartre adopts the phenomenological method, which is a means of offering 'a description of transcendental consciousness investigated through an intuition of essence', and crucially 'the object of phenomenology is *transcendental*, not in any mystical sense but rather in so far as it is not identified with any particular individual' (7). Therefore, 'the phenomenological method is intuition—not in the general sense of insight, but in the philosophical sense of what is apprehended by the mind as immediate evidence' (8). By 1943, Sartre discounts both realism and idealism, and instead chooses to focus on a return to the 'phenomenon of being' [*le phénomène d'être*] (Gardner 2009: 55). And with this method, Sartre proposes a total rejection of the notion of the unconscious (Rabaté 2020: 121). Indeed, 'Sartre is in full agreement with phenomenology in so far as it attempts to avoid dualism, to refuse any notion of an unknowable essence (the Kantian noumenon) underlying appearances' (Howells 1988: 14). However, Sartre's steadfast adherence to the phenomenological method is not to say that he was a naïve realist. Sartre sought to highlight the radical contingency of consciousness, and he set up a sophisticated and original philosophical framework within which he claimed love is impossible for the subject.

Sartre pitted love against freedom, and by extension, permanence against contingency, and it is for this reason that love is impossible. According to Sartre's dialectic of self and other, and, as a result of his ontological account of *for itself* and *in itself*, love falls on the side of permanence and fixity and is both an impossible and futile passion. As I intimated above, the early Sartre was an exemplary philosopher of contingency. The subject is destined to choose between his/her/their radical freedom and any rooted stability or permanence, and it was for this reason that Sartre rejected the concept of love so forcefully. Because love is a quasi-metaphysical force that only weighs the subject down, slows them, and roots them in the world, and, although my analysis of Sartre's philosophy of love might sometimes appear truculent, this is not the case. I am not unsympathetic to Sartre's early philosophy, and I believe, as I outline early in chapter one, Sartre's account of love in *Being and Nothingness* is pivotal to the birth and development of Lacanian psychoanalysis. Moreover, many twentieth-century philosophers owe Sartre a great debt, notably Lacan and Deleuze. However, it is also my contention that Sartre's account of love did not consider the metaphysical malleability of the concept in quite the same way as Lacan had, for example. Sartre did not sufficiently complicate his philosophy of love. As Rabaté highlights, Lacan once 'quipped, what distinguishes Sartre in his often brilliant, suggestive, but misleading descriptions, is a "wonderful talent for side-tracking"' (Rabaté 2020: 124; and Lacan in Rabaté 2020).

From chapter three onwards, then, I turn to Lacan as a result of the ostensible claim of the metaphysical insufficiency of Sartre's treatment of the concept of love. For Lacan, love signifies many things at different times, and this makes any discussion of love in Lacan's philosophy quite complicated—as we will see.[2] If Sartre did not sufficiently complicate love, Lacan sought to overcomplicate it, but, as I suggested above, Sartre and Lacan are not as far apart as is sometimes suggested. As Leguil details, there are many connections between these two thinkers (2012: 17). Indeed, as Howells argued in *Mortal Subjects* (2011), Lacan shares Sartre's view of love and desire to some extent—with important differences (131). Therefore, I contend that it is not an unusual move to read these two thinkers together, and, for my part, I show a possible connection between these two by appealing to Schelling's middle philosophy in order to draw onto-theological connections between both thinkers. Schelling's highly speculative, onto-theological reading of God both connects the metaphysical aspect of love with the Sartrean fascination with freedom, as well as opening a possible path to Lacan's onto-theological view of love.

Lacanian Fables

Lacanian psychoanalysis is not a science, nor does it claim to be one. At a 1975 conference held at Yale University, Lacan, taking questions from students, stated:

> I do not imagine myself doing science when I am plainly doing literature. [...] It is literature because it is written and it sells; and it is literature because it has effects, and effects on literature (*Scilicet* 32).

[2] In *L'Amour Lacan* (2009), Jean Allouch attempts to chronicle all the different Lacanian interpretations of love. In what follows, I do not adopt Allouch's strategy; instead, I try and focus on one interpretation of love.

Lacan was a fabulist, a fantastical storyteller, and a master of language, as we will see, and, unlike Sigmund Freud, Lacan did not seek to understand the biological world, nor did he attempt to discover verifiable, falsifiable, or quantifiable claims about mental processes. None of Lacan's theories are empirically true, but they could be said to resonate as philosophically true. Furthermore, Lacanian psychoanalysis is not a branch of cultural studies in the sense that its focus is not solely on a socio-historical analysis of the world. Equally, Lacan's work is not a work of pure philosophy: if anything, as Lacan famously suggested, he produced a kind of 'anti-philosophy' (*AÉ* 314).[3] As Rabaté succinctly puts it, this time in *Psychoanalysis and the Subject of Literature*, '[Lacan] continued to criticise philosophy for an original sin that consisted in placing consciousness as the origin of meaning' (2001: 15), and so, as we will see, Lacan is interested in meaning and its connections to knowledge, and Lacan's method often swerves into metaphysical speculations in order to assert transcendental claims. For Lacan, following Freud, consciousness is not even the site of subjective self-understanding. It is my contention that Lacan concocted a psychoanalytic discipline that sought to posit a set of transcendental (this time, in the fully mystical sense) markers to define subjectivity and its pitfalls, and Lacan's intellectual strategy engages with all the disciplines mentioned above.

One of Lacan's central contributions to the history of French philosophy was his introduction of the three psychoanalytic realms: the Real, the Symbolic, and the Imaginary (R.S.I.). According to Lacan, the Imaginary

---

[3] As Colette Soler remarks in "*Lacan en antiphilosophe*," the term '*antiphilosophe*' [antiphilosopher] was a popular slur in the eighteenth-century, deployed predominantly against non-Enlightenment philosophers (2006: 121). Anti-philosophy, then, is a pertinent description of Lacan's philosophical project, since Lacan's ideas are opposed to the Enlightenment. The differences between Lacan and the Enlightenment are most evident in the many parallels between Lacan's philosophy and F.W.J. Schelling's onto-theology and speculative metaphysics, as well as in the anti-Enlightenment themes of Lacan's "Kant with Sade," as we show later. Therefore, we contend that Lacan's 'anti-philosophy' is undoubtedly a work of philosophy, and in *SXXV, Le Moment de conclure* [*The Moment to Conclude*], Lacan clearly refers to his psychoanalytic practice as a work of philosophy:

> What I am doing here (as Althusser noticed [...]) is philosophy. [...] Philosophy is all we know how to do. My Borromean knots are also philosophy. It is philosophy that I have handled as best I could by following the current, if I may say so, the current that results from Freud's philosophy (28).

contains and contextualises the ego and their demands and needs. The Symbolic is the realm of the subject, intersubjective relationships, and the subject's relationship with the big Other in language. And, the Real describes that which exists outside symbolisation. For Lacan, without these three interrelated concepts, philosophy mistakenly remains in the Imaginary realm, unable to capture the transcendental Real which may lie beyond mere phenomena of appearances—'without the recognition of the symbolic order, we are caught in the imaginary' (Leguil 2012: 312). Importantly, the concept of the Imaginary is not shorthand for the imagination, the Symbolic is not social constructivism, and the Real is not another word for reality, nor is it the underlying "reality of reality," or some hidden wisdom that underscores our existing world.

At its heart, Lacanian psychoanalysis's primary concern is to conceptualise the relationship between knowledge [*savoir*] and truth [*vérité*], and Lacan proceeds to treat this relationship at different times from many different angles. For example, the distinction Lacan draws between the Symbolic and the Real is one way he treats the problem of the relationship between knowledge and truth. Another way Lacan handles this relationship is through his conceptualisation of sexual difference, or *sexuation*. Crucially, however, sexual difference does not aim to uncover the essence of sexuality, and Lacan's theory of sexual difference does not refer to anatomy, physiology, or biology. Lacan's intellectual interests is partly in linguistics, namely through the works of Ferdinand de Saussure and Roman Jakobson, and it should, therefore, come as no surprise that Lacan's treatment of sexual difference refers to problems in language, to elucidate the ontological and epistemological consequences of the Symbolic and the Real, for example, the effect of *there is no sexual relationship* [*non-rapport*] on the subject.

It might seem an obvious point, but it is also essential to mention that Lacan worked in the French language, and this fact played a significant role in the way that Lacan's psychoanalysis developed. Lacan recognised the importance of the French language to his philosophy in *SXXIII, Le Sinthome*, when he stated: 'my *lalangue*, specifically French' [*lalangue* mienne, à savoir le français] (*SXXIII* 3, translation modified/11). For Lacan, recognising the centrality of the French language to his philosophy is not to privilege one language over another; for example, he is not seeking to build a hierarchal system of languages where some languages are intrinsically more privileged in accessing the Real, but instead, Lacan wished to highlight the centrality of the subject's mother tongue in their relationship to the inaccessible *lalangue.* As Julia Kristeva explains in *Passions of Our Time,* for Lacan, 'the speaking being is subjected to the influence of the family linguistic code, and every mother tongue imprints itself on the organization of the "own," including one's own body' (Kristeva 2013: 74). *Lalangue* is one word that Lacan employs to designate those moments in our subjective experience that exist beyond the subject's conscious recognition of them, or we could say outside symbolisation, others include the unconscious, *~~La~~ femme* [~~The~~ Woman], and *l'Amour* [Love], as we will see.

As Jean-Claude Milner explained in *For the Love of Language* (1978), '*lalangue* is thus one language among others, to the extent that once postulated, it prevents by incommensurability the construction of a class of languages which includes it; its most direct figuration is indeed the mother tongue' (1990: 61). Therefore, all subjects get a sense of *lalangue* in their maternal language, and Lacan is notoriously tricky to understand because he manipulates the French language for a French audience in order to illustrate the French 'bits of' *lalangue.*[4] The bifurcation of the French language at Lacan's hand resembles a strategy that, according to Lacan, Joyce managed to pursue in the English language, 'Joyce wrote in English in such a way that the English language no longer exists' (*SXXIII* 3). Concomitantly, manipulating language in this way is Lacan's means of dissolving *le langage,* and a method of appreciating *lalangue* for his French auditors. It is difficult, if not outright impossible, to approach the Lacanian corpus without bearing in mind the particularly enigmatic manner by which Lacan handles and deploys his mother tongue.

One of the tasks in this book is to demonstrate the asymmetric relationship Lacan builds between knowledge and truth, a task that, as I have said, Lacan describes as the relationship between the Symbolic and the Real. I do this to situate the concept of love in Lacan's psycho-philosophical

[4] I write "bits of" because when Lacan discusses the Real, which is to say those bits of subjective experiences that exist outside symbolisation, Lacan specifically says 'bouts de réel.' Because, for Lacan, we can only access the Real in a piecemeal way. See (*SXXIII* 104).

project and extrapolate a Lacanian theory of love that responds to the challenge laid down by Sartre in *Being and Nothingness*. Lacan also treats the problem of the incongruity of knowledge and truth in terms of the uneasy relationship between necessity and impossibility, and this formulation will be the angle through which I will predominantly tackle the question here. I have chosen to focus on the relationship between necessity and impossibility from the frame of 'love' and '~~The~~ Woman,' rather than from the angle of the 'unconscious,' for example. In many ways, Lacan agrees with Sartre that love is an attempt to become *in itself for itself*, except that Lacan discusses this in terms of *~~The~~ Woman* and argues that the subject must identify with 'her' as a necessary by-product of the impossibility of love. Whereas, for Sartre, attempting to become *in itself for itself* is the impossible wish to become God himself, as he puts it in *Being and Nothingness,* 'in-itself-for-itself [is] a consciousness that has become substance, a substance that has become its own cause, a Man-God' (*BN* 746). Whereas, in Lacan's baroque psycho-philosophical project, the subject must identify with God herself, we could say Woman-God, and this book hopes to show why trying to identify with 'her' is the necessary impossibility I call love.

For Lacan, then, love is not necessarily a redemptive or optimistic concept. Indeed, as Howells explains, 'love is doomed to disappoint us, for it can never measure up to the demands of unconditionality we make of it. It makes promises of union and permanence that it can never keep, and is ultimately a *tromperie,* a deception' (2011: 131). As I will show, for Lacan, love is the impossible deception of reuniting with this Woman-God, and the only modest addition I make in this book is to suggest that this deception (and the resultant alienation) is necessary for any subjective insight within the Lacanian frame.

To explicate this complex Lacanian onto-theology, I explore Lacan's notions of *jouissance* and the idea that *there is no sexual relationship,* and I explain these concepts by continuous reference to subject formation. Chapter two sets the scene with Sartre's concomitant view of love and desire as impossible and futile passions, as well as highlighting his view that the subject's wish to become *in itself for itself* is doomed from the start. Later in chapter two, I compare Sartre with Schelling to show the relevance of onto-theological speculation concerning Sartre's philosophical account of the world in *Being and Nothingness*, since Schelling's earlier philosophy was similarly faced with an insurmountable problem concerning an ungrounded *for itself*. By comparing these philosophers, I suggest that Schelling's philosophical reinterpretation of the Fall of Man might be an appealing solution to Sartre's negative challenge about love, desire, and the impossibility of *in itself for itself*. The third chapter directly emerges from the conclusions from the second and seeks to further problematise the premise underlying the Sartrean *in itself* by introducing Lacan's baroque metaphysical speculations. We begin by investigating what I call Lacan's method of *temporary detours* to highlight the importance of Lacan's reliance on metaphysical solutions to conceptual problems. By discussing the importance of the notion of language to Lacan's conceptual scheme, I offer a preliminary account of some of the key philosophical issues with which he wrestles. The aim of this chapter is to show the validity of the Schellingian-Lacanian underdetermination of *in itself* and I argue through the metaphor of the decorator crab that the *in itself for itself* is not a concept that can entirely be excluded as simply impossible. *In itself for itself*, or God, haunts Sartre's philosophy, and it seems to me that the concept returns as *feminine jouissance* in Lacan's later work, as I will show. Chapter four investigates the Lacanian corpus in substantial detail and offers a careful reconstruction of Lacanian psychoanalysis as it relates to the formation of the subject in the Symbolic Order. Since Lacan makes numerous references to Madeleine de Scudéry's *Map of Tender* throughout the seminars, I analyse this seventeenth-century map of loving friendship alongside Lacan's graph of desire.[5] Both the map and the graph are strikingly visually similar, and it is vital to show the extent of Lacan's uncanny semblance with Scudéry for appreciating his baroque and literary style. Finally, in the final chapter, I reconnect Lacan's onto-theological turn with its roots in Sartre's fascination with the passions, notably love. In the end, this book hopes to show Lacan's view that the lover's task is a necessary one. Lacan believes that we must insist on loving, even if we know this to be a futile and impossible task.

[5] See Figs. 4.10 and 4.11 on pages 119 and 120.

References

Howells, Christina. 1988. *Sartre: The Necessity of Freedom*. Cambridge: Cambridge University Press.

———. 2011. *Mortal Subjects: Passions of the Soul in Late Twentieth-Century French Thought*. Cambridge: Polity.

Kristeva, Julia. 2013. *Pulsions du temps*. Paris: Fayard. English edition: Kristeva, J. 2018. *Passions of Our Time* (trans: Borde, C and Malovany-Chevallier, S.) New York: Columbia University Press.

Leguil, Clotilde. 2012. *Sartre avec Lacan: Corrélation antinomique, liaison dangereuse*. Paris: Navarin.

Lacan, Jacques. 1966. *Écrits*. Paris: Seuil. English edition: Lacan, J. 2006. Écrits. (trans: Fink, B.) London: W.W. Norton & Company.

———. 1975a. *Le Séminaire de Jacques Lacan, Livre XX, Encore (1972–1973)*. Paris: Seuil. English edition: Lacan, J. 1998. The Seminar of Jacques Lacan. Book XX, Encore, (1972–1973). (trans: Fink, B.) London and NY: W.W. Norton & Company.

———. 1975c. Conférences et entretiens dans des universités nord-américaines. In *Scilicet n° 6/7*, 32–37. Paris: Seuil.

———. 1978. *Le Séminaire de Jacques Lacan, XXV, Le Moment de Conclure (1977–1978)*. Patrick Valas, unpublished transcript. http://www.valas.fr/IMG/pdf/s25.pdf. Accessed 4 Apr 2023.

———. 2001. *Autres écrits*. Paris: Seuil.

———. 2005. *Le Séminaire de Jacques Lacan, Livre XXIII, Le Sinthome (1975–1976)*. Paris: Seuil. English edition: Lacan, J. 2016. The Seminar of Jacques Lacan, Book XXIII, The Sinthome (1975–1976). (trans: Price, A.R.) Cambridge: Polity.

Miller, Jacques-Alain. 2012. Préface. In *Sartre avec Lacan: Corrélation antinomique, liaison dangereuse*, ed. Clotilde Leguil, 7–10. Paris: Navarin.

Milner, Jean-Claude. 1978. *L'Amour de la langue*. Paris: Seuil. English edition: Milner, J-C. 1990. For the Love of Language (trans: Banfield, A.). New York: The Macmillan Press.

Rabaté, Jean-Michel. 2020. Jacques Lacan's Evanescent Affects. In *Affects and Literature*, ed. Alex Houen. Cambridge: Cambridge University Press.

Sartre, Jean-Paul. 1934. *La Transcendance de l'ego*. Paris: Vrin. English edition: Sartre, J-P. 1960. Transcendence of the Ego (trans: Williams, F. and Kirkpatrick, R.). New York: Hill and Wang.

———. 1943. *L'Être et le néant*. Paris: Gallimard. English edition: Sartre, J-P. 2021. Being and Nothingness (trans: Richmond, S.). London and NY: Routledge.

Schelling, Friedrich Wilhelm Joseph von. 1997. *Ages of the World: Die Weltalter/ The Abyss of Freedom (second draft, 1813)*. Trans. Judith Norman. Ann Harbour: University of Michigan Press.

Soler, Colette. 2006. Lacan en antiphilosophe. *Filozofski vestnik XXVII* 2: 121–144.

2

Ontologically Sick—Sartre's Challenge

'He Was My Teacher'

> The for-itself tries to escape its *de facto* existence, in other words its being-there, as an in-itself of which it is not in any way the foundation, and that this flight takes place toward an impossible and constantly pursued future where the for-itself might be in-itself-for-itself, i.e., an in-itself that would be its own foundation in relation to itself (Sartre).

Gilles Deleuze, in a short but compelling piece on Jean-Paul Sartre's influence on French post-war thought "He Was my Teacher" (1964), places Sartre at the heart of the more radical developments of French philosophy after the Liberation. For Deleuze, Sartre was '[one of those teachers] who [brought] us something radical and new. […] in those days, who except for Sartre knew how to say anything new? Who taught us new ways to think?' (*Islands* 77). For Deleuze, Sartre's philosophy ushered in a new way of thinking about freedom, and a new way to think in general; to think *with* literature, to blur the boundaries of classical philosophy and related disciplines. Sartre, Deleuze argues, forced philosophy ('proper') to change its place: 'philosophy was changing its arena, leaving the sphere of judgement' (*Islands* 78). Deleuze is right of course, Sartre's

S. Richards, *Dialectics of Love in Sartre and Lacan*, The Palgrave Lacan Series,
https://doi.org/10.1007/978-3-031-45798-2_2

influence stretches far beyond the confines of philosophy and literature, and into all aspects of French thought and culture.

Sartre's literary method of focusing on particular instances of human interaction—such as the look [*regard*] of another—or of attempting to determine what the movements of certain beings say about their ontological identity—as with the café waiter—demonstrates his unique ability to extend the abstract into an imaginative reading of the human, which amounts to an attempt to try and uncover the origins of the *for itself*. According to Deleuze, these novel interventions in the history of philosophy motivated future thinkers to work within Sartre's more representative, less abstract framework, Deleuze says, 'and every time, essence and example would enter complex relationships that gave a new style to philosophy' (*Islands* 79). For example. Lacan's focus on the gaze, intersubjectivity, and shame in *SI, Freud's Papers on Technique*, owes a substantial debt to Sartre's *regard*—as Lacan acknowledged: 'I cannot refrain at this point from referring to the author [Sartre] who has described this play in the most magisterial manner' (*SI* 215).[1] It is important to appreciate the continued importance of Sartre's philosophy to the developments of twentieth-century French thought, and it is fitting that I should begin with *Being and Nothingness*, to retrace an account of love that heavily influenced Lacan, which he enlisted and refashioned.

In this chapter, then, I elucidate Sartre's account of love and desire and ask whether his claim that love is impossible is justified. In 1943, Sartre makes an original and complex argument to demonstrate how these two forces are 'doomed to failure' (*BN* 502). Overall, Sartre maintains that love and desire are impossible, and that they end in failure. For Sartre in *Being and Nothingness*, love and desire are impossible for three interconnected reasons:

1. Love and desire are impossible by virtue of being two examples of the alienation we feel as a result of being-for-others; Sartre's insight is that love and desire are merely two attempts to try and achieve the impossible as *in itself for itself*. In effect, this amounts to the impossi-

[1] Moreover, Jean-Michel Rabaté explains in *Psychoanalysis and the Subject of Literature* (2001) that 'Lacan names three authors he has used at various points of his career in order to invent and refine notions: Poe, […], Racine, […]; and Sartre's political plays' (4).

bility of love and desire at an ontological level. As we will see in the final chapter, I contend that Lacan's assertion that ~~*The*~~ *woman* does not exist is closely related to this ontological deadlock described by Sartre in *Being and Nothingness.*

2. For Sartre, in loving another, while attempting to achieve the ideal as *in itself for itself,* the subject ends up renouncing their subjectivity to serve the subjectivity of their lover, which leads to masochism.
3. Desiring another necessarily objectifies the other, and since what the subject desires is the free subjectivity of the other that is perpetually beyond their reach, their touch immediately makes the other an object for them, which leads to sadism.

In this chapter I engage these three arguments and question whether we are content for love and desire to carry the negative hue bestowed onto them by Sartre.

In order to appreciate Sartre's account of love and desire, a general account of his philosophical project must first be considered, with an emphasis on the relationship between *in itself* and *for itself* explored in *Being and Nothingness*'s introduction and conclusion. Sartre splits being into two regions, *in itself* and *for itself,* and I will investigate how Sartre relates being to freedom. I reconstruct some of the core arguments in *Being and Nothingness* to suggest towards the end of this chapter that Sartre has not managed to make both regions communicate in quite the way in which he had hoped. Sartre's ideal of *in itself for itself* is pivotal to my reconstruction of the (im)possibility of love, and in the latter half of this chapter, I will also contrast *in itself for itself,* as well as Sartre's broader ontological scheme, with F.W.J. Schelling's split in being from his second draft of *Ages of the World* [*Die Weltalter*]. This comparison will show how both Sartre and Schelling are investigating similar philosophical themes. However, in juxtaposing both philosophers' arguments in relation to being I will suggest that what underpins Sartre's ontological account of *in itself* and *for itself*—and the resultant impossibility of *being-for-others,* love, and desire—leaves Sartre vulnerable to the charge that everything outside his account of *in itself* is the product of an illusion. This philosophical challenge addressed to Sartre will prepare the turn to Lacan's psychoanalysis to consider his arguments about the (im)possibility of love.

Preambling Love and Desire in Sartre's *Being and Nothingness*

The centrality of Sartre's concept of freedom is notoriously implacable in *Being and Nothingness* and in many of his other writings. For Sartre, freedom is at the very core of humankind and, by extension, man's place in the world. Freedom is where one will inevitably end up, regardless of whether we appreciate or recognize it. Sartre is unequivocal on this point precisely because it is central to his project, and he even says: 'freedom is [...] the fabric of my being' (*BN* 576). The 'fabric' or 'stuff' of my being, Sartre argues, is nothing other than freedom itself. For Sartre, to *be* is to exist, and existing is necessarily to exist freely.

It might be unsurprising to state that *Being and Nothingness* is Sartre's attempt to (successfully or unsuccessfully) resolve multiple philosophical problems that have haunted the history of Western philosophy since at least Descartes. In the first instance, Sartre's moves are that of semantic and intellectual 'ground clearing' (Gardner 2009: 41). Sartre imports from Husserl and Heidegger a phenomenological lexicon and a novel method of doing philosophy. He says from the first sentence of *Being and Nothingness* that: 'by reducing the existent to the series of appearances that manifest it, modern thought has made considerable progress' (*BN* 11). For Sartre, the phenomenological focus on the phenomenon is a convincing way to avoid problematic dualisms—inside/outside—and Sartre's aim in *Being and Nothingness* is to carry forward this phenomenological legacy without falling into the traps of either realism or idealism. As Sartre often reads him, Husserl falls into idealism, and Heidegger, though often on the right lines, is fundamentally mistaken by having removed consciousness from Dasein. Sartre says:

> Being is everywhere. Admittedly, we could apply to consciousness the definition that Heidegger reserves for Dasein, and say that it is a being for whom, in its being, its being is in question—but one would have to

> complete it and formulate it roughly like this: *Consciousness is a being for whom in its being there is a question of its being, insofar as this being implies a being other than itself.* (*BN* 23).

Sartre's task, therefore, is a deceptively simple one. He wants to ask: does the world exist pre-consciously? And, what is consciousness's role in the structuring of the world? Having weaved consciousness back into Dasein, Sartre has radically re-conceptualized it. In so doing, Sartre has reintroduced a problem that Heidegger had sought to eliminate in the first instance. The problem is that, with the introduction of consciousness into being, how are we to explain the relationship between phenomenon and consciousness? For Sartre, consciousness does not create being; being just simply *is*. Indeed, being, too, does not bring about consciousness. Instead, Sartre is keen to point out that being is characterized by a *transphenomenality* of being (*BN* 7). For Sartre, when I apprehend this pencil, for example, I apprehend the phenomenon of the being of the pencil in one state; from this one angle, in this light, along these particular circumstances. However, I also appreciate that the being of the pencil possesses a multiplicity of possible particular appearances, which makes it what it is. Therefore, the pencil's being is transphenomenal. Sartre stresses that this is not a backhanded way of alluding to a Kantian Noumenon, that somehow behind the pencil's given being there is a transcendental truth beyond the reach of humans: 'that does not mean that being is hidden behind the phenomena […] nor that the phenomenon is an appearance that refers to a being distinct from it (the phenomenon has being qua appearance, i.e., it indicates itself on the foundation of being)' (*BN* 7–8). For Sartre, this reintroduction of consciousness into Dasein does not restate the aforementioned problem since it has been accounted for appropriately. This problem, as outlined in traditional philosophical terms [explaining the relationship between phenomenon and consciousness], is uncouth for Sartre. As Howells explains, 'consciousness and phenomena do not exist in isolation: consciousness is always *of* something; phenomena always appear *to* consciousness' (Howells 1988: 15). Crucially, however, for Sartre, the relationship that exists between phenomena and consciousness is not one of coincidence or identity. Rather, the relationship is characterized by difference and opposition: 'if consciousness is always *in* and *of* the world, this is not to say that it is one *with* the world; on the contrary, its relationship with the world is one of negation' (Howells 1988: 15). Indeed, Sartre says:

> There is nothing substantial about consciousness; it is a pure "appearance," where this means it exists only to the extent to which it appears. But it is precisely because consciousness is pure appearance, because it is a total void (since the entire world is outside it), because of this identity within it between its appearance and its existence, that it can be considered as the absolute (*BN* 16).

Since consciousness is never characterized by self-coincidence but rather by difference and opposition, Sartre is keen to attribute to consciousness a negating ability; at the heart of consciousness is a *nothingness.* He says, 'nothingness must be given in the heart of being' (*BN* 57). Indeed, Sartre also says that this is because 'if negation did not exist, it would be impossible to raise any question at all—in particular the question of being' (*BN* 57). Consciousness, then, is the non-substantial absolute, which carries at its heart: nothingness. Being itself must be in perpetual questioning through negation, and negation has referred Sartre to nothingness [*le néant*].

Sartre is able to distinguish between *being in itself* and *being for itself* through consciousness and nothingness. The being *in itself* is a thing that possesses a fullness of being; it is identical to itself and is positive. The table at which I am sitting is as it appears. It possesses a self-identification with itself—it's being table and has no consciousness. Whereas, as I said earlier, consciousness is a being not characterized by self-coincidence; so, it is 'the being that is its own nothingness' (*BN* 86). This, Sartre calls *being for itself.* The *for itself,* forms the early architectonics of Sartre's conception of the subject in *Being and Nothingness,* and it is a being who, Sartre says, simply is. 'The for-itself is. It is, as some may say, even if its way of being is such that it is not what it is and it is what it is not' (*BN* 129). What is clear is that this conception of the subject as fundamentally unprivileged—i.e., that holds no special relation to itself, is a prescient anticipation of much post-war French philosophy. Indeed, anticipating Lacan, Sartre gives the radical incommensurability of (not) knowing oneself an extraordinary velocity in the development of the subject in contemporary French thought.

Returning to *Being and Nothingness*, for Sartre to build a concrete phenomenological picture, the two forms of being—*for itself* and *in itself*, must be taken together to build a coherent whole: the two units of analysis form a coherent, concrete synthesis. Sartre says:

> The preceding reactions have in particular allowed us to distinguish two absolutely distinct regions of being: the being of the *prereflective cogito* and the being of the phenomenon. But although the concept of being is, therefore, characterized by its division into two incommunicable regions, we must still explain how these two regions can be placed under the same heading (*BN* 25).

This, then, is Sartre's task, and, following Heidegger, Sartre appropriates *being-in-the-world*. He says, 'what is concrete is man in the world, with the specific union of man with the world that Heidegger, for example, names "being-in-the-world"' (*BN* 34). With this in mind, Sartre suggests that in order to move forwards all we need to do is simply open our eyes: 'we need only open our eyes and interrogate, from a standpoint of naïveté, the totality that is man-in-the-world' (*BN* 34). This allows Sartre to link his (relatively) abstract ontological structure with particular instances of human conduct, and through this liaison he argues for the centrality of negation, and ultimately nothingness.

Being for *Others* and *In Itself For Itself*

Towards the end of "He was my Teacher," Deleuze, somewhat surprisingly, chooses to focus on Sartre's (fictitious) friendship with Pierre. Deleuze says, 'above all my friend-Pierre-who-was-never-there [...] Ever and always to the friend Pierre-who-is-never-there' (*Islands* 79–80). Pierre is a mysterious figure in the context of Sartre's *Being and Nothingness,* he is never really there, in a sense he is absent—or lacking. References to Pierre are nearly always mounted when Sartre needs to illustrate some of the more abstract ontological concepts in *Being and Nothingness,* to illuminate these *through* our friend Pierre. The figure of Pierre is constantly referred to as the reader and Sartre's mutual friend—a feeling that Deleuze seems to share: 'above all *my* friend-Pierre (*Islands* 79: my emphasis). Deleuze's repeated references to Pierre in "He was my Teacher" suggests that the role he plays is more than merely that of an illustrative figure in *Being and Nothingness.* Pierre is, in a sense, the perfect synecdoche for Sartre's entire project of *being-for-others. Being-for-others* is characterised by its impossible dimension, as we will see; love and desire are vital movements in the *for itself*'s coming-to-be, or realisation, for-others, but these end in failure. And so, allegorically, Deleuze's example of Pierre shows how our mutual friend is always 'almost,' in *becoming,* our relationship with Pierre is in the process of realisation, yet, in effect, governed by the very same impossibility.

Sartre's Pierre is the perfect other; other than Sartre, and other than us. However, Pierre is also us, we are Pierre, in the sense that we could be the figure of Pierre in relation to Sartre within the confines of *Being and Nothingness,* or indeed, that Pierre could be an *being-for-itself* in his own right, in the same way that we are, or that Sartre is. The tension between each of our differing being(s)-for-other(s) is fundamental to the famously conflictual descriptions of love and desire in *Being and Nothingness.* In short, conflicts arise because *for itself(s)* clash against one another, to preserve their being in the face of adversity. Even Sartre's relationship with Pierre is characterised by a certain uneasiness—a feeling of never really knowing what constitutes Pierre's *other-subject,* only his *other-object in-the-world.* Sartre says:

> When Pierre looks at me, I know without doubt that he is looking at me: his eyes—things in the world—are riveted on my body—a thing in the world; that is the objective fact of which I can say "It is." But it is also a fact that belongs to the world. The meaning of this look is not, and that is what bothers me. Whatever I do—smile, promise, threaten—nothing can win me the approval, the free judgment I am seeking. I know that it is always "beyond" (*BN* 106).

Sartre argues that we must forever keep in mind that all attempts to love or to desire are basic attempts to overcome the original alienation in our being. In short, *being for itself* is characterised by a radical disunity of (not)knowing itself—there is a lack in the *for itself.* Anticipating Lacan somewhat, we might already be able to see how these two philosophers are deeply connected. A lack of self-identity/self-coincidence is precisely what the *in itself* does not suffer from since it is instead characterised by a fullness of being. According to Sartre, love and desire force the *for itself* to attempt to fill this lack—projecting itself towards something which would give the *for itself* the characteristics that are usually held by the *in itself,* which is to say the features of stability and wholeness. To achieve this ideal (otherwise known as the metaphysical impossibility that is *in itself for itself*) would be to become God himself, to have achieved the unachievable. Sartre says in *Being and Nothingness:*

> The for-itself as nihilation of the in-itself temporalizes itself as *flight toward.* In effect, it surpasses its facticity—or its being *given*, or its past, or its body—toward the in-itself that it would be if it were able to be its own foundation. This could be put into terms that are more psychological—and that are, for this reason, incorrect, even if they are perhaps clearer—by saying that the for-itself tries to escape its *de facto* existence, in other words its being-there, as an in-itself of which it is not in any way the foundation, and that this fight takes place towards an impossible and constantly pursued future where the for-itself might be in-itself-for-itself, i.e., an in-itself that would be its own foundation in relation to itself (*BN* 480).

Attempting to achieve the impossible as *in itself for itself* would be unintelligible; it is, as I have mentioned, the perfect coincidence that is reserved for God himself. Sartre argues that the *for itself* is haunted by its inability to become this totalised ideal:

> The ideal fusion—in the shape of an unrealizable totality—of the missing item with what that missing item is missing from, haunts the for-itself and constitutes it in its very being as a nothingness of being. That, as we said, is the in-itself-for itself—or value. [...] the in-itself-for-itself is a possibility that belongs to the for-itself. It haunts the world as an unrealizable (*BN* 273–4).

It is in the context of the ideal of *in itself for itself* that we first appreciate that love and desire are impossible since love and desire are two forms of attempting to reconcile *for itself* with *in itself* as *in itself for itself.* Put simply, achieving *in itself for itself* would be to have successfully married freedom and identity, which is, for Sartre, the original ontological impossibility. In other words, love and desire are the impossible off-shoots of the original impossibility of the *for itself*'s trying to become *in itself for itself*. Though impossible, *in itself for itself* remains crucial since it is what Sartre claims is of value for the *for itself*, or so the *for itself* mistakenly imagines (*BN* 273). *In itself for itself* is the totalised value that in love can never be achieved, and this un-realisability always haunts the *for itself*. Sartre again makes plain the importance of *in itself for itself* in the *Notebooks for an Ethics*:

> The historical act by which being negates itself into the for itself is a fall and a memory of Paradise Lost. Myth of the fault in every religion and in folklore. It is not necessary to see here either a dialectical necessity as with Hegel, where the first individual relationship is necessarily that of the master and the slave, or a totally incomprehensible caprice. Rather an original fault that one can clarify through consideration of the original event. The appearance of the for itself is properly speaking the irruption of History in the world. The spontaneous movement of the for itself as a lack (on the plane of the unreflective) is to seek the in itself for itself (*NFE* 11).

For Sartre, we must clarify the *for itself*'s original mistake, the Fall of Man, by considering the original event [*événement originel*]. Somehow, being nihilates itself [*se néantise*] and is transformed into *for itself*, and according to Sartre, the *for itself* searches to reconnect with the *in itself* as *in itself for itself*. We contend that this original error [*faute originelle*] is central to Sartre's philosophy in relation to the impossible. Moreover, Sartre's task of investigating the original events following the original error [*faute originelle*] resembles the task that Schelling had previously attempted in the early nineteenth-century, except that Schelling had tried to think the original event at the level of *in itself* rather than at the level of *for itself*, and I return to this later on in this chapter. Lacan, too, picks up the theme of examining the ways that being is affected by an original error [*faute originelle*]; Lacan says original sin [*première faute*], and I discuss this in greater detail in the final chapter to tie together my claim that Schelling, Sartre, and Lacan are investigating similar concepts in their work (*SXXIII* 5).

Sartre argues in *Being and Nothingness* that the fusion of *in itself* with *for itself*, though ontologically impossible, is nevertheless pursued by beings attempting to achieve the union of *in itself for itself*. Sartre claims that desire is an absence of being, [*le désir est manque d'être*] (*BN* 746/*EN* 664), that in desiring another, the *for itself* tears itself away from *in itself*, and latches onto another in order to grasp for wholeness, to square the circle of one's identification with oneself. For Sartre, 'as such, it is immediately *directed on* the being that it lacks. This being [...] is in-itself-for-itself, a consciousness that has become substance, a substance that has become its own cause, a Man-God' (*BN* 746). The *for itself* ultimately desires to be both whole and free, all the while attempting to secure its grip on what constitutes the *in itself*—stability and permanence. The implication is that it is evident from the beginning that, framed in this way, the *for itself*'s attempt to become *in itself for itself* is impossible.

Sartre explains in his discussion concerning *being-for-others* that the impossible union of freedom and fixed identity, as *in itself for itself*, is problematic by virtue of the difficulties we encounter in our relationship with others. Sartre complicates our relationship with the other by granting the other a privileged position over the subject. The other, in directing their look towards the subject, alienates the subject from their being—so that the subject's *being-object* only exists in the safety of its being seen by another. This means that the other holds a privileged position with regards to the subject's being and knows something about the subject which is perpetually beyond their reach.

> The Other *looks at* me and, in so doing, he holds the secret of my being; he knows what I *am*. Thus the innermost meaning of my being is outside me, imprisoned in an absence; the Other has the advantage over me (*BN* 481).

In *Being and Nothingness*, Sartre often casts intersubjective relationships in confrontational terms, whereby encountering the other evokes a fear of the other in the subject. Sartre highlights the limitations others can place on the subject's freedom. The other's freedom is precisely what limits my freedom (*BN* 359). Dealings with another can yield many pitfalls, wherein the relationship is always characterised by a certain precarity, as though Pierre, as well as being our mutual friend, can also enslave us through his freedom (*BN* 366). The relations between beings, then, for Sartre, as it is for Hegel, are primarily focused on conquest and power.

The intersubjective relationships formed with another brought to the fore by the look, yield in the *for itself* an uncomfortable option between two incompatible modes of being. The look is a moment which places the *for itself* on the back foot—the argument is that I am caught out in a compromised position in-the-world. In Sartre's example, while succumbing to my desire to be a voyeur, and so spying on lovers through a keyhole in an act of non-thetic self-consciousness, utterly unaware of myself as a voyeur (*BN* 355), I am thwarted the moment I hear footsteps in the hall. At that moment, even if the footsteps were to continue up the stairs, and so never to catch me in the act (*BN* 375), the mere threat of being caught triggers a chain of events which leads me to recognise my shame. Feeling shame, according to Sartre, is the *for itself* recognising that it has knelt before the other and realising that it has lost ground. The freedom of the *for itself* has been captured, and the impulse now is that it desperately needs back what has been taken away. Indeed, Sartre stresses shame is a fundamental human attitude which can exist only in relation to others: 'pure shame is not the feeling of being this or that reprehensible object but, in general, of being *an* object, i.e., of *recognizing* myself in that degraded, dependent, and frozen being that I am for the Other' (*BN* 392). If the other catches (or threatens to catch) the subject in a compromised position in the world, the conflict and shame elicited in the subject will force the subject to confront their being-for-others. Sartre summarises in *Baudelaire* (1947): 'that's the true prostitution—you belong to everyone' (*B* 149, translation modified). In other words, Pierre belongs to me, and I belong to Pierre. In many ways, there are similarities between Sartre's conceptualisation of others as they bear on the subject and Lacan's formulation of the big Other. For Lacan, as we will see in the next chapter, those feelings of shame felt by the mere threat of being caught, is the power of the big Other par excellence.

The result of such a conflictual situation leads the *for itself* to react in one of two ways; firstly, the *for itself* could try and return the look, this is done in order to override the other's freedom exercised in their look, and Sartre's argument here is that in the returned look we are attempting to bend the *being-object* that the other has attempted to reduce me to, back onto them. In effect, we are attempting to force the other to be seen by me as *being-object*, in turn. Sartre shows how this conflictual strategy manifests itself in attitudes such as pride and vanity; the *for itself* in these instances wants to regain some of its subjectivity and diminish the *other-subject* into *other-object* (*BN* 395). Secondly, the *for itself* can react to intersubjective conflicts by trying to assimilate itself into the freedom of the other, through love. Love is an attempt to square the circle—to be absolutely free whilst being the foundation of such freedom. Put another way, love is an attempt to become *in itself for itself*. Sartre makes clear that the *for itself* as a nihilation [*néantisation*] of the *in itself* is a flight [*fuite*] towards another *in itself* that could be its own foundation (*BN* 480). Therefore, loving the other, in an attempt to achieve *in itself for itself*, is the second way the *for itself* can react to the conflict elicited by the look of the other who puts the subject's freedom in jeopardy.

Establishing the *for itself's* freedom is central to Sartre's entire ontological scheme. Sartre claims that freedom is the very 'stuff' of existence: 'freedom is [...] the fabric of my being' (*BN* 576), as I stated earlier. So, Sartre claims that to be is to exist, and existing is necessarily to exist freely. However, somewhat paradoxically, for Sartre, freedom itself is not free to be unfree, nor can unfreedom exist: 'freedom is not free to not be free and that it is not free to not exist' (*BN* 635), and here Sartre is attempting to sidestep a metaphysical problem that necessarily arises in trying to define freedom: how can freedom not be free not to exist if it were truly free?[2] In a highly original move, Sartre develops what he calls the nihilating step back [*recul néantisant*] to preserve freedom's pure contingency, 'through the nihilating step it takes back, freedom establishes a system of relations' [*par son recul néantisant, la liberté fait qu'un système de relations s'établisse*], Sartre says (*BN* 636/*EN* 567). Therefore, the *recul néantisant*, the nihilating step back, is the process whereby consciousness withdraws from being, and it is this process of withdrawal that Sartre attaches to freedom, thereby attempting to preserve freedom's quality of pure contingency. Sartre says, 'that does not mean that human-reality exists *first*, in order to be free *afterward*' (*BN* 634). Consciousness can recede and withdraw from the self—in effect the *for itself* choosing to withdraw from the *in*

[2] See: (Heidegger 1985: 48).

itself: 'to be, for the for-itself, is to nihilate the in-itself that it is' [*être, pour le pour soi, c'est néantiser l'en soi qu'il est*] (*BN* 576). In practical terms, this means that the *for itself* is always free to constitute itself differently, to create new meaning for itself, and it is this radical conception of freedom, at the heart of consciousness, that always engenders with it an awareness of the freedom of self. For Sartre, the self is an object of consciousness, and so when I reflect on it, I am inadvertently reflecting on my freedom, too—this is why Sartre claims that 'freedom is […] the fabric of my being' (*BN* 576). However, crucially, this freedom resides in *for itself* which is also characterised by a radical incompatibility of (not)knowing itself, as a result of the nihilating step back [*recul néantisant*] from the *in itself*, and, as we will see shortly, Sartre is careful not to explain this mechanism of withdrawal—leaving him vulnerable to the charge that the *for itself* is ungrounded. Sartre says, 'each human-reality is at the same time the direct project to metamorphose its own for-itself into the in-itself-for-itself, and the project to appropriate the world as the totality of being-in-itself, in the form of a fundamental quality' (*BN* 707). And so, it is precisely this very freedom, that is at the core of the *for itself*, that needs to be protected from the *other-subject* that stares so ferociously, attempting to make the *for itself* merely a *being-object*. The constriction of freedom felt by the *for itself* puts the subject's freedom in jeopardy in their relationships with others, and the subject's freedom must be protected or re-established at all costs as a result.

The *for itself* pursues a twofold strategy in its attempt to achieve the impossible goal of *for itself in itself*, and, for Sartre, both are destined to fail. On the one hand, as already noted, the *for itself*'s tactic is a flight away from an *in itself* that could not be its own foundation, in a sense the *for itself* is attempting to out-run its past, its facticity; and, on the other hand, the *for itself*'s strategy is also a pursuit towards the *in itself* which falsely promises to be its own grounding—transcendence. So, the *for itself* is caught in this double dance of both flight and pursuit, never to be reconciled, unable to close the circle. Sartre says:

> The for-itself tries to escape its *de facto* existence, in other words its being-there, as an in-itself of which it is not in any way the foundation, and that this flight takes place toward an impossible and constantly pursued future where the for-itself might be in-itself-for-itself, i.e., an in-itself that would

> be its own foundation in relation to itself. Thus, the for-itself is at the same time a flight and a pursuit; at the same time it flees the in-itself and it pursues it; the for-itself is a pursuing-pursued (*BN* 480).

However, as noted, this double dance of both flight and pursuit is always haunted by the spectre of the impossible. In short, the whole strategy of running after *in itself* involves making a grave and fundamental error, for the circle can never be closed. One cannot be one's own foundation according to Sartre; indeed, he shows how the second of these strategies, to take up an attitude of love, to grasp for transcendence as it were, is a futile passion—an attempt to grasp a wholeness that is available only to God. Nevertheless, Sartre argues, we pursue and engage with love and desire because as soon as another body exists in the world, these attitudes simply manifest themselves: 'from the moment that "there is" a body and "there is" the other, our reaction is one of desire, of love—and the derivative attitudes that we have cited' (*BN* 536). We will return to this metaphysical question of why we love and desire the other at the end of this chapter.

In Sartre's earlier philosophy, the impossible dimension of love is originally found in the *for itself*'s wanting to become *in itself for itself*, the original unrealisable ideal. Concomitantly, Sartre argues that the impossibility of love is also a direct result of the impossibility of being-for-others. The examples of love and desire, while given their own original arguments by Sartre, are impossible from the start by virtue of their ontological articulations in the *for itself's* relationship with *being-for-others,* and the futile wish to become *in itself for itself.* It is at this ontological level that a systemic problem arises with Sartre's account of the impossible. I suggest that the accounts that Sartre gives with regards to the foundations of *for itself* are perhaps unstable, and I return to this argument in more detail, by way of a comparison with Schelling, in the second half of this chapter.

Impossible Love

For Sartre, love is doomed from the start, and it emerges from a situation of conflict with one's lover. Sartre says, 'the following descriptions [in relation to love] should therefore be envisaged within the perspective of *conflict*. Conflict is the original meaning of being-for-the-Other' (*BN* 482–3). In what follows, we take our lover to be Pierre—in our case, to err towards both stretching the opening analogy too far, and to play with the figure of Pierre, whom we now know quite intimately. When Pierre confronts me with his love, our necessary conflict emerges, to borrow language from Baudelaire's "To a woman passing by;" *One lightning flash… then night! Sweet fugitive/Whose glance has made me suddenly reborn* [*Un éclair… puis la nuit!—Fugitive beauté/Dont le regard m'a fait soudainement renaître*] (1998:198/1868: 270). However, this rebirth, the first encounter with the other's love, Sartre argues, has taken me by surprise: 'but when one of the passers-by suddenly looks up, the observer finds that he is observed, *the hunter hunted*' (*B* 150: my emphasis. Translation modified). Pierre attracts me towards his freedom, but, I too, pull him towards mine. Conflict is inescapable—*the hunter hunted*. We both recognise that to experience our respective being-for-others, we must seize the other as possession:

> I am possessed by the Other; the Other's look models my body in its nudity, gives birth to it, sculpts it, produces it as it is, sees it as I will never see it. The Other holds a secret: the secret of what I am. He makes me be and, in so doing, he possesses me—and this possession is nothing other than his consciousness of possessing me. As for me, in recognizing my objecthood, I feel that he has this consciousness. As a consciousness, the Other is for me at the same time someone who has stolen my being, and someone who brings it about that "there is" a being that is my being. […] I am responsible for my being-for-the-Other but I am not its foundation (*BN* 483).

Love and desire are not synonymous for Sartre; instead, these two concepts are radically incompatible—though, they do end up in the same place. Desire is closely aligned with the need to reduce the other to *other-object* that I noted earlier.

In love, the subject necessarily pursues an intersubjective strategy that attempts to assimilate itself into the other's freedom, which involves an attempt to preserve one's freedom while simultaneously choosing its foundation, in order to control, possess and direct it. For Sartre, this means to assimilate oneself into the alterity of the other—the subject wholly identifying themselves as subject being-seen by Pierre, while Pierre maintains his freedom through the look he gives the subject. Since the only intersubjective link we share in this allegedly loving relationship is Pierre's look confronting my *being-object* it is necessarily unstable, 'this object-being is the only instrument I can use to bring about the assimilation of the other freedom with myself' (*BN* 484). In trying to assimilate myself into Pierre's freedom, in effect, attempting to take on features of *in itself* by anchoring my subjectivity in another subject, I am forgetting that this is merely an ideal (*in itself for itself*), which is impossible because I am simultaneously sacrificing my freedom, and I am turning myself into an inert being, an *in itself*, since I am foregoing my *for itself* in exchange for my lover's gaze. The subject is unable to surmount the original problem, that there is no internal, symmetrical relation between two subjects in love: 'the Other establishes himself as other from me and the negation through which I establish myself as other from the other' (*BN* 484). In short, I am unable to renounce my subjectivity, my freedom, and allow my being to be degraded to the being-seen of the other, as an *object* for his *subjectivity*. In the event of love, the two parts are not in harmony, they do not, together in love, form a complementary or coherent whole.[3] The parts attempting to be unified are asymmetrical; two rugged pieces that do not fit neatly together. Sartre's radical dislocation between the two lovers is also remarkably close to how Lacan interprets the same dilemma, as I will show. For Sartre, the individual parts (the two *for itselfs*' attempting to fuse together) are not malleable, and the loved subject is unable to diminish, mould, or renounce their freedom to accommodate Pierre's gaze. Pierre, in his love for me, would like me to bend my freedom towards his, to be at the service of his freedom. Sartre

[3] As Aristophanes argued in Plato's *Symposium*, for example (Plato 2008: 24) § 191a; § 191d.

says, 'what would be required therefore—since my being for the Other involves a double internal negation— would be to act on the internal negation through which the Other transcends my transcendence and makes me exist for the other, i.e., to act on the Other's freedom' (*BN* 485). Therefore, according to Sartre, love is necessarily a descent into masochism because one has to accept to become the other's slave. Sartre explains the subjective conflict that emerges in the loving relationship thus: 'so far this description fits Hegel's famous description of the relations between master and slave quite well. What Hegel's master is for the slave is what the lover wants to be for his loved one' (*BN* 490). However, Sartre is keen to stress that the analogy ought not be stretched too far. Love's necessarily conflictual relationship, then, is how Pierre wants to enslave me through his love for me. Pierre wants nothing more than to capture my freedom; attracting it, luring and stealing it from me. However, Pierre is equally misguided since in love, Pierre is pursuing nothing other than the subject's *perceived* objectivity to be captured by his subjectivity, and the subject's freedom to be assimilated into his, yet the subject is unable to renounce their freedom, which exists necessarily, and, therefore, the end of such unions, for Sartre, 'becomes frozen into a dead-possibility' (*BN* 498). When a couple are in love, then, each is trying to become an object in the eyes of the other, at the service of the other's freedom. Each carries forward an alienation within themselves, and they are pursuing contradictory ideals—ones which contradicts the freedom their *for itself* necessarily contains.

Furthermore, according to Sartre, the problem of being-for-others cannot be solved with more love. Therefore, love is problematic for three reasons:

> In the first place it is, in essence, an illusion [*duperie*] and an infinite referral [...]. The more someone loves me, the more I lose my *being*, and the more I am returned to my own responsibilities and my own possible way of being. In the second place, it is always possible that the other will wake up: she can at any moment summon me before her as an object: hence the lover's constant insecurity. In the third place, love is an absolute that is constantly being *relativized* by others. One would have to be alone in the world with one's loved one for love to retain its character as an absolute axis

> of reference: hence the lover's constant shame (or pride—which in this case comes to the same thing) (*BN* 498–9).

According to Sartre, the only coherent outcome of a loving relationship is that it must end up 'frozen into a dead-possibility' (*BN* 498). Love is an attempt by the other to beguile the subject's freedom and render it inoperable, 'the more someone loves me, the more I lose my *being*,' Sartre says. Love is a dead-end, characterised by constant insecurity, a precarity which cannot be assuaged in-the-world, it is impossible. I contend that we should approach Sartre's pessimistic account of love with some scepticism. Although Sartre's primary aim was to expose our ontological insecurities towards the other in love, Sartre's tripartite account of love winds up looking quite bleak ['frozen into a dead-possibility' (*BN* 498)].[4] Moreover, I contend that Sartre leaves unsettled the central metaphysical question implied by his account of love: *why* does the subject pursue a futile goal? It is this metaphysical question which foregrounds my investigations of Lacan's psychoanalysis in the following chapters. Sartre, having demonstrated love's ultimate failure, believes that he has given an account of the world in which love is impossible. Can this satisfy us?

Of course, Sartre is not claiming that love does not serve a purpose in the subject's everyday life. However, I am more concerned with Sartre's own teleological discussion of the endpoint of love. Sartre claims that love fails *in the end.* Love's final destination is, Sartre says, *in itself for itself*—the impossible. By being part of being-for-others, 'it follows that love, as a fundamental mode of being-for-the-Other, contains in its being-for-the-Other the seeds of its own destruction' (*BN* 498). So, since Sartre is engaging with the articulation of the final destination of love, I contend that we are justified in taking Sartre on his own terms in the analysis concerning love's final meaning and destination. I follow, and naively ask: why pursue love if it fails in the end? Why does love 'haunt the world as an unrealizable' (*BN* 274)? Sartre does not convincingly answer these concerns, and, as we will see later in this chapter, it is the ungrounded ontological foundations of *being-for-itself* and *being-for-others* that render Sartre's account of love unstable.

[4] As Sartre himself recognised, see Sartre 1981 p. 13.

Impossible Desire

Sartre's account of desire differs from his account of love, but it ends up in the same place—in impossibility. As Howells puts it, 'desire is *trouble,* it disturbs both body and consciousness' (Howells 2011: 32). Sartre stresses that love does not take precedence over desire, that desire is not secondary to love simply by virtue of its being treated second in *Being and Nothingness*. Rather, they are both put in motion as a result of being-for-others (*BN* 501). However, while love, in a sense, may follow a more "optimistic" path to destruction, desire follows an antithetical one. According to Sartre, I cannot both love and desire Pierre at the same time, these two drives are separate. Furthermore, I choose to desire. Sartre says: 'consciousness chooses itself as desire. Of course, for that to happen there will normally be a motive: I do not desire just anyone, at any time' (*BN* 515). For Sartre, the subject is not automatically considered a sexual being by mere virtue of possessing sexual organs, instead sexual desire is intentional in the Husserlian sense (*BN* 509). For example, a penis might mean that a man can act on a desire in a particular way; Sartre says: 'neither penile turgescence nor any other physiological phenomenon (or the mere fact of being conscious of these physiological modifications) will ever be able to explain or to provoke sexual desire' (*BN* 506). Sartre is taking aim at both the empirical psychologists and the 'existential philosophers,' Heidegger included, who would have it that sexual desire is instinctual (Howells 2000: 87). For Sartre, sexual desire falls firmly into the realm of philosophy. Moreover, desire occurs not as a result of another's particular bodily attributes, but as a result of the 'complete figure,' Sartre goes on: 'better still, to a figure *in situation*' (*BN* 510). And it is *I* who desires, 'without doubt, *I am* the one who desires, and desire is a distinctive mode of my subjectivity' (*BN* 510). This desire manifests itself in consciousness, and we feel it bodily, according to Sartre, it 'seems to become "thicker" [*empâtée*]'. Desire is to consent to an impulse or drive; there is a choice to be made (*BN* 512). And yet, somehow, if I dare to resist desire, I begin to feel myself heavier, 'we will "wake up" and find ourselves lucid, but with a heavy head and a pounding heart,' my consciousness becoming corporeal (*BN* 513). As Howells argues, 'desire compromises the *pour soi* [for itself], and is a fall into complicity with the body [...]. In a word, consciousness becomes bodily' (Howells 2011: 31), and this also highlights that desire is not simply the pursuit of the other's body, but also the revelation of my own body:

> In desire, the body—instead of being no more than the contingency from which the for-itself flees toward its own possibles—simultaneously becomes the for- itself's most immediate possible: desire is not only a desire for the Other's body; it is, within the unity of a single act, the non-thetically lived pro-ject of sinking into one's body. [...] it is indeed an appetite *toward* the Other's body, which is lived as the for-itself's vertigo in relation to its own body; and the being who desires is a consciousness *making itself body* (*BN* 513).

The other becomes flesh for me, through my touch, which is more than simple contact, it is an incarnation of the other whom I desire (*BN* 514). But not just for the pleasure of climax, that would be nonsensical since simple egocentric pleasure could be abated in masturbation. For Sartre, to satisfy one's desire for another with the other is an attempt to grasp both body *and* soul.

> The Other's flesh did not exist for me explicitly, since I apprehended the Other's body in situation [...] Out of my caress the Other is born as flesh—for me and for herself (*BN* 515).

> Desire is an action whose aim is to cast a spell [...] its point, since I am able to grasp the other only in her objective facticity, is to mire her freedom within that facticity: it must be made to "set" within it—as we might say of a custard that it has "set"—so that the Other's for-itself reaches to the surface of her body, so that it extends throughout her body and so that, in touching this body, I can at last touch the other's free subjectivity. That is the true meaning of the word "possession" (*BN* 519).

And it is precisely here, that we can see that desire fails, that it falls irremediably into the abyss of the impossible. I want to possess the other's body, in the sense outlined above. I want to possess a body that is itself possessed, a body which is itself conscious of others, and identified by its own freedom. In short, to possess the free transcendence of the other as pure transcendence and yet still in bodily form, which would amount to: 'reduce the other to her mere *facticity*, because then she exists in the midst of my world' (*BN* 520). However, a body in my world apprehended in its simple facticity would be to radically modify my own being to accommodate them: 'the moment I throw myself in the direction of another's facticity, the moment I want to set aside her actions and her duties in order to reach her in her flesh, I incarnate myself' (*BN* 521). Desire ends in failure, Sartre says this explicitly: 'desire is itself doomed to failure' (*BN* 522), because the desire to appropriate the embodied consciousness of the other incarnated in the touch, quickly loses its subjectivity—it becomes object:

> The Other's body, surpassed toward its potentialities, descends from the level of *flesh* to that of a pure object. It is implicit in this situation that the reciprocal incarnation—which was, precisely, desire's distinctive goal—will be broken. The other [...] is a flesh that I can no longer apprehend through my own flesh, a flesh that is no longer anything but a *property* of the object-other, and not the incarnation of an other-consciousness (*BN* 525).

The other that I desire becomes an object through my touch, they become pure object and lose their subjectivity, the objectivity of the body has taken over. 'Desire, for Sartre, is of course intentional: it is a mode of consciousness [...] it is a primary ['*originelle*'] mode [...] fundamental not contingent' (Howells 2011: 31). Which is why desire ultimately fails to overcome the need for the *for itself* to be its own foundation. Desire is an illusory attempt to really possess and sublimate the freedom of the other into my own. Pierre is by nature unseizable, he defies possession: 'the Other eludes me as a matter of principle: when I seek him, he runs away from me and, when I run away from him, he possesses me' (*BN* 538, translation modified). As Judith Butler put it in a different context, the 'desire to be,' is ultimately to be 'forced to desire the impossible' (1987: 98).

Why Love?

Earlier I intimated my potential dissatisfaction with Sartre's contention that we love and desire one another simply because we can; 'from the moment that "there is" a body and "there is" the other, our reaction is one of desire, of love—and the derivative attitudes that we have cited' (*BN* 536). Sartre does not much allow for metaphysical discussions as to *why* we engage with certain phenomena, preferring to focus on ontological descriptions. Indeed, at various points in *Being and Nothingness,* Sartre avoids metaphysical questions altogether. However, in the conclusion to *Being and Nothingness,* Sartre does engage in 'some metaphysical observations' (*BN* 798). Though, here, once again, Sartre only critiques Hegel and Heidegger's forays into metaphysics, and does not engage in much metaphysical speculation himself. 'All "why" questions,' Sartre says, 'are in fact subsequent to being, and presuppose it. Being is, without reason, without cause, and *without necessity*' (*BN* 800–1, my emphasis). It is clear that Sartre is unwilling to negotiate the minefield that is metaphysical speculation. Nevertheless, the question as to *why* we love and desire is a pertinent concern for me here, I am not content for love to be an impossibility which, by the end of *Being and Nothingness,* Sartre has clarified as being a perpetual attempt at an ultimate failure. In other words, love is the thwarted attempt to try and effectuate the impossible, actioned simply because *we can try to fail.* To achieve the impossible in love and become *in itself for itself* would be to attempt to diminish the radical freedom with which we are condemned to live: it is *because* we are condemned to freedom that we cannot love. I argue that this is an unsatisfactory conception of why subjects love, and, it is evident that Sartre, too, shared this anxiety:

R: *Then do you think you deserved to be reproached for idealism, as has rather frequently been charged?*

Sartre: No, not idealism but rather, bad realism. That part of *L'Être et le néant* [*Being and Nothingness*] failed.

P: *One often has great difficulty with your analyses of love, of the "for-others." You yourself have said that in L'Être et le néant* [*Being and Nothingness*] *you depicted above all negative love.*

> **Sartre:** Yes, certainly. Beginning with *Saint Genet* I changed my position a bit, and I now see more positivity in love.
> **P:** *Sadism and masochism are quite normal aspects of human love*:
> **Sartre:** Yes, that was what I wanted to say. I would still maintain the idea that many acts of human love are tainted with sadism and masochism, and what must be shown is what transcends them. I wrote *Saint Genet* to try to present a love that goes beyond the sadism in which Genet is steeped and the masochism that he suffered as it were, in spite of himself (Sartre in 1981: 13).[5]

Sartre agrees, as it were, that he has portrayed a predominantly negative view of love in *Being and Nothingness.*[6] My task is to attempt to supply a view of love which takes into account its metaphysical underpinnings—why do we love? I contend that love is both as necessary as it is impossible, describing an always unfinished task that we could qualify as a form of cruel optimism.[7] This oxymoronic conclusion, typical of Lacan's psychoanalysis, will become more evident as we develop our understanding of his philosophy. If, as it is for Sartre in *Being and Nothingness,* love and desire are key movements in the *for itself's* coming-to-be, or realisation, then, the concepts of love and desire form a relatively substantial part of human subjectivity and the subject's relationship with others. Therefore, 'if, as we have tried to establish, it is true that human-reality becomes acquainted with itself and defines itself through the ends it pursues' (*BN* 723), then, we contend, it is worthwhile to investigate why subjects pursue love as one of their subjective goals. Furthermore, we are concerned with the ways in which the concept of love as Sartre developed it in *Being and Nothingness* emerges in Lacan's psychoanalysis.

I now turn to the many connections between Sartre and Schelling. The intuition for this comparison is twofold; firstly, Schelling's critique of Hegel, and later philosophy more generally, anticipates a manifold of

[5] This is an excerpt from an interview Sartre conducted for publication in the series *Library of Living Philosophers,* towards the end of his life. The interview, though conducted in French, was translated for publication into English as *The Philosophy of Jean-Paul Sartre* (1981).

[6] It is worth noting that Sartre's view of love develops substantially from *Saint Genet* onwards, as Sartre says. However, regretfully, this is beyond the scope of this book.

[7] I borrow this term from Lauren Berlant who argues that 'a relation of cruel optimism exists when something you desire is actually an obstacle to your flourishing' (2011: 1).

themes that are to plague and inform French philosophy throughout the twentieth century.[8] Secondly, Schelling's speculative middle philosophy offers us a creative solution to the problems we have encountered in Sartre's account of love and desire in *Being and Nothingness*. In what follows, my central view will be to suggest that Sartre's hypothesis of the impossibility of love in *Being and Nothingness* is an only illusory impossibility.

Thinking the Fall: Ontologically Sick

> Our knowledge is incomplete, that is, it must be produced piecemeal in sections and degrees (Schelling).

Little has been written on Sartre's relationship to Schelling, though their works share similarities (Frank 2004b: 151; Gardner 2006: 271),[9] and in order to put pressure on Sartre's account of the impossible, we consider Sartre alongside Schelling. This comparison is not designed to minimise Sartre's original contributions to the history of philosophy but is instead envisaged to resurrect the metaphysical reflections that were unconvincingly buried by Sartre in *Being and Nothingness*. Moreover, the highly speculative aspects of Schelling's middle philosophy echo the late Lacan's onto-theological arguments from around *Seminar XX, Encore,* onwards.

Schelling's highly speculative discussion concerning the origins of God in *Ages of the World* [*Die Weltalter*] (1813), informs my reading of Sartre, and this reading enables me to challenge the confines of Sartre's closed philosophical system. Strikingly, Sartre often alludes to the Fall of Man in *Being and Nothingness*, and this comparison makes more sense than it ought for a thinker who consistently considered himself an atheist.[10] The atheistic dimension of Sartre's humanistic philosophy needs to be re-

[8] See (Butler 1987) for more on the reception of Hegel in twentieth-century French thought.

[9] Further notable exceptions are: (Frank 1992)—not available in English, though some excerpts from (Frank 1992) have been translated in *The New Schelling*, Norman and Welchman 2004—and (Gardner 2005), (Gardner 2006), (Gardner in Webber 2011).

[10] As I will show later, for Lacan, it is the pious who are the best atheists.

oriented towards an onto-theological reading of his notorious condemnation to freedom.[11] Schelling, like Sartre, separates being into two regions, and for Schelling freedom is found at the heart of *in itself*; thereby allowing Schelling to invest freedom with ontological primacy. Whereas by investing freedom in the *for itself*, Sartre has left himself open to the charge that everything contained outside *in itself* is the product of a systematic illusion (Gardner 2006: 261), including Sartre's highly creative solution for the pure contingency of freedom, the nihilating step back [*recul néantisant*], since the relationship between *in itself* and *for itself* has not been properly accounted for. Furthermore, since this dilemma underpins Sartre's entire account of love, as it was outlined previously, I claim that Sartre's account of love is unstable at a primary ontological level.

Many studies have highlighted Sartre's philosophical connections to Hegel,[12] and these works unavoidably open a discussion on Sartre's relationship to Hegel.[13] However, I am less interested in revisiting the Hegelian debt that Sartre may or may not owe, and instead suggest that Sartre is replying, in part, to questions that motivated both Hegel and Schelling. And, since Schelling had also formulated an earlier critique of Hegel, we are justified in comparing the two philosophers.

[11] Onto-theology to be understood as 'a philosophical position that regards the intelligibility of our and the world's being as bound up metaphysically with the concept of a highest being (God) conceived as having at least some attributes of personality, mind, or subjectivity, in some sense and to some degree. Onto-theology therefore does not coincide with (classical) theism' (Gardner 2006: 268).

[12] For example: (Hartmann 1966) and (Seel 1995). For a concise but comprehensive discussion on Hegel and Sartre see also: (Verstraeten in Howells 1992).

[13] Ronald Hayman claims that according to the library register at the École normale supérieure, Sartre read Fichte and Hegel during his third year at the ENS (1986: 55). Bruce Baugh's *French Hegel* makes a more complete assessment, though he does say: 'despite what Sartre and others have claimed, even during the ascendancy of neo-Kantianism, Hegel's philosophy did not pass into complete obscurity. There were Alain's courses on Hegel at the Lycée Henri IV from 1923–1928 which were attended by Hyppolite and students of the École Normale, including perhaps Sartre' (2003: 14). Baugh also states that the often-asserted claim that Sartre learnt all he knew of Hegel by attending the Kojève lectures on Hegel is characterised by having 'no good evidence' (2003: 98). Nonetheless, I take it as given that Hegel was very important to Sartre: 'the great importance of Hegel for Sartre is manifest in the terminology and on almost every page of *Being and Nothingness*, throughout which Sartre is engaged in an extended argument with Hegel—not of course with Hegel alone, but it is Hegel, rather than Husserl or Heidegger, whose general metaphysical views Sartre is most keen to contest' (Gardner 2006: 264–5).

For Paul Tillich, Schelling can be considered to be the 'first great existentialist' philosopher of the modern period (1972: 437). For Tillich, Schelling's reconfiguration of German Romanticism pushed it onto surer existential ground (438). Furthermore, Schelling's Berlin lectures were so important that Tillich claims: 'there is hardly one category in twentieth-century existentialist poetry, literature, philosophy, and indirectly the visual arts, which you cannot find in these lectures' (446). Indeed, Sartre's notion of freedom from his earlier philosophy is comparable to Schelling's notion of the absolute (Gardner 2006: 261).[14] And so Manfred Frank is able to deploy Sartre's language to explicate and reinterpret Schelling in light of *Being and Nothingness* (Frank 2004b: 151). Therefore, in adopting Frank's method, I compare Sartre with Schelling to force open the possibility of love. However, before further attempting to link Schelling to Sartre we first need to contextualise Schelling's thought and development.

Schelling developed his philosophy of freedom in an attempt to replace his earlier identity philosophy—his account of absolute rational idealistic monism—that he considered to be a total failure. By the turn of the nineteenth-century, Schelling had recognised that his identity system lacked an adequate epistemology, and was, therefore, fundamentally weak. Schelling attempts (and fails) to resolve these questions in the *Ages of the World* [*Weltalter*] texts. In these ambitious texts, Schelling attempts to build a philosophical account of the nature of time and creation (Norman: in *Weltalter* 107), and as Judith Norman notes, Schelling's multiple drafts of *Weltalter* are all unfinished fragments: 'Schelling barely got further than book I, which treated the first "age of the world," the past. [And] he would eventually abandon the project' (ibid). Understanding the historical context is crucial to appreciating the hesitant nature of Schelling's philosophical project. As Jean-François Marquet explains in *Liberté et existence, études sur la formation de la philosophie de Schelling* (1973), 'the story of the *Ages of the World* is that of an unknown masterpiece—the story of enthusiasm, despair and sacrifice' (449).

[14] Schelling's philosophy is notoriously schismatic, and he assigns similar concepts different names in the various phases of his thought. For my limited purposes here, with the aim of no great reconstruction of Schelling's philosophy, it is enough to signal that Schelling's 'Absolute' denotes roughly what Sartre means by 'Freedom.' However, the Absolute is also God, for Schelling.

Schelling's project consisted in seeking to implement a philosophical revolution that could provoke a theological revolution, since the theological aspect was thought to be a more important or significant goal. As Marquet says:

> Schelling believed that a revolution in philosophy was merely a prelude to a revolution in Religion [...] his ambition remained the same—to overcome the unilateral vocabulary of philosophy and translate the truth into a popularized language; the only place where it could be really itself. An immemorial language which belongs to no-one (1973: 449).

The language that Schelling develops from 1809 takes on an increasingly theosophical flavour. As Marquet puts it: Schelling begins deploying 'the only eternal language, the "language of the people," the biblical language of God.' (ibid 450).

Schelling believed that in his earlier identity philosophy, the principle of freedom had not been substantiated strongly enough. As Martin Heidegger summarises in his essay *Schelling's Treatise on the Essence of Human Freedom* (1985), Schelling's dilemma was that he had not adequately accounted for freedom; for the German Idealists a 'system' consisted of 'the totality of Being in the totality of its truth and the history of the truth' (48), and yet with such strong requirements, how could a fluid concept like 'freedom' be integrated into, or form the central part of, a constricting 'system'? In effect, Heidegger contends, if 'freedom, [...] is groundless and breaks out of every connection, [how could it be] the centre of [a] system?' (ibid). Therefore, Heidegger formalises Schelling's primary dilemma thus: 'a system of freedom appears to be impossible from both sides. There are two fundamental difficulties: (1) either "system" is retained, then freedom must be relinquished; or (2) freedom is retained, which means renunciation of "system"' (49). Schelling's motivation was to try and achieve true freedom without constraining it within the prison of a system, and this moment marks the beginning of Schelling's philosophy of freedom, the seeds of which are present from *Philosophy and Religion* (1804). By the time Schelling begins work on the first draft of his freedom text from 1809—*Ages of the World* [*Die Weltalter*]–Schelling has completely shifted focus towards concepts of 'eternity,' 'freedom,' and 'God' (Tillich 1972: 444). Schelling intended this fragmentary text to correct the failures of his earlier identity philosophy, and, concomitantly, they form part of Schelling's critique of Hegel, which as Heidegger put it, are 'the treatise which shatters Hegel's *Logic before* it was even published!' (1985: 97).

The problem of human freedom, as outlined above, forms only one part of a tripartite problem that Schelling recognised had emerged from his earlier work, the aforementioned anxiety that his identity philosophy lacked an adequate epistemology. The two other variants of this problem are: how to derive the finite from the infinite and the problem of evil. In brief, the former being the idea that if everything is to be contained within God, and God cannot create something outside himself, God may exist but how does there come to be a world? And, the latter, why is it that evil exists? Heidegger says, 'the question of the nature of human freedom becomes the question of the possibility of evil' (1985: 97). At its core, the premise of the problem states that for human beings to have real freedom, it must be that evil has reality (Snow 1996: 157). Schelling's philosophical rationale was that evil needed to be real, otherwise there is nothing to choose between, and freedom becomes essentially meaningless. Taken together, these are three strands of the same problem viewed from different angles, and we can say that, together, these questions constitute Schelling's riddle of human freedom. Schelling believed the tripartite questions were co-dependent, not unlike Lacan's Borromean knot, and that in answering one, he could provide answers for all three. For Schelling, the only freedom that is important is the freedom that is exercised by subjects in moral choices; Schelling contends that a morally significant choice between alternatives means that there must be at least two choices for the subject—a good one and an evil one.

In *Philosophy and Religion*, Schelling attempts to resolve the problem of freedom under the guise of the problem of deriving the finite from the infinite, which is to say deriving *for itself* from *in itself.* Schelling argues that since God, the Absolute, has created the world in his image, following Christian doctrine, the image that he has created that Schelling calls the *Gegenbild,* becomes a counter or mirror-image of God himself. Schelling argues that God, or the absolute, has to share its absolute freedom with something that is not itself—the *Gegenbild,* or counter-image.

For Schelling, the split is thought to be at the heart of the absolute itself. Schelling argues:

> The exclusive particularity of the Absolute lies in the fact that when it *bestows its essentiality upon its counter-image*, it also *bestows upon it its self-dependence*. This being-in-and-for-itself, this particular and true reality of the first-intuited, is *freedom*, and from that first self-dependence outflows what in the phenomenal world appears as freedom, which represents the last trace and the seal [*Siegel*], as it were, of divinity in the fallen-away world (*PR* 27–8, my emphasis).

Schelling has effectively split God into two halves ['bestows its essentiality upon its counter-image']. However, an important problem arises when God, who now wants to verify the *Gegenbild*, discovers that he can only do so from the position of the counter-image itself—which is to say that the view God desires needs to be immanent to the image itself. And, in a flash, God *falls* from himself—he falls from the seat of the absolute, into the abyss of the counter-image. God *becomes human* in the fall into the *Gegenbild, (counter-image)*. Recall Sartre's description in *Being and Nothingness* concerning the *for itself*'s desire to become *in itself for itself*, Sartre said: 'this being […] is in-itself-for-itself, a consciousness that has become substance, a substance that has become its own cause, a Man-God' (*BN* 746), Schelling is, in effect, giving a theosophical account of Sartre's impossible *in itself for itself*. Whereas the early Schelling had argued that all finite things in the world remained within God, the middle Schelling now argues that the world, in becoming conscious of itself as something distinct from the absolute, falls from God:

> The counter-image, as an absolute entity and having all its attributes in common with the originary [*sic*] image, would not truly be in itself and absolute if it could not grasp itself in its selfhood [*Selbstheit*], in order to have true being as the *other* absolute. But it cannot be as the *other* absolute unless it separates itself or falls away from the true Absolute (*PR* 28).

For Schelling, the split at the heart of the Absolute describes the need to separate *ground* from *existence*. Importantly, this intuition, as we have seen, employs theosophical language and ideas; the split at the heart of the Absolute has a clear echo to the beginning of the biblical story, the Fall. For Schelling, God created Adam and Eve, and they remained within him. However, God also had to invest them with some of his own freedom which enabled them to re-exercise their freedom to think themselves as separate from God, and according to Schelling's metaphysical depiction of the Fall of Man, *that fallen condition* is the condition of the world. The created world has thought itself apart from God and has, therefore, fallen from the seat of God. As Gardner argues, this narrative of the fallen world closely resembles Sartre's account of the subject, '[Sartre] encouraged us to think of human being[s] as a "fallen," negated form of being-in-itself' (Gardner 2006: 254). Recall the passage we quoted earlier from the *Notebooks for an Ethics* (1983), in which Sartre made explicit the importance of the narrative of the Fall:

> The historical act by which being negates itself into the for itself is a fall and a memory of Paradise Lost. Myth of the fault in every religion and in folklore. It is not necessary to see here either a dialectical necessity as with Hegel where the first individual relationship is necessarily that of the master and the slave, or a totally incomprehensible caprice. Rather an original fault that one can clarify through consideration of the original event. The appearance of the for itself is properly speaking the irruption of History in the world. The spontaneous movement of the for itself as a lack (on the plane of the unreflective) is to seek the in itself for itself (*NFE* 11).

Sartre is clear about the need to investigate the original sin at the heart of being, and that we should do so by considering the original (pre-ontological) events. Sartre also employs the language of the Fall of Man on several occasions in *Being and Nothingness* to explain the alienation felt at the heart of our being. Earlier, in my discussion concerning being-for-others, the look and the shame that it could engender, I argued that for Sartre, our being was being stolen by another in shame, a theft from which we desperately needed to recover. However, in the same passage, Sartre had also put it thus:

> Shame is the feeling of an *original fall*, not in virtue of my having committed this or that misdeed but merely by virtue of having "fallen" into the world, in the midst of things, and of needing the Other's mediation to be what I am (*BN* 392).

Shame is the *original fall* [*chute originelle*], the sudden realisation that I, in shame, have fallen into the world, in the middle of the situation and at the mercy of the other; the similarity in metaphorical language between Sartre and Schelling is inescapable. Moreover, both Sartre and Schelling characterise being in ominous terms; Sartre sought to characterise our human condition as a '*sickness*' [*une maladie*] (BN 803/*EN* 669), which resonates with Schelling's consistent use of the word 'contraction' in describing the split between *ground* and *existence*. For Schelling, God *contracts* Being, and Schelling means it in the sense of contracting a disease; since we are sick. As Marquet explains:

> Once freedom had been thought in its "inapproachable purity", it could not remain retained there, [freedom] inevitably passed into existence—inevitably, that is, in a blind and involuntary way. As the German term [anziehen] used by Schelling puts it very well, it "attracted" or "contracted" being, as one contracts a disease or as one attracts an unpleasantness (1973: 541).

Slavoj Žižek develops Marquet's reading and states:

> God unavoidably, of blind necessity that characterises the workings of fate, "contracts" Being, that is, a firm, impenetrable Ground. (Schelling, of course, plays upon the double meaning of the term *contraction*: to tighten-compress-condense *and* to catch, to be afflicted with, to go down with [an illness]; the primordial Freedom "contracts" Being as a painful burden that ties it down) (1997: 16).

The metaphor that both Sartre and Schelling are grasping for is a similar one; being is a sickness or disease [*maladie*] to be *contracted*—our human condition truly governed by a *condition*. The ultimate account of the human subject is catastrophic for them both, something must have "gone wrong" here—pre-ontologically—at the very heart of being itself.[15] Sartre is unambiguous on this point, we must try to *illuminate* this condition, he says: 'an original fault that one can *clarify* through consideration of the original event' [*une faute originelle qu'on peut* éclairer *par la consideration de l'événement original*] (NFE 11/*CPM* 18). Sartre agrees with Schelling, and the aspect of Schelling's philosophy under consideration here deals with his attempts to think, as Sartre puts it, 'the original event' [*l'événement original*].

Schelling has evidently distanced himself from his earlier identity philosophy, and instead argues that 'the ultimate goal of the universe and its history is nothing other than the complete reconciliation [*Versohnung*] with and reabsorption [*Wiederaufladung*] into the Absolute' (*PR* 31). This reconciliation ought to be understood as the conditions for our redemption, our finding a cure for our *condition/sickness* [*maladie*], and it is Schelling's attempts to speculate on the absolute origins of *for itself* and *in itself* that I am most concerned with elucidating. Schelling clearly demonstrates the mechanism by which the *for itself* comes to exist from *in itself*. The freedom contained within God is shared with the *Gegenbild* [counter-image], and freedom is therefore granted the ontological primacy that is crucial to Schelling's account of freedom. In the next section, I further investigate how Sartre's reluctance to give a metaphysical account of how and why the *for itself* is a nihilation found at the heart of *in itself* leaves him open to the charge that the examples he gives of love and desire, as well as of *for itself* and *being-for-others* more generally, rest on unstable foundations. In effect, this means that Sartre's arguments do not properly account for everything outside *in itself*, and, therefore, Sartre's philosophy in *Being and Nothingness* could be said to be the expression of a vast illusion (Gardner 2006: 261). I extend this critique to explicitly encompass love and desire, therefore reopening the possibility of love.

[15] I discuss this ontologically sick subject at some considerable length in my forthcoming book, *Homo alienatus: Freedom and Psychosis in Lacan and Fanon*.

Sartre's Atheistic Pause, or the Illusion of the Impossibility of Love

For Sartre, love and desire are the mistaken attempts to reconcile the *for itself* with features of stability and permanence that are available only to the *in itself*. Indeed, I stressed, as Sartre himself does in *Being and Nothingness*, that achieving this self-coincidence, that Sartre called the *in itself for itself*, is a futile attempt to become God himself. However, this is precisely where the later Schelling found his place in my reconstruction, since Schelling attempted to think the impossible in the Sartrean sense. For Schelling, the primordial wound at the heart of being is greater than with Sartre, because it is precisely God himself who is irremediably lost to himself, he has fallen from the seat of the absolute. For Schelling, to achieve the impossible as *in itself for itself* would be, in a sense, to be back to square one, to be lost once again, this time *as* God himself—there is no self-coincidence in Schelling's version of pure *in itself for itself*, God is nothing but a fragmented vessel.[16] Schelling takes a speculative leap from where Sartre has taken pause, he leaps into the abyss of trying to think pre-ontologically. No doubt, this sounds paradoxical and, perhaps, even nonsensical, yet what Schelling has created is a profoundly original, and completely innovative set of new metaphysical reflections that could be said to chime in step with Sartre's own radical originality. However, Schelling's is a leap in the direction of the onto-theological, as opposed to Sartre's atheistic pause (Gardner 2006: 260).

To see how this comparison makes sense, let us consider Sartre's discussion in *Existentialism is a Humanism* of atheism:

> For if it is true that existence precedes essence, we can never explain our actions by reference to a given and immutable [*figée*] human nature. In other words, there is no determinism—man is free, man is freedom. If, however, God does not exist, we will encounter no values or orders that can legitimize our conduct. Thus, we have neither behind us, nor before us, in the luminous realm of values, any means of justification or excuse. *We are*

[16] I borrow this phrasing from Walter Benjamin (1999: 79).

> *left alone and without excuse*. That is what I mean when I say that man is condemned to be free (*EH* 29: my emphasis).
>
> [...]
>
> Existentialism is not so much an atheism in the sense that it would exhaust itself attempting to demonstrate the nonexistence of God; rather, it affirms that *even if God were to exist, it would make no difference*—that is our point of view. It is not that we believe that God exists, but we think that the real problem is not one of his existence; what man needs is to rediscover himself and to comprehend that nothing can save him from himself, not even valid proof of the existence of God (*EH* 53–4: my emphasis).

Sartre describes our ontological condition as characterised by a necessary alienation. Sartre says, '*we are left alone and without excuse*,' and concludes the chosen extract with his existential slogan: 'man is condemned to be free.' Though, what is arguably more interesting is the way that Sartre seems to sketch God as only tangentially, or better, parenthetically, relevant to human reality '*even if God were to exist, it would make no difference*,' he says. Yet, Sartre's condemnation *to* freedom, which holds that existence persists even without the support of God, is in the middle Schelling the opposite, which is to say that in Schelling's project freedom is found *in* God. Sartre is right when he characterises his project as fundamentally optimistic, even though he does not allow for love to have true intersubjective value since in this quite formal sense, our radical freedom ought to be fully exercised: 'in this sense, existentialism is optimistic,' Sartre says (*EH* 53). But Schelling's account is precisely that the radical non-self-coincidence found in Sartre's version of *for itself* can, in a sense, be extended to be thought in God himself. God is apprehensive, radically dis-unified, uncertain of himself and of his act of Creation. God, too, is condemned to his absolute freedom, he is alienated, afraid, and without excuses. This conclusion yields a more intrinsically pessimistic view, a figure of God—an *in itself for itself*—that is properly dethroned.

Speaking of God in this way is, no doubt, unfashionable to our contemporary intuitions, perhaps even objectionable to our atheistic sensibilities—as well as being both Eurocentric and Christian-centric. However, it must be noted that, for Schelling, these are not simply difficult philosophical problems that we are attempting to resolve, or interesting detours to entertain in our human reality. These problems, the tension of the irremediable non self-coincidence of our subjectivity, are the very schism found at the core of God, and this ought to be taken as a synecdoche of our human condition. For Schelling, the "soul" is a significant matter, and it is precisely what is at stake. Schelling says in the second draft of his *Weltalter*:

> Man must be granted an essence outside and above the world; for how could he alone, of all creatures, retrace the long path of development from the present back into the deepest night of the past, how could he alone rise up to the beginning of things unless there were in him an essence from the beginning of times? (114).

For Schelling, attempting to speculate upon the origins of the world, time, and the universe is crucial to understanding both God and Man. This speculation is, in a sense, the metaphysical goal which, if adequately resolved, will alleviate the burden of our human condition—our original, pre-ontological sickness—Man will be redeemed from the catastrophe of the Fall. Schelling's *Ages of the World* is characterised by its sense of urgency, possessing all the hallmark drama of German Romanticism. And, for Schelling, in total contrast to the Enlightenment philosophers, we must go back to 'the deepest night,' no longer revel in the cleansing sunlight of Enlightened reason and rationalism (*Weltalter* 114). This seemingly doomed search through darkness is not as reactionary, or conservative, as it may appear since Schelling's work offers us a wholly reconfigured God—one who has shared his absolute freedom with Man. Schelling is undertaking a profoundly different analysis in this text by attempting to speculate on the 'original fault' that Sartre argued 'one can *clarify* through consideration of the original event' (*NFE* 11). As we will see, there are many echoes to Lacan's psychoanalysis here, notably with "Kant with Sade" and concerning *jouissance féminine,* which we will explore in later chapters.

Schelling holds that man is privy, by virtue of his essence, to a glimpse of the origins of the world. However, this is, Schelling says; 'the unfathomable' (*Weltalter* 14). For Schelling, the 'prehistoric age rests in this essence; although it faithfully protects the treasures of the holy past, this essence is in itself *mute* and cannot express what is enclosed within it' (ibid, my emphasis). For Schelling, we arrive at an impasse, subjects know that there is something to know about the origins of the world, but how do we grasp the inner core of it? All of knowledge, science, and history, for Schelling, succeeds only in unravelling the "facts" of available "data," so that, for Schelling: 'the history of nature has its monuments,' these are 'thoroughly researched, in part genuinely deciphered, and yet they tell us nothing but rather remain dead' (116), until such a time that we can think the inner core of the thing, the primordial "something to know," by which Schelling means the moment of creation, or the "holy past." Schelling's discussion of time proposes a view of time which is unlike anything we understand it to be in the quotidian. The Past is not, for Schelling, a linear succession of "presents;" 'most know only of that [past] which grows within each moment through precisely that moment, and which is itself only becoming, not being' (*Weltalter* 120). So, when Schelling discusses the past, he means something closer to what is best described as the biblical past:

> Thus, everything remains incomprehensible to man until it has become inward for him; that is, until it has been led back to precisely that innermost [aspect] of his essence which for him [is] the living witness of all truth (*Weltalter* 116).

Thus, for Schelling, to think *this* past is to make progress in metaphysics; it is, in contrast to Hegel's *Logic*, possible to think the historical past in this way: 'these lofty representations might protect him [Schelling referring to himself as philosopher] from the belaboured concepts of a sterile and dispirited dialectic [which is presumably criticism of Hegelian doctrine]' (*Weltalter* 117). It is to accept that 'our knowledge is incomplete, that is, it must be produced piecemeal in sections and degrees' (ibid). Schelling is eager to ascribe modesty to these reflections, and to the feasibility of the task at hand, first to think the 'infinite manifold [that] is ultimately produced from the greatest simplicity of essence,' Man 'must experience it in himself' (ibid). However, Schelling knows this to be an extremely taxing task:

> But all experiencing, feeling, and intuiting is in and of itself mute and requires a mediating organ to gain expression. If the intuiter [*sic*] does not have this, or if he intentionally pushes it away from himself so that he might speak immediately from his intuition, he thereby loses the measure necessary to him: he is one with the object and, to a third [party], like the object itself. For precisely this reason, *he is not master of his thoughts; he is caught in a futile struggle, expressing without any certainty what is nonetheless inexpressible*; he encounters what he might, though without being sure of it, without being able to place it securely before him and, as it were, to reinspect it in the understanding as if in the mirror (*Weltalter* 117–8, my emphasis).

Schelling's decisive insight is that the subject is 'not master of his thoughts,' and in a reverberating pre-echo to Sartre (Lacan, and much of the structuralist movement), '[the subject] is caught in a futile struggle.' Therefore, Schelling says, in order to understand the past, we must posit the unconscious grounds of the beginning: 'unconscious presence of the eternal, science leads it up to the supreme transfiguration in a divine consciousness' (*Weltalter* 119).[17] Ominously, Schelling adds, 'this is still a time of struggle' (*Weltalter* 120). The general process is one of radical re-orientation, thus, in typical grandeur, Schelling announces that:

> The man who cannot separate himself from himself, who cannot break loose from everything that happens to him and actively oppose it—such a man has no past, or more likely he never emerges from it, but lives in it continually (*Weltalter* 120).

Schelling demands us to follow him in suspending the present as constitutive in representing anything other than the appearance of quotidian empirical reality—what I earlier called "data." And instead, Schelling's wager is that we must attempt to separate ourselves from ourselves, draw closer to our divine essence, and try to think the historical Past. It should be noted that this is a radical subversion of philosophy as it stood at the turn of the nineteenth-century; Schelling is

[17] As I will show in later chapters, this description of the unconscious closely resembles Lacan's view of the same concept.

demanding from us a wholesale reconceptualisation of time and metaphysics itself, in order to re-orient us towards a theosophy. This new conception of 'the past,' for Schelling, is 'what came before the world' (*Weltalter* 121), and, for Schelling, the evidence of this biblical past exists all around us. For Schelling, to comprehend this past, we must ask ourselves *how* are we to form a conception of the birth of the world, the oldest stamps of the age of the world, without first positing these as 'unconscious.' For example, Schelling asks: how can we understand the oldest geological formations, which have their birth before humanity, without first positing them as an unknown event, an 'unconscious' beginning of the world (*Weltalter* 121)? In *The Abyss of Freedom*, Žižek explains that 'Schelling's fundamental thesis is that, to put it bluntly, *the true Beginning is not at the beginning*: there is something that precedes the Beginning itself' (1997: 14). Schelling is searching for the 'beginning of the beginning,' as Žižek puts it, Schelling proclaims that there exists a primordial 'something to know,' of which we have an inkling by virtue of our essence, and which our task is to think. In other words, Schelling's attempts to comprehend the 'beginning of the beginning' is to locate what Sartre had called the 'original fault' (*NFE* 11). However, the difference with Sartre is that Schelling locates the true beginning in *in itself*, the original catastrophe is that it is the absolute, God himself, who has to learn to come to terms with himself.

Schelling argues that in order to understand the absolute past, and the resultant relationship between *in itself* and *for itself*, we need to appreciate that time itself is constituted by two motions. One which propels time forwards, the other a slowing mechanism that attempts to prevent it from going too fast:

> Whoever takes time only as it presents itself feels a *conflict of two principles* in it; one strives forwards, driving towards development, and one holds back, inhibiting [*hemmend*] [*sic*] and striving against development (*Weltalter* 123, my emphasis).

This is important for Schelling since if this inhibiting element did not exist then time would take place in an 'uninterrupted flash' (*Weltalter* 123). Moreover, if the inhibiting element were to exercise itself too much then the world would be at total rest, and there would be only stillness. Therefore, it is the dynamic interplay of the continual conflict between the two elements that allows for time to be characterised as it appears to us (*Weltalter* 123). Crucially, this insight, adduced through time, is quickly enlisted to explain being; Schelling now argues that 'it is necessary to conceive of these principles in everything that is—indeed, in being' (*Weltalter* 123). This idea, distilled from the speculation on time, has clear bearings on our human subjectivity, Schelling argues. The conflict at the heart of being, which for Sartre in *Being and Nothingness* is the conflicting relationship between the two incommunicable regions—*in itself* and *for itself*—is in Schelling's *Weltalter* the 'original conflict of principles within being, which generates conscious subjectivity, and in so doing transposes itself into the relation of subject to world' (Gardner 2006: 253). In a sense, Schelling's speculations, adduced through time, have rendered explicit the relationship between the two forms of being; it is the continual dynamic interplay between *in itself* and *for itself* that generates conscious subjectivity. Furthermore, Schelling's account of freedom is secure, since he invests the *in itself* with freedom—as we detailed in the last section—which is then reinvested into *for itself* through the fall of the absolute into the *Gegenbild.*

Sartre's task in *Being and nothingness* is a similar one; Sartre is attempting to build a concrete phenomenological picture where the two forms of being—*for itself* and *in itself*—communicate with one another. He claims that these must be taken together in order to form a coherent whole: the two units of analysis form the concrete synthesis. Sartre claims that the *in itself* is beyond understanding, that it just *is*: 'the in-itself has no secret [...] It is what it is [...]—being-in-itself *is*' (*BN* 28–9). So, Sartre writes:

> A host of unanswered questions still remain: What is the fundamental *meaning* of these two types of being? What are the reasons for their both belonging to *being* in general? What is the meaning of being, insofar as it includes within it these two radically distinct regions of being? If both idealism and realism fail to explain the relations that in fact unite these regions—which are in principle incommunicable—what other solution to this problem can we find? (*BN* 29).

Sartre's task is to answer these questions throughout *Being and Nothingness.* He says: '[we have] reached a dead end because we have not been able to establish a connection between the two regions of being we have discovered' (*BN* 33). Sartre attempts to answer this by somehow linking *in itself* with *for itself,* following Heidegger in appropriating *being-in-the-world* and elucidating it through anthropogenetic reading of humans: 'what is concrete is man in the world, with the specific union of man with the world that Heidegger, for example, names "being-in-the-world"' (*BN* 34). And, although Sartre's suggestion that in order to move forward all we need to do is simply open our eyes—stating that: 'we need only open our eyes and interrogate, from a standpoint of naïveté, the totality that is man-in-the-world' (*BN* 34) –, this has perhaps not really allowed Sartre to answer his own question in a way which is sufficient, namely that of rendering intelligible the communication between *in itself* and *for itself.* Sartre writes:

> In our Introduction, we discovered that consciousness is a call for being, and we showed that the *cogito* immediately refers us to a being-in-itself as the *object* of consciousness. But after describing the in-itself and the for-itself it seemed difficult to establish a connection between them, and we were afraid of falling into an insurmountable dualism. This dualism also threatened us in another way: to the extent that we were able to say, in effect, that the for-itself is, we found ourselves faced with two radically distinct modes of being, the being of the for-itself, that has what it is to be (i.e., it is what it is not and is not what it is), and the being of the in-itself, that is what it is. We wondered then whether the discovery of these two types of being might not lead us to establish a hiatus, splitting Being (as a general category belonging to all existents) into two incommunicable regions, in each of which the notion of Being would have to be taken in an original and particular sense (*BN* 798).

To avoid confusion, Sartre, of course, does explain that the *in itself* and *for itself* have been shown to relate to each other in some way throughout the course of *Being and Nothingness,* that 'the for-itself and the in-itself are joined by a synthetic bond that is nothing more than the for-itself itself,' which Sartre clarifies as being 'a tiny nihilation that originates within being' (*BN* 799). Sartre argues that this enables him to bat away the question as to *how* this union effectuates itself in the heart of being: 'it is not therefore relevant to ask ourselves how the for-itself is able to unite with the in-itself, since the for-itself is in no way an autonomous substance' (*BN* 800). However, what Sartre had called 'decompression of being' (*BN* 27) in his introduction is now under pressure—for it is the actual decompression itself that is not explained in any meaningful sense, nor does Sartre claim that the birth of the *for itself* from *in itself,* by virtue of the nihilation [*néantisation*] at the heart of being, can be assumed to be a brute ontological fact:

> For example, [Sartre] takes care to say [...] that the for-itself is a nihilation which *has its origin* in being, not that it is in being; so the question is expressly left open concerning the ground in being of the nihilation which the for-itself consists in (Gardner 2006: 251).

Therefore, Sartre has touched upon a problem that he, too, recognises; 'there is space therefore for a metaphysical problem here, which we can formulate like this: Why does the for-itself arise on the basis of being?' (*BN* 801). To answer this question, Sartre simply restates the, he argues, vital distinction between ontology and metaphysics; 'the relation of metaphysics to ontology is like that of history to sociology. We saw that it would be absurd to ask why being is' (801). Indeed, Sartre goes on to say that 'all "why" questions are in fact subsequent to being, and presuppose it. Being is, without reason, without cause, and without necessity' (*BN* 801–2). For Sartre, the only questions that we should concern ourselves with are ontological questions to try 'to explain an event, and not to describe the structures of a being' (*BN* 802). This is what we earlier referred to as Sartre's atheistic pause.

Sartre's reconstruction of two differing regions of being both striving for communication with each other is in Schelling the radical separation of *ground* from its *existence*. Both thinkers, it would seem, are attempting to grasp 'how individual self-conscious subjectivity can arise out of pre-self-conscious being' (Gardner 2011: 68). Yet, Schelling is willing to take the leap into speculative metaphysics to answer Sartre's 'why does the for-itself arise on the basis of being?' (*BN* 801), whereas Sartre leaves the full weight of his conclusions in suspension, and without explication. It is for this reason that Schelling is included here, since the attempt to think the absolute is one speculative leap beyond Sartre, in the direction of an onto-theology, as the philosopher Sebastian Gardner puts it (Gardner 2006: 253). Schelling's elaborate scheme is to try and uncover the origin of the *for itself* in *in itself*, and Schelling manages to do so whilst maintaining Sartre's 'emphasis on the non-intentional character of the upsurge of the for-itself' (Gardner 2006: 253). Whereas Sartre explains the upsurge of the *for itself* as somehow a 'tiny nihilation that originates within being' (*BN* 799), this is 'reconceptualized in Schelling's idealistic terms, as the absolute or eternity' (Gardner 2006: 253). And so, 'at the point where what Sartre calls being-in-itself gives rise to the upsurge of the for-itself, being-in-itself *is* what onto-theology calls the highest being' (ibid). Schelling's insights are guaranteed by his deferral to 'the Absolute,' 'the eternal,' or 'God,' whereas Sartre's vast ontological programme does not have such a safety net. Sartre based everything on the *néantisation* at the heart of being. For Sartre, freedom *is* the very stuff of our existence, so that freedom and existence are synonymous, yet guaranteed by nothing—while simultaneously being the synecdoche for everything. The result is that Sartre's entire system outside of *in itself* is vulnerable to the charge that, 'while fully coherent, may nevertheless be merely the expression of a vast *illusion*' (ibid: 261). Gardner argues:

> Thus it remains entirely possible that all of Sartre's theory of nothingness, freedom, the mode of being of the for-itself, etc., is simply the expression of a systematic illusion: it is possible that Sartrean belief in the reality of everything over and above being-in-itself—everything which his ontology of the for-itself comprehends—is empty, and that in reality there is nothing but being-in-itself (ibid).

Schelling does not have this problem since he endows freedom with ontological primacy in *in itself*, whereas Sartre relegates freedom to an ontologically secondary position, as residing in the *for itself*. For Schelling, as we have seen, God himself has *fallen* from himself, he has freely chosen the catastrophe of the Fall, and as such has freely fallen from the absolute. Therefore, God's choice remains an acutely *free choice* found right at the heart of the absolute, or the Sartrean *in itself*. In Schellingian terms, this is the 'decompression of being' that would explain the connection between *in itself* and *for itself* which would substantiate the real, instead of falling into the charge of illusion.

The comparison with Schelling has unearthed how Sartre's ontological account could be said to have a crucial metaphysical problem; if Sartre refuses to accept the charge that everything outside the *in itself* is ungrounded and illusory, he nevertheless suffers with the insurmountable consequences of an unfounded metaphysical system. On the other hand, Sartre could relinquish his atheistic pause and follow Schelling in the direction of an onto-theology—which, as Gardner points out, would not be inconsistent with Sartre's atheistic desires.[18] Nevertheless, the impossibility of love, as propounded in Sartre's ontological account of the *for itself*, could be extended to being the *illusion of the impossibility of love*, opening, once again, the meaningful possibility of love and desire as not governed by the impossible characteristics endowed onto them by Sartre in *Being and Nothingness*.

In what follows, I undertake a detailed investigation of Lacan's psychoanalysis with the problematics outlined in this chapter in mind in order to demonstrate how Lacan's complex view of love brings us back full circle to its impossibility, with the caveat that love is impossible but necessary.

References

Baudelaire, Charles. 1993. *The Flowers of Evil*. Trans. J. McGowan. Oxford: Oxford University Press.

Baugh, Bruce. 2003. *French Hegel: From Surrealism to Postmodernism*. London/New York: Routledge.

[18] Gardner argues:

There is in fact no contradiction between an onto-theology of the appropriate kind, and Sartre's 'humanistic' claim for our total and exclusive self-responsibility. A form of onto-theology like Schelling's, in which the will does not follow from 'the understanding', and in which it is held that the transition from the being of God to that of the human subject is not a relation of purposive creation through which human beings are bound to a concept of an end lying in the divine mind, supplying them with an essence which precedes their existence, does not contradict Sartre's axiom of human freedom (Gardner 2006: 263).

Benjamin, Walter. 1999. *Illuminations*. Trans. Harry Zorn. London: Pimlico.

Berlant, Lauren. 2011. *Cruel Optimism*. Durham: Duke University Press.

Butler, Judith. 1987. *Subjects of Desire: Hegelian Reflections in Twentieth Century France*. New York: Columbia University Press.

Deleuze, Gilles. 2002. *L'Île déserte et autres textes: Textes et entretiens (1953–1974)*. Paris: Minuit. English edition: Deleuze, G. 2004. Desert Islands and Other Texts (1953–1974). (trans: Taormina, M.). Los Angeles: Semiotext(e).

Frank, Manfred. 1992. *Der Unendliche Mangel an Sein: Schellings Hegelkritik Und Die Anfänge Der Marxschen Dialektik*. Munich: Wilhelm Fink Verlag.

———. 2004a. *The Philosophical Foundations of Early German Romanticism*. Trans. E. Millàn-Zaibert. New York: State University of New York Press.

———. 2004b. Schelling and Sartre on Being and Nothingness. In *The New Schelling*, ed. Judith Norman and Alistair Welchman. London/New York: Continuum.

Gardner, Sebastian. 2005. Sartre, Intersubjectivity, and German Idealism. *Journal of the History of Philosophy* 43 (03): 325–335.

———. 2006. Sartre, Schelling, and Onto-Theology. *Religious Studies* 42 (03): 247–271.

———. 2009. *Reading Being and Nothingness*. London: Continuum.

———. 2011. The Transcendental Dimension of Sartre's Philosophy. In *Reading Sartre on Phenomenology and Existentialism*, ed. Jonathan Webber. New York/London: Routledge.

Hayman, Ronald. 1986. *Writing Against: A Biography of Sartre*. London: Weidenfeld and Nicolson.

Heidegger, Martin. 1985. *Schelling's Treatise on the Essence of Human Freedom*. Trans. J. Stambaugh. Ohio/London: Ohio University Press.

Hartmann, Klaus. 1966. *Sartre's Ontology: A study of Being and Nothingness in the light Hegel's Logic*. Illinois: Northwestern University Press.

Howells, Christina. 1988. *Sartre: The Necessity of Freedom*. Cambridge: Cambridge University Press.

Howells, Christina. 2000. "Desiring the Impossible," in *Philosophy and Desire*, ed. Silverman, H J. New York and London: Routledge.

Howells, Christina. 2011. *Mortal Subjects: Passions of the Soul in Late Twentieth-Century French Thought*. Cambridge: Polity.

Lacan, Jacques. 1975. *Le Séminaire de Jacques Lacan, Livre I, Les Écrits techniques de Freud (1953–1954)*. Paris: Seuil. English edition: Lacan, J. 1991. The Seminar of Jacques Lacan Book I, Freud's Papers on Technique (1953–1954), (trans: Forrester, J.) London/New York: W.W. Norton & Company.

Norman, Judith, and Alistair Welchman. 2004. *The New Schelling*. London/New York: Continuum.

Plato. 2008. *The Symposium,* ed. M.C Howatson, tr. Frisbee C. C. Sheffield. Cambridge: Cambridge University Press.

Rabaté, Jean-Michel. 2001. *Psychoanalysis and the Subject of Literature.* Basingstoke: Palgrave Macmillan.

Sartre, Jean-Paul. 1943. *L'Être et le néant.* Paris: Gallimard. English edition: Sartre, J-P. 2021. Being and Nothingness (trans: Richmond, S.). London/New York: Routledge.

———. 2007 [1946]. *L'Existentialisme est un humanisme.* Paris: Folio Gallimard.. English edition: Sartre, J-P. 2007. Existentialism is a Humanism (trans: Macomber, C.). New Haven: Yale University Press.

———. 1947 [1975]. *Baudelaire.* Paris: Folio Gallimard.. English edition: Sartre, J-P. 1967. Baudelaire (trans: Turnell, M.). New York: New Directions Paperbook.

_____. (1981) is QUOTED IN: Schilpp, Paul Arthur. 1981. *The Philosophy of Jean-Paul Sartre*. Illinois: Open Court Publishing Co.

———. 1983. *Cahiers pour une morale.* Paris: Gallimard. English edition: Sartre, J-P. 1992. Notebooks for an Ethics (trans: Pellauer, D.). Chicago: The University of Chicago Press.

Schelling, Friedrich Wilhelm Joseph von. 1997. *Ages of the World: Die Weltalter/The Abyss of Freedom (second draft, 1813).* Trans. J. Norman. Ann Harbour: University of Michigan Press.

———. 2010. *Philosophy and Religion (1804).* Trans. Kaus Ottmann. Connecticut: Spring Publications Inc.

Schilpp, Paul Arthur. 1981. *The Philosophy of Jean-Paul Sartre.* Illinois: Open Court Publishing Co.

Seel, Gerhard. 1995. *La dialectique de Sartre.* Trans. E. Müller, Ph. Muller & M. Reinhardt. Lausanne: L'Age de l'Homme.

Snow, Laurence. 1996. *Schelling And The End Of Idealism.* Albany: State University of New York Press.

Tillich, Paul. 1972. In *A History of Christian Thought, from Its Judaic and Hellenistic Origins to Existentialism*, ed. Carl E. Braaten. New York: Simon and Schuster.

Verstraeten, Pierre. 1992. Appendix: Hegel and Sartre. In *The Cambridge Companion to Jean-Paul Sartre*, ed. Christina Howells. Cambridge: Cambridge University Press.

Žižek, Slavoj. 1997. *The Abyss of Freedom/Ages of the World: Die Weltalter (second draft, 1813).* Trans. Judith Norman. Ann Harbour: The University of Michigan Press.

3

The Decorator Crab—Lacanian Misunderstandings

Lacan, *the Master Supposed to Know*

> *Language entirely operates within ambiguity, and most of the time you know absolutely nothing about what you are saying.* (Lacan)

Lacan's contributions to the history of French philosophy are both wide-ranging and complex. The young Lacan first trained as a psychiatrist, and after having completed his medical doctorate, he sat the *'concours du médicat'* exam in 1934 to qualify to become a 'médecin-chef des asiles' [lead psychiatric consultant] (Roudinesco 1993: 115/1997: 80). Lacan almost failed this exam, and in their examiners' report, his examiners noted that Lacan was "a tiresome young man," (1997: 80) [*ce garçon nous ennuie* (1993: 114)]. And while Lacan did qualify, he never took up the intended post; instead opting to continue running his psychoanalytic practice (1997: 80). His first seminars, *L'Homme aux loups, L'Homme aux rats*, took place between 1951–1953, and these seminars were held at Lacan's home. These are the only seminars that were not stenographed, and so are unavailable for scrutiny. Lacan's last public seminar took place in August 1980, in Caracas, Venezuela, a year before his death (Krutzen 2009: XI).

S. Richards, *Dialectics of Love in Sartre and Lacan*, The Palgrave Lacan Series,
https://doi.org/10.1007/978-3-031-45798-2_3

Lacan is known for his many grandiose and controversial statements (notably: the unconscious is structured like a language, there is no sexual relationship, and The woman doesn't exist), as well as for his notoriously opaque writing style and eccentric presentation. As Jean Allouch remarks in *L'Amour Lacan,* there are long stretches in Lacan's seminars where nothing interesting happens for months, and times when his ideas develop very rapidly (2009: 251). This strategy is perhaps unsurprising since Lacan's ideas developed incrementally and in full public view, and, throughout the seminars, Lacan would make categorical statements one year only to correct himself the following year. This spasmodic style presents us with many challenges as we approach the Lacanian corpus. However, as we will see in more detail, Lacan's endless equivocation means that we cannot very convincingly pin him to anything. Although far from being problematic, we contend that we should enter into this ambiguous intellectual spirit—devoid of certainty—to see that that is, in fact, the goal of Lacan's practice. As my final chapter will show, equivocation becomes central to Lacan's concept of *the sinthome.*

Lacan's public persona was that of an omniscient Master, and we contend that we ought to understand his public personality, practice, and philosophy ironically. Just like his brand of psychoanalysis, Lacan's idiosyncratic persona contains its auto-critique. For example, Lacan presented himself as the absolute master,[1] yet in *SXI*, *The Four Fundamental Concepts in Psychoanalysis*, he develops the *Subject Supposed to Know* (SSK), and although Lacan affirms the subject's implacable need for a master, evidently the master who is supposed to know applies to Lacan, also. For Lacan, the Subject Supposed to Know (SSK) is a charlatan and a fraud but one who kick starts the process of transference between teacher and student by adopting the position of an allegedly all-knowing master. So, Lacan adopts the position of a charlatan and a fraud, whilst simultaneously affirming: 'now, it is quite certain, as everyone knows, that no psycho- analyst can claim to represent, in however slight a way, a corpus of absolute knowledge' (*SXI* 232), and of course that includes Lacan himself. Therefore, Lacan's presentation as an all-knowing *master* should be understood as parody—his seminars merely perform this persona of the Master. For example, in *SVII*, *The Ethics of Psychoanalysis,*

[1] I borrow this term from Borch-Jacobsen's *Lacan*: *Le Maître absolu* (1990).

Lacan begins the November 25th session by flippantly declaring: 'honey is what I am trying to bring you, the honey of my reflections' (*SVII* 19), and in the many available audio recordings of these seminars Lacan's auditors often laugh as he makes these increasingly ridiculous jokes.[2] This aspect of Lacan's seminars gets lost in the published versions, and we mention this here since it is, we contend, crucial to understanding the performative dimension of Lacan's practice.

Lacan's psychoanalytic project in relation to theories of subjectivity is governed by his desire to unravel the maxim that the subject is not his own master [*m'être*] (*SXVII* 152) but is instead governed by a master [*maître*]. Lacan's philosophy relies on the idea that subjective insight is not located where philosophers have traditionally argued it ought to be, or where classical philosophy had placed the self prior to the advent of Freudian psychoanalysis. Mind-body dualism was abandoned by Freud (*SIII* 240), and Lacan argues that psychoanalysis's most significant early contribution to the understanding of subjectivity had been that the subject itself is not the site of the problem. Subjectivity, the location of the subject, and the ambiguous relation of being to consciousness will be my primary topics of interest in Lacan's early work.

The early Lacan, working on the Imaginary and the Symbolic, distinguishes the ego from the subject.[3] For Lacan, the ego exists in imaginary relations, 'if the *ego* is an imaginary function, it is not to be confused with the subject' (*SI* 193). However, Lacan does not suggest that they are not related, 'everything pertaining to the *ego* must be realised in what the subject recognises as himself' (*SI* 195). Therefore, the structure of the ego allows humans to enter the Symbolic through the Imaginary. I take this birth of the subject in the Symbolic as my starting point, and my aim is

[2] See also Rabaté (2001: 5).

[3] This is reminiscent of Sartre's claim in *Transcendence of the Ego* that the subject can only ever apprehend himself in fleeting moments, 'the ego never appears, in fact, except when one is not looking at it [...] behind the state, at the horizon, the ego appears. It is, therefore, never seen except "out of the corner of the eye"' (88). Indeed, as Clotilde Leguil argues in *Sartre avec Lacan*, these two thinkers are not the strange bed-fellows they are often cast as: 'notre analyse conduit à affirmer qu'il [Lacan] a aussi formulé son retour à Freud en empruntant à Sartre certaines de ses thèses et quelques-uns de ses concepts' (2012: 22). While Sartre influenced Lacan in many ways, Lacan also draws inspiration from other contemporaries: Heidegger, Kojève, Hyppolite, and Jakobson. The influence of Freud, Hegel (albeit, via Kojève and Hyppolite (Žižek 2012: 507), and Saussure cannot be overstated (see: Roudinesco 1993 [on Saussure]: 51, [on Kojève]: 94, [on Hyppolite]: 222, [on Heidegger]: 291/298, [on Jakobson]: 304.)

to build a coherent account of Lacan's argument that ultimately reaches the impasse expressed in his famous slogan: *there is no sexual relationship* [*non-rapport*].[4] Lacan's *non-rapport* suggests that there is a deadlock at the heart of subjectivity, which emerges in the relations between two subjects, for example, Man and Woman.[5] For Lacan, the absent sexual relationship is the by-product of a myriad of interrelated problems. We reconstruct a partially chronological account of Lacan's argument as it mirrors incremental developments in his thought through the yearly seminars.

For Lacan, if sexual relations were successfully achieved between subjects, the Other would be annihilated, the subject who achieved such a state would instantly transform themselves into the mythical Father of unregulated desire [*le père de la horde*], and would have foreclosed the master signifier (*SXVII* 111–12). In what follows, I aim to unpack these jargon-laden Lacanian assertions and explain why Lacan arrives at these conclusions. In the second half of this chapter, after having reconstructed the necessary Lacanian framework, I aim to complicate Lacan's argument by reintroducing onto-theology in discussions with Lacan on God. I will argue, by exploiting the now open possibility of love from the previous chapter in relation to Sartre's conception of *in itself for itself*, that, since God himself has fallen from the seat of the Absolute, God can now be conceptualised differently. Schelling's construal of the metaphysical Fall of Man, we suggested, created difficulty for Sartre's argument that *for itself* is founded on a decompression of being from *in itself*. If Schelling is correct and God has fallen from the seat of the Absolute, we are now able to consider Schelling's fallen God alongside Lacan's suggestion that God is potentially pernicious and evil; a God who only maintains the *appearance* of himself as stable and permanent.

Beginning with Descartes's *Fourth Meditation*, Lacan makes the argument that God (or, *in itself for itself*) might be deceiving us, which means that the empirical world is governed only by an appearance of stability and permanence. I engage Lacan into a discussion with Schelling and argue that since God has fallen from the seat of the Absolute, perhaps

[4] Lacan frequently discusses the *non rapport sexuel*, especially in the later seminars from *SXV* onwards. See for example *SXX* p. 17 and *AÉ* p. 455.

[5] 'Man' and 'Woman' are to be understood as psychoanalytic concepts linked to sexual difference but not based on anatomy/ gendered difference.

God's deception is double—both as the perceived deceit of a stable world, and as the perceived deceit of his own stability and permanence.

Love remains a possibility as *in itself for itself*, since it is precisely *in itself for itself*, the Other, that we know nothing about. However, for the moment, given that we love precisely because we do not know, love is possible because we will never know. I argue that the best way to conceptualise *in itself for itself* in relation to love is akin to the figure of the decorator crab. A crab which having camouflaged itself to look like a rock [*une pierre*], and so taking on the appearance of an inanimate object characterised by 'stability' and 'permanence' (*in itself*), suddenly sprouts legs and begins to rush off the beach (*in itself for itself*). The decorator crab is a metaphor for the pernicious God, who, after having fallen from the seat of the absolute is scared and alone. The crab's final act on his descent from the heavens was to seemingly render the world empirically stable and hide amongst his creation. Analogously, attempting to love, trying to achieve *in itself for itself*, is not impossible because, ultimately, we would not be attempting to grasp at the static and the infinite, rather we would be grasping for an unknown, which is a theological leap of faith. This leap could very well end in failure, but it is not (yet) impossible. Sartre would be incorrect, since the metaphor of the decorator crab illustrates the potential for the unknown in the guise of what looks like *in itself*.

In order to construct a cogent account of Lacan's ideas on philosophical themes, I undertake a comprehensive analysis, by no means exhaustive, of his work on language, psychosis, as well as mapping out the complex system that Lacan elaborates throughout the developments of his thought. For now, I omit Lacan's work on transference.[6]

The Problem with Language

According to Lacan, the central psychoanalytic insight stems from the 'recourse to the letter' (*SIII* 239). Simply put, this slogan is a note on the use of language. The psychoanalytic tradition appreciates that, while language is an imperfect substitute for what the subject is really trying to say,

[6] Indeed, there is much on Lacan I omit, for now, since the literature on love and psychoanalysis is extensive. For example (not-exhaustive): Copjec (1994), David-Ménard (1997), Morel (2000), Soler (2003), Balmès (2007), Allouch (2009), Monnier (2011), Žižek (2012).

we must nevertheless take the subject at her/his/their word—since the language deployed by any given subject contains the inexpressible kernel that eludes even the subject themself. The psychoanalytic task, then, is to grasp these moments from the unconscious and bring them into consciousness. 'Everything stems from here. Who is this other who speaks in the subject, of whom the subject is neither the master nor the counterpart, who is the other who speaks in him? Everything is here' (*SIII* 239). From this point, we are able to extrapolate quite a significant portion of Lacan's early thinking—namely the triad: Imaginary, Symbolic, and Real.

It is fair to say that Freud heavily influenced Lacan, and Lacan considered himself a Freudian right up to his death—stating as late as 1980 in Caracas, Venezuela: 'Me, I am a Freudian'[7] (*SXXVII* 2)—and, throughout his teachings, Lacan remains mostly faithful to Freud's central idea that subjectivity is somehow defective. Therefore, it is unsurprising that Lacan inaugurated his practice with a plea for a return to Freud. However, as Lacan says: 'the meaning of a return to Freud is a return to Freud's meaning' (*É* 337), which means that his 'return to Freud' is his *own* profoundly original return to what Lacan thought Freud meant. Lacan reads Freud quite liberally, and his engagement with Freud's writings illustrate Lacan's view about the instability of language itself.

If Lacan's philosophy has a core, it would be the idea that language is ambiguous and actively duplicitous, as he says: 'language entirely operates within ambiguity, and most of the time you know absolutely nothing about what you are saying' (*SIII* 115–16). However, Lacan affirms the ambiguity of language in clear language, which paradoxically allows for a reading of the ambiguity of language as straightforward (*SIII* 162–3)—and so taking language at its word. This complication is essential since it allows, according to Lacan, for *temporary misunderstanding* in his psychoanalysis. Lacan's method of understanding is through this essential detour. 'Quite literally' [*au pied de la lettre*] (*É* 342/411) Lacan stresses, because it illustrates his keen belief in disassociating the subject from her/his/their conscious speech. Lacan explicitly refers to language as untameable, yet we must work within its bounds, 'if psychoanalysis inhabits language, in its discourse it cannot misrecognize it with impunity' (*SIII* 144). What is

[7] Though, we should not take this statement too seriously either.

clear is that language is 'a marker of absence,' that 'illusion and imagination have an important role to play in self-understanding' (Howells 2011: 134–8). Lacan's primary aim is not necessarily to promote clarity of expression—for Lacan clarity of expression is, in a sense, a decoy; false security that does everything to obfuscate the nature of complex concepts. In *Écrits,* Lacan explains:

> Writing is in fact distinguished by a prevalence of the *text* in the sense that we will see this factor of discourse take on here—which allows for the kind of tightening up that must, to my taste, leave the reader no other way out than the way in, which I prefer to be difficult. (412)

Lacan goes to great lengths to, on the one hand, prevent misunderstandings, while simultaneously maintaining the ambiguity of language itself. 'I'm approaching, as you can see, in small steps' [*J'approche, vous le voyez, par petites touches*] Lacan says in the unpublished manuscript of *SXV, L'Acte psychanalytique*. He goes on:

> I can't say these things in clear terms—as it were. Not at all because I don't occasionally practice this, but because here in this delicate matter, what must be avoided at all costs is misunderstanding [*ce qu'il s'agit d'éviter avant tout, c'est le malentendu*]. (22)

Misunderstandings are to be avoided, through an only temporary misunderstanding. The temporary lapse in clarity of expression and the temporary misunderstanding is essential to the Lacanian method. Lacan argues we should read other philosophers in this way too, for example Aristotle's *Nicomachean Ethics*:

> Read the *Nicomachaen Ethics* [...]. There are no doubt a number of difficulties to be found at the level of the text, in its digressions and in the order of his arguments. But skip over the passages that seem too complicated or acquire an edition with good notes that refers you to what it is sometimes essential to know about his logic in order to understand the problems that he raises. Above all, don't overburden yourself by trying to grasp everything paragraph by paragraph. Try instead to read him from beginning to end and you will certainly be rewarded. (*SVII* 22)

There is no need to grasp every sentence and every word. For Lacan, 'read'! The reader will surely gain something from an insufficient first reading. Of course, Lacan's final aim *is* to transmit a fullness of comprehension of delicate concepts that speech and writing themselves make difficult and butcher—he clarifies: 'what is important is to understand what one is saying. And in order to understand what one is saying it's important to see its lining, its other side, its resonances, its significant superimpositions' (*SIII* 115). Therefore, for example, Lacan seeks to read *into* Freud, which is why Lacan believes he has provided a 'return to the *meaning* of Freud.'

Lacan's methodological approach is a form of hermeneutic exegesis of the language the subject deploys. It is for this reason that Lacan suggests we should follow a strategy of temporarily misunderstanding in order to finally understand his meaning because, at first glance, his ideas seem incomprehensible or counterintuitive. In *SXVIII, D'un discours qui ne serait pas du semblant,* Lacan offers his readers hope by remarking to his critics who claim that he is incomprehensible: '"we don't understand any of it", they tell me. Notice how it's already a lot. Something you don't understand offers all the hope in the world, it's a sign that you've been affected by it' (*SXVIII* 105). For Lacan, the comprehension of difficult concepts is possible in language; yet language is not what it seems. Lacan contends that the Real does not easily manifest itself in language: 'this tells you to what extent one must avoid the illusion that language is modelled on a simple and direct apprehension of the real' (*SIII* 118), and according to Lacan, the subject needs to work hard to get a sense of the Real in language.

Lacan impresses upon us that the radical inexpressibility of language mimics the radical inexpressibility of the unconscious, and it is for this reason that the unconscious is structured like a language (*SIII* 167). Lacan says, 'the unconscious is fundamentally structured, woven, chained, meshed, by language' (*SIII* 119). Language ultimately leaves subjects feeling wanting, since it is an imperfect tool for understanding the unconscious:

> The obscurity, the confusion, in which we live and due to which, whenever we spell something out, we always have this feeling of discordance, of never

being completely up to what we want to say. This is the reality of discourse. (*SIII* 155)

Obscurity is woven into discourse, and confusions are a necessary part of expression in itself, and Lacan cautions us not to blindly trust in words and labels. In *SVII*, *The Ethics of Psychoanalysis,* he says: 'but we must be careful. One must not always trust words and labels'—relying on words and labels is dangerous for Lacan, it obstructs both the 'liberating truth' [*vérité libératrice*] as well as the location of truth (*SVII* 32, translation modified). Language is problematic; it partly carries the liberating truth while disguising it, also—which is why Lacan urges us to proceed cautiously. The "problem with language" sets the intellectual ground for the quilting point [*point de capiton*], that becomes central to Lacan's conception of the big Other from the 1950s onwards. This discussion also sets the scene for understanding how the not-all [*pas-toute*], is meaningless yet envelops all truth and knowledge.

The Birth of the Big Other and the Oedipus Complex

At the outset of this chapter, I highlighted the view that Freudian psychoanalysis dethroned the subject from its position in classical thought.[8] Freud postulated the unconscious and revealed that central aspects of our subjectivity resided in the unconscious. This psychoanalytic idea shares

[8] Of course this is too cursory; while Freud is generally considered to have popularised the notion of a 'split subject' (conscious/ unconscious)—'no twentieth-century discussion of what the subject is and where it comes from has been untouched by the theories and vocabulary of Freudian psychoanalysis' (Mansfield 2000: 25)—it is useful to contextualise Freud himself. It is unclear if Freud read Schelling, but it is clear that he read Kant. Freud did not always see Kant as a willing partner; Freud rejected Kantianism 'because of the associated "transcendental" qualities of its epistemology' (Tauber 2010: 10). However, Freud's division of the mind into 'unconscious' and 'conscious' faculties, with biological characteristics of the 'unconscious'—subject to natural causation, and rational characteristics of our 'conscious' faculty—independent of natural cause, meant that Freud followed a Kantian construction of epistemological partitioning in order to engender our self-understanding (ibid 117). Therefore, Freud is heavily indebted to nineteenth-century developments in Kantian, and post-Kantian philosophy. See: Longuenesse (2012), Tauber (2010), and Nicholls and Liebscher (2010). For more on the lineage and developments of the unconscious see: Whyte (1960), Henry (1993), and Bell (2005). Lacan also acknowledged his debt to Kant, see (*SIII* 110).

the ambivalent structure that Lacan assigns to language, which is to say that language mediates subjective understanding, and, therefore, subjectivity must also share some of the obscurity of language. Lacan says, 'the unconscious is a concept forged on the trace [*trace*] left by that which operates to constitute the subject' [*l'inconscient est un concept forgé sur la trace de ce qui opère pour constituer le sujet*] (*É* 703/830). The unconscious shapes the subject, and the unconscious is structured like a language, in language itself. It is language 'which makes us subjects rather than mere animals' (Howells 2011: 134), and language necessarily implies language *for* someone else; 'language, prior to signifying something, signifies for someone' [*le langage avant de signifier quelque chose, signifie pour quelqu'un*] (*É* 66/82, translation modified). According to Lacan, despite the ambiguities of language, we are still able to communicate with one another since when subjects communicate, they ignore the fundamental ambiguity of language. We prevent the discordance between our experience of language as ambiguous, untrustworthy, and duplicitous, and the everyday use of language by ignoring the fundamental ambiguity of language in interlocution with another (*É* 66/82).

For Lacan, language is made up of signs, 'this experience is, first, some language, a language—in other words, a sign' (ibid), and signs are constituted by signifiers, and signifiers are understood in relation to the Symbolic Order. Therefore, the Symbolic Order is the domain of language for the subject, and Lacan says:

> That a name, however confused it may be, designates a specific person, is exactly what makes up the transition to the human state. If one has to define the moment at which man becomes human, we can say that it is the moment when, however little it be, he enters into the symbolic relation. (*SI* 155)

Subjects enter the Symbolic Order as soon as they are interpellated by name, which is to say as soon as they are named as infants (or before), and at that moment they become human. For Lacan, subjectivity is not necessarily located in conscious speech, as I showed earlier, and Lacan is contesting the idea that the subject is the site of his/her/their subjectivity (*SIII* 36). Subjects partake in the Symbolic Order through language, and human beings intersubjectively share the faculty of language. However, it does not necessarily follow that language or conscious speech is the location of the subject or subjective insight. The subject can attempt to articulate and describe language's structure by deploying words, and the subject can utilise language to explain and describe specific symptoms, delusions, or psychotic episodes, yet, fundamentally, language's first function is to necessarily imply an other, someone else, which is to say that language does not exist without the relationship between subject and other. Earlier, I explained how for Lacan, language before signifying something, must signify *for someone,* 'language, prior to signifying something, signifies for someone' (*É* 66). This 'someone' must be other than me, and, therefore, 'from the moment the subject speaks, the Other, with a capital O, is there' [*du moment que le sujet parle, il y a l'Autre avec un grand A*] (*SIII* 41/52). Lacan's highly original move is to suggest that the spoken word of an other inaugurates the big Other, and this big Other, to put it in crude terms, is the stand-in for the Symbolic Order.[9] Therefore, the big Other is a necessary counterpart to language, and, for Lacan, subjects not only interact with each other but always with the big Other:

> Within the generalized notion of communication, I state what speech as speaking to the other is. It's making the other speak as such. [...] We shall, if you like, write that other with a capital O. (*SIII* 48, translation modified)

For Lacan, it hardly matters if there is an empirical other person to consent to the subject's use of language or their speech, because there always exists a 'third,' a big Other who hears what we have to say, who consents to our use of language and our speech, thereby reinforcing our obedience to the Symbolic Order.

According to Lacan, the Symbolic Order overlaps with the Imaginary and the Real, and these three realms interact with each other in several ways. For example, Lacan characterises the ego as unstable and aggressive, depicting it as rivalrous and jealous, and, according to Lacan, the ego will necessarily attempt to establish its dominance over other egos in the

[9] Which is why in the graph of desire Lacan illustrates the "Voice" as partly constituting the big Other for the subject.

imaginary realm. However, in the Symbolic Order, the big Other acts to regulate these aggressive egos through a process that creates and forms the subject, transforming their ego-ideal into the Ideal-Ego.

Lacan explains that the desiring subject emerges from a series of incoherent desires that are themselves rooted in the incoherent set of desires that the egos form based on the desire of the other. Lacan says:

> Human objects are characterized by their neutrality and indefinite proliferation. They are not dependent on the preparation of any instinctual coaptation of the subject, in the way that there is coaptation, housing, of one chemical valency by another. What makes the human world a world covered with objects derives from the fact that the object of human interest is the object of the other's desire. (*SIII* 39)

The object of human interest is the object of desire of the other, and, according to Lacan, this interest in the desire of the other is an incoherent desire. Therefore, Lacan claims that the body is fragmented at the mirror stage because, in the Imaginary, the ego necessarily predicates itself on an *alter ego.* Lacan says: 'the initial synthesis of the ego is essentially an alter ego, it is alienated' (*SIII* 39). In the sentence that immediately follows, Lacan shifts from the ego to the subject in the Symbolic: 'the desiring human subject is constructed around a centre which is the other insofar as he gives the subject his unity' (*SIII* 39). So, the subject partly emerges from an original incoherence which is found in the subject's ego in the Imaginary realm.

It might seem paradoxical for Lacan to jump from the ego in the Imaginary to the subject in the Symbolic, but Lacan is simply highlighting the linguistic elevation from one realm to the other. An aggressive tension characterises egos in the Imaginary, and this, Lacan says, leaves its mark on the big Other in the Symbolic: 'the aggressive character of primitive competition leaves its mark on every type of discourse about the small other, about the Other as third party' (40). This move enables Lacan to claim that the subject's object of desire is the other's object of desire, because 'the human ego is the other' (ibid). I will explain this in much greater detail as it relates to the Symbolic Order in the next chapter, suffice to say for now that the middle Lacan argues that the subject, in early childhood and adolescence, models him/herself/themselves on others before their own wishes and desires emerge through a process called subject formation (ibid).

As I said, the ego's strategy of modelling its desire on the desires of the other is rooted in an incoherent set of desires, and this is based on the ego's fallacious belief that the other has a more coherent set of desires than its own. As a result, for Lacan, the ego is a fragmented body, and the emergence of its own character ['emergence of his own tendency' (ibid)] is trapped in the imaginary relationship it builds with the world at the mirror stage; 'it suffices to understand the mirror stage in this context as an identification, in the full sense analysis gives to the term: namely, the transformation that takes place in the subject when he assumes [*assume*] an image' (*É* 76). The infant does not recognise their body as fragmented in their mirror image; instead, they assume the '*ego-ideal* of the (imagined) seemingly coherent and fully formed image which is being reflected back at them. When egos stare at themselves in the mirror, they are confident that they exist, and egos see themselves as possessing a full being. However, Lacan argues that this stable relationship between the ego and its mirror image is only imagined; an imagined ego-ideal replaces the incoherent, fragmented body that is staring back at us in the mirror. However, the infant's identification with the ego-ideal reveals the tension between the missing object of the infant's desire and the other's object of desire, inaugurating, for Lacan, a dualism at the heart of the ego.

Our relationship with the other takes place in our communications with the other, and this communication is predicated on jealousy and rivalry (not to mention confusion): 'all human knowledge stems from the dialectic of jealousy, which is a primordial manifestation of communication' (*SIII* 39). For Lacan, the instability of this 'primordial communication,' cemented at the mirror stage in relation to desire and the other, is the distinction between the Imaginary and the Real (*SIII* 39). Lacan is careful to say, 'primordial communication' and not language, because language belongs to the subject in the Symbolic, and, at this stage, he is primarily describing egos in the Imaginary. Therefore, the aggressive relationship between egos is at the heart of all primordial communications with the other; 'speech is always a pact, an agreement, people get on with one another, they agree—this is yours; this is mine, this is this, that is that. But the aggressive character of primitive competition leaves its mark' (*SIII* 39–40). Lacan argues that, if taken to its limit, this aggressive tension in primordial communication would mean that it is possible to quash the other [*d'annuler l'autre*]:

> For one simple reason. The beginning of this dialectic being my alienation in the other, there is a moment at which I can be put into the position of being annulled myself because the other doesn't agree. The dialectic of the unconscious always implies as one of its possibilities, struggle, the impossibility of coexistence with the other. (*SIII* 40, translation modified)

Lacan then deploys this 'dialectic of the unconscious' to draw parallels with Hegel's Master and Slave dialectic. The connections to Sartre are also stark since 'the impossibility of coexistence with the other' is clearly influenced by Sartre's discussions of the impossibility of love and desire in *Being and Nothingness* that we explored earlier. Importantly, for Lacan, subjects vie in a contest for true recognition from the big Other but no subject will ever be vindicated in their struggle, since there is no adjudicator, no judge; no one subject will win since the big Other is vacuous and unknown, and yet the big Other remains paramount for all signification and maintains the Symbolic Order.

In order to develop the function of this third other, the big Other, I now turn to the antagonisms in intersubjective relationships at the cusp between the Imaginary and Symbolic realms. For Lacan, the aggressive tension between egos is central to all relationships, including erotic relationships, and the mirror stage brings to the fore the same tension which is, correspondingly, inherent to the ego (*SIII* 93). Lacan says:

> If the aggressive relation enters into this formation called the ego, it's [...] because the ego is already by itself an other, and because it sets itself up in a duality internal to the subject. The ego is this master the subject finds in an other, whose function of mastery he establishes in his own heart. In every relationship with the other, even an erotic one, there is some echo of this relation of exclusion, it's either him or me, because, on the imaginary plane, the human subject is so constituted that the other is always on the point of re-adopting the place of mastery in relation to him, because there is an ego in him that is always in part foreign to him, a master implanted

in him over and above his set of tendencies, conduct, instincts, and drives. (*SIII* 93)

Lacan argues that when the ego apprehends itself in the Imaginary, it is unwittingly constituted by the other's object of desire—creating a duality between the ego's object of desire and the other's object of desire, as we have already identified. For Lacan, 'the ego is this master the subject finds in an other,' by which he means that the subject is necessarily unstable since the subject's ego is to be found in the other, who is its master. This duality at the heart of the ego resembles the one that is at stake in erotic relations; for example, in the breakdown of a loving relationship, the sudden withdrawal of one's former lover can often be painful because our previous partner seemingly held our ego securely ['the ego is this master the subject finds in an other'], which has now been squashed and left in ruin. For Lacan, the ego in the Imaginary realm is fighting two wars, one internally and one with others. In erotic relations, the other can quash [*annuler*] the ego, and be his/her/their master, and, conversely, the ego is always ready to regain its mastery over the other, and in so doing, the ego could quash the other. Moreover, since the other is the master of the subject's ego in the Imaginary realm, and the other seems to possess all their tendencies [*l'ensemble de ses tendances*]—behavioural traits, instincts, and drives that are merely implanted in the ego—the other could easily hijack the ego [*c'est lui ou moi*].

However, in the internal conflict between the drives, Lacan argues, the ego must choose which drives and tendencies it should embody, and which ones it should discard. As egos, we do not know why we choose what we choose, there are some drives and tendencies we adopt and some we do not, but regardless of the choices we make; the 'synthesis of the I' is never accomplished. 'Synthesis' is not coherent in the Imaginary, and Lacan suggests, 'we would do better to call

it a function of mastery' (*SIII* 93). The 'function of mastery' we adopt is always made in relation to the big Other's desire, who is both inside and outside the ego. It is for this reason that any equilibrium reached with another ego is characterised by a fundamental instability (*SIII* 93).

> He will never be completely unified precisely because this is brought about in an alienating way, in the form of a foreign image which institutes an original psychical function. The aggressive tension of this either me or the other is entirely integrated into every kind of imaginary functioning in man. (*SIII* 95)

The aggressive tension between egos (or, the dialectic of the unconscious) necessarily precludes any co-existence with the other. Relations between egos in the Imaginary are necessarily unstable as a result, and, if left to their own devices, this would result in totally unregulated mayhem. Therefore, something needs to structure the Imaginary, and Lacan argues that this void is filled by the big Other, language, and the Symbolic Order; without which the aggressive relations in the Imaginary between egos would lead to a complete collision: 'everything smashed to a pulp. [...] This is only a fable designed to show you that the ambiguity and the gap in the imaginary relation require something that maintains a relation, a function, and a distance. This is the very meaning of the Oedipus complex' (*SIII* 96). Therefore, for Lacan, the Oedipus complex emerges as a result of the aggressive tensions between egos at the heart of the Imaginary relations.

Without the Oedipus complex, the aggressive tension between egos would be laced with incestuous drives and would lead to further conflict and ruin. For humans to have the most "normal" relations a 'third' needs to intervene, and the 'third' needs to be the model for a successful relationship, 'the model of a kind of harmony' (*SIII* 96, translation modified). According to Lacan, this model of harmony must be an injunction enshrined in law, the Law of the Symbolic Order:

> The intervention of the order of speech, that is, of the father. Not the natural father, but what is called the father. The order that prevents the collision and explosion of the situation as a whole is founded on the existence of this name of the father [*nom du père*]. (*SIII* 96)

Lacan insists the *Nom-du-Père* [Name-of-the-Father] is the master signifier in the signifying chain that reigns over the Symbolic Order. This signifier (Name-of-the-Father [*Nom-du*-Père]) is identical to the other signifiers that regulate Symbolic life, for example, the *fear-of-God, the Phallus, the Father,* etc. These signifiers found the symbolic law, the structure, within which subjects are allowed to operate, 'the symbolic order has to be conceived as something superimposed, without which no animal life would be possible for this misshapen subject [*sujet biscornu*] that is man' (*SIII* 111). The Symbolic Order is fundamental, it is what makes human life possible, and it contains language, the law, and the signifying chain. Lacan says, 'it is in the *name of the father* [*nom du père*] that we must recognize the basis of the symbolic function which, since the dawn of historical time, has identified his person with the figure of the law' (*É* 230). The role it plays in the Oedipus complex is key since it regulates the subject's desires. I now turn to what happens when this Symbolic Order is mis-structured for the subject, which results in the pre-psychotic subject.

Psychosis, Foreclosure, and Sexual Difference

Psychosis and foreclosure are fundamental concepts in Lacan's conceptual scheme, and, in order to develop an understanding of *sexuation* and sexual identity that informs much of the second half of this chapter in relation to Lacan's famous slogan *there is no sexual relationship* [*il n'y a pas de rapport sexuel*], I begin by discussing foreclosure [*forclusion*]. It is precisely the absence of phallic meaning (or, the master signifier) in psychosis that informs our understanding of Lacan's view of sexual difference and love, and, as is often the case with Lacan's work, a *temporary detour* is essential: 'if this doesn't seem obvious to you, confirmation by its contrary is, as usual, so much more obvious,' Lacan says (*SIII* 37).

Though we encounter the Symbolic Order at the original level of naming (and so language), we are only properly inculcated into the Symbolic Order from early childhood onwards. It is during this process that subjects are either properly oedipalized or not. Subjects are exposed to certain signifiers (*the Phallus/ Fear of God/ The Father/ Name-of-the-Father*) that are either recognised or misidentified, which results in a structuring or mis-structuring in the subject's relationship with the Symbolic Order, and, according to Lacan, this has severe consequences for subject development. The Symbolic Order is 'beyond all understanding, which all understanding is inserted into, and which exercises such an obviously disruptive influence over human and interhuman relationships' (*SIII* 8). Much like the interrelated concept of language, the Symbolic Order is both beyond all comprehension, and the mechanism by which all comprehension is apprehended, 'the understandable [*compréhensible*] is an ever-fleeting and elusive term [...]. Begin by thinking you don't understand. Start from the idea of a fundamental mis-understanding' (*SIII* 20). This is why Lacan refers to the big Other as something about which we know nothing, 'the Other,' Lacan says, 'in so far as it's not known' (*SIII* 40). The big Other belongs to the Symbolic, and in crude terms, it is the misstructuring of the subject's relationship with the big Other which leads to psychosis.

Lacan aims to show how the subject experiences foreclosure by studying the clues offered by psychotic subjects and their manifestations in psychotic breakdowns. According to Lacan, foreclosure is a specific mechanism located at the origin of psychosis and predicated on the subject's rejection of specific foundational signifiers (Laplanche and Pontalis 2014: 163). Lacan's *SIII, The Psychoses,* attempts to interpret Freud's '*Verwerfung*' as 'foreclosure' by undertaking a close exegesis of Daniel Schreber's *Memoirs of my Nervous Illness* (1903). Schreber's text had been the subject of a detailed analysis by Freud, whose efforts were directed towards understanding psychotic symptoms at the turn of the twentieth century. Lacan criticised the prevailing clinical view of Schreber's psychosis as having remained at the level of unconscious drives, and subsequent repression of homosexual tendencies: 'you know that psychoanalysis explains the case of President Schreber, and paranoia in general, by portraying the subject's unconscious drive as nothing other than a homosexual tendency' (*SIII* 29). Instead, Lacan argues that Schreber was not properly inculcated into the Symbolic Order at the oedipal stage. In simple terms, Schreber experienced foreclosure, a rejection of the primordial signifiers, which resulted in delusions and dysfunctional intra-human relationships. Schreber's psychosis, according to Lacan, was prompted by a defective inculcation into the Symbolic Order, a schism which only appeared at a later moment in Schreber's psychic development:

> It's possible that at the outset the stool doesn't have enough legs, but that up to a certain point it will nevertheless stand up, when the subject, at a certain crossroads of his biographical history, is confronted by this lack that has always existed. To designate it we've made do until now with the term *Verwerfung* [foreclosure]. (*SIII* 203)

Psychosis and foreclosure do not indicate that Schreber did not identify with *a* symbolic order, which is why the stool holds up for so long; Lacan insists on this point. Against prevailing theories, Lacan interprets Schreber's delusions from the perspective of Schreber's unique identification with God, because this relationship reveals his connection with *a* symbolic order. Schreber's psychotic delusions, Lacan argues, are comprehensible from within the triadic schema, Real/ Symbolic/ Imaginary, precisely because Schreber's delusions signal a fractured inculcation into symbolic coordinates, and these are translatable into comprehension. Therefore, for Lacan, Schreber's "delusions" were not so delusional after all, and Lacan is seemingly taking his cue from Schreber himself who noted in *Memoirs of my Nervous Illness*:

> Science seems to deny any reality background for hallucinations, judging from what I have read for instance in Kraepelin, PSYCHIATRY, Vol. 1, p. 102 ff., 6th Edition. In my opinion this is definitely erroneous, at least if so generalized. (Schreber 2000: 269)

In 'typical' subject development, the subject's symbolic castration offers her/him/them the chance to form "normal" libidinal relations with others, and, in order for this to happen, the subject must renounce the mother's unregulated desire, or in other words, the subject 'gives up some jouissance' (Fink 1995: 99). If they do not, they risk being faced with the big Other's *jouissance,* which is utterly incomprehensible from the subject's standpoint.

For Lacan, it is the "normal" structuring of desire in the phallus economy that enables the "normal" subject to form libidinal relations with others. Crucially, since the relinquishment in castration is of *jouissance* and not the penis, this applies to both sexes (Fink 1995: 99). In the case of the psychotic, the foreclosure of the *Nom-du-Père* [*Name-of-the-Father*] indicates an absence of phallic meaning which results in forming dysfunctional libidinal relations.

The Father, the signifier that structures the truth of the thing [*la vérité de la chose*], is defective in the pre-psychotic, which precipitates the pre-psychotic's descent into psychosis. However, what happens to the subject when the father, *qua* actual empirical being, is himself missing or defective? '*What happens*' Lacan asks, '*when the truth of the thing is lacking, when there is nothing left to represent it in its truth, when for example the register of the father defaults?*' (*SIII* 204: emphasis in original). Lacan clearly disassociates the signifiers (The Phallus; Fear-of-God; The Father; Name-of-the-Father) from actual empirical beings, individuals, or for example one's father. Reading the paternal function in relation to empirical beings, or understanding 'The Phallus' literally, for example, would be to have missed the point of Lacan's argument.[10] Lacan argues that the process of oedipalisation, symbolic castration, and the general inculcation into the symbolic by way of the signifiers, can be achieved (or forfeited) simply by an exposure to the image of the signifier itself—*A-father* [*Un-père*].[11] 'Let's suppose,' Lacan argues, 'that this situation entails for the subject the impossibility of assuming the realization of the signifier father at the symbolic level. What's he left with? He's left with the image the paternal function is reduced to' (*SIII* 204). The image of the signifier (*A-father*) [*Un-père*] is more important than the empirical person that assumes the position of the signifier in the Symbolic Order. 'how can the Name-of-the-Father be summoned by the subject to the only place from which it could have come into being for him and in which it has never been? By nothing other than a real father, not at all necessarily by the subject's own father, but by A-father [*Un-père*]' (*É* 481, translation modified).

Lacan demonstrates the priority of the image in the Symbolic Order (representation) with the case of 'history' vs. 'History.' There is, Lacan argues, a distinction between 'l'histoire de France' [history of France],

[10] See, for example, "Cosi fan tutti" in Irigaray 1977. I discuss the irony of Lacan's practice in "'I am a clown': Lacan's Difficult Literary Dandyism," *Paragraph*, forthcoming.

[11] It should be noted that, in French, 'un-père' is homophonous with 'impair,' which is to say not divisible by two, or simply: *odd*. Whereas, father, or 'père' is homophonous with 'pair,' in French, which is to say *even*.

and 'l'Histoire de France' [History of France], whereby in the former 'truth' may reside, whereas in the latter 'truth' may be relegated in favour of the decisive symbolic articulation of the History of France. 'What interests us are the decisive moments of symbolic articulation, of history, but in the sense in which we say the History of France' (*SIII* 111). What counts, Lacan argues, in our attempts to understand the psychotic, is not so much the truth of the thing, but the signifier that structures the Truth of the thing in its symbolic articulation, or simply, its image (*A-father* [*Un-père*]):

> One day Mlle de Montpensier was at the barricades. She was there perhaps by chance, and perhaps this was of no importance from a certain point of view, but what is certain is that this is all that remains in History. She was there, and a meaning, whether true or not, has been given to her presence there. Besides, the meaning is always a bit truer at the time, but it's what has become true in history that counts and operates. (*SIII* 111, translation modified)

Mlle de Montpensier could have or could not have actually been at the barricades that day, but what counts, 'counts and operates,' is that we understand the position of the image of the signifiers with regards to the Symbolic Order more generally. The disassociation of the (empirical) father from the image of *A-Father* [*Un-père*] is crucial for Lacan. The properly castrated subject experiences the same inculcation into the Symbolic Order as a subject that has been inculcated by the image of the signifier (*SIII* 204). However, Lacan associates the psychotic with the secondary form of paternal identification, which is to say with the identification with the image of the father. The subject who is exposed to the image of the signifier could experience a radical and alienating inculcation into the Symbolic Order. Therefore, the subject can be captured by the specular, limitless image of paternal authority:

> The image, on its own, initially adopts the sexualized function, without any need of an intermediary, an identification with the mother, or with anything else. The subject then adopts this intimidated position [...] The imaginary relation alone is installed on a plane that has nothing typical

> about it and is dehumanizing because it doesn't leave any place for the relation of reciprocal exclusion that enables the ego's image to be founded on the orbit given by the model of the more complete other. (*SIII* 205)

The defective identification could mean that the pre-psychotic subject forecloses the signifier, by misperceiving the captivating image that is without limits and so manifests him/herself/ themselves 'in the order of strength and not in that of the pact' (*SIII* 204). The pact with the father is the normal resolution of the Oedipus complex, the child would be said to have been properly castrated. The subject's exposure to, and subsequent realisation of, a father who had rightful possession of the mother is central to the subject's resolution of the Oedipus complex, the child having ascended to the normal model of virility (*SIII* 204–5). Conversely, the subject who forecloses would not be able to model themselves on the more complete Other (the father), and therefore relates to a Symbolic Order characterised by an absent core.

This problem, the original misstructuring of the Symbolic Order (the pre-psychotic), is carried forth throughout the subject's life until prompted into a full psychotic breakdown triggered by specific events in her/his/their life. 'The situation may be sustained for a long time this way, psychotics can live compensated lives with apparently ordinary behaviour considered to be normally virile, and then all of a sudden, mysteriously, God only knows why, become decompensated' (*SIII* 205). The psychotic subject forecloses and annihilates herself/himself/themselves through a misidentification with the Other's desire. However, the pre-psychotic (*homo alienatus*) subject descends into madness proper only after a traumatic moment that triggers the underlying psychosis in the subject's life, which had been a life of normal functioning until the onset of delusions (Richards, Forthcoming-b). Since the pre-psychotic, Schreber for example, is plainly in *a* symbolic order, not *the* Symbolic Order, any attempt to resolve the question of the father or the problems of his sexual identity are being undertaken at the wrong level. And so, it takes an encounter with the Name-of-the-Father [*Nom-du-Père*] for a psychotic, like Schreber, to break down: 'for psychosis to be triggered, the Name-of-the-Father—*verworfen*, foreclosed, that is, never having come to the place of the

Other—must be summoned to that place in symbolic opposition to the subject' (*É* 481). A confrontation with the Name-of-the-Father [*Nom-du-Père*] summons the subject to recognise her/his/their opposition to the Symbolic. The sheer weight of this summoning causes the subject to break down psychologically. This actualisation, brought on by exposure to the signifier, uncovers their absence and demonstrates their lack of sexual identity. In Schreber's case, the absence of a primordial male signifier was hidden for a long time, 'he looked as if he, like everyone else, were upholding his role as a man and of being somebody' (*SIII* 252). And, since virility signified something essential for Schreber, it is unsurprising, for Lacan, that the onset of his psychosis was triggered by having discovered that his wife was newly pregnant and that his election to the position of a Judge at the local judiciary was complete; igniting in him the fear of castration. 'The delusion's development expresses the fact that for him there is no other way of realizing himself, of affirming himself as sexual, than through admitting he is a woman, transformed into a woman' (*SIII* 252). This meant that the missing signifiers came to light in the guise of his desire to be a woman undergoing sexual intercourse; 'virility [is] the object of [Schreber's] very lively protestations at the time the delusion erupts, which initially presents itself in the form of a question over his sex [...]—"*how nice it would be to be a woman undergoing intercourse*" (*SIII* 252). Schreber's delusion was that he could only construct the realities of the world, the cosmos, according to the idea that he must be the universal God's wife (ibid). The decompensation that Schreber suffered occurred because he realised that he felt he could not become a 'Father;' the phallic signifier had not been correctly installed in his psychic economy (*SIII* 320–1).[12]

[12] Schreber was also a distinguished legal scholar, as Peter Goodrich shows in *Schreber's Law* (2018). Moreover, Patricia Gherovici argues in *Transgender Psychoanalysis* (2017) that 'Schreber [...] thought that he was becoming a woman rather than expressing a demand for a sex change' (91). Gherovici explains further: 'Schreber was *certain* that he was becoming a woman. He would become God's bride, a consenting prey to God's voluptuous pleasures. Freud interprets Schreber's paranoia as a defence against homosexuality while Lacan centres his analysis in what he calls Schreber's transsexual drive and, most importantly, his transsexual enjoyment. This should not surprise us [...] Lacan conducted a psychotherapy with a transgender person and was well aware of the differences between transsexuality and homosexuality' (92).

Building on the previous understanding of subjective inculcations into the Symbolic Order, I should note that the typical subject is not any more complete than a psychotic subject simply because they are named at birth, and so initiated into a relationship with the Symbolic Order; Schreber, too, was named. Rather, it is the process of castration and a subject's relationship with the big Other that structures the "normal" functioning of the Symbolic Order. The clinical tools, such as foreclosure, which Lacan develops from case-studies of psychotics like Schreber, are not inserted to wedge a distinction between "normal" and "abnormal," as though only psychotics are abnormal through the identification of a symptom. Hence, Lacan remains philosophically minded since he makes both an ontological and a clinical point.

Earlier, I suggested that subjects are initially inculcated into the symbolic at the original level of naming. We are spoken to, thus interpellated, and so initiated into a relationship with the various processes governing the Symbolic dimension. However, it is important to note that even though this might be 'typical,' it does not follow that it is successful. This is Lacan's ontological discovery concerning subjectivity. Our 'typical' inculcation into the Symbolic Order necessarily represents a failure. In Žižek's terms:

> The subject *is* the retroactive effect of the failure of its representation. It is because of this failure that the subject is divided—not into something and something else, but into something (its symbolic representation) and nothing, and fantasy fills the void of this nothingness. And the catch is that this symbolic representation of the subject is primordially *not its own*. [...] The speaking subject persists in this in-between, prior to nomination, there is no subject, but once it is named, it already disappears in its signifier—the subject never is, it always *will have been*. (2016: 210)

In order to understand why our inculcation into the Symbolic Order represents a failure; I turn to Lacan's arguments of the signifiers themselves. I will show how the subject disappears into its signifiers by looking at Lacan's qualifications of the signifiers themselves as meaningless and fake.

The Quilting Point

Lacan is unambiguous that the master signifier (Φx), for example, the phallus, is not something that we can possess. Moreover, the phallus is not restricted to men—the phallus is 'baladeur' [portable], it is elsewhere (*SIII* 359). Lacanian psychoanalysis has sometimes been erroneously characterised as phallocentric, and, according to this characterisation, the phallus belongs solely to the father and the father alone can possess it—the phallus becomes shorthand for oedipal domination by patriarchal power over feminine sexuality.[13] However, this argument is dissipated by recalling that symbolic articulations, as we have seen, are established without the physical signifier, and by relying on the image of the signifier. Lacan says:

> The father has no function in the trio, other than to represent the carrier, the holder of the phallus. The father, as father, has the phallus—a point: that's all. (*SIII* 319, translation modified)

It is a misconception to assume that the Lacanian concept of the phallus is a stand-in for a patriarchal theory of libidinal relations in psychoanalysis. For Lacan, the phallus-as-signifier is not determined by the father's penis; Lacan illustrates the concept of the phallus-as-signifier with reference to the celestial sphere (*SIII* 310). The master signifier is spectral, denoting nothing but a glimpse of the Symbolic Order itself—as the manifestation of the law in a symbol. This master signifier is not gendered *per se;* it is un-gendered par excellence because it can take on any form (for example: the Fear-of-God). Lamentably, we live in a patriarchal society, and that is why, for Lacan, the signifier is phallic since the phallic

[13] Jacqueline Rose argues in *Feminine Sexuality* (1982) that 'there is, therefore, no question of denying here that Lacan was implicated in the phallocentrism he described' (56). Furthermore, Emily Zakin argues: 'here we arrive at the phallocentrism, if not the patriarchalism, of Lacan's thought, the central role of the phallus in his thinking about subjectivity and sexual difference. [...] Lacan centres human experience not on the supposed biological fixity of anatomical distinctions, but on a representational economy, the phallus retains its associations with masculinity and remains the focal point of sexual identity.' see: (Zakin 2011); see also (Irigaray 1977).

signifier is Lacan's *ironic* description of current social power rather than Lacan's *prescription* for how society *ought* to be. Lacan is not suggesting we should keep the phallus, but that any signifier can take-on the structure of the master signifier. Lacan's use of the term phallus is an ironic, quasi-comical, take on societal formations, which seeks to undermine patriarchal power rather than to strengthen it. As Rabaté puts it in *Jacques Lacan: Psychoanalysis and the Subject of Literature*:

> The phallus is fundamentally a comical notion since it is intimately bound up with the genre of comedy that begins with Aristophanes, reaches its maturity with Molière and culminates with Jean Genet [...]. No need, therefore, to believe that [Lacan] remains caught up in a nostalgic fascination for the phallus, or to understand it just as the "signifier of lack" to which it has too often been reduced, since the phallus provides an introduction to a fundamentally funny, even ludicrous version of a bloated, excessive, impossible and symptomatic sexuality from which we are saved—but condemned at the same time—because we are "speaking beings" whose fate has been written in advance. (13)

Moreover, the comical aspect of the phallus is picked up by Lacan in *SXIX, ... Or Worse,* where Lacan says: 'today, we can indulge in some fun [...] we can have a bit of a laugh [...] The phallus is no small matter [...] the phallus is signification [...], the phallus is that by which language signifies. There is only one *Bedeutung*, and it's the phallus' (*SXIX* 55–56). How can a statement like "*Bedeutung* [meaning] is the phallus" be taken in any other manner than the intended comical, humiliating even, description of macho masculinity? Crucially, Lacan emphasises that the master signifier is fastened at a certain quilting point in the construction of the Symbolic Order, which is to say that he is offering a *description* of psychical reality.

In such a paradigm of meaning, the fulcrum that binds the set together does not need to be real, or true. In order for a community of people to communicate on a shared topic, the shared master signifier does not need to exist. Moreover, Lacan suggests that the master signifier does even not require meaning:

> It's a question of the transmission of something empty that wearies and exhausts the subject. At their first appearance these phenomena are situated at the limit of meaning, but they soon turn into quite the contrary—residue, litter, empty bodies. (*SIII* 259, translation modified)

This master signifier that guarantees the big Other is an empty signifier without a contentful signified. Žižek explains:

> Suffice it to recall how a community functions: the master signifier that guarantees the community's consistency is a signifier whose signified is an enigma for the members themselves—nobody really knows what it means, but each of them somehow presupposes that others know it, that it has to mean "the real thing," and so they use it all the time. This logic is [also at work] in some Lacanian communities, where the group recognises itself through the common use of some jargon-laden expressions whose meaning is not clear to anyone, be it "symbolic castration" or "divided subject"—everyone refers to them, and what binds the group together is ultimately their shared *ignorance*. (Žižek 2002: 58)

We can see the logic of shared ignorance in Lacan's concept of the *quilting point*. The *quilting point* is Lacan's first major qualification to the structure of the big Other that he effectuates in the mid-1950s during his work on psychosis (Žižek 2002: 58). The second revision that Lacan makes in relation to the big Other is in *SXX, Encore,* in the 1970s, where he uses the logic of the 'not-all' and the 'exception constitutive of the universal' (Žižek 2002: 58).

In order to make his point about the *quilting point,* Lacan shows how the master signifier, this time under the guise of the '*fear-of-God,*' was quilted by Racine's *Athalie:*

> The fear of God isn't a signifier that is found everywhere. Someone had to invent it and propose to men, as the remedy for a world made up of manifold terrors [...] To have replaced these innumerable fears by the fear of a unique being who has no other means of manifesting his power than through what is feared behind these innumerable fears, is impressive [*c'est fort*]. (*SIII* 267, translation modified)

Lacan argues that in order to invent a system structure with a master signifier like that of the *fear-of-God,* one must be either a prophet or poet: 'at least by the grace of Racine, [...] does this major and primordial signifier' come into being (*SIII* 267). For Lacan, Jean Racine effectuates a sleight-of-hand that transmutes normal fear into a faith in God, which guarantees an end to everyday normal fear by supplanting it with the master signifier: the *fear-of-God.* This transformation gives the subject enough faith to confront normal fear; however, Lacan points out that the master signifier (*fear-of-God*) is a fabrication (God) signifying nothing—an empty container:

> The virtue of the signifier, the effectiveness of this word *fear*, has been to transform the *zeal* at the beginning, with everything that is ambiguous, doubtful, always liable to be reversed, that this word conveys, into the faithfulness of the end. This transmutation is of the order of the signifier as such. No accumulation, no superimposition, no summation of meanings, is sufficient to justify it. (*SIII* 267)

As we have seen, the signifiers hardly need to be real in order for them to function as signifiers, and that argument underpins the *quilting point.* The *fear-of-God* is not founded on any real fears; *fear-of-God* does not signify anything in reality. Lacan maintains that God is merely an imagined construction of poets and prophets, and yet, he does not mean to suggest that faith should be ridiculed or ignored. On the contrary, faith is a foundational signifier that governs human actions. Faith operates the same machinery of the Symbolic Order; God is its master signifier. The pious refer to God, and what binds them together is their shared *ignorance* of what constitutes God as a master signifier, or as the big Other. Which is why at the end of the previous section I stated that the subject disappears into the signifier, because the signifier is a fake; and yet, the master signifier is the very mechanism of apprehending the world in the Symbolic Order for the subject.

The case of the psychotic has enabled us to see how symbolic castration is essential at the Oedipal stage to the development of desire. The properly formed subject will acquire a sexual identity at this stage, and the absence of phallic meaning in psychosis is pivotal to Lacan's conceptualisation of sexual difference. I have also qualified the signifier in order to transmit Lacan's insistence on the vacuity of the big Other. The master signifier is not something we can know anything about; this insight becomes crucial in tying together my view of the possibility of love as an attempt at becoming *in itself for itself* (or God—the unknown), later in this chapter. I now turn to Lacan's conception of sexual difference, and his discussion in *SXX, Encore,* of the not-all [*pas-toute*]; Lacan's second qualification of the status of the big Other as unknown enables my argument that love is possible as an unknown leap of faith.

The Absence of the Sexual Relationship

> To these children, Ladies and Gentlemen will henceforth be two homelands toward which each of their souls will take flight on divergent wings, and regarding which it will be all the more impossible for them to reach an agreement since, being in fact the same homeland, neither can give ground regarding the one's unsurpassed excellence without detracting from the other's glory. (Lacan)

Previously, I showed how the quilting point fastened a master signifier in language, and I said this master signifier was paramount to all signification, but that the master signifier was only an empty container whose primary function is to regulate the language the subject used in the Symbolic Order. In "The Instance of the Letter in the Unconscious, or Reason Since Freud," from *Écrits*, Lacan further develops the signifier by advancing the complicated relationship between the signifier and the signified in his philosophy, in order to advance his argument concerning the split between the subject and the subject of the unconscious, (this is an early iteration of a corresponding difference that Lacan develops, using different terms, in his later seminars) (Figs. 3.1 and 3.2).

Lacan criticises and complicates Saussure's famous tree schema to clarify the relationship between the signifier and the signified. The 'famous Saussurean algorithm (S/s—signifier over signified)' shows that the signifier and the signified are separated by a bar' (Zupančič 2017: 57). Whereas, Lacan's schema differs by replacing the signifier, 'Tree' in

Fig. 3.1 Saussure's tree schema

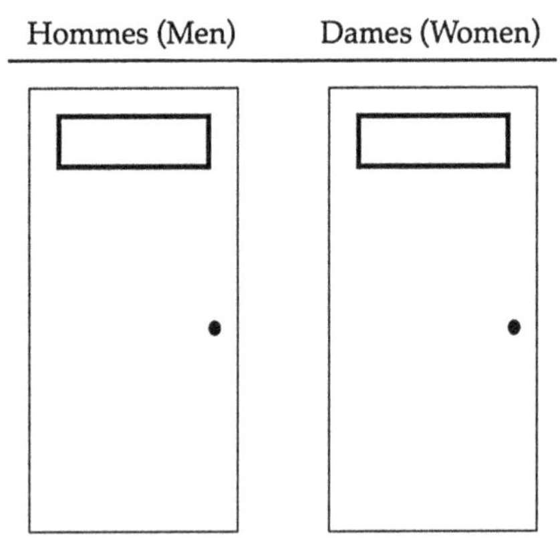

Fig. 3.2 Lacan's two doors

Saussure's classical schema, with 'Men and Women.' In *What is Sex?*, Alenka Zupančič contextualises Lacan's original move:

> The central theme of structural linguistics is the emphasis on pure differentiality (as Saussure famously puts it in his *Course in General Linguistics*: in language there are only differences without positive terms, and signifiers

> "make sense," or produce meaning, only as parts of differential networks of places, binary oppositions, etc.), as well as the emphasis on the arbitrariness of the sign: the signifying chain is strictly *separated* from the signified, which is what the bar in the Saussurean algorithm indicates. [...] The signifier "tree" would serve (albeit arbitrarily) to represent some signification. This is the conception that Lacan refutes as erroneous. (2017: 57–8)

Unlike for Saussure, according to Lacan, the signifier enters the signified. Lacan says: 'the signifier in fact enters the signified—namely, in a form which, since it is not immaterial, raises the question of its place in reality' (*É* 417). I should note here that, as we saw earlier, and as Rabaté argued, Lacan is taking his cue here from Jean-Paul Sartre (Rabaté 2020: 121). In amending Saussure's illustration, Lacan is differentiating his practice from structural linguistics, arguing that the important relationship is not the separation between the signifier and signified, nor is it the sign's relationship to 'representation' in the signifying structure. Instead, Lacan highlights that it is the 'signifier and the unconscious [which] are inseparable concepts; the signifying order [...] and the constitution of the unconscious are one and the same thing' (Zupančič 2017: 58). The crucial difference between Lacan and Saussure is that, for Lacan, the signifier itself is qualified as lacking, and this lack opens the space for the subject of the unconscious. To show this, Lacan adapts Saussure's tree schema to include 'two twin doors' (*É* 417) in lieu of Saussure's illustration of a tree—to designate the signified. And, as Zupančič explains, 'what do we have here? Two different names written above (the repetition of) the same thing, a door. In other words, we have differentiality (two different signifiers), but there is nothing different in the realities to which they refer. And yet they are not one reality, but reality as split' (59). I begin with this schema from *Écrits* since it succinctly illustrates the idea that Lacan's theory of sexual difference occurs at the level of the split signifier and not at the level of the signified (or the referent).

Lacan divorces the signifier from the signified by introducing the *quilting point,* 'every real signifier is, as such' he says in *SIII,* 'a signifier that signifies nothing' (*SIII* 185). Therefore, Lacan's conceptualisation of *sexuation* and sexual difference is not at the level of biology or alleged anatomical differences between the sexes. Rather, it could be said that, according to Lacan, the sexes are twin—the two doors in the schema above are the same; 'Men' and 'Women' are twins. For Lacan, sexual differences exist at the level of the Symbolic Order; differences exist as a result of the two sexes' operations concerning language, the big Other, and the lack in the signifying chain. Lacan explains the paradox of sexual difference as it relates to a fundamental lack through the story of a young sister and brother in a train, pulling into a train station:

> A train arrives at a station. A little boy and a little girl, brother and sister, are seated across from each other in a compartment next to the outside window that provides a view of the station platform buildings going by as the train comes to a stop. "Look," says the brother, "we're at Ladies!" "Imbecile!" replies his sister, "Don't you see we're at Gentlemen". (*É* 417)

For Lacan, this story illustrates the radical failure of signification, the deadlock of the subject's perception, and Lacan says:

> One would have to be half-blind to be confused as to the respective places of the signifier and the signified here, and not to follow from what radiant center the signifier reflects its light into the darkness of incomplete significations. For the signifier will raise Dissension that is merely animal in kind, and destined to the natural fog of forgetfulness, to the immeasurable power of ideological warfare, which is merciless to families and a torment to the gods. To these children, Gentlemen and Ladies will henceforth be two homelands toward which each of their souls will take flight on divergent wings, and regarding which it will be all the more impossible for them to reach an agreement since, being in fact the same homeland, neither can give ground regarding the one's unsurpassed excellence without detracting from the other's glory. (*É* 417)

For Lacan, then, the signifiers 'Ladies and Gentlemen' offers a kind of ideological phoney war in language, and, seen from the perspective of each side, they each pull in their direction. However, they are 'two souls' of the *same flight* ['being in fact the same']. As Zupančič explains, 'in other words, the 'Ladies and Gentlemen' example is not so much an example of the logic of the signifier as the example "illustrating" the constitutive gap and contradiction at the very core of the signifying logic'

(2017: 60). So, although Lacan is trying to maintain the differences between the sexes at the level of the signifier, there is a sense in which Lacan is also arguing that they are, in fact, the same, or it would be more accurate to say: twin. The discord at the heart of the signifier illustrated by 'Ladies and Gentlemen' mimics the difference between the subject and the subject of the unconscious I mentioned at the outset of this section. For Lacan, 'Ladies and Gentlemen' highlights the primary gap (or, discord) between the conscious subject and their unconscious, and, therefore, we might already be able to see why there is no sexual relationship [*il n'y a pas de rapport sexuel*].

As early as 12 April 1967, in *SXIV*, *La Logique du fantasme* [*The Logic of Fantasy*], Lacan says that 'the great secret of psychoanalysis is that there is no sexual act' [*le grand secret de la psychanalyse c'est qu'il n'y a pas d'acte sexuel*] (355). Years later, he formalises this thought into his famous slogan 'there is no sexual relationship,' wherein he does not mean to suggest that sex is impossible—'does not imply that there is no relationship to sex' [*n'implique pas qu'il n'y ait pas de rapport au sexe*] (*AÉ* 464)—but that the relationship (interaction in the realm of ideas) between the sexes is not possible (Fink 1995: 104). At the symbolic level—at the level of 'Gentlemen,' and 'Ladies' as signifiers—sex is not possible. Furthermore, the *non rapport sexuel* should not be read as a denial of the potentially existing difference between the sexes—we are not talking about biology here. Lacan says 'I'm not denying the difference that there is, from the earliest age, between what are known as a young girl and a young boy. This is even my starting point' (*SXIX* 5). But Lacan is very careful to emphasis he does not mean biological characteristics: 'I'm not talking about the notorious small difference for which, with respect to one of the two, when [they] become sexually mature' (*SXIX* 5). Characteristically, Lacan's *non-rapport sexuel* is both a provocation and a container for an idea that requires extrication:

> *There is no such thing as sexual relation* is proposed, therefore, as a truth. However, I've already said that truth can only come half-said [*mi-dire*]. So, what I'm saying is that, all in all, it's about the other half saying worse [*l'autre moitié dise pire*]. (*SXIX*, 5–6, translation modified)

Sexuality, for Lacan, does not simply describe certain characteristics of human reality; instead, we should understand sexuality as an ontological category, where *castration,* for example, designates specific conditions of the universe, that would classically have been denoted as *finitude* or *limitation* (Žižek 2012: 739).

In my reconstruction of Lacan's psychoanalysis, I have purposefully avoided drawing a marked distinction between the sexes, since, earlier, it would have complicated matters. In Lacanian psychoanalysis, the concepts of men and women are not tied to biology. Instead, men and women are psychoanalytic concepts. We could even argue that "Men" are not necessarily "male," and "Women" are not necessarily "female." Lacan distinguishes the sexes in relation to language, and so *sexuation* is intimately linked to language, 'when I say that *there is no such thing as sexual relation*, I'm asserting precisely the truth that sex does not define any relation in *speaking beings*' (*SXIX* 5, my emphasis). In other words, the speaking being has no sexual relationship with another speaking being. Lacan links the *non rapport sexuel* to language once again in *Talking to Brick Walls*:

> There is no sexual relationship seems a bit nuts, a bit *effloupi* [Lacanian neologism]. One would just have to get down to some good fucking to demonstrate to me the contrary. Unfortunately, this is something that demonstrates absolutely nothing of the sort because the notion of relation does not altogether coincide with the metaphorical use that is made of the unqualified word *relation*, as in *they had sexual relations*. One can only speak seriously in terms of relation, not simply when a discourse establishes relation, but when relation is stated. The real is there before we think about it, but relation is far more doubtful. Not only do you have to think it through, but also you have to write it down. If you're not fucked to write it down, there's no relation. (*TBW* 26–27, translation modified)

Lacan asserts the connection of *il n'y a pas de rapport sexuel* to language very clearly; sex is not at stake for Lacan, 'the real is there before we think about it,' he says. The *rapport,* Lacan argues, is of the realm of the metaphorical. The *rapport* must not only be *thought,* it must also be *written*, otherwise, 'you're fucked'—thus forced into the realm of language, and ultimately the Symbolic. Without formalisation in writing, there is no *rapport* at all, and yet *can* it be written?

Lacan clarifies there is no sexual relationship [*il n'y a pas de rapport sexuel*] in relation to speaking beings in *SXX*. Lacan develops *mathemes* in an attempt to formalise key concepts in psychoanalysis, with constant reference to the schema (Fig. 3.3) below.[14] Lacan says, regardless of biological sex, a speaking being will be in either one of the two boxes at the top of the schema; 'every speaking being situates itself on one side or the other' (*SXX* 79):

Everything we have seen so far, symbolic castration, the phallic function, foreclosure, and the successful (or unsuccessful) resolution of the Oedipus complex, is primarily tied to psychoanalytic conceptions of Man. However, as earlier indicated, it does not follow that empirical women are not also predisposed to the same development since, in Lacan's illustration, the two doors were twin at the level of signification. If, as I have said, castration (the function that produces "Man") is Lacan's word for *finitude*, then we can already see that ~~*The*~~ *woman* is produced by *infinitude,* and, therefore, we can begin to appreciate why she is impossible. Whereas, for Lacan, all finite subjects are properly alienated in language and marked by the psychic construction I have so far laid out. They are tied to the limits of language, and thus subject to the prohibitions of the Symbolic Order, organised around the master signifier Name-of-the-Father [*Nom-du-Père*] and its corollary injunction of the 'no!' of the father ['*non!* *du père*].[15]

Lacan's *mathemes* seek to express sexuality in logical denotations; he expresses the 'masculine' under the remit of the phallic economy, as $\forall x \Phi x$ (as seen Fig. 3.3 above, in the top left square); where '$\forall$' is the function for 'all,' or the 'whole,' x is the 'subject,' or part thereof, and 'Φx' is the phallic function for the subject that precedes it (*SXX* 73–4). We can

[14] The history of the Lacanian mathemes are interesting. Solange Faladé, the Franco-Beninois psychoanalyst and close personal friend of Lacan, had proposed the term 'algorithms' for Lacan's use of algebra. 'Algorithms' strikes me as a much more pertinent description for what Lacan was trying to do. For more on Solange Faladé's life, work, and algorithms, see my article (Richards 2023: 448).

[15] In French, the 'Name-of-the-Father,' *Nom du Père*, is homophonous with the 'No!-of-the-Father,' *Non du Père*.

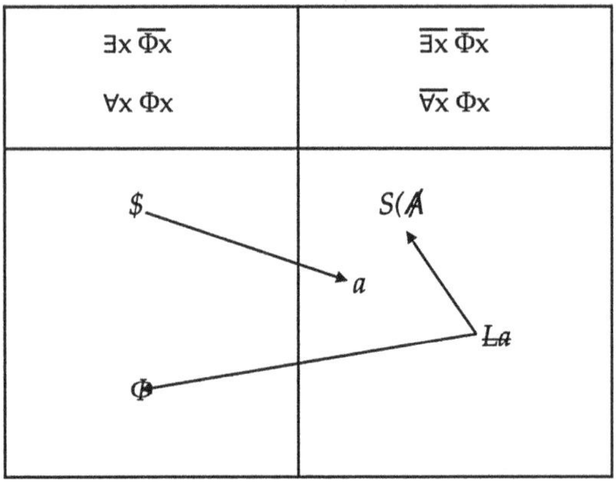

Fig. 3.3 Lacan's formulas of sexuation

translate this Lacanian logic as: the whole subject ($\forall x$) is governed by the phallic function (Φx), and is, therefore, prey to the power of the signifier in the Symbolic Order. '$\forall x \Phi x$ indicates that it is through the phallic function that man as whole acquires his inscription' (SXX 79). However, Lacan says, 'with the proviso that this function is limited due to the existence of an x by which the function Φx is negated [*niée*], $\exists x \overline{\Phi x}$' (*SXX* 79).[16] Men are governed by an ultimate limit ($\overline{\Phi x}$), and it is for this exact reason that they can be considered whole, '$\exists x$: there exists some x [some subject or part thereof] such that $\overline{\Phi x}$, the phallic function is foreclosed' (Fink 1995: 109). In simple terms, the Name-of-the-Father [*Nom-du-*Père] (with its associated signifiers, the mythical primordial father, *le Père,* etc.), or $\exists x \overline{\Phi x}$, envelops man's desire and so it is whole—man's incestuous desire has been castrated, and is therefore foreclosed.[17] The limitless father, the psychotic who sees all women as indiscriminately accessible is $\exists x \overline{\Phi x}$, ($S_1$). And the son who has been properly castrated is $\forall x \Phi x$, (S_2), 'every male is serf to the phallic function' (*SXIX* 92). The primordial psychotic father (S_1) is the only one who is able to have unrestricted sexual relations with a woman, 'enjoy[ing] a woman's body,' which is one reason why *il n'y a pas de rapport sexuel.*

[16] The "bar" across the top of the matheme means "not."

[17] In *What is Sex?,* Alenka Zupančič puts it thus: 'the logic at stake here is nicely summed up by the following joke: "There are no cannibals here, we ate the last one yesterday"' (2017: 51).

An exemplary case of the psychotic father (S_1) appears in Pedro Almodóvar's *Women on the Verge of a Nervous Breakdown* [*Mujeres al borde de un ataque de nervios*] (1988). In the opening scene, the mythical primordial father, Iván (himself, very appropriately devoid of a surname, master signifier par excellence), confronts an endless conveyer belt of women, finding them indiscriminately accessible. As he gallivants from woman to woman, flirting with each according to their ostensible stereotypes, he indulges in a form of unregulated enjoyment.[18] To a woman in traditional Spanish dress, he quips: 'life means nothing without you.' Then he mocks a nun: 'will you marry me?'. 'One thousand and one nights wouldn't be enough,' he says lustfully to a harem girl. 'I love you; I desire you, need you,' Iván rehearses. As a geisha walks by: 'you are the geisha of my life. Sayonara.' He does not stop there: 'let's get married again,' he says to his ex-wife. Finally, Iván deigns to tell a prostitute: 'I accept you as you are.' 'Great' she replies. Iván acts on unregulated impulse, just like the father of the mythical hoard; no phallic function (Φx) exists to restrict his *jouissance.* Iván's unregulated enjoyment and desire demonstrates the absence of prohibition, and, according to Lacan, 'the father of the horde' is an impossible myth that no human subject can embody, 'The father of the horde—as if there has ever been the slightest trace of it' (*SXVII* 112).

To undergo proper castration, the son (S_2) must renounce unstructured, limitless *jouissance,* which is to say that, unlike Iván, the son must make choices. Lacan says; 'Phallic jouissance is the obstacle owing to which man does not come [*n'arrive pas*], I would say, to enjoy woman's body, precisely because what he enjoys is the jouissance of the organ' (*SXX* 7). The exclusion of incest allows for an inclusion of everyone else—creating a whole. Unrestricted sexual relations are only possible from the position of the mythical father who is able to truly enjoy woman [*jouir de la femme*], the entirety of the woman. All properly castrated men (S_2) can only achieve a maximum of jouissance of the organ—in effect, the sexual relationship amounts to the enjoyment of only one part of the Other's body (*SXX* 23). Therefore, (S_2) is qualified by the features of limitation and finitude, and, for Lacan, all subjects are (S_2).[19]

---

[18] See: https://youtu.be/7femT8pLeFA?t=58 (last accessed 17 April 2023).

[19] ['On ne peut jouir que d'une partie de corps de l'Autre, [...], c'est pour ça qu'on en est réduit simplement à une petite étreinte, comme ça, à prendre un avant-bras ou n'importe quoi d'autre—ouille!' (*SXX*: 26).]

Women, on the other hand, are not necessarily restricted by the same phallic function (Φx). They *are* captured by the phallus, but not in exactly the same way and potentially not to the same degree. Of course, women are not lesser than men, nor are women unable to have a host of sexual relations with men (or indeed, women) in the symbolic articulation of the phallus economy; 'because in the end the absence of sexual relation clearly doesn't prevent liaisons, far from it, but rather provides them with their conditions—[…] the enthralling acts […] are necessitated by the absence of relation' (*SXIX* 11). The *non-rapport* does not denote the impossibility of the physical act; instead, Lacan suggests that the *non-rapport* is the condition of possibility for 'the enthralling acts' (*SXIX* 11). Furthermore, Lacan does not suggest that the psychoanalytic concept of 'women' necessarily corresponds to being anatomically perceived as female, just as he did not earlier designate 'men' as anatomically perceived as male. Sex is not related to *sexe.* Moreover, according to Lacan, we *can-be-not* our designated biological sex.

Returning to Fig. 3.3, Lacan denotes women as $\overline{\forall x}\Phi x$, where $\overline{\forall x}$ denotes the not-all (*pas toute*) subject, x, that is governed by the phallic function (Φx):

> On the other side, you have the inscription of the woman portion of speaking beings. Any speaking being whatsoever, as is expressly formulated in Freudian theory, whether provided with the attributes of masculinity—attributes that remain to be determined—or not, is allowed to inscribe itself in this part. If it inscribes itself there, it will not allow for any universality- it will be a not-whole, insofar as it has the choice of positing itself in Φx or of not being there [*de n'en pas être*]. (*SXX* 74)

If the woman chooses *not* to recognise the mastery of the signifier (Φx), then the expression would be written, $\overline{\exists x \Phi x}$, and she would not *Be* [*n'en pas être*]. Lacan says that all speaking beings, regardless of their anatomical attributes (or those yet to be determined), remain in the clutches of the Phallus as master signifier. Lacan makes a few exceptions: namely mystics like him. The expression $\overline{\exists x \Phi x}$ designates no possible being. 'Or of not being there' in the Symbolic Order means that the woman $\overline{\exists x \Phi x}$

would have foreclosed (having rejected the primordial signifier, *the phallus*), and would live as a psychotic subject beyond signification.

Before returning to the implications of the not-all [*pas-toute*] and the transcendental logic of feminine *jouissance* which enables my re-introduction of a pernicious God in the next section, my final task in this section is to tease out what the *non-rapport* implies in relation to knowledge and truth. Lacan's main aim in introducing the logic of the *non-rapport,* from *SXIV* onwards, is to demonstrate the limits of the logic of truth, and the incompleteness of truth itself (Chiesa 2016: 77). Lacan stresses that the *non-rapport* is related to language and writing: 'not only do you have to think it through, but also you have to write it down. If you're not fucked to write it down, there's no relation' (*TBW* 26–27). So, Lacan says once again 'this non-relation, if I can put it like that, needs to be written. It needs to be written at any cost' (*SXIX* 20). Lacan argues that the *rapport sexuel* is impossible precisely because it cannot be formalised in symbolic structures. Thus, in being un-formalizable, the *rapport sexuel* does not exist.

> The sexual relation remains in the last term only from writing. The essence of the relation is an application, *a* applied to *b*—*a* → *b*. If you don't write it down as *a* and *b*, you don't hold the relation as such. (*SXVIII* 65)

So, for Lacan, from a purely linguistic and logical standpoint, there is no sexual relationship: 'that there is no sexual relationship, I have already fixed it in this form, that there is no way to write it' (*SXVIII* 83). Therefore, language forces a disjunction between Man and Woman, and it is impossible to formalise the *non-rapport,* ('by the effect of language, inscribed in the disjunction of the man and the woman') (*SXVIII* 75). The central question of the *non-rapport,* that Lacan investigates in these seminars is: how to formalise the unformalizable? Which, in many ways, resembles Schelling's view of the unfathomable that I identified earlier.

In adopting the *mathemes,* Lacan tries to overcome these difficulties in formalising *sexuation* by attempting to express the relationship of Men and of Women to the symbolic as $\forall x \Phi x$ and $\overline{\forall x}\Phi x$, respectively (*SXX* 78–9). Clearly, the problem of language articulated earlier is systemic to the entirety of Lacan's conceptual thinking:

> The alleged sexualization of the functions that can be called subjective that the Freudian doctrine would accomplish, on the condition of situating them in the order of language, consists essentially in this, that what should result from language, that is to say that the sexual relation can be inscribed in it in any way, shows precisely, and this in fact, its failure. It is not inscribable. [...] For example, we recall that I say that the sexual relation fails to be stated in language. But precisely, it is not *stated* [*énoncé*] that I said, it is *inscribable* [*inscriptible*]. (*SXVIII* 132)

The problem of formalising *sexuation* does not make discussions of sex or love impossible. Indeed, as Lacan puts it: 'we have done nothing but speak of love in analytic discourse [...] to speak of love is in itself a jouissance' (*SXX* 83). Lacan explicitly denotes sex: F(x), 'symbolized in the simplest way, namely this, F, in a certain relation to x, is F(x)' (*SXVIII* 132). However, we are unable to effectively *inscribe* the resolution of the sexual relationship, and thus unable to merge the two poles—Man and Woman:

> It cannot be that this inscription is what I define as the effective inscription of what would be the sexual relation insofar as it would put in relation the two poles, the two terms that would be entitled man and woman [...] in a being that speaks, in other words, who inhabits language, finds itself drawing from it this use that is that of speech. (*SXVIII* 132)

Lacan explains the *non rapport sexuel* from the logical standpoint of language itself. Man and Woman are disjunctive and non-complementary; the two poles of sexuation (Man and Woman) organised around the phallic function make any inscription untenable, 'this phallic function now makes sexual bipolarity untenable, and untenable in a way that literally volatilizes what can be written about this relationship' (*SXVIII* 67). Ultimately, psychoanalysis offers a new track for thinking about sexuality:

> Let's say that, here, we find ourselves faced with the splintering apart of the notion of, let's call it, sexuality. Without a doubt, sexuality lies at the centre of everything that happens in the unconscious. However, it lies at the centre in so far as it is a lack. In other words, in the stead of anything whatsoever of sexual relation that could be written as such, impasses arise, impasses

> which are generated by the function of sexual jouissance, in so far as it appears as the point of mirage that Freud himself makes a note of somewhere as absolute jouissance. And it's true that, precisely, this jouissance is not absolute. Jouissance is in no sense absolute because, first of all, as such it is doomed to these different forms of failure constituted by castration for male jouissance and by division for female jouissance. (*TBW* 29)

The impasse reached in the *non-rapport* is the renunciation of unrestricted *jouissance* at the original level of castration. Pure *jouissance* would entail a return to the unregulated desire of the Father of the mythic hoard. By renouncing this *jouissance*, we are instead left with the semblance of *jouissance,* only able to enjoy part of the body. The true sexual relation would be effectively inscribable, precisely because it is absolute, incomprehensible, and ungoverned by formal structure or language. What remains is a semblance of the real, and we are nothing but 'fictional beings' in an incomplete structure of a fiction (*SXVIII* 132). In the fiction that we perceive as real, we play our gendered identification, and our identity is rendered "stable." Lacan says, 'for the boy, it is a question, in adulthood, of *making-man* [*de faire-homme*],' and this functions identically for girls and women, they 'make-women' (*SXVIII* 32: my emphasis). 'The sexual identification does not consist in us believing ourselves to be men or women [*ne consiste pas à se croire homme ou femme*], but in taking into account that there are women, for the boy, that there are men, for the girl' (*SXVIII* 34). Ironically, while gender identity is built on a relationship between Men and Women, the construction is founded on the relation of an un-relation of the *non-rapport sexuel.* Lacan removes completeness and essence from Men and Women (*SXVIII* 32). 'When thought of as outside of symbolic institutions and the phallic function that sustains them, man and woman can only designate sex as a *real* "unknown"' (Chiesa 2016: 80). Ultimately the logic of *sexuation* in Lacan's construction is that subjectivation occurs around the symbolic identification with the signifier (Phallus), which is structured differently for Men and Women among speaking beings, 'yet at the same time always presupposes the other sex [...], man becomes a man only against the background of woman, just as woman becomes a woman only against the background of man' (Chiesa 2016: 106). *Il n'y a pas de rapport sexuel* expresses a recognition of the limits of psychoanalysis. Lacan's slogan recognises that psychoanalysis will not be able to produce scientific laws of nature, that are repeatable and predictable in all subjects and their development. Geneviève Morel states 'psychoanalysis cannot write the universal law of this relationship, nor give the rules, because they do not exist' (Morel 2000: 19).

The dislocation that sexuality exposes through the *non rapport sexuel* is Lacan's equivalent of the ontological gap which, according to Žižek, finds its earliest expression in Kant's *Critique of Pure Reason,* and envelops the whole of German Idealism, most notably in the philosophies of Schelling and Hegel (Žižek 2012: 739–40). Lacan 're-ontologizes' sexual difference, so that it no longer simply designates 'a particular ontic sphere of human reality' but instead 'stands for a certain displacement, an anamorphic distortion, whose status is strictly formal. [...Sexuality,] does *not* have its own "proper" sphere, because it is primordially "out of joint," marked by a constitutive gap or discord' (ibid).[20] In *SXX*, Lacan clearly identifies this ontological gap as the difference between phallic *jouissance,* and the other (feminine) *jouissance.* 'Only phallic enjoyment is (f)actual, actually existing, while the other (feminine) *jouissance* is counterfactual' (Žižek 2016: 296). Žižek uses the term counterfactual to designate the difference between what I have so far exposited as the phallic master signifier of masculine sexuality (finitude), and the not-all [*pas-toute*] to which I now turn (infinitude). I also turn to the corollary discussion of Lacan's God hypothesis, which finds its earliest expression in *SIII, Les Psychoses.* The aim now is to demonstrate how love is ultimately possible, *contra* Sartre, as the symptomatic expression of an *unknown*—and, therefore, speculatively thinkable through Schelling's metaphysical construal of the Fall of Man.

[20] The fundamental ontological question here and ultimate potential weakness of the argument I develop is: (to put it in Sartrean language) can we introduce sexual difference in the *for itself*? For Jacques Derrida, the answer is an emphatic no. Derrida repeatedly treats this philosophical problem in Heidegger in his three-part "Geschlecht" books, and although, there is much to say on the question, this would demand a sustained treatment in a second work on the subject. Suffice it to say for now, the argument I develop, by adopting Sartrean language, is an argument contained to Lacan's psychoanalysis and his view of love. For more, see: Derrida (1990, 2018).

The Paradoxes of the Not-All, or God's Deception

In keeping with his method of temporary detours, Lacan's distinction between phallic and feminine *jouissance* is mostly designed to shed light on the former, just as, at the outset of the previous section, the subject was clarified thanks to the comparison with the subject of the unconscious. If we translate Lacan's intellectual strategy into Kantian language, we can see that Lacan posits a *noumenal* unknown (feminine *jouissance*) in order to flesh out the *phenomenal* known (*jouissance phallique*). For Lacan, feminine *jouissance* is both not possible and not required, formalised thus: $\overline{\exists x \Phi x}$, and pursuing feminine *jouissance* would result in in-existence; it is 'the jouissance that shouldn't be' [*la jouissance qu'il ne faudrait pas*]. Lacan continues, 'that is the correlate of the fact that there's no such thing as a sexual relationship, and it is the substantial aspect [*le substantiel*] of the phallic function' (*SXX* 59). Feminine *jouissance* is not only prohibited but entirely inaccessible for the subject in Lacan's thought because it describes a mere illusion, and yet, this fiction is necessary for the phallic function.

> If there were another than phallic jouissance, it would have to not be this one [...] "if there were another:" there is no other than phallic jouissance. Except for the one about which the woman does not breathe a word [*sauf celle sur laquelle la femme ne souffle mot*], perhaps because she does not know it, the one that made her *not-all*, in any case. Therefore, it is wrong, eh, that there is another. [...] Assuming that there is another one, but precisely there isn't, and at the same time, it's not because there isn't another one... and that's that what the "it shouldn't be" depends on... so that the knife doesn't fall any less cleanly [*pour que le couperet n'en tombe pas moins sûr*]. Well, this one which is not the other, that one from which we left, it is necessary that that one is wrong, notice the guilt, and fault of the other, of that which is not. (*SXXa* 140–1)

> S'il y en avait une autre que la jouissance phallique, il ne faudrait pas que ce soit celle-là [...] "s'il y en avait une autre:" il n'y en a pas d'autre que la jouissance phallique. Sauf celle sur laquelle la femme ne souffle mot, peut-

> être parce qu'elle ne la connaît pas, celle qui la fait *pas toute* en tout cas. Il est donc faux, hein, qu'il y en ait une autre. [...] À supposer qu'il y en ait une autre, mais justement il n'y en a pas, et du même coup, c'est pas parce qu'il n'y en a pas...et que c'est de ça que dépend le "il ne faudrait pas" ... pour que le couperet n'en tombe pas moins sûr. Eh bien celle-lÀ qui n'est pas l'autre, celle dont nous sommes partis, il faut que celle-lÀ soit faute, entendez-le culpabilité, et faute de l'autre, de celle qui n'est pas. (*SXXa* 140–1)[21]

In much the same way as the un-relation of the *non rapport* created the connection between Man and Woman in the previous section, Lacan posits the other (feminine) *jouissance* ['assuming that there is another one, but precisely there isn't'] in order to say something about *jouissance phallique.* Lacan jokes that while we may think that it is only *jouissance phallique* that exits, *la femme* knows better and is a tease ['the one about which the woman does not breathe a word']. Once again, Lacan is employing his strategy of temporary misunderstandings through a speculative fiction in order to illustrate its opposite ['therefore, it is wrong, eh, that there is another']. Lacan argues that 'there exists no *x* that is not (Φx)' [there is no subject that is not enthralled to the phallic function], all the while stressing that it does not necessarily follow that 'all *x* is (Φx)' [all subjects are enthralled to the phallic function]. In other words, both statements suggest that there is no woman that is *not* in some way linked to the phallic function, Φx. However, this should be taken in conjunction with: 'not-all of the woman is linked to this function (Φx)' (David-Ménard 1997: 139: my translation). Therefore, some part of the woman *is* linked to the phallic function but not all of her is linked to the phallic function. Lacan says, 'when any speaking being whatsoever situates itself under the banner "women," it is on the basis of the following—that it grounds itself as being not-whole in situating itself in the phallic function' (*SXX* 72). This paradox is Lacan's (fictional) logic of the *not-all.* Women comply with the 'demands of the one' [*exigence de l'Un*]

[21] I rely on the stenographed transcript, *SXXa*, published online by Patrick Valas: http://www.valas.fr/IMG/pdf/s20_encore-2.pdf . In many ways these are less mediated than the published version edited Jacques-Alain Miller (Seuil), which can often stray too far from Lacan's word. *cf.* footnote 92, p. 247.

(universal phallic function), and yet *do not* do so universally, but rather one by one [*une par une*] (*SXX* 10)—a countable infinity and, therefore, not a totality. Women, in their status as *pas-toute,* are only able to be enthralled by the masculine sex (and so phallically) one-by-one, putting them at odds with universality. However, Lacan states that in her status as not-all [*pas-toute*] she possesses a 'supplementary jouissance' that is something that means she possesses Man in his entirety: 'c'est quand même elles qui possèdent les hommes, [...] le phallus, son homme comme elle dit' (*SXX* 68–9). As Chiesa puts is: 'woman is, at the same time, infinite and countable, or better, she becomes countable precisely insofar as she exposes the count as nontotalizable' (Chiesa 2016: 4).

However, Lacan, never wishing to be outdone, suggests that this impossible thing that does not exist, ~~*La*~~ *femme* [~~The~~ *woman*] (or, $\overline{\exists x \Phi x}$, the *pas-tout* foreclosed), is at the same time a line of flight that could reach outside the totalised enclosure of phallic *jouissance*—while remaining impossible in practice and not being required. Therefore, although the feminine *jouissance* is a fiction created to make *jouissance phallique* more concrete, and, therefore, a necessary counterpart for *jouissance phallique*, feminine *jouissance* nevertheless persists spectrally, beyond the reach of the subject, haunting him/her/them as a *possible impossibility*. Just like the concept of the quilting point, Lacan says: 'there is a jouissance that is hers [*à elle*], that belongs to that "she" [*elle*] that doesn't exist and doesn't signify anything' (*SXX* 74). If we read Lacan's infamous slogan of 'woman does not exist' [il n'y a pas *la* femme] (*SXX* 7) alongside the logic of the quilting point, we can see how her nonexistence and nonsignification renders the slogan itself *not real*, a lie that is deployed for another purpose. As I said earlier: the quilting point [*point de capiton*], the *fear-of-God* is not real, it does not signify something in reality. Lacan's frequent use of '*il n'y a*' [*there is not*] works in the same way, '*il n'y a*' [*there is not*] introduces a fiction which gives necessary intellectual supports for the actual. It is for this reason that *il n'y a pas de rapport sexuel* resembles '~~*La*~~ *femme*' (*SXX* 68), because in both cases Lacan is inventing (then, denying) the opposite in order to make more concrete the opposing idea.

Lacan's late thought is highly speculative, and, in many ways, resembles Schelling's fragmentary text I exposited earlier. Lacan's ontologizing of gendered difference is not unlike the conceptual deadlock that is present in the enigma of human freedom, where Schelling tried to think finitude through infinitude, or: how is there something rather than nothing? In what follows, I conceptualise Lacan's *not-all* as one of the names for God—following Lacan's argument that God is a woman from *SXXIII, The Sinthome*: 'the woman in question is another name of God, and it is in this respect that she doesn't exist' (*SXXIII* 5). Both God and the Woman's existence, are the intellectual bedrocks that support Lacan's system, which Lacan calls '*the God hypothesis*' [*l'hypothèse Dieu*]:

> What makes up [*supplée*] for the sexual relationship is, quite precisely, love. The Other, the Other as the locus of truth, is the only place, albeit an irreducible place, that we can give to the term "divine being," God, to call him by his name. God [*Dieu*] is the locus where, if you will allow me this wordplay, the *dieu*—the *dieur*—the *dire*, is produced. With a trifling change, the *dire* [to say] constitutes *Dieu*. And as long as something is said, the God hypothesis will persist [*Et aussi longtemps que se dira quelque chose, l'hypothèse Dieu sera là*]. (*SXX* 45)

Although God is inexistent, according to Lacan, he can only in-exist as a fiction in, *stricto sensu*, the manner explored previously. For Lacan, God persists in this way because we can say the word 'God,' and so God persists in language. This fact haunts us, and we are only able to experience ourselves as free of God because we can safely ignore the concept of God, appropriately maintaining *the theistic logic of our atheism*. This insight ties in with the idea that we must have a concept of God in order to reject that concept. Paradoxically, 'that is why, in the end, only theologians can be truly atheistic, namely, those who speak of God' [*il ne peut y avoir de vraiment athées que les théologiens, c'est à savoir ceux qui, de Dieu, en parlent*] (*SXX* 45). Since faith relies on a lie, faith is a paradox that exemplifies the logic of the fiction I described earlier concerning the *non rapport sexuel* and ~~La~~ *femme*, which Žižek calls 'counterfactual:'

> If we take as our starting point a false premise that we can clearly see the true in its proper contours, [...] it is only from a counterfactual premise that we can grasp the truth of the factual. The big problem of the cognitive process is thus not simply to get rid of the lies and illusions, but how to

select the right lie, a lie which eventually can enable us to arrive at the truth—if we want to go directly for truth, we lose the truth itself. (Žižek 2016: 298–9)

'Selecting the right lie' is the central idea which governs Lacan's thinking on *sexuation*, love, God, and the Real. It underscores Lacan's argument of 'there is no Other of the Other' [il n'y a pas d'Autre de l'Autre] (*SXXIII* 108), to which I will return in chapters four and five.

Jean-Luc Nancy understood Lacan when he summarised the central Lacanian insight thus: 'psychoanalysis is founded, Lacan tells us, on the following principle: "there is no sexual relationship" […] or, simply, its other variant formulation: jouissance in impossible' (2001: 9). The *non rapport sexuel* is intimately linked to the unbearable feminine *jouissance*, and its corollary impossibility of being not-all. We could say that the *not-all* of feminine sexuality is another way of expressing the impossible fiction explored earlier, which guarantees the Symbolic Order. Its totality envelops the master signifier (the Phallus) in relation to masculine sexuality. The not-all is outside, inaccessible, it exists as 'bits of the real' [*des bouts de réel*] (*SXXIII* 104, translation modified) for the subject; the not-all is the exception that guarantees the rule. Or, to put it another way, it is the truth of incompleteness—a Lacanian paradox: 'the real is what is entailed in the fact that, in the most commonplace function, you are swimming in significance, yet you cannot grasp all the signifiers at the same time. This is forbidden by their very structure' (*SXIX* 19, translation modified). Therefore, as I suggested earlier, God, the not-all of feminine sexuality, is Lacan's second major qualification of the big Other (Žižek 2002: 58).

As I showed earlier, for Lacan, God could be based on a lie, and the truth of God is an incomplete truth that is not guaranteed by the totality of a universal. The split for the subject exists at a primary, ontological level of being, whereas the transcendental logic of feminine *jouissance* is beyond the phallic function. These speculative insights that Lacan, developed more seriously in *SXX*, *Encore*, find their origin in *SIII*.

In *SIII*, Lacan focuses on God and his potential for deceit, starting with Descartes's "Fourth meditation." Descartes's theory considers that while human doubt renders ideas both incomplete and dependent, at the very least, we may form an idea of a clear, distinct God, and conclude that he exists absolutely. We can know with certainty that God guarantees our existence:

> *Cùmque attendo me dubitare, sive esse rem incompletam & dependentem, adeo clara & distincta idea entis independentis & completi, hoc est Dei, mihi occurrit; & ex hoc uno quòd talis idea in me sit, sive quòd ego ideam illam habens existam, adeo manifeste concludo Deum etiam existere, atque ab illo singulis momentis totam existentiam meam dependere, ut nihil evidentius, nihil certius ab humano ingenio cognosci posse confidam.* (IV)[22]

Descartes further argues that this God is not duplicitous, nor is he deceitful. God maintains the world as empirically stable; Descartes elaborates:

> *In primis enim agnosco fieri non posse ut ille me unquam fallat; in omni enim fallaciâ vel deceptione aliquid imperfectionis reperitur; & quamvis posse fallere, nonnullum esse videatur acuminis aut potentiae argumentum, proculdubio velle fallere, vel malitiam vel imbecillitatem testatur, nec proinde in Deum cadit.* (IV)[23]

Descartes argues that although God might have the ability to deceive us, he does not do so because, logically, a benevolent God would never do such a thing. Lacan questions this Cartesian logic, arguing that nothing protects the subject from God's potential malice.

Therefore, as early as *SIII,* Lacan makes a rudimentary case for the logic of the *non rapport sexuel,* and the concomitant argument for the deceptiveness of the big Other. There is, Lacan says, in the triad of the Real, Symbolic, Imaginary, the basic condition of all relationships; 'it's the basic condition of any relationship' (*SIII* 64). Lacan argues that the

---

[22] 'And when I consider the fact that I have doubts, or that I am a thing that is incomplete and dependent, then there arises in me a clear and distinct idea of a being who is independent and complete, that is, an idea of God. And from the mere fact that there is such an idea within me, or that I who possess this idea exist, I clearly infer that God also exists, and that every single moment of my entire existence depends on him. (Descartes 1996: 37).

[23] 'To begin with, I recognise that it is impossible that God should ever deceive me. For in every case of trickery or deception some imperfection is to be found; and although the ability to deceive me appears to be an indication of cleverness or power, the will to deceive is undoubtably evidence of malice or weakness, and so cannot apply to God.' (Descartes 1996: 37).

Imaginary, Symbolic, and Real realms reflect the registers of the subject: speech, the order of alterity as such, and of the Other. 'Vertically, there is the register of the subject, speech, and the order of otherness as such, the Other' (*SIII* 64). The pivotal point of the function of speech is the subjectivity of the Other, who is capable of lying: 'the hub of the function of speech is the subjectivity of the Other, that is to say, the fact that the Other is essentially he who is capable, like the subject, of convincing and lying' (*SIII* 64). However, the Cartesian wager was that there must be a non-deceptive core of reality at the heart of the big Other. 'The dialectical correlate of the basic structure which makes of the speech of subject to subject speech that may deceive is that there is also something that does not deceive' (*SIII* 64). Indeed, modern science has done much to demonstrate the repeatability, and, therefore, perceived stability of the world, 'the notion that the real, as difficult as it may be to penetrate, is unable to play tricks on us [*jouer au vilain avec nous*] and will not take us in on purpose, is, [...] essential to the constitution of the world of science' (*SIII* 64). But Lacan reminds us that the core of the Real is always already a function of speech, and there is absolutely nothing that guarantees the original step of all scientific investigations as anything other than an act of faith—God maintaining the world as empirically stable:

> We have in fact never observed anything that would show us a deceiving demon at the heart of nature. But that does not prevent its being a necessary article of faith for the first steps of science and the constitution of experimental science. It need hardly be said that matter does not cheat, that it has no intention of crushing our experiments or blowing up our machines. This sometimes happens, but only when we have made a mistake. It's out of the question that it, matter, should deceive us. This step is not at all obvious [Ce pas, ce n'est pas du tout-cuit]. (*SIII* 64–5)

Lacan does not share the certainty found in Descartes's *Fourth Meditation.* Lacan sees God as a potentially pernicious in-itself who forces the world to react maliciously and manipulates the order of things to render our world duplicitous. For Lacan, every empirical development in modern science rests on those 'bits of the real' that we know nothing about, onto which we project 'stability' and 'permanence;' the phenomenological approach of taking things as they appear is invalid, according to Lacan. Recall the opening lines of *Being and Nothingness,* 'by reducing the existent to the series of appearances that manifest it, modern thought has made considerable progress' (*BN* 11). Yet, Sartre's view does not take into account Lacan's argument that there is always the possibility of a deceptive God who is playing with the 'appearances' which manifest themselves in the world.

The Decorator Crab

Sartre had argued that in loving another, we would effectively be attempting to become *in itself for itself*—which would amount to wanting to become God –, and, as I showed, this metamorphosis is both impossible and incomprehensible for Sartre because ultimately, we would have to partially renounce freedom to acquire the features of stability and permanence from God, and this is impossible. According to Sartre, we are condemned to our own freedom. However, Lacan's double qualification of the big Other, in *SIII* and *SXX*, demonstrated that the concept of *in itself for itself* as God is complex, and prone to subterfuge. I contend that Lacan's Other *jouissance* (feminine *jouissance*) is comparable to Sartre's *in itself for itself,* and it takes on two dimensions in Lacan's work. On the one hand, there is the big Other of the mythical hoard—the Father of unregulated desire—the *Père* [Father] who enables us to act in relative harmony in language, so long as we are dupes. On the other, for Lacan, there is the limitlessness of feminine *jouissance;* the meaningless and unnecessary lie (fiction) which supports the structure of the Symbolic, and, therefore, the entire empiricism of modern science. And, it is in the big Other of feminine *jouissance*, not in the big Other of the mythical psychotic father, that we can safely conclude that to love would be to want to discover the unknown, to stab in the dark.[24]

The dualism at the heart of the big Other resembles Schelling's argument that God had fallen from the seat of the absolute. As we saw in the

[24] I will contextualise this in chapter four in my discussion with Scudéry's *Map of Tender*.

previous chapter, Schelling held that God (or the Absolute) had to share his absolute freedom with something that was not himself—the *Gegenbild*:

> The counter-image [*Gegenbild*], as an absolute entity and having all its attributes in common with the originary [*sic*] image, would not truly be in itself and absolute if it could not grasp itself in its selfhood [*Selbstheit*], in order to have true being as the *other* absolute. But it cannot be as the *other* absolute unless it separates itself or falls away from the true Absolute. (*PR*, 28)

To put it in Lacanian terms, Schelling's philosophy attempted to conceptualise the Other of the not-all, and we could further develop his speculative account of the Fall into our understanding of God as unknowable, an *in itself for itself* that enables the technical possibility of love. As we saw, Lacan argued that God could be deceptive and could have chosen not to render the world empirically stable or permanent. Unlike Sartre, who argued that *in itself* was governed by the characteristics of stability and permanence, we can now say that *in itself* is governed only by an *appearance* of stability and permanence. The entirety of our knowledge is predicated on that which only has the *appearance* of truth and stability, which, thus, amounts to what is unknown. If God is capable of deceiving us about *in itself*, would it not then follow that he is also able to deceive us about *in itself for itself*? Therefore, God's deception could be double—indeed, following Lacan, we have little logical proof for *in itself*'s stability or permanence, other than an act of faith. As Lacan puts it: 'it's the radicality of *Judaeo-Christian* thought on this point that made possible this decisive step, for which the expression *act of faith* is not out of place, which consists in supposing that there is something absolutely nondeceptive' (*SIII* 65).

If the pre-historic ontological scene were a deserted beach, we can imagine beach shrubs, driftwood, and rocks amassing on the sand dunes on the backshore. A small crab who has camouflaged itself to look like a rock—taking on the appearance of an inanimate object characterised by stability and permanence—suddenly sprouts legs and begins to rush off the beach. This almost imperceptible movement is our pernicious God himself, who, after having fallen from the seat of the absolute, is both scared and alone. God's fall from the heavens was the result of his own narcissistic attempt to verify the *Gegenbild,* Schelling had argued. However, what if God's final act on his descent from the heavens was to also render the appearance of *in itself* as permanent and stable so that we could not find him lying afraid on the beach—an eternity of camouflage and deceit? The decorator crab camouflaged as a rock is the problematic Sartrean *in itself for itself,* and mistaking the crab for a rock would amount to being unaware of its deceit. *For Lacan, that is the position the world of science is in.* What Lacan has shown, by employing the same radical speculation that Schelling had earlier, is that the *in itself* need not be stable and permanent. Therefore, there is no conflict in potentially marrying freedom and permanence as *in itself for itself* in love. Schelling's and Lacan's move is to posit such an unknown fiction, the decorator crab that looks like *in itself* but is potentially *in itself for itself.* Lacan's doubt retroactively throws the human condition into sharp relief. Could this be the reason why Sartre finds Pierre so disconcerting in *Being and Nothingness*?:

> When Pierre looks at me, I know without doubt that he is looking at me: his eyes—things in the world—are riveted on my body—a thing in the world; that is the objective fact of which I can say "It *is.*" But it is also a fact that belongs to *the world.* The meaning of this look is not, and that is what bothers me. Whatever I do—smile, promise, threaten—nothing can *win* me the approval, the free judgment I am seeking. I know that it is always "beyond". (*BN* 106)

For Sartre, Pierre is beyond, impossible to love as *for itself.* To love Pierre would be to renounce one's radical freedom. However, what if instead, we gave Pierre the features of *une pierre* [*a stone*] as decorator crab?[25] What if *une pierre* (or, stability and permanence) was the fictional lie that sustains the truth of the world? What if half of Pierre, as our decorator crab, is one of the names of God? For Lacan, the impossibility of love is necessary, the subject needs this fiction, the impossible concept of the Other of the Other, *jouissance féminine*, God, even if it does not exist. Postulating God's existence is taking a *leap of faith,* and, as I will show in the next two

[25] The name Pierre and a 'pierre' [the name Peter and a 'stone'] are homonyms.

chapters, this false hope, the temporary detour through speculative fiction, is, for Lacan, necessary for the subject to *be* in the world.

References

Allouch, Jean. 2009. *L'Amour Lacan*. Paris: EPEL.

Balmès, François. 2007. *Dieu, le sexe, et la vérité*. Ramonville: Érès.

Book XXIII, The Sinthome (1975–1976). (trans: Price, A.R.). Cambrige: Polity.

Borch-Jacobsen, Mikkel. 1990. *Lacan: Le Maître absolu*. Paris: Flammarion.

Chiesa, Lorenzo. 2016. *The Not-Two: Logic and God in Lacan*. Cambridge, MA: MIT Press.

Copjec, Joan. 1994. *Supposing the Subject*. London: Verso.

David-Ménard, Monique. 1997. *Les Constructions de l'universel*. Paris: Presses Universitaires de France.

Derrida, Jacques. 1990. *Heidegger et la question de l'esprit et autres essais*. Paris: Flammarion.

———. 2018. *Geschlecht III: Sexe, race, nation, humanité*. Paris: Seuil.

Descartes, René. 1996. *Descartes Meditations on First Philosophy, with Selections from the Objections and Replies*. Trans. John Cottingham. Cambridge: Cambridge University Press.

Fink, Bruce. 1995. *The Lacanian Subject*. Princeton: Princeton University Press.

Gherovici, Patricia. 2017. *Transgender Psychoanalysis*. London and New York: Routledge.

Goodrich, Peter. 2018. *Schreber's Law: Jurisprudence and Judgment in Transition*. Edinburgh: Edinburgh University Press.

Henry, Michel. 1993. *The Genealogy of Psychoanalysis*. Stanford: Stanford University Press.

Howells, Christina. 2011. *Mortal Subjects: Passions of the Soul in Late Twentieth-Century French Thought*. Cambridge: Polity.

Irigaray, Luce. 1977. *Ce sexe qui n'en est pas un*. Paris: Minuit.

Krutzen, Henry. 2009. *Jacques Lacan, séminaire 1952–1980, index référentiel*. Paris: Economica.

Lacan, Jacques. 1966. *Écrits*. Paris: Seuil. English edition: Lacan, J. 2006. Écrits. (trans: Fink, B.) London: W.W. Norton & Company.

———. 1973a. *Le Séminaire: Livre XI, Les Quatre concepts fondamentaux de la psychanalyse (1963–1964)*. Paris: Seuil. English edition: Lacan, Jacques. 1981. The Seminar of Jacques Lacan, Book XI, The Four Fundamental

Concepts of Psychoanalysis (1963–1964) (trans: Sheridan, A.). London and NY: W.W. Norton & Company.
———. 1973b. *Le Séminaire de Jacques Lacan, XXa, Encore (1972–1973).* Patrick Valas, unpublished transcript. http://www.valas.fr/IMG/pdf/s19.ou_pire.pdf. Accessed 30 July 2022.
———. 1975a. *Le Séminaire de Jacques Lacan, Livre XX, Encore (1972–1973).* Paris: Seuil. English edition: Lacan, J. 1998. The Seminar of Jacques Lacan, Book XX, Encore, (1972–1973). (trans: Fink, B.). London and NY: W.W. Norton & Company.
———. 1975b. *Le Séminaire de Jacques Lacan, Livre I, Les Écrits techniques de Freud (1953–1954).* Paris: Seuil. English edition: Lacan, J. 1991. The Seminar of Jacques Lacan Book I, Freud's Papers on Technique (1953–1954). (trans: Forrester, J.). London and NY: W.W. Norton & Company.
———. 1978a. *Le Séminaire de Jacques Lacan, XV, L'Acte psychanalytique (1967–1968).* Patrick Valas, unpublished transcript. http://staferla.free.fr/S15/S15%20L%27ACTE.pdf. Accessed 4 Apr 2023.
———. 1978b. *Le Séminaire de Jacques Lacan, XXV, Le Moment de Conclure (1977–1978), Patrick Valas*, unpublished transcript. http://www.valas.fr/IMG/pdf/s25.pdf. Accessed 4 April 2023.
———. 1980. Le Séminaire de Jacques Lacan, *XXVII, La Dissolution*, Caracas (12/7/1980), Patrick Valas, unpublished transcript. http://www.valas.fr/IMG/pdf/lacan_caracas_12_7_1980_bis_.pdf. Accessed 4 April 2023.
———. 1981. *Le Séminaire de Jacques Lacan, Livre III, Les Psychoses (1955–1956).* Paris: Seuil. English edition: Lacan, J. 1993. The Seminar of Jacques Lacan Book III, The Psychoses, (1955–1956). (trans: Grigg, R.). London and NY: W.W. Norton & Company.
———. 1986. *Le Séminaire de Jacques Lacan, Livre VII, L'Éthique de la psychanalyse (1959–1960).* Paris: Seuil. English edition: Lacan, J. 1992. The Seminar of Jacques Lacan, Book VII, The Ethics of Psychoanalysis, (1959–1960). (trans: Porter, RD London and NY: W.W. Norton & Company.
———. 1991. *Le Séminaire: Livre XVII , L'Envers de la psychanalyse (1969-1970).* Paris: Seuil. English edition: Lacan, Jacques. 2007. The Seminar of Jacques Lacan, Book XVII, The Other Side of Psychoanalysis (1969–1970). (trans: Grigg, R.). London and NY: W.W. Norton & Company.
———. 2001. *Autres Écrits.* Paris: Seuil.
———. 2005. *Le Séminaire de Jacques Lacan, Livre XXIII, Le Sinthome (1975-1976).* Paris: Seuil. English edition: Lacan, J. 2016. The Seminar of Jacques Lacan,

———. 2007. *Le Séminaire de Jacques Lacan, Livre XVIII, D'un discours qui ne serait pas du semblant (1970–1971)*. Paris: Seuil.

———. 2011a. *Le Séminaire de Jacques Lacan, Livre XIX, … Ou pire (1971-1972)*. Paris: Seuil. English edition: Lacan, Jacques. 2018. The Seminar of Jacques Lacan, Book XIX, …Or Worse, (1971–1972). (trans: Price, A.R.). Cambridge: Polity.

———. 2011b. *Je Parle Aux Murs*. Paris: Seuil. English edition: Lacan, Jacques. 2017. Talking to Brick Walls. Cambridge: Polity.

———. *Le Séminaire de Jacques Lacan, XIV, La Logique du fantasme (1966-1967)*. Patrick Valas, unpublished transcript http://www.valas.fr/IMG/pdf/S14_LOGIQUE.pdf. Accessed 14 Apr 2023.

Laplanche, Jean, and J.-B. Pontalis. 2014. *Vocabulaire de la psychanalyse*. Paris: PUF.

Leguil, Clotilde. 2012. *Sartre avec Lacan: Corrélation antinomique, liaison dangereuse*. Paris: Navarin.

Longuenesse, Béatrice. 2012. Kant's 'I' in 'I Ought To' and Freud's Superego: Freud and Philosophy. *Proceedings of the Aristotelian Society* IXXXVI: 19–39.

Mansfield, Nick. 2000. *Subjectivity: Theories of the Self from Freud to Haraway*. New York: New York University Press.

Marquet, Jean-François. 1973. *Liberté et existence, études sur la formation de la philosophie de Schelling*. Paris: Galimard.

Monnier, David. 2011. *Le Réel de l'amour, trois modèles lacaniens*. Rennes: Presses Universitaires de Rennes.

Morel, Geneviève. 2000. *Ambiguïtés sexuelles*. Paris: Anthropos.

Nancy, Jean-Luc. 2001. *L'"Il y a" du rapport sexuel*. Paris: Galilée.

Nicholls, Angus, and Martin Liebscher. 2010. *Thinking the Unconscious: Nineteenth Century German Thought*. Cambridge: Cambridge University Press.

Rabaté, Jean-Michel. 2001. *Psychoanalysis and the Subject of Literature*. Basingstoke: Palgrave Macmillan.

———. 2020. Jacques Lacan's Evanescent Affects. In *Affects and Literature*, ed. Alex Houen. Cambridge: Cambridge University Press.

Richards, Sinan. 2023. A lesson for the world: Solange Faladé's anti-colonial multiracialism, Modern & Contemporary France, 31: 4, 435–450, https://doi.org/10.1080/09639489.2023.2264217

Rose, Jacqueline. 1982. Introduction—II. In *Feminine Sexuality: Jacques Lacan and the École Freudienne*, ed. Jacqueline Rose and Juliet Mitchell. London: The Macmillan Press.

Roudinesco, Élisabeth. 1993. *Jacques Lacan: Esquisse d'une vie, histoire d'un système de pensée.* Paris: Fayard. English edition: Roudinesco, Élisabeth. 1997. Jacques Lacan (trans: Bray, B.). New York: Columbia University Press.

Sartre, Jean-Paul. 1934. *La Transcendance de l'ego.* Paris: Vrin. English edition: Sartre, J-P. 1960. Transcendence of the Ego (trans: Williams, F. and Kirkpatrick, R.). New York: Hill and Wang.

———. 1943. *L'Être et le néant.* Paris: Gallimard. English edition: Sartre, J-P. 2021. Being and Nothingness (trans: Richmond, S.). London and New York: Routledge.

Schreber, Daniel Paul. 2000. *Memoirs of my Nervous Illness.* Trans: Ida Macalpine and Richard A. Hunter. New York: NYRB.

Soler, Colette. 2003. *Ce que Lacan disait des femmes.* Paris: Éditions du Champ Lacanien.

Tauber, Alfred I. 2010. *Freud, the Reluctant Philosopher*. Princeton and Oxford: Princeton University Press.

Whyte, Lancelot Law. 1960. *The Unconscious Before Freud.* London: Tavistock Publications.

Žižek, Slavoj. 2002. The Real of Sexual Difference. In eds. Susanne Barnard and Bruce Fink, *Reading Seminar XX: Lacan's Major Work on Love Knowledge, and Feminine Sexuality*. New York: State University of New York Press.

ŽiŽek, Slavoj. 2012. *Less Than Nothing, Hegel and the Shadow of Dialectical Materialism*. London and New York: Verso.

———. 2016. *Disparities*. London: Bloomsbury.

Zupančič, Alenka. 2017. *What is Sex?* Cambridge, MA: MIT Press.

4

A Momentary Folly—The Wish to Be Loved

The Quilting of Meaning

In this chapter, I investigate Lacan's concept of *jouissance* as it relates to the notions of desire, fantasy, and pleasure. In previous chapters, I investigated the quilting point, and argued that this could qualify the master signifier, Φx, as deceitful since the signifier's meaning was only fixed arbitrarily. If the master signifier, Φx, is not outright deceitful, it is characterizable as at least partially untruthful. Lacan identified the quilting point in his third Seminar, and he continued to rework the notion throughout his teachings. The quilting point is central to Lacan's graph of desire (see Fig. 4.1), and I begin the first part of this chapter by contextualising and analysing this graph.

The graph of desire's main explanatory power resides is in its ability to schematically illustrate subject development in language. The graph introduces a distinction between the Subject of Language and the Subject of *Jouissance* (the lower and upper parts of the graph, respectively). The graph visually illustrates the core components of our understanding of Lacan's psychoanalytic theory of subject development. The analysis of the graph will lead the argument to Lacan's concept of *jouissance* which I

S. Richards, *Dialectics of Love in Sartre and Lacan*, The Palgrave Lacan Series,
https://doi.org/10.1007/978-3-031-45798-2_4

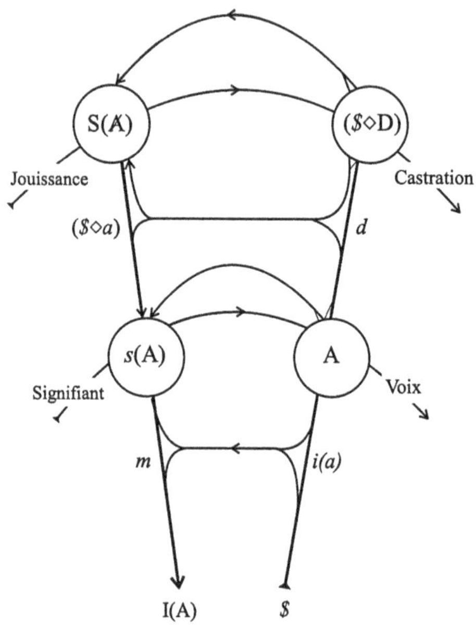

Fig. 4.1 Lacan's complete graph of desire

explore through discussions of *das Ding* and the ethics of psychoanalysis. This chapter also contextualises the abstract concepts with some examples: I analyse Madeleine de Scudéry's *Map of Tender* to exemplify the Lacanian fantasy screen and the disintegration of the subject's psychic life in the pursuit of *jouissance*. I also discuss Sartre's philosophical strategy "*loser wins*" and ask if we can relate this concept to Lacan's psychoanalysis to highlight the desolation of the subject and the closed circle of symbolic coordinates, the non-dupes err [*les non-dupes errent*]. Finally, I demonstrate *jouissance*'s relevance to the theory of love that I am sketching concerning Lacan's psychoanalysis. I argue that love, in Lacan's work, is both necessary and impossible. Lacan does not explicitly treat love as this essential leftover, which is impossible to subsume, however, I claim that not only is this an appealing Lacanian definition of love, but that love is the necessary metaphysical leftover of Lacan's psychoanalytic practice itself.

In Lacan's early teachings, the clinical aspects of his psychoanalytic theory took priority. Lacan's first seminar on Freud, *Les Écrits techniques de Freud,* engages in a sustained close reading of what he calls 'Freud's technical papers' to sketch the parameters of the psychoanalytic clinic (*SI* 18). In *SI* Lacan investigates the Symbolic Order to highlight the centrality of this register to his clinical practice (*SI* 343), and by Lacan's third seminar, on psychosis, he contends that psychosis is a diagnosable symptom within the Symbolic Order and, therefore, in need of broader analysis. By Lacan's seventh seminar, *L'Éthique de la psychanalyse*, his strategy begins to shift. His seminars become increasingly popular with auditors, and he delivers his lessons to a popular, philosophically minded, audience, and not just clinicians. For example, in *The Ethics of Psychoanalysis* Lacan introduced ethical concerns, drawing heavily from Freud's *Civilisation and Its Discontents*. Lacan stretched his clinical interpretations to apply them to society, effectively turning this aspect of his practice into a branch of social philosophy.

Responding to his changing audience, Lacan focuses on literature, electing to analyse Sophocles' *Antigone* as a means of performing the psychoanalytic ethic he describes. Lacan does this by referring to the law and tragedy. Lacan pursued a similar strategy the previous year in his sixth seminar, *Le Désir et son interprétation,* offering a sustained analysis of Shakespeare's *Hamlet.* Lacan will continue this method in his later seminars, most notably with Joyce in *SXXIII*, *Le Sinthome,* to which I will return in the final chapter. As we saw in the previous chapter, Lacan's ideas and teaching style resist easy categorisation, and this makes it challenging to systematise his work. Lacan is also a difficult author to systematise because what he means keeps 'sliding' around at different moments, and any investigation of Lacan's psychoanalysis will aim to identify the 'quilting point' in his work; the point at which a set of theses, said to be "Lacanian," could intersect.[1] By the time of Lacan's eleventh seminar, *The Four Fundamental Concepts of Psychoanalysis,* his lectures will have moved from Saint Anne Hospital in Paris [*L'Hôpital Sainte-Anne*] to

[1] 'Sliding' because, as we will see, meaning emerges from the clipping together of the free sliding around of signifiers. Moreover, as we saw earlier, Lacan kept changing his mind, for example, he qualifies the big Other twice, first in *SIII*, then in *SXX*, effectively changing what he meant.

a room [Salle Dussane] at the École normale supérieure de Paris, and from *SXI* onwards we can detect an even more pronounced shift in Lacan's teaching style. As I showed in the previous chapter, towards *SXX*, *Encore*, Lacan became increasingly obsessed with formal logic and continued the transformation of his teachings into dense *mathemes* and graphs, and these have eluded me as often as they have clarified his concepts.[2] I will only focus on graphs and mathemes if these help to clarify Lacan's argument.

In what follows, the graph of desire is treated systematically with continuous reference to "The Subversion of the Subject and the Dialectic of Desire in the Freudian Unconscious" from *Écrits*.[3] However, before entering this dense and complex text, I turn to *SV*, *The Formations of the Unconscious* [*Les Formations de l'inconscient*], where Lacan first mentions the graph of desire. Lacan begins by briefly summarising his teachings to date (1957), stressing the importance of the quilting point and his third seminar on psychosis more generally: 'In the third year of my Seminar, I spoke about psychosis insofar as it's founded on a primordial deficiency of a signifier' [*carence signifiante primordiale*] (*SV* 6). The *carence* (lack or deficiency) of the primordial signifier is comparable to what I have called the sickness [*maladie*] in Being, following from Sartre and Schelling. Moreover, as I intimated earlier, Lacan universalised the pre-psychotic's experience of this lack to demonstrate the broader subjective experience of the lack and its role in symbolic subject development. He says in *SV*:

> I nevertheless believe that the Seminar on psychosis made it possible for you to understand, if not the ultimate mainspring, at least the essential mechanism by which the Other, the big Other, the Other as the seat of speech, is reduced to the imaginary other. It involves the temporary replace-

---

[2] In *L'Œuvre claire* (1995), Jean-Claude Milner argues that this shift is a shift from what he calls 'the first Lacanian classicism [*le premier classicisme Lacanien*] to 'the second Lacanian classicism' [le second classicisme Lacanien], which pivots on Lacan's move towards the formal logic expressed in the mathemes: 'the pivot of the second classicism is the notion of the mathematic' [*le pivot du second classicisme est la notion de mathème*] (122).

[3] Lacan refers to and explains the graph of desire in many other texts including *SV, SVI, SXIII, SXVI*, and *SXX*, (this list is non-exhaustive). I will treat the graph thematically and so will draw from a comprehensive set of sources. However, my primary source text will be *Écrits*.

> ment of the symbolic by the imaginary [*C'est une suppléance du symbolique par l'imaginaire*]. (*SV* 6, translation modified)

As we saw, Lacan's 'essential mechanism' is a reference to those aggressive egos in the imaginary realm, who vie for the attention of the big Other thereby inaugurating the big Other's omnipotent power as the regulator who will prevent the unregulated mayhem of the egos ['[preventing] everything [from being] smashed to a pulp' (*SIII* 96)]. For Lacan, this recognition of the big Other's role and power enables an analytic shift of focus from the subject's ego in the Imaginary to the development of the subject in the Symbolic Order. According to Lacan, once in the Symbolic, some subjects might foreclose the master signifier, which is psychosis by definition. The psychotic subject denies the big Other in the process of their subjective development, and this foreclosure is instrumental in the psychotic subject's dysfunctional development. Lacan sums up further:

> I think, therefore I am, as we say, intransitively. Assuredly, this is where the difficulty lies for the psychotic [*psychosé*], precisely because of the reduction of the duplicity [*duplicité*] of the Other with a capital O and the other with a little o, the Other as the seat of speech and guarantor of truth, and the dual other, the one whom the subject finds himself faced with as his own image. The disappearance of this double aspect is precisely what makes it so difficult for the psychotic to maintain himself in the human real, that is to say, in the symbolic real. (*SV* 6)

The psychotic subject misidentifies the Symbolic Order, and this leads them to experience a psychological breakdown when they realise that they had misrecognised the big Other. As a result, the psychotic [*psychosé*] identifies with the "wrong" big Other, and, upon realising this, the psychotic collapses since their 'guarantor of truth' has failed to hold symbolic reality together. In short, the psychotic denies a specific symbolic reality, and the subject who pursues pure *jouissance* ends up in the same place.

The crucial implication for Lacan's social philosophy is that the Symbolic Order, which I understand to mean the incomplete marriage of truth and knowledge in language, needs to be governed by a big Other that acts as the guarantor of truth. Truth is quilted and expressed in the big Other whose role is to prevent the free fall of meaning (*jouissance*), Lacan says, 'there does have to be some point, effectively, at which the fabric of one becomes attached to the fabric of the other, so that we know where we stand, at least with respect to the possible limits of the sliding' (*SV* 7). The quilting point is the point at which the fabric of reality is sewed together, knotted, or clipped, to prevent further sliding on the signifying chain. Lacan adopts this idea from Ferdinand de Saussure's *Course in General Linguistics* (1916), where Saussure argues: 'the signifier, though to all appearances freely chosen with respect to the idea that it represents, is fixed, not free, with respect to the linguistic community that uses it' (2011: 71). Clearly, Lacan's argument for imposed meaning is taken directly from Saussure's idea; the quilting point possesses a fixity that is implicit in the imposed Saussurian model. Furthermore, Saussure is clear that the meaning of the signifier is conferred by a social body, which Saussure names 'the collectivity,' that arbitrarily imposes meaning. In Saussure's terms:

> The arbitrary nature of the sign explains in turn why the social fact alone can create a linguistic system. The community is necessary if values that owe their existence solely to usage and general acceptance are to be set up; by himself the individual is incapable of fixing a single value. (Saussure 2011: 113)

The quilting point synthesises symbolic power on the one hand with the arbitrary aspect of language on the other. The resulting master signifier, Φx, is only fixed by the choice and tacit consent of 'the collective.' The graph of desire's descriptive strength resides in schematically representing the arbitrary marriage of truth and reality in the process of subject formation. The process of subject formation throughout Lacan's work is always contingent on the big Other, which takes hold from the mere clipping together of signifiers. The quilting of meaning could have been otherwise, but it was not, and, therefore, from the subject's perspective, the big Other is a void which now appears whole.

The Graph of Desire

The graph of desire stitches together the various aspects of subject formation and development described in the previous chapter, illustrating the relationship between the subject and the signifier, and, once understood, the graph of desire succinctly represents much of Lacan's early conceptual scheme. Lacan defines the graph of desire's intended aim: 'it will serve here to show where desire is situated in relation to a subject defined on the basis of his articulation by the signifier' (*É* 681). Lacan claims that desire exists in relation to the signifier, articulating itself against the signifier. Lacan introduces the graph of desire in *SV* in its most rudimentary form (Fig. 4.2).

The graph is intended to be read backward, or *retroactively*, beginning from the lower right corner. Briefly, because I will comment on this later, the central horseshoe (right-to-left) vector represents subject development from birth and ends up in what I will call, for now, the *affected subject of experience*. Therefore, the right-to-left horseshoe vector illustrates a subject who has been affected by the weight of symbolic life. The left-to-right vector, which cuts across the top of the horseshoe vector, represents the quilting of the signifiers in language. Lacan's disparate theoretical threads find their realisation in this rudimentary schema.

Before commenting further on the graph, Lacan explains that a key question for psychoanalysis is whether both 'truth' and 'knowledge' can

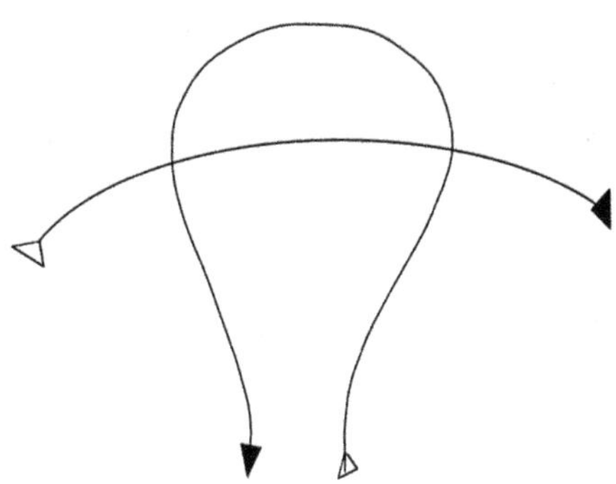

Fig. 4.2 Lacan's Rudimentary graph of desire

ever be quilted together. Lacan is taking his cue from Hegel, and the latter's quest for Absolute Knowledge. Lacan says, 'I am talking about its [psychoanalysis's] philosophical relevance, for that is, in the end, the schema Hegel gave us of History in *The Phenomenology of Mind*' (*É* 671). Leaving to one side the controversy surrounding Lacan's reading of Hegel, as well as Hegel's twentieth-century French reception more generally, which is subject to endless discussion, Lacan is entrusting psychoanalysis with a primary task of situating the subject in a relationship to knowledge [*un rapport au savoir*]. Accordingly, Lacan states that psychoanalysis's task is to demonstrate the 'ambiguity of such a relationship' [*demontrer l'ambiguïté d'un tel rapport*] (*É* 671–2).

Traditionally, the subject was not always thought to be in an ambiguous relationship with knowledge, and this is why Lacan sees the psychoanalytic task as one of subverting the question of the subject because the subject introduces doubt (*É* 672). However, what does the subject desire from all this? Do they want to be subverted? For Lacan, the primary relationship between the subject and knowledge arises from the relationship between the subject and the Other which is characterised by radical insecurity. Lacan says: '"*Che vuoi*?," "What do you want?," is the question that best leads the subject to the path of his own desire, assuming that, thanks to the know-how of a partner known as a psychoanalyst, he takes up that question, even without knowing it, in the following form: "What does he want from me?"' (*É* 690). The subject does not know what he/she/they want, and subjects will instead ask: *Che vuoi?* 'What do you want from me?' which pushes the subject to start asking the right questions about their desire in their search for knowledge. However, before they begin asking the right questions ('thanks to the know-how of a partner known as a psychoanalyst'!) the subject wrongly pursues the desire of the Other. Therefore, in the process of subject formation, subjects first have to accept the desires of the Other before they can know what they want.

Lacan appeals to the Copernican Revolution in "Subversion of the subject" to explain how the subject exists in an ambiguous relationship with the truth. For Lacan, modern science is just one of many subjects of knowledge, with psychoanalysis representing another example, he says, 'in and of itself, this warrants our speaking of a subject of science' (*É*

672). Lacan interferes in the epistemological debate of identifying the subject of science because he believes that psychoanalysis is better placed to subvert the question of the subject, to better capture the ambiguous relationship between the subject and knowledge.[4] Lacan discusses the subject of science through the example of Copernicus's paradigm shift from a geocentric to a heliocentric universe. Lacan argues that, in postulating a heliocentric universe, Copernicus ended up splitting 'empirical' truth from 'divine' truth. The result was that, far from getting closer to the truth, Copernicus *simply forced the truth to multiply*. Lacan says, 'Does anything make it seem that the other truth, if we may so term revealed truth, has seriously suffered as a result?' (*É* 674). For Lacan, the Copernican revolution has a linguistic legacy, 'the use of Copernicus's name as a reference has more hidden resources [*l'emploi du nom de Copernic à une suggestion langagière*] [...]. The revolution is no less important even though it concerns only "celestial revolutions"' (ibid). 'Meaning' is continually sliding around, and the nomination 'Copernicus' merely quilts the intended concept, 'has more hidden resources that touch specifically on what has already just slipped from my pen regarding our relation to the true' (ibid). The knotting together of truth and knowledge that formed in the naming of 'Copernicus' is only a formal exercise in the semantic restructuring of reality. Lacan argues in *Écrits*:

[4] Analytic philosophers of science have generally ignored twentieth-century French philosophy and social theory. The early Anglo-American debates surrounding the demarcation of science, corroboration, realism/antirealism, and falsification are impoverished by the blind refusal to read Canguilhem, Bachelard, Foucault, and Lacan. Lacan develops a psychoanalytic tradition which actively works against "science" in its purely empirical, measurable, quantifiable, and repeatable vein. He explicitly states that: 'what qualifies me to proceed along this path is obviously my experience of this praxis. [...] [which] while presenting no danger to the praxis itself, result, in both cases, in a total absence of scientific status' (*É* 672). Indeed, Lacan also argues that 'this can be gauged by crosschecking the contribution made by psychoanalysis to physiology since its inception: its contribution has been nil, even as far as the sexual organs are concerned. No amount of fabulation will prevail against this balance sheet' (*É* 680). Lacan advocates for a psychoanalytic discipline that stands totally independently from the empirical sciences and one which could respond to the same "scientific" questions from a different paradigm. Lacan's approach is unlike Freud's who insisted on the biological nature of psychoanalysis, and its supposed claims to scientism. For example, we should read Lacan alongside Popper (1998), Kuhn (1996), Lakatos (1998), and Feyerabend (1993) in the epistemological debates in the philosophy of science.

> From that point on, to dwell on it no longer means simply revoking some idiotic [*révoquer une sottise*] notion stemming from the religious tradition, which, as can be seen well enough, is none the worse for it, but rather of tying more closely together the regime of knowledge and the regime of truth [*nouer plus intimement le régime du savoir à celui de la vérité*]. (ibid)

Lacan's paradoxical conclusion is that, in having corrected the religious geocentric view of the universe, the Copernican revolution's only result was to have created a new subject of science. For Lacan, the Copernican revolution achieved nothing but the arbitrary knotting together of knowledge and truth in a novel way. The Copernican revolution did not develop a more accurate understanding of "the truth," but only created a *new subject of the truth*. Lacan suggests that this is the form of subversion that psychoanalysis can offer.

As I explained in the last chapter, Lacan claimed there to be a radical discontinuity at the heart of the signifier, which, according to Lacan, illustrated the difference between the subject and the subject of the unconscious. Against Saussure, I showed that, for Lacan, the relationship between signifier and signified is ambiguous because there is a discord at the level of the signifier. Lacan demonstrated this radical separation between the signifier and the signified in the schema he adapted from Saussure's tree schema, with 'Ladies and 'Gentlemen' followed by two identical doors (Fig. 4.3).

As demonstrated earlier, Lacan argued that the concept of *sexuation* was founded on this split at the heart of the signifier. However, there is also a difference between the signifier and signified, and this is a general concept in Lacan's psychoanalysis, 'we analysts must bring everything back to the cut [*coupure*] qua function in discourse, the most significant being the cut that constitutes a bar [*fait barre*] between the signifier and the signified' (*É* 678). And, according to Lacan, the split in the signifying chain is the only evidence we have of the discontinuity of the subject in the Real: 'the cut made by the signifying chain is the only cut that verifies the structure of the subject as a discontinuity in the real' (ibid). This means that the symbolic structures of language are not connected to the objects to which they supposedly refer, and it is this structure of discontinuity which follows the structure of the unconscious. This is why Lacan

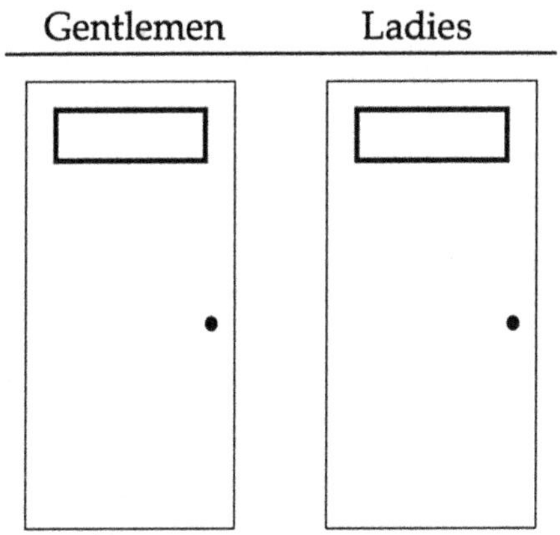

Fig. 4.3 Lacan's two doors schema

repeatedly states that the unconscious is structured like a language because the unconscious is equally discontinuous (*SIII* 119), and this idea of discontinuity is closely related to the *non-rapport sexuel*.[5] Lacan says, 'if linguistics enables us to see the signifier as the determinant of the signified, analysis reveals the truth of this relationship by making holes in meaning the determinants of its discourse' (*É* 801).

The argument that Lacan is deploying is that the 'gaps in our understanding' affect any truth which might emerge from discourse, which is Lacanian jargon for the truth is always incomplete (in full Lacanian jargon it is said to be *mi-dit* [half-said]). The focus on discontinuity is an early formulation of what will later become the *non-rapport sexuel*. The necessary relation of the *non-rapport* is riddled with gaps, making any coherent, rational, or systematised sense impossible. However, I stress that this is a *necessary* non-relation. But why? Because the attempt to make sense of the *non-rapport* is a necessary one: even Lacan is attempting to make some sense of it in his discussions of the *non-rapport sexuel*. There might not be a *rapport sexuel* but subjects need some symbolic/

[5] It is for this reason that Didier Anzieu was wrong to criticise Lacan's concept of the unconscious. The reference to the unconscious's structure as mimicking the structure of language is not a kind of linguistic determinism. Lacan does not mean that the unconscious *is* language. Rather, he means that the very instability and discontinuity of language mimics the unconscious (see Anzieu and Tarrab 1990: 43).

fictitious/ conceptual sexual relationship to exist in the first instance for the truth of this relation to be qualified as 'non' or impossible. As we saw earlier, only a true believer can be a good nonbeliever. The arbitrarily posited fiction *retroactively* generates some truth. This fiction of retroactive truth is illustrated in the graph of desire; by starting on the right-hand side of the right-to-left vector, Lacan is suggesting that the graph already presupposes "a subject," named at birth, that is ready to be affected by the world.

The graph of desire's explanatory strength is that it schematises the quilting (see Fig. 4.4), knotting the signifier and the signified together. Once this process has taken place, we are left with a decisive, though arbitrary and cunning, master signifier. Arbitrary and cunning because there are holes in the discourses from where the master signifier emerges. Figure 4.4 develops the previous graph (Fig. 4.2) by adding Lacan's labelling from *Écrits*, 'this is what might be called its elementary cell'. Lacan says: 'in it is articulated what I have called the "quilting point" [*point de capiton*] by which the signifier stops the otherwise indefinite sliding of signification' (*É* 681, translation modified). The updated graph shows the process by which the signifier is quilted and how meaning takes on currency. Lacan places the prelinguistic subject at 'Δ,' this is the fictitious animal being who is *retroactively* seeking to make sense of the world. '$' refers to the fully formed barred subject, one who has been through the process of subjectivation in language and on whom the signifiers have

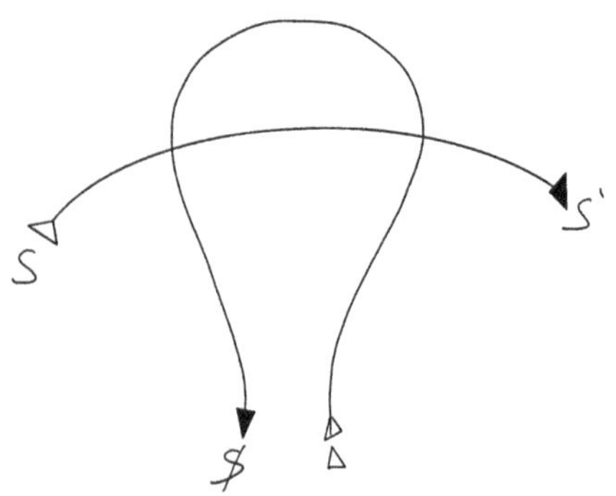

Fig. 4.4 Graph of desire stage 1

been impressed. The left-to-right vector ($\overrightarrow{S.S'}$) which cuts across the top of the main vector ($\overrightarrow{\varnothing\$}$) represents the signifying chain in language. The main vector, ($\overrightarrow{\varnothing\$}$), demonstrates the meaning-making process of subject formation. As already noted, this graph should be read *retroactively*; the retroactive mechanism of subject formation will become ever more crucial to Lacan's conceptual scheme. Therefore, the graph should be read by beginning from (Δ) and ending in ($), after having been impressed at (S) and (S′). Confusingly, Lacan will later transform S and S′ into S1 and S2 (respectively) following the mathemes (Fink 2004: 114), as explored in the previous chapter, and so, the horizontal vector ($\overrightarrow{\varnothing\$}$) intersects at S1 and S2, as shown in Fig. 4.5 below:

The graph displays the process of subject formation with all three psychoanalytic realms (R.S.I.) present in the graph, as will become apparent as I explain the graph in more detail. The quilting point [*point de capiton*] is located where ($\overrightarrow{S1.S2}$) intersects with ($\overrightarrow{\varnothing\$}$).

Lacan further complicates the graph by changing the labelling once again (see Fig. 4.6), and claims that both (*s*(A)) and (A) are 'the locus of the treasure trove of signifiers' [*le lieu du trésor de significant*]. *s*(A) 'is what may be called the punctuation, in which signification ends as a finished product,' and, Lacan adds, 'let us observe the dissymmetry between the one, which is a locus (a place, rather than a space), and the other, which is a moment (a scansion, rather than a duration) (*É* 682). At both intersections along the signifying chain [*s*(A) and (A)], the big Other acts to tame the subject to the arbitrary will of the Signifier.

To contextualise this highly abstract discussion, let us imagine a child who is journeying merrily along the path of subject formation [$\overrightarrow{\$.I(A)}$],

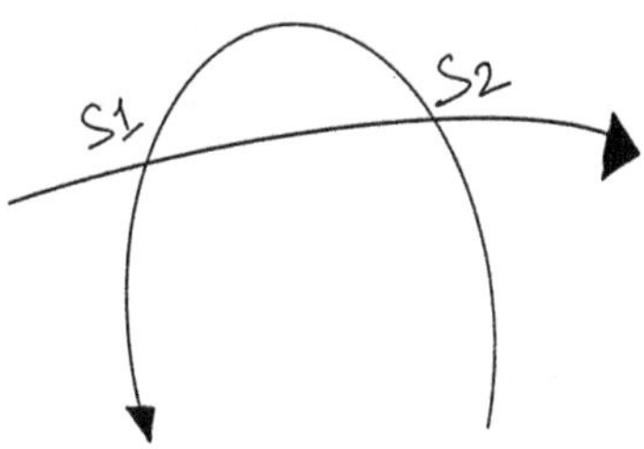

Fig. 4.5 Rudimentary graph with labelling

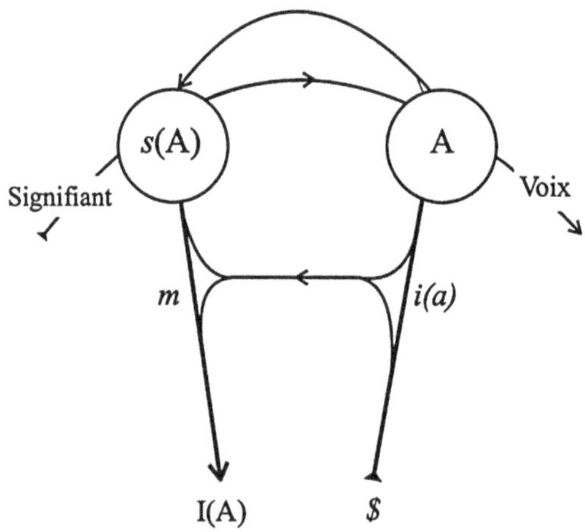

Fig. 4.6 Intermediary graph of desire

and suddenly finds themselves confronted with the big Other (A). In childhood, a subject's parents personify the big Other (A). When the child's parents first impose a strict restriction on their child, they inadvertently coerce the child into submitting to the power of the Other. The parents might rationalise with the child to convince them to submit to authority, by stressing the immediacy of a danger which might risk the child's life. Therefore, a threat will often follow a prohibition; sometimes "under pain of death" to guarantee its proper installation. The parent might say: "do not cross the road if the 'red man' lights up. You could get run over by a car, so watch out!" When a parent warns their child in this way, compelling them to wait for the traffic signal as they cross the road, the parent is nothing but a vector for the desire of the big Other, in this case, personified by the local authority or the State. However, the severity of the symbolic injunction has been forcefully impressed upon the child; Lacan represents this moment of confrontation with the big Other as (A) on the graph. The next time the child confronts a road crossing, with or without her/his/their parents, the memory of the symbolic injunction to "Wait!" is so severely installed in the child that they will wait. Lacan labels this child with the symbolic awareness of the finished product of the signifier '*s*(A)', the child (*s*) with an awareness of the prohibition of this big

Other (A). After this event has taken place, we can say that the Signifier has quilted, and it is representable on the chain of signification. The signifier's quilting is a two-stage process; both moments involve a certain amount of interaction with the other. The feedback loop begins with (A), the primary exposure to the symbolic demand, then the installed symbolic restriction at *s*(A) feeds back to (A) and is passed on to future subjects.

> The subject's submission to the signifier, which occurs in the circuit that goes from s(A) to A and back from A to *s*(A), is truly a circle, inasmuch as the assertion that is established in it—being unable to close on anything but its own scansion. (*É* 682)

This demonstrates the insignificance or lack of meaning of the signifier; 'in other words, failing an act in which it would find its certainty—refers back only to its own anticipation in the composition of the signifier which is in itself meaningless [*insignifiante*]' (*É* 683). Since the content of the restriction is totally arbitrary, in this case, the rules of the road in the UK, we could imagine a society where cars do not obey the "green man" (traffic signal) rule. Moreover, in the example I have laid out to explain the graph, Lacan illustrates the interplay between the three psychoanalytic realms. The child and her/his/their imaginary ego journeying along the path, fighting off other children to the road's edge, the parent and the weight of symbolic authority forcing the ego into language and the symbolic law, and, finally, the real of having your life flash before your eyes as you're about to be squished by oncoming traffic, now forced to escape language through death.

One difference between Figs. 4.5 and 4.6 is that the big Other (A) replaces S2. Lacan says that to square the circle, and for the graph to make sense, (A) need not be a complete and contentful signifier, it only needs to look complete and contentful (*É* 683). Lacan again argues that (A), the big Other, is characterised by the incompleteness I explored in the previous chapter. Lacan characterises the big Other as lacking a fullness of being, and it is wrong, according to Lacan, to presume that the big Other is a complete and truthful thing. If we do, we reduce the big

Other to a mere formalism and diminish the graph to a pure expression of Game Theory, which gives the subject calculable choices:

> This allows us to see that this Other is but the pure subject of modern game strategy, and is as such perfectly accessible to the calculation of conjecture—in the sense that the real subject, in making his own calculations, need not take into account any so-called subjective (in the usual, that is, psychological, sense of the term) aberration. (*É* 806)

Squaring this circle is impossible, Lacan says:

> This squaring of the circle is nevertheless impossible, but solely because the subject constitutes himself only by subtracting himself from it and by decompleting it essentially, such that he must, at one and the same time, count himself here and function only as a lack here. (*É* 683)

When the subject confronts the big Other, they subtract their desire from the equation and submit to the big Other to simultaneously come into being against it and allow the big Other to function as a lack in their subjective economy.

This confrontation is the necessary and impossible logic of the big Other. On the one hand, it demands from the subject the complete submission to its law and the subtraction of the subject's desire only to then require that the subject propagate its vacuous law, reinforcing its power. It is worth noting that this is not a Lacanian *prescription,* but a mere *description* of the world of signification. Translating this abstract analysis into the language of our example, the child, in confronting the big Other, subtracts his/her/their desire: to cross the street unobstructed at whim and will. The subject becomes an *affected subject* when they have installed the desire of the Other in their subjective economy. The child essentially sacrifices their desire for nothing concrete in return because the big Other is unable to offer a definite, cast-iron, guarantee that vehicles will *always* stop at red traffic lights. Of course, it would not be unreasonable to assume that a car would probably stop if a child ran out into the road, provided the driver was paying sufficient attention and stopped. However, it is not inconceivable that a car could run the child over, and the big

Other cannot provide a solid guarantee to the contrary. Lacan argues that, in this example, the law acts to preserve the Law itself, and not the child's life. The "green man" is not a failsafe guarantee that the child will never be run over. It is a game of chance and probability. What the local government's rules of the road provide is a *semblance of law and order*, a set of rules which inaugurates the subject's guilt, creates prosecutable offences, and, as such, the big Other always wins. The child gives up some desire to a vacuous and deceptive big Other. The child has staked their entire being on the incoherence and vacuity of the big Other. However, Lacan does not (yet) lament this structure. There is no other viable way for societies to function, and for this reason, it is *necessary*. And, for Lacan, we must be dupes to these lies, the non-dupes err [*les non-dupes errent*].

The Big Other and the Ego-Ideal

The existence and structure of the master signifier precede the subject's relationship with it, as the example of the child illustrated. For Lacan, the symbolic law is always already present, and he says the big Other is a 'preliminary site of the pure subject of the signifier, occupy[ing] the key [*maîtresse*] position here, even before coming into existence here as absolute Master—to use Hegel's term with and against him' (*É* 683). The structure of the pure signifier of signification is sovereign, and codes exist in our world even before we have uncovered them, or entered into a relationship with them; they are always already operative:

> One cannot even speak of a code without it already being the Other's code; something quite different is at stake in the message, since the subject constitutes himself on the basis of the message, such that he receives from the Other even the message he himself sends. Thus the notations A and s(A) are justified (*É* 683).

Lacan stresses that the big Other is the locus [*lieu*] of Speech (*É* 683); this confirms the logic of Lacan's conceptual scheme because it is only within the Symbolic Order that a subject can speak. Speech always already inculcates the subject into the Symbolic Order, and this is so because naming the subject in language necessarily includes them in the relation. However, Lacan adds a caveat that the big Other 'nevertheless emerges as Truth's witness' (*É* 683). The concept of Truth is further complicated: not only is the Truth multiple, as demonstrated earlier concerning Copernicus's heliocentric universe, but now Lacan argues that the Truth is born, constructed, and continually related to lies.

To show this Lacan makes a comparison between the 'feint' [*feinte*] which might overcome an animal and the deceit [*tromperie*] which a signifier in Speech might undertake.

> The deceptiveness of Speech would be indistinguishable from the feint, which, in fighting or sexual display, is nevertheless quite different. [...] But an animal does not feign feigning. It does not make tracks whose deceptiveness lies in getting them to be taken as false, when in fact they are true—that is, tracks that indicate the right trail. (*É* 683)

There is a difference between preparing decoys to throw a hunter off-scent as a survival mechanism, as found in the animal kingdom, which is how I have understood Lacan's example of feint [*feinte*] in animals, and the deceit [*tromperie*] of the signifiers themselves: 'animals [...] manage to throw their pursuers off the scent by briefly going in one direction as a lure and then changing direction' (*É* 683). However, the deceit of the signifier is greater, it is inscribed in the signifiers themselves and for-themselves.[6]

> But it is clear that Speech begins only with the passage from the feint to the order of the signifier, and that the signifier requires another locus—the locus of the Other, the Other as witness, the witness who is Other than any of the partners—for the Speech borne by the signifier to be able to lie, that is, to posit itself as Truth. (684)

[6] Lacan's *tromperie* is a refashioning of Freud's joke from *Jokes and their Relation to the Unconscious* about two Jews who meet in a railway carriage at a station in Galicia. Freud explains:

> "Where are you going?" asked one. "To Cracow," was the answer. "What a liar you are!" broke out the other. "If you say you're going to Cracow, you want me to believe you're going to Lemberg. But I know that in fact you're going to Cracow. So why are you lying to me?" (Freud 1960: 115)

The decoy enables Speech to ascend to the rank of the signifier. Lacan says that the Other is invoked to bear witness to this transformation, thereby elevating the animal decoy to the deceit [*tromperie*] of the signifier. In simpler terms, the decoy enables the lie to enter into Speech, in effect endowing Speech with the capacity to lie (*tromperie*), and through the lie, Speech converges with the signifier to pass itself off as Truth. The reason that the deceit of the signifier is greater than the animal decoy is that Speech *sells* Truth in language.[7] Lacan says, 'thus Truth draws its guarantee from somewhere other than the Reality it concerns: it draws it from Speech. Just as it is from Speech that Truth receives the mark that instates it in a fictional structure' (*É* 864). Further, 'the instauration of the lie in reality is brought about by speech' (*SI* 228). What makes the structure of the big Other and its relation to the lie relevant to us? Why does Lacan include all this in his discussion of the second stage of the graph of desire?

The big Other is not an innocuous force in subject formation, and the master signifier (Φx) is linked to the big Other and it is central to subject formation as the graph shows. The right-to-left horseshoe vector represents the movement of subject creation as subjects are impacted by the big Other, chiefly at (A) and *s*(A), see Fig. 4.6. At (A), the big Other is effectively taming the subject, commanding the subject: barking orders, telling him/her/them how they ought to live, what they ought to do, and how they ought to feel. In *The Great Dictator*, Chaplin's final speech echoes the way the subject can experience the dictates of the big Other. Chaplin says:

> Don't give yourselves to brutes—men who despise you—enslave you—who regiment your lives—tell you what to do—what to think and what to feel! Who drill you—diet you—treat you like cattle, use you as cannon fodder. Don't give yourselves to these unnatural men—machine men with machine minds and machine hearts! (Chaplin 1940)

Except, for Lacan, that is precisely what subjects do, they acquiesce to the machine heart of the big Other, they are enslaved by the big Other. Lacan says, 'the first words spoken decree, legislate, aphorize, and are an oracle;

[7] This is Lacanian jargon for: language contains its own perfidy.

they give the real other its obscure authority' (*É* 684) The big Other issues the regulative principles which affix the codes that emerge from the quilting [*capitonnage*] of meaning at point (A). For example, if a young boy is hurt after a minor fall, a parent might deploy the widely espoused symbolic demand: "big boys don't cry," and, in effect, the parent is invoking the big Other's obscene power which seeks to modulate basic emotions, inculcating the boy into a system structure which focuses on the repression of his emotions. Another example is Malcolm X's succinct capturing of the big Other's obscene strategy in exposing how Black Americans are deliberately exploited, disadvantaged, and disenfranchised by the White Man in the United States:

> It's like when you go to the dentist, and the man's going to take your tooth. You're going to fight him when he starts pulling. So they squirts some stuff in your jaw called novocaine, to make you think they're not doing anything to you. So you sit there, and because you've got all of that novocaine in your jaw, you suffer—peacefully. Blood running all down your jaw, and you don't know what's happening. Because someone has taught you to suffer—peacefully. (Malcolm X 2003: 124)

For Lacan, the big Other's power, in this case, wielded by structural White Supremacy, is precisely that power which slowly inculcates and bends its subject to its will; forcing one to suffer peacefully. "Big boys don't cry" works in the same way; it is founded on a lie because, plainly, all children (and adults) cry. This shameless power is the power of castration in the oedipal process, and as we will see in the final chapter, this is the strategy which creates pre-psychotic subjects.

Nevertheless, a parent might employ such a strategy, borrowing some of the big Other's obscene power, because it is successful in achieving the desired result: the boy will most likely stop crying and might repress future cries. The boy wants to satisfy the desire of the Other and if that desire is for "men" not to cry, and the boy wants to become that "man," as defined by the desire of the Other, then, the boy will *will* himself into submission.[8] In a similar vein, women are subject to the so-called "bio-

[8] Of course, this conclusion does not apply in quite the same way to Malcolm X's analogy, which is a much more complicated deployment of the big Other's obscene power.

logical clock" symbolic demand which states that women should "hurry up" should they wish to have children, this is an equally perverse injunction deployed to invoke the same power of the big Other to regulate women's lives, bodies, and mould our final Ideal-Ego. These examples demonstrate the power the signifiers hold in subject formation. All signifiers are not necessarily true, *in fact they are lies*, and yet, these oracles legislate their fictions and demand the subject's strict adherence to their codes of speech. And this is central to the graph of desire and Lacan's theory of subject formation because these demands are willingly internalised by subjects as their Ideal-Ego.

The Second Mirror Stage

Unlike the Ideal-Ego, which is formed by the demands and desires of the big Other, the imaginary ego-ideal is formed during the second phase of the mirror stage. Lacan tweaked the mirror stage in *SVIII, Transference* (1960–61), five years before the publication of *Écrits* (1966). He says, 'a necessary modification to psychoanalytic theory, given the path it followed whereby the ego was used as I indicated earlier—this is what I teach you, or rather taught you, under the heading of the mirror stage' (340). The mirror stage part II has not been subject to as much scrutiny as the original, which I discussed earlier. Lacan elaborates on this notion alongside the ego-ideal, in chapters thirteen and fourteen of *SVIII, Transference.*

In the subject's search for self-understanding, Lacan says that an essential misunderstanding comes to the fore. As is often the case with Lacan, the subject prepares for self-consciousness via an essential detour through misunderstanding. 'Here arises the ambiguity of a misrecognizing that is essential to knowing myself [*un meconnaitre essentiel au me connaitre*]. For, in this "rear view," all the subject can be sure of is the anticipated image—which he had caught of himself in his mirror' (*É* 684). After having recognised the specular image of her/his/their reflection for the first time, the child looks back at their parents for reassurance. The child seeks to corroborate the discovery of their *"I"* in the "eye" of the parent. It is at this moment that the child will begin internalising the desires of the Other (A), in this case, personified by the desires of the parent. These could be, for example, the set of future expectations for the child. These parental desires are continually seen in the subject's rear-view-mirror and act to encourage specific actions, behaviours, and desires. These parental commands are not expressed directly but rather proliferate ambiguously; these commands lead the child toward a myriad of misunderstandings in their search for self-understanding. Lacan extrapolates this insight from subject formation into broader considerations of intersubjective relations in society. All subjects act to fulfil the desires of the Other without necessarily knowing what those desires are, instead we all act on approximations of the tacitly accepted suggestions of the big Other. Lacan cautions us to be wary of the simple rehashing of the mirror metaphor because in its second variation it does not hold as evident a visual representation. The original Mirror Stage is, after all, a "scientifically" observable phenomenon: that of a (pre-linguistic) infant in front of a mirror enamoured by the recognition of their reflection for the first time. Whereas in its second variation this is not the case, as Lacan explains:

> What is based on mirrors goes much further than the model. […] But beware: this [second] schema is a bit more elaborate than is a child's concrete experience in front of a real surface […]. What is represented here as a flat mirror has a different use. The schema is of interest to us because it introduces the function of the Other with a capital O, whose initial, in the form of the letter A [for Autre, meaning Other], designates the flat mirror apparatus here [*mis au niveau de l'appareil du miroir plan*]. (*SVIII* 351)

In looking over their shoulder, after recognising their specular image, the child recognises the big Other standing behind them. However, this recognition does not introduce the big Other into the world, since the big Other was always already there, but this recognition brings in an awareness of the big Other in the subject's life. Skipping ahead slightly, the child, in recognising its self-consciousness against the desires of the big Other, begins to understand the extent of its unawareness and its lack of knowledge. The subject's spontaneous reaction will be to begin asking the big Other: *che vuoi?,* or "what do you want from me?!" Backtracking a bit, Lacan explains:

> There is something in images that transcends the movement and changeability of life, in the sense that images live on after the death of living

> beings. According to Antiquity's *nous*, this is one of the first steps of art: that which is mortal is immortalized in statuary. This is also the function that is served in a certain way by the subject's image in my theory of the mirror [stage]. When this image is perceived by a child, something is suddenly proposed to him whereby he does not merely receive the sight of an image in which he recognizes himself; this image already presents itself as an ideal *Urbild*, as something that is both ahead of him and behind him, as something that has always existed, as something that subsists by itself, and as something before which he senses his own fissures as a prematurely born being and experiences himself as still insufficiently coordinated to correspond to it in its totality. (*SVIII* 413)

What the subject recognises in their rear-view [*rétrovisée*] is a coherent 'ideal *Urbild*,' which I have understood as a pre-image ideal or archetype. Lacan is clear that this is already present because the 'ideal *Urbild*' does not merely include the desires and expectations of parents but also the comprehensive set of past and future societal expectations which are or will be internalised by the subject. The comprehensive set includes the demands of the master signifier. The subject internalises an entire system structure. This realisation happens, echoing Heidegger, as a thrown-ness in the world ('something that is both ahead of him and behind him') inaugurated as the child looks back to his/her parent.[9] As Lacan explains:

---

[9] In §38 of *Being and Time* (1927), Heidegger discusses being-thrown-in-the-world. In *Ontologie et temporalité,* Jean Greisch explains:

> "Non seulement l'être-jeté n'est pas un "fait fixe", mais il n'est pas non plus un fait accompli [...]. Il appartient à sa facticité que le *Dasein, aussi longtemps qu'il* est ce qu'il est, reste dans le jet et est entraîné par le tourbillon dans l'inauthenticité du On" (SZ *179*). Hamlet, dont le nom signifie d'ailleurs "tourbillon," pourrait en offrir une illustration littéraire. L'analytique existentiale aborde ici une expérience que d'autres philosophes, Schelling notamment, ont théorisé sous le titre de "vertige spéculatif". On peut en effet se demander si un *Dasein* aussi foncièrement "piégé" par lui-même [...] qui "se perd" aussi vertigineusement lui-même [...] (SZ *179*), dispose encore d'un quelconque moyen pour accéder à une existentialité authentique. La réponse de Heidegger à cette question est paradoxale à souhait: loin de constituter un obstacle *contre* l'existentialité, la déchéance est "plutôt la preuve la plus élémentaire à l'appui de l'existentialité du *Dasein*". (BT *179*) (Greisch 1994: 227/8)

Stitching together aspects of Schelling, Heidegger and Lacan, the subject thrown-in-the-world could be said to be locked in an infinite whirlwind of oncoming decay ('le tourbillonnement infini de la déchéance'). This Heideggerian insight is the same one which pushed Schelling to describe being as something the subject "contracts" (see chapter one). The subject is irremediably lost, and Lacan captures this subject in the '*Urbild* idéale.'

> Let me exemplify this with a movement made by children in front of mirrors [...]. A child, who is being held in the arms of an adult, is expressly confronted with his image. [...] Referring to the Other nevertheless clearly comes to play an essential role here. [...] What can come from this Other, insofar as the child in front of the mirror turns around to look at him? I would say that the only thing that can come from him is the sign "image of a" [*i(a)*]—a specular image that is both desirable and destructive, that is effectively desired or not desired. This is what comes from the person toward whom the child turns, to [*à*] the very place with which he identifies at that moment, inasmuch as he sustains his identification with the specular image. (*SVIII* 415)

Lacan argues that from this moment on the child's Ego-Ideal, I(A), is born, and acts to regulate the ego. From the moment of self-recognition the ego is simply a good student waiting to be mastered, 'the ego is thus a function of mastery, a game of bearing, and constituted rivalry' (*É* 685), to be mastered by the big Other.

Graph II (Fig. 4.6) represents the mastering of the subject by the big Other. The subject begins his/her/their journey at *\$* and entertains imaginary relationships with "small others" (traditionally known as intersubjective relations, *i*(*a*)) (*É* 810). The intersubjective relationships are said to be imaginary because, as part one of the mirror stage showed, all egos are imagined, and the subject soon realises these small others are only *semblants* of his/her own ego, shell characters, expressed as *i*(*a*), 'that is, to the semblable connoted by a lowercase *a*' (É 810). The subject who has refused to settle for a mere *semblant*, *i*(*a*), is exposed to the big Other, (A), and, as a result, becomes a subject of the big Other, expressed '*s*(A).' In simpler terms, the subject's ego is produced by first being exposed to their parents (A), thereby accepting the demands of the Other, which makes them install the *s*(A). In turn, this now *processed* child is denoted '*m*' for '*moi*' [ego], on the graph (Fig. 4.6) which ends in the full transformation of the ego into the Ego-Ideal, I(A). Note how there is a shortcut on the graph, which avoids the (A), the Symbolic Order, altogether, from $\overrightarrow{i(a) \text{ to } m}$, this represents the unregulated mayhem ['everything smashed to a pulp' (*SIII* 96)] of the conflict between egos without the decrees and legislation of the big Other. Instead, Lacan focuses on the journey to the Ego-Ideal through the Symbolic Order, taming and regulating the subject's ego through the desires of the big Other.

At the outset of this chapter, I described the subject's transformation into the Ideal-Ego, I(A) as the *affected subject of experience*—a subject who has been affected by *the weight of symbolic life*. Lacan explains:

> This imaginary process, which goes from the specular image to the constitution of the ego along the path of subjectification by the signifier, is signified in my graph by the $\overrightarrow{i(a).\mathrm{m}}$ vector, which is one-way but doubly articulated, first as a short circuit of the $\overrightarrow{\$.\mathrm{I}(\mathrm{A})}$ vector, and second as a return route of the $\overrightarrow{\mathrm{A}.s(\mathrm{A})}$ vector. This shows that the ego is only completed by being articulated not as the *I* of discourse, but as a metonymy of its signification. (*É* 685)

Lacan draws a distinction between the $\overrightarrow{i(a).\mathrm{m}}$ vector and $\overrightarrow{\$.\mathrm{I}(\mathrm{A})}$ vector. The $\overrightarrow{i(a).\mathrm{m}}$ vector represents a short circuit that bypasses the quilting of the signifiers, and, therefore, is designated an unsuccessful means of arriving to the Ego-ideal, 'I(A).' It is for this reason that we cannot chop the graph in half, since the process of subject formation must go through (A) and then *s*(A), the now quilted signifiers, to be completed (Fig. 4.6). We can now understand why 'I(A)' expresses a subject which has been impacted by the weight of symbolic demands and expectations. Lacan argues that the subject must go through the metonymy of signification (quilting or '*capitonnage*') by pursuing the strategy expressed in the whole $\overrightarrow{\$.\mathrm{I}(\mathrm{A})}$ horseshoe vector. There is no shortcut in the formation of the subject.

To get beyond the lower half of the graph of desire to the upper half, Lacan depicts the subject and Other in a relationship of conflict, and he is, once again, taking his cue from Hegel's *Phenomenology of Spirit.* Lacan returns to the Master and Slave dialectic and relates this to his understanding of intersubjective relations in psychoanalysis (*É* 685–86). Lacan deploys the classic Hegelian theme of conflict to discuss the relationship between the subject on the one hand, and his/her/their needs and demands on the other. Lacan locates 'demand' in relation to signifiers so that demands only exist in their articulation against the big Other's desires, once the quilting of meaning has affected the subject. Lacan says:

> Yet it is impossible, for those who claim that discordance is introduced into the needs assumed to exist at the subject's origins by the way demand is received, to neglect the fact that there is no demand that does not in some respect pass through the defiles of the signifier. (*É* 687)

For Lacan, while 'needs' always pre-exist and are directed at the big Other to be fulfilled, some specific demands cannot be satisfied by the big Other nor by the quilting of the signifiers, and this 'leftover' demand opens the subject up to her/his desire (*d*) and, eventually, *jouissance* (Fink 2004: 119).

For Lacan, subject formation occurs as a result of the subject's relationship with others, and, therefore, her/his/their needs and demands are necessarily intersubjective. Moreover, the subject's desires are only ever generated as a result of the by-product produced by the big Other's having fulfilled the subject's needs and demands, effectively having satisfied the subject's needs and demands. Therefore, in this relationship, the subject's desires emerge from the subject's conflict with the big Other. Moreover, once the subject is confronted with this leftover desire, they are unable to entertain it for long, and will, instead, be expected to acquiesce to the clear and straightforward edicts of the big Other in exchange for having fulfilled the subject's demands.

For clarity, I have, so far, avoided the distinction Lacan draws between the Ideal-Ego and the ego-ideal, opting to treat them separately. I have avoided this distinction because I have so far chosen to focus on the subject's Ideal-Ego in the Symbolic, stemming from the subject's relationship with the Other, and expressing what the Other wants from the subject. The lower half of the graph of desire has the primary function of representing the Symbolic Order's signifying structure as it relates to subject formation, illustrating the mastery of the subject by the Other. However, the lower half's second function is to show how leftover demand is generated and transformed into the subject's desires, and this leftover desire prompts Lacan to re-investigate the subject's ego-ideal, opposed to the subject's Ideal-Ego, arguing that the subject's primary interest is in their desires.

On social media, for example, users articulate and sharpen their ego-ideals. Only after users have intensively vetted the way they will be represented do they authorise the use of their virtual *semblant.* Subjects ensure that they are content with what they have constructed, selecting the right profile pictures, ones that will satisfy their ego-ideal, and subjects further sharpen their ego-ideal in preparing the accompanying text/speech which they consider to be original and exciting. Subjects say and do things which express what they believe their ego truly *is*—their ego-ideal—whereas the Ideal-Ego is what the Other wants from the subject. It is this distinction that opens the next section of the graph of desire, to which I alluded earlier. As subjects develop a plethora of 'needs,' they increasingly begin 'demanding' satisfaction and pleasure. Lacan is clear that the subject is a demanding subject. She/he/they needs things from others; for example, we might need our parents to feed us as young children. However, what is leftover from the requests of these needs is an insatiable demand, an unquenchable thirst, and it is this surplus that Lacan calls desire (*d*).

Desire Is a Trap

For Sartre, desire forces the subject to confront the impossible abyss of failure; the desiring touch reduces the other to an object, and, therefore, is always in vain. Sartre said: 'desire is itself doomed to failure' (*BN* 522), However, Lacan says in *Écrits*:

> In other words, to such an extent that these needs have passed over into the register of desire, with everything it forces us to face in this new experience of ours: the age-old paradoxes desire has created for moralists and the mark of the infinite that theologians find in it, not to mention the precariousness of its status, as expressed in its most recent form by Sartre—desire, a useless passion (*É* 687).

Unlike Sartre, Lacan argues that desire is not useless, and, opting to make a platitudinous comment, Lacan jokingly says that desire is a natural function which serves to maintain the propagation of the species (*É* 687). Moving the argument onto surer ground, Lacan argues that the question of desire brings the subject back to the role of the Father and prompts us to ask, 'what is a Father?' (688). Lacan contends that Freud proclaimed the Father dead, but we did not take notice: '"It is the dead Father," Freud replies, but no one hears him; and it is regrettable that, due to the mere fact that Lacan takes it up again under the heading of the "Name-of-the-Father," a situation that is hardly scientific should still deprive him of his normal audience' (ibid).[10] The *Name-of-the-Father* returns as a structuring principle which enables the normal functioning of desire, for Lacan. This argument corroborates our reconstruction of Lacan's argument concerning desire from the previous chapter. I said that the subject renounced the unrestricted enjoyment of the Other, and, in the broader process of symbolic castration, the subject accepted the partial enjoyment of the Other's body; the subject seeks the *objet petit a* (the object cause of desire) but will never find it. The big Other is the master signifier personified, and the present investigation seeks to demonstrate how and why this big Other can wield so much power. I argued that the big Other (or its connected master signifier) is a lie, and yet, the lie functions as truth. The lie governs subject development and installs the Symbolic Order. And, now, Lacan goes further in qualifying and characterising this big Other:

> No authoritative statement has any other guarantee here than its very enunciation, since it would be pointless for the statement to seek it in another signifier, which could in no way appear outside that locus. I formulate this by saying that there is no metalanguage that can be spoken, or, more aphoristically, that there is no Other of the Other. And when the Legislator (he who claims to lay down the Law) comes forward to make up for this, he does so as an impostor. But the Law itself is not an impostor, nor is he who authorizes his actions on its basis. (*É* 688)

According to Lacan, conferring the authority of the Legislator onto the master signifier "the Father" is an act of perfidy/duplicity. The question of

[10] Lacan often refers to himself in the third person.

desire is a question of first uncovering the desires of the Other in order to guarantee the Other's love for the subject.

> It will seem strange that—in opening up here the incommensurate space all demand implies, since it is a request for love—I didn't allow for more "making" and debating on this point. And that instead I focused it on what closes shy of it, due to the same effect of demand, to truly create the place of desire. Indeed, it is quite simply, and I am going to say in what sense, as the Other's desire that man's desire takes shape, though at first only retaining a subjective opacity [*opacité subjective*] in order to represent need in it. (*É* 688–89)

The subject spends a substantial amount of time imagining what it is that the Other desires from them, and motivating the subject is simply *a wish to be loved*, the subject acquiesces to the desires of the Other because they simply want to be loved. Moreover, this *wish to be loved* will reappear in *SXX, Encore.* The subject's wish to be loved ignites their search for their true desire, pushing the subject beyond the desires of the Other (ibid). The 'subjective opacity' [*opacité subjective*] is simply Lacanian jargon for the subject's desire which has not yet been fully formed, what I earlier called 'leftover,' following Bruce Fink's designation. The subject's desire can only materialise against the backdrop of the desires of the Other, and that is why there are two stages to the graph of desire. Louis Malle's *The Lovers* [*Les Amants*] (1958) illustrates the *wish to be loved* as the site of the subject's pure desire convincingly. In *Les Amants,* Jeanne suffers in an unhappy marriage, her husband never shows Jeanne any love or affection, and, although he supports her with her *needs* and *demands* in exchange for her silence and obedience to the patriarchal norm, Jeanne's *wish to be loved* persists. Her wish for love prompts her to seek her leftover desires elsewhere, which she eventually discovers with Bernard (Malle 1958), and Lacan represents Jeanne's search for love beyond her husband, in the upper level of the graph.

The lower part of the graph maintains the subject in a clear relationship with the big Other—this is the Subject of Language. If the subject can work out what the Other wants from him/her/them, that subject can try and satisfy the desires of the Other: for example, children who fulfil the desires of their parents, or Jeanne who suffers quietly, living with her husband and looking after his children. However, Lacan is simultaneously developing a general intersubjective theory of the subject's desires at the Symbolic level, and he argues that desire is what befalls the subject when their demands diverge from their needs; 'desire begins to take shape in the margin in which demand rips away from need' (*É* 689). The split pushes the subject away from the formal structures of language and the symbolic, and drives the subject closer to *jouissance,* S(Ⱥ). In many ways, this split in desire is a re-articulation of the split investigated in the previous chapter as the difference between the subject and the subject of the unconscious, which was drawn from the split signifier 'Ladies and 'Gentleman.'

However, the subject finds that this path to *jouissance,* S(Ⱥ), is a dead end, because there is never any escape from language. The subject's search for their true desire necessarily leads the subject to the fantasy ($\$\lozenge a$), and this is what Jeanne discovers at the end of *Les Amants*: she is desperately unsure of herself, and seemingly wishes for the restoration of the Symbolic fantasy which she has denied in her relationship with Bernard. The push towards desire runs the subject close to *jouissance.* The small '*a*' in '$\$\lozenge a$' is the *objet petit a*—object cause of desire. Graph 3 (Fig. 4.7) illustrates the difference between the desire of the Other and the subject's desire. The subject recognises this split through the question '*Che vuoi?*' The subject is led to ask: what do you want from me? The left-to-right, *s*(A) to (A), vector denotes the subject's search for the desires of the Other, while the lines which split off towards ($\$\lozenge a$) illustrates the subject's search for his/her/their own desire which necessarily ends in the fantasy.

> 'Fantasy' Lacan says, 'is defined by the most general form it receives in an algebra I have constructed for this purpose—namely, the formula $\$\lozenge a$, which the lozenge $\lozenge$ is to be read as "desire for," being read right to left in the same way, introducing an identity that is based on an absolute non-reciprocity'. (*É* 653)

($\$\lozenge a$) states that the barred subject's desire is for the object *a,* 'it relates the pleasure that has been replaced by an instrument (object a in the formula) here to the kind of sustained division of the subject that experience orders' (ibid). And, for Lacan, this desire for object *a* is the *fantasy* par excellence, because object *a* resides in the *jouissance* of the Other, which is both impossible and deceitful.

According to Lacan, anxiety (*angoisse*) results from our never being able to reach the *objet petit a*, and so anxiety ensnares the subject because the subject has a 'need' which cannot be satisfactorily or universally fulfilled (*É* 689). Therefore, we experience anxiety's grip as 'trampled by the elephantine feet of the Other's whimsy [*caprice de l'Autre*]' (É 689). The perceived whims of the Other are internalised and introduce in the subject, as Lacan says: 'the phantom of Omnipotence—not of the subject, but of the Other in which the subject's demand is instated' (ibid). It is for this reason, according to Lacan's psychoanalysis, that all rejection is painful. The pain a subject experiences in rejection is not directly caused by the subject who rejects them, but is the result of a need which will now go unfulfilled by the big Other. The subject experiences this loss as the arbitrary whim of the big Other's elephant feet trampling on one's heart. The all-powerful big Other rejects the subject's need to be loved. The request for love is unconditional and necessarily puts the subject in a

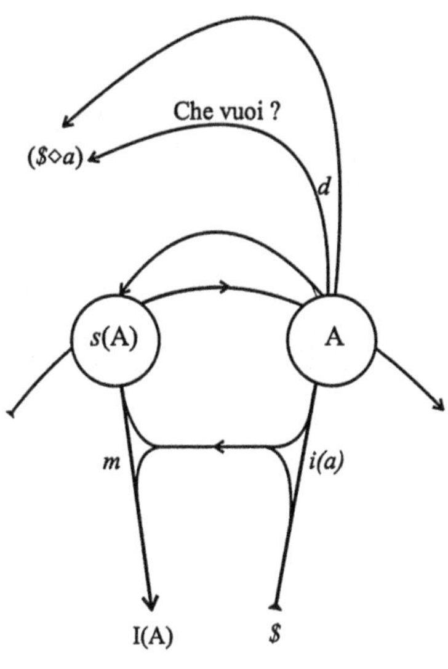

Fig. 4.7 Graph of desire with Che Vuoi?

relationship of subjection to the big Other, 'the subject remains subjected to the Other [*le sujet reste dans la sujétion de l'Autre*]' (ibid), and it is under this subjection that the subject discovers its proper desire:

> This is why the Other's question [*la question* de *l'Autre*] —that comes back to the subject from the place from which he expects an oracular reply—which takes some such form as "*Che vuoi?*," "What do you want?," is the question that best leads the subject to the path of his own desire, assuming that, thanks to the know-how of a partner known as a psychoanalyst, he takes up that question, even without knowing it, in the following form: "What does he want from me?". (690)

What does this person want from me? This question launches the subject onto the path to fantasy, which ends the journey represented in the upper part of the Graph (Fig. 4.7). As the subject descends from the top of the graph, they are exposed, once again, to the quilted signifier, and this forces the subject to translate their pure desire into language, making them feel the full weight of symbolic commands. The sheer weight of the signifier, *s*(A), re-structures the subject's ill-fated attempt to exercise its desire. The process re-fashions the subject's desire into the appropriate Ego-Ideal arrived at by way of re-integrating the desire of the Other.

This is the same strategy and insight, expressed in different terms, as symbolic castration ($\$\Diamond D$). We can now understand that as the subject is impacted by the big Other, (A), and discovers their desire, (*d*), they are forced to submit to symbolic castration ($\$\Diamond D$). In so doing, the subject gives up a bit of *jouissance,* S(Ⱥ), and enters the fantasy inaugurated by their wish to fulfil their desires ($\$\Diamond a$); this necessarily leads the subject back to the desire of the Other, *s*(A), which the ego, (*m*), has now accepted. The ego installs the desires of the Other as the subject's own desire and this ends the formation of the subject's desires; with the ego having been refashioned as the Ideal-Ego, I(A).

As noted previously, the lower half of the graph depicts the relationship the subject has with the big Other and so with language, the Symbolic Order, and results in the subject's Ego-Ideal. Whereas, the top of the graph deals with what the subject would like for her/him/themselves. '*Che vuoi?*' is the moment that the subject begins asking about their place in the construction of their subjectivity, but this only happens because the subject refuses to give up on her/his/their desire. Lacan concludes *SVII* with his famous slogan: '*ne pas céder sur son désir*' [do not give ground relative to one's desire] which is directly related to this move from the lower level of the graph of desire to the upper level. Lacan says, 'I propose then that, from an analytical point of view, the only thing of which one can be guilty is of having given ground relative to one's desire' (*SVII* 319). If the subject feels guilt, it is because she/he/they have effectively sacrificed her/his/their desire, 'in the last analysis, what a subject really feels guilty about when he manifests guilt at bottom always has to do with—whether or not it is admissible for a director of conscience—the extent to which he has given ground relative to his desire [*c'est toujours, à la racine, pour autant qu'il a cédé sur son désir*] (*SVII* 319). Repressing one's desires and pursuing desire in someone else's name or in the "name of the good" inflicts guilt upon the subject because they are refusing to accept their desires. Lacan says, 'doing things in the name of the good, and even more in the name of the good of the other, is something that is far from protecting us not only from guilt but also from all kinds of inner catastrophes' (*SVII* 319). Subjects do themselves great psychological harm by relinquishing their desire in this way; they elicit the guilt they feel, and this catastrophic error denies them the formation of normal libidinal relations:

> Either the subject betrays his own way [*trahit sa voie*], betrays himself, and the result is significant for him, or, more simply, he tolerates the fact that someone with whom he has more or less vowed to do something betrays his hope and doesn't do for him what their pact entailed—whatever that pact may be, fated or ill-fated, risky, short-sighted, or indeed a matter of rebellion or flight, it doesn't matter. (*SIII* 321)

Subject formation is betrayed by the subject's incapacity to submit to her/his/their own desire; what the subject should do, according to Lacan, is renounce the desire of the Other which characterises the lower half of the graph of desire. Abandoning the desire of the Other forces the subject to follow her/his/their own desire, and yet this 'leftover' desire leads the subject to renounce unrestricted *jouissance*, and this renunciation is the successful resolution of the Oedipus complex. The process allows the subject to be castrated symbolically and for the forfeited *jouissance* to be surrendered at S(Ⱥ).

According to Lacan, desire does not promise the subject any means of escape from the Symbolic Order. Instead, the pure desire (*d*) wished for by the subject is actually an elaborate trap, and the process of symbolic castration contains no real solution for the subject since the subject that emerges is necessarily captured by the symbolic structure. The grand Lacanian irony is that not giving ground relative to one's desire [*ne pas céder sur son désir*] is actually the appropriate mechanism by which the subject is coerced into re-entering the symbolic structure, after they traverse the fantasy, and the big Other demands from the subject that she/he/they actually exchange her/his/their desire for the desires of the Other, thereby re-integrating the commandments of the big Other and the power of the law itself. It is for this reason that the subject is always already guilty before the law, and it allows the law to exact a high price from all subjects. The paradox is that, for Lacan, desire is necessarily destined to fail, which is strikingly similar to Sartre's claim that 'desire is itself doomed to failure' (*BN* 522). Lacan and Sartre are making similar points, for both Lacan and Sartre the failure is a *necessary* one. It is necessary to go through the process and fail. Moreover, as I will show in the next section, failure allows for the process of symbolic castration ($\$\diamond D$), and it is this necessary mechanism that allows subjects to remain within the linguistic structure, the Symbolic Order.

S(Ⱥ)

According to Lacan, S(Ⱥ), or, simply, an aspect of *jouissance*, describes the lack in the Other itself, 'the lack of which makes the Other inconsistent' (*É* 694), and as the final chapter will clarify, S(Ⱥ) is the impossible *in itself for itself* with which we have been wrestling since Sartre introduced it earlier. S(Ⱥ) expresses the inconsistency in the big Other, 'it is here in S(Ⱥ) and read as: signifier of a lack in the Other' (*É* 693). S(Ⱥ) emerges for the subject in the clash between the Symbolic Order and *jouissance*, exposing the signifier of the lack in the Other, which is to say that there is no Other of the Other, no God that guarantees our existence. Lacan says, 'the lack at stake is one I have already formulated: that there is no Other of the Other' (*É* 693), and, strictly speaking, this lack in the Other is the impossible *objet petit a* that the subject desires.

Therefore, the pure desire (*d*) that the subject discovers takes him/her/them to a point where enjoyment [*jouissance*] has to be forfeited to continue on the path of identification. However, $S(\cancel{A})$ is itself barred, confirming what I described in the previous chapter as the inconsistent lying, arbitrary, unknown, master signifier. This traumatic reality can only be digested via the medium of fantasy ($\$\Diamond a$) which provides the subject with the appropriate lenses to survive this traumatic reality. Which is why exposure to $S(\cancel{A})$ necessitates a renunciation of $S(\cancel{A})$ and an acceptance of fantasy, because at $S(\cancel{A})$ we are not directly in language, but close to the edges of language. The fantasy screen hides the Real which states that our God is a liar, the decorator crab hiding in plain sight. The fantasy screen is the camouflage that God, $S(\cancel{A})$, employs to keep his inconsistency secret. However, $S(\cancel{A})$, as the impossible *in itself for itself,* also updates *in itself for itself,* because the process is a necessary one. $S(\cancel{A})$ is a conventional operation in the process of subject formation, part of the resolution of the Oedipus complex and, concomitantly, part of the process of symbolic castration ($\$\Diamond D$).

As soon as a subject begins demanding more than the desires of the Other, the subject's desires mutate and are no longer simple leftover demands but rather, Lacan says, these demands become drives [*pulsions*]. The transformation occurs in the process of *Che Vuoi,* where the subject asks, "what do you want from me." Lacan says:

> But while my complete graph allows us to situate the drive as the treasure trove of signifiers [*trésor des signifiants*], its notation, ($\$\Diamond D$), maintains its structure by linking it to diachrony. The drive is what becomes of demand when the subject vanishes from it [*quand le sujet s'y évanouit*]. (*É* 692)

The lower half of the graph expresses the meaning that is guaranteed by the big Other, *s*(A), this meaning is quilted and continuously upheld by the master signifier, for example, the incest prohibition as contained in the signifier the Father [*le Père*]. However, at the upper level of the graph of desire, there is no longer a guaranteed big Other, no big Other which could convincingly answer our questions. Therefore, the sheer fabric of meaning fragments, and one can no longer pin the signifiers to the signified, and this radical instability is *jouissance* itself, which is characterised by a lack. It is precisely this lack that love seeks to fill to re-establish meaning and coherence.

S(Ⱥ) expresses the inconsistent and lying master signifier, the *in itself for itself*, or God himself, and S(Ⱥ) also expresses the related notion that there is no Other of the Other, no God's God. Therefore, S(Ⱥ) describes a primordial lack. It is the missing piece. The humble realization that Lacan's psychoanalysis offers no easy truths, only some Faithless truth [*du Sans-Foi de la verité*] which can offer no guarantees:

> The lack at stake is one I have already formulated: that there is no Other of the Other [*qu'il n'y ait pas d'Autre de l'Autre*]. But is this characteristic of truth's Faithlessness [*Sans-Foi de la vérité*] really the last word worth giving in answer to the question, "What does the Other want from me?" when we analysts are its mouthpiece? Surely not, and precisely because there is nothing doctrinal about our office [*notre office n'a rien de doctrinal*]. We need not answer for any ultimate truth, and certainly not for or against any particular religion [*Nous n'avons à répondre d'aucune vérité dernière, spécialement ni pour ni contre aucune religion*]. (*É* 693)

The task of the analyst is not to tell the analysand what he expects from them, rather analysis has a much more modest aim which is to remind us how destitute our subjectivity really is. The Faithless truth is symptomatic of Lacan's overall method, characterised by its continuous revisions. In the previous chapter, I described the big Other and the master signifier as the regulative principle of the Symbolic Order; I discussed the Name-of-the-Father [*Nom-du-Père*] as the principle which guaranteed the existence of the Symbolic Order. However, the middle Lacan quoted here from the final chapters of *Écrits* has very enthusiastically claimed that there is 'no Other of the Other,' that is to say no regulative principle of the big Other itself, which is what a subject tries to uncover in *jouissance*. It is this kind of revision that makes Lacan so difficult to read and pin down: he continually changed his mind, and the only way to approach Lacan, therefore, is to read 'Lacan against Lacan' as Miller had suggested in his seminars (Figs. 4.1 and 4.8).

Contextualising the Fantasy with Scudéry's Clelia

> But it is a momentary folly, that I look upon as a toy, which hath it may be either some gallantry or novelty for those whose Spirits are well tuned to understand it. (Scudéry)

Thus far, our discussions on Lacan's graph of desire, the process of subject formation, the Father's Law, and love and desire, as both necessary and impossible, has been both highly abstract and theoretical. In this section, I turn to Madeleine de Scudéry's *Map of Tender* (Fig. 4.8) to contextualise our discussion and illustrate Lacan's distinction between the Symbolic and the Real, and the concomitant difference between signifier, (Φx), and *jouissance,* S(A̸).

Scudéry's *Map of Tender* first appeared in *Clelia* (1654–1660), and it illustrates a lover's journey, plotting the possible emotional responses to friendship. I contend that we can read Scudéry's *Map* in the light of Lacan's *Graph of Desire.* I synthesise Scudéry's *Map* with Lacan's *Graph* to adapt it to include Lacan's view that there is no sexual relationship [*il n'y a pas de rapport sexuel*]. And, although our argument seeks to dig into Scudéry's *Map*, it is mainly a discussion on Lacan's distinction between the signifier (Φx) and *jouissance* S(A̸), which I argue parallels Scudéry's division between *The Dangerous Sea* and the *Unknown lands.* Our comparison with Scudéry's *Map* aims to show how Scudéry's *Unknown lands* foreshadowed Lacan's concept of *jouissance,* and the inclusion of Scudéry's *Clelia* is designed to show how the late Lacan's philosophy is, therefore, not as abstract as might appear at first glance.

I begin by showing how Lacan's graph is a reimagining of Scudéry's *Map.* Then, I track the rhetorical and linguistic similarities between Lacan's practice and Scudéry's salon. I do this to demonstrate how Scudéry's *Map* challenged the seventeenth-century French social order, thereby highlighting the value of Lacan's practice as a form of social

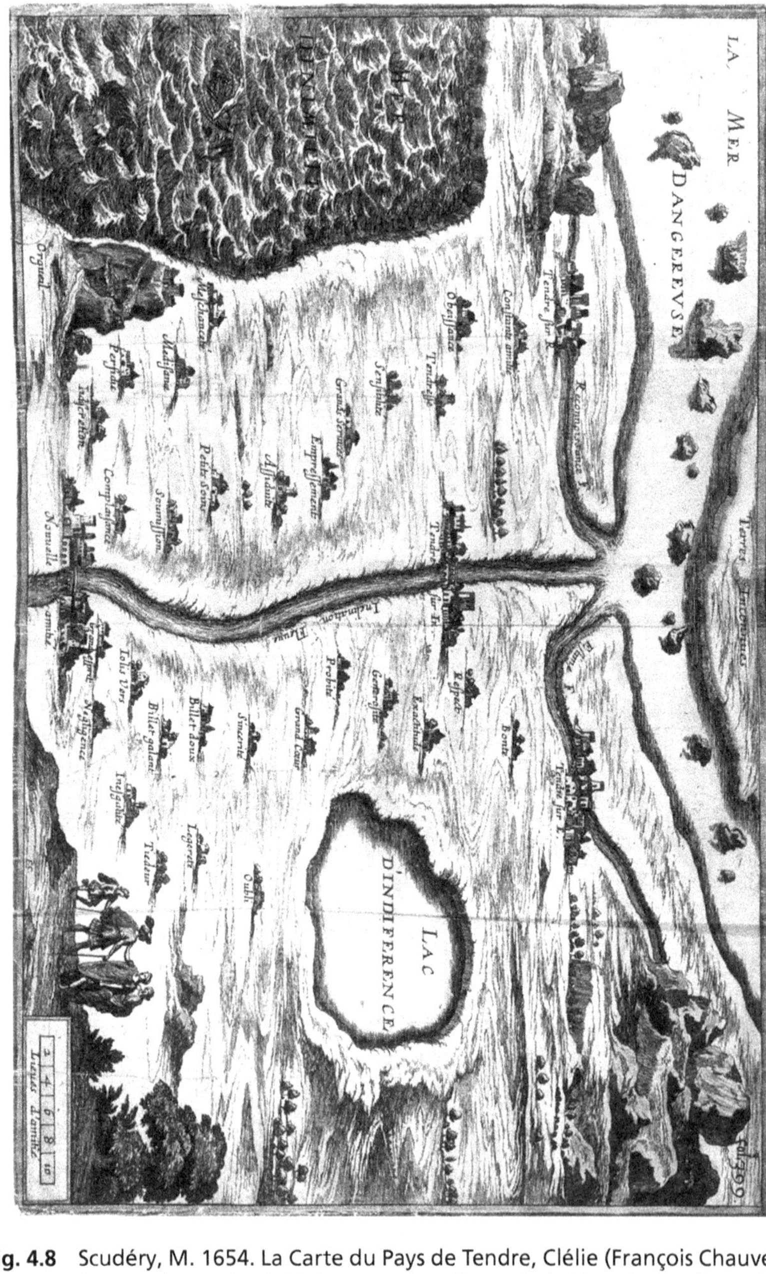

Fig. 4.8 Scudéry, M. 1654. La Carte du Pays de Tendre, Clélie (François Chauveau, La Carte du Pays de Tendre (1654), engraving, from Madeleine de Scudéry, Clélie, Histoire romaine. Paris: Courbé. Public domain, via Wikimedia Commons)

theory. I contend that we can only appreciate Scudéry's threat to the language of reigning power from a Lacanian standpoint, where Scudéry's *Map* pointed not just to the signifiers but also *jouissance,* and it was for this reason that Scudéry's language caused such anxiety to seventeenth-century masculine *doxa*. Scudéry threatened to expose what *doxa* needed to keep hidden to strengthen its symbolic power, and by illustrating these unknown lands, Scudéry made visible what *doxa* wished to remain invisible, namely the fragility of masculine power. Scudéry's "Real" move was to use the *Map* to defy male authorship and writing, threatening the sheer symbolic fabric of patriarchal relations because such an act highlights the inconsistency of reigning power. This illustration is crucial since, for Lacan, the *non-rapport sexuel* is shorthand for such a move, which can also be described as the trauma of the Real. This trauma reveals that the Symbolic was but a mere fiction offering only an illusion of stability and coherence. This move prepares my discussion in the final chapter of the difference between phallic *jouissance* and feminine *jouissance,* in order to show how love is aligned with the latter and, therefore, impossible. However, as the discussion of Scudéry's *Map* will show, the impossible *jouissance* (or *Unknown lands*) is a necessary fiction which supports *jouissance phallique* (or, *The Dangerous Sea*) and, therefore, preserves the subject's symbolic libidinal economy in the process of subject formation. Furthermore, the Lacanian reading I offer of Scudéry's writings, as both threatening and preserving symbolic power, bolsters our understanding of Lacanian psychoanalysis's vital relationship to language and writing.

Map of Desire

Both Scudéry's *Map* and Lacan's Graph of Desire share visual and conceptual similarities, and, although not much has been written on the visual similarities between these two illustrations, Lacan did note multiple connections between his work and the *Map*.[11] Saying in *SIII*: 'many things become clear if we take them in this register—for example, the curious onset of Schreber's psychosis with the curious expression soul

[11] For example: *É* 407; *SI* 238 & 295; *SVII* 175 (non exhaustive).

murder he employs, a most unusual echo, you'll agree, of the language of love in the technical sense I have just been highlighting for you, love at the time of the *Map of Tender*. This sacrificial and mysterious symbolic soul murder is formed at the onset of psychosis according to the *precious* language' (*SIII* 254–5). In *SVII, the Ethics of Psychoanalysis*, Lacan says again: 'so as to imagine the extremely rarefied and complex organization concerned, think of the seventeenth-century *Map of Tender* [*Carte du Tendre*], although what one finds there is a far more pallid version; the Précieuses, too, at another historical moment placed the emphasis on a certain social art of conversation' (SVII 146–7, translation modified). In *SXIX, Or… Worse*, Lacan states again the importance of the Précieuses to his thinking and philosophy, saying: 'this was why I called upon the testimony of Les Précieuses who, as you know, remain a model for me, Les Précieuses who, if I may say so, define so admirably the *excès au mot*, the excess in the word' (*SXIX* 9). And, as Jacques-Alain Miller has maintained, Lacan and the Précieuses complement each other: 'Lacan, against Molière, was on the side of the "Précieuses *ridicules*" [Ridiculous Précieuses] and the "Femmes Savantes" [Learned Women]' (Miller 2011: 336). Therefore, I seek to investigate the Graph of Desire in light of Scudéry's *Map*, to see what can be discovered about each from this comparison since both illustrate the subject's desires and emotions as they interact with social rules and expectations.

Lacan's Graph of Desire expresses an emotional journey comparable with the one found in Scudéry's *Map*. However, Lacan's graph also depicts the process of subject formation as the subject interacts with language and the Other, *s*(A), while Scudéry's *Map* focuses on intersubjective relationships. Although, I contend, both show the subject's relationship with the big Other.

Scudéry's *Map* illustrates the debates surrounding amorous relationships in seventeenth-century France. For Scudéry, the *Map* does not reflect love as it necessarily relates to sexual desire, since these are usually considered to be separate in the bulk of the geographic area visualised by the *Map*:

> Allegorically, it is a map of an imaginary land called Tenderness. As the novel's heroine teaches her audience how to read it, the map is revealed to

be a course in gallantry, giving men the woman's perspective on both the ways to win her heart [...] and the ways to lose it. (DeJean 1991: 57)

By contrast, Lacan's graph is revealed to be a lesson in subject formation. While Lacan's graph does allude to the sexual act, like Scudéry's map, it does so only parenthetically. The graph separates love and sex, and it is organised into an upper and lower-level, separated by the left to right vector *Signifiant* [Signifier] –> *Voix* [Voice]. As we saw, the Subject of Language [*l'être parlant*] is expressed below this arrow, at the lower level. Above this arrow, at the upper-level, Lacan depicts the Subject of *Jouissance* [*parlêtre*], and, remarkably, both Scudéry and Lacan banish sex to the top of their respective illustrations. It is at the upper level of the graph that the sexual relationship would occur if it were possible, and where physical acts partially occur. The sexual relationship is characterised by a *non-rapport* because the Subject of *Jouissance* is not submitted to the symbolic restrictions of language or the dictates of the big Other, which is why the sexual relationship is inexpressible. Instead, the subject is in the free fall of *jouissance*, where unregulated enjoyment operates. Subjects cannot forge relationships outside of language and speech; the sexual act cannot be inscribed, written, or translated convincingly.[12]

Burrowing around in the *Unknown lands* has returned something closely resembling the Subject of *Jouissance*, a subject that exists beyond all societal restrictions—as opposed to the Subject of Language, encountered in the central landmass, *Tendre*, which describes a subject as tied to the signifiers. As we saw, the signifier entraps this latter subject through language and, since language always already contains societal expectations, it inevitably wears the subject down. According to Lacan, Subjects of Language are oblivious to societal pressures and do not recognise them as such, which is why Lacan states wryly: 'Speaking beings are happy' [*les êtres parlants sont heureux*] (*AÉ* 556). As we saw, the upper level of the graph describes a subject who, in pursuing their leftover desires, attempts to reach *jouissance*. This journey ends in the fantasy ($\$\Diamond a$) because *jouissance* is much too excessive and incoherent to bear directly; therefore, the subject is forced to return from the upper-level to the lower-level of the

[12] *cf.* Milner (2009: 91).

graph, through the fantasy. Paradigmatically, in Scudéry's *Map,* the traveller is coerced into staying behind the Dangerous Sea [*Mer dangereuse*] (Φx). In both illustrations, the desiring subject is compelled to fashion a fantasy screen, enjoying *jouissance* or the *Unknown lands,* S(Ⱥ), only from a safe distance. The fantasy screen is built to sustain the subject's self-image and to prevent them from getting too close to *jouissance*. Understood this way, we could say that the lower level of the *Map* is a fantasy screen, it is a lover's ideal designed to sustain the fantasy of courtship, friendship, and the loving relationship uncorrupted by sex (*SI* 213). However, the paradox of the *Map* is that in wilfully excluding sex from the map it becomes about the *non rapport sexuel.*

Both Lacan's *jouissance* and Scudéry's *Unknown lands* are located at the upper levels of the respective illustrations. Scudéry intended to relegate sex to the realm beyond *The Dangerous Sea,* placing the sex act beyond a treacherous and dangerous sea: Scudéry says, 'because it is dangerous for a woman to go a bit beyond the limits of friendship' [*parce qu'il est assez dangereux à une femme, d'aller un peu au-delà des dernières bornes de l'amitié*] (*Clelia* I 42/ *Clélie* 184). Though, for Scudéry, the sexual prohibition begins right at the edge of friendship ('a bit beyond'), and so, directly in *The Dangerous Sea*; we are not quite in the *Unknown lands* yet: 'beyond this Sea is that we call *Unknown lands*' (42). Therefore, the *Unknown lands* hint at something else, not necessarily sex but unregulated desire, or *jouissance.* Similarly, for Lacan, the *non-rapport* is hidden behind the dangerous arrow of *jouissance –> Castration*. Scudéry does not attempt to discuss what might take place in the *Unknown lands*, 'in effect we know not what they are, and that we believe no person can go further than *Hercules* his pillars' (ibid). And, if it is *The Dangerous Sea* [*Mer dangereuse*] that prohibits sex, then what is in the *Unknown lands*? Understood in this way, the *Unknown lands* become analogous with Lacan's realm of *jouissance* beyond the Real of *there is no sexual relationship* [*il n'y a pas de rapport sexuel*].

A notable difference between the *Map* and the Graph is that the graph is descriptive, not prescriptive. Lacan is not sketching a perfect subject; instead, he is expressing the subject's troubled journey. First, the subjugation by the signifiers, then, the desolation felt at the loss of unregulated desire, and, finally, the integration of the fantasy which gives the subject enough will to continue doing the big Other's bidding. The graph expresses a subject who has agreed to society's restrictions and expectations. I argue that this reading of the graph mirrors the role played by the lower half of the *Map*. Both illustrations describe a journey whose travellers are cautioned to respect its laws and customs. In Lacan's graph, subjects are invited to renounce *jouissance* and restore the fantasy screen to tacitly accept the excessive power of the big Other—the *Name-of-the-Father* [*Nom-du-Père*]. In the *Map,* the traveller is warned against crossing the bounds of friendship, and they are invited to renounce their curiosity for the *Unknown lands* to maintain the fantasy of a genuinely tender relationship—the *Mer*(*e*) *dangereuse* [*The Dangerous Sea/Mother*].[13]

The Dangerous Sea marks the acceptable limit of social relations in the *Map,* and as such everything (allegedly) becomes about avoiding it. Claude Filteau argues that for Scudéry's *Map* 'everything is based on the form and content of a speech' (1979: 38). Language and speech are the essential characteristics of amorous relationships, and these are privileged over bodily relations.

> The Précieuses share the lessons that Pascal draws from his reading of Montaigne: because no truth is definitive, an assertion can be valid only by posing it in relation to others which are contrary to it: this is why *The* Précieuses privilege the word and the dialogic genre. (ibid)

The radical view Scudéry shares with Pascal, Montaigne, and Lacan, is that the truth is unstable and affirmed only relationally. The "truth" needs the support of conventional social norms and rules, as well as the contradictions and arguments which disputation then reinforces. *The Dangerous Sea* is the restrictive social limit which should not be violated by those who follow the map. The signifier *Mer(e)* [Sea/ Mother] enables complex amorous events to take place in language, just like the *Nom-du-Père* [Name-of-the-Father] enables the complex intersubjective relationships to take place in language. In other words, *The Dangerous Mother* is the very condition of possibility of the *Map of Tender.* Earlier, Lacan

[13] The word 'Sea' [*Mer*] in French is homophonous with 'Mother' [*Mère*]. In our context, *The Dangerous Sea* contains the signifier *The Dangerous Mother*, which tacitly convinces the subject in the *Map* to remain within the land of *Tender* and not exceed the limits to access the *Unknown lands.*

suggested that the *non-rapport* was the very condition of possibility for 'the enthralling acts (*SXIX* 11),' and almost identically, Scudéry's prohibiting the sexual act enables the tender friendship found in the map, and so, paradoxically, the map largely becomes about this prohibition.[14] Accordingly, I contend that in Scudéry's *Map*, we could say that the master signifier (Φx) is the "*Mère dangereuse*," ["*Dangerous Mother*"] who is both mostly absent and excessively present, just like the *Nom-du-Père*.

The central logic of Scudéry's map is contained and preserved by the use of water, *The Lake of Indifference* [*Lac d'indifférence*], *The Sea of Enmity* [*Mer d'inimité*], and *The Dangerous Sea* [*Mer dangereuse*]; the liquid, material, element of the signifying chain expressed in the *Mère dangereuse,* and just as in Lacan's graph, subjects are only ever formed against their signifier, which appears to regulate them. In Lacan's case, the master signifier is Name-of-the-Father, [*le-Nom-du-Père* or, *Non!-du-Père/ les-Non-Dupes-Errent*]. The very condition of possibility for the intelligibility of the Subject of Language [*l'être parlant*] rests in this signifier. The symbolic structure contains the law and sets the parameters for social interactions. In Scudéry's *Map*, the water is meant to signal the "natural" limit, but also the principal direction of travel, orientating the travellers in the land of *Tender*. All three rivers bend towards the *Dangerous Sea* [*Mer dangereuse*] and so, perilously close to the *Unknown lands*.[15]

The rivers drift in the direction of the *Mer dangereuse*, where the waters suddenly run still and are no longer characterised by the natural movement of the rivers—making the sexual act, for Scudéry, a matter of *will*,

[14] As Milner argues, 'what for the speaking being is the site of the impossible is also the site of a prohibition' [*ce qui pour l'être parlant est lieu d'impossible, est aussi lieu d'une prohibition*] (1990: 98/ 2009: 64).

[15] 'La rivière d'Inclination se jette dans une mer qu'on appelle la Mer Dangereuse' (*Clélie* 184).

because a boat is required.[16] Therefore, crossing the *Mer dangereuse* is only achievable by those who exercise the agency of their desires. As Jörn Steigerwald argues: 'in any case, it is necessary to take a boat, that is to say the "major trope" of the metaphors, to go to the "Unknown Lands"' (2008: 241). The Unknown Lands do not mark the destination of the journey expressed in the *Map*, but they do indicate the general direction of the drifting rivers. If the waters were allowed to carry an inanimate player, one would necessarily end in muddy (emotional) waters. Scudéry's *Map* contends that the water is an overwhelming natural force, both an uncontrollable element and a wild compulsion which, if left unchecked, would enable natural impulses to carry a player outside language and the symbolic regulations of the *Map*. This watery 'wild compulsion' mimics Lacan's argument that the drives develop out of the leftover desire, which was discussed earlier, further reinforcing the connection between the *Map* and the Graph of Desire (*É* 692). The water metaphor highlights the subject's relationship between nature and their drives. However, as Steigerwald explains, lovers need to make their journey across *The Dangerous Sea* [*Mer dangereuse*] by boat; the boat highlights the human agency of our desire to reach these unknown lands. Effectively, subjects who journey to these *Unknown lands* would have breached the prohibi-

[16] Katherine Ibbett has argued in "Productive Perfection: The Trope of the River in Early Modern Political Writing" that the trope of the river runs through early modern political writing. 'The [...] rhetorical deployment of the river was frequent in the literature of reason of state that circulated in early modern Europe. [...] This use of the river as a forceful grounding point for simile occurs again and again in Renaissance texts' (44). Ibbett also makes the point that 'watery tropes' were deployed by some early modern writers to develop core analyses. The 'figurative river is accompanied by—and perhaps facilitates—something more prosaically productive, allowing us to admire the works of man as well as those of God.' (53). Water, and rivers more specifically, were, in their rhetorical deployment, a powerful conceptual tool. In the language of the present study we could say the 'watery trope' is a signifying chain. Ibbett begins her article with an ominous warning of the danger that rivers could present. Ibbett writes: 'In "Le Torrent et la rivière" [La Fontaine] sketches the history of a man escaping from robbers who, with some trepidation, crosses a dangerous torrent to get away. The man discovers that his fears are unfounded, for the torrent is less dangerous than it seems. [...] He continues, still pursued by the robbers, and comes to a much more reassuring sight, a peaceful river [...] The man crosses the river, but though he manages to escape the robbers, he does not get out of the clutches of the river, and he drowns. La Fontaine adds darkly that the man and his horse are thus doomed to cross otherworldly rivers, and concludes, succinctly, that "Les gens sans bruit sont dangereux": when still waters run deep, they are dangerous' (Ibbett 2008: 44). As a parable echoing *la Mer(e) dangereuse*, I could seldom do better than Ibbett's channelling of La Fontaine.

tion expressed in the signifier *Mère dangereuse* [Dangerous Mother]. And, this compulsion to violate the law is not against their will; the desire to reach these Unknown Lands is not the result of some animal instinct, it is a reasoned and spoken attempt to cross the *Mer(e) dangereuse* [Dangerous Mother/Sea], and a deliberate violation of the command expressed in this signifier.

The traveller's *wish* is to find love by building the sexual relationship in language, which, as Lacan stated, is impossible. It is this attempt for subjects to connect in speech and writing that is doomed to fail. Not sex *qua* physical act, which is never really risked in the *non-rapport.* It is precisely the subjective desire to relate to lovers in language, to inscribe sex in speech, or writing that is impossible. Filteau maintains his analysis of the *Map* at the lower level of the graph, where tenderness is only expressed against symbolic structures, therefore ignoring the Real. However, I argue that we can meld this separation by speculatively reading the *Map's* meaning beyond the *Mer(e) dangereuse.* I want to suggest that we should shift our reading away from only viewing the map as related to the signifiers, to the map as also related to *jouissance* S(Ⱥ); this move allows us to recognise the centrality of *jouissance* to the entire Lacanian schema.

The Temporary Detour (*A Momentary Folly*)

In opposition to the standard critical cliché which sees the *Map* as a lover's game, a frivolous map illustrating how to win over a woman's heart, Joan DeJean and Jeffrey Peters see the *Map* as a powerful expression of proto-feminist power.[17] Lacan makes a similar point in *The Ethics of*

[17] DeJean is credited with coining 'salon-writing.' See: Beasley (2000) p. 69. See also, Peters (2004).

Psychoanalysis.[18] DeJean rejects Molière's (as well as the post-Molière) characterisation of the Précieuses as ridiculous.

> The leaders of seventeenth-century salon society have generally been portrayed as silly, frivolous women who frittered away their time and that of the male aristocrats. [... Where] all products of salon culture are only social games, shallow amusements of the idle rich. What if, however, the *précieuse* salons were thus ridiculed precisely because they were far more than a superficial pastime? (DeJean 1991: 86)

I wholeheartedly agree with DeJean that the Précieuses were ridiculed because they offered something far more than the superficial characterisation put forth by conservative critics. However, DeJean, like Filteau, maintains her analysis of Scudéry's proto-feminist influence at the level of symbolic structures when it is argued that the leaders of seventeenth-century salon culture helped to shape and precipitate the developments of a meritocratic French society. For DeJean, the accusations of frivolity and ridiculousness needed to be contested from within the remit of prevailing cultural and political *doxa*:

> Scudéry's tender geography has been enshrined in literary history as a mere bagatelle, the frivolous pastime of idle aristocrats. This recollection is founded on a deliberate forgetting, that of the political content of Scudéry's Tenderness. (ibid 78)

Scudéry's 'novels provide the clearest illustration' of salon writing (ibid 73). The collaborative literary exercise of shared production in Scudéry's

---

[18] Lacan says:

> It presents itself to us in a much more refined form ... as a "*Map of Tender*," since in short *The Précieuses*, at another moment in history, have brought to the forefront a certain social art of conversation. Here it is a question of things which are all the more surprising to see arise, that they arise in a time whose historical coordinates show us that on the contrary nothing seemed there—far from it—to answer what one could call a *promotion*, even the liberation of women. (SVIIa 301)

The published version, *SVIII* [*Seuil*], is erroneous on this point. Therefore, I have chosen to cite the unpublished transcript.

salon 'operated in effect as social levellers to blur the demarcations of a normally rigid class system' (ibid 76). The melding of aristocratic and bourgeois artists in the salons, of which Scudéry's was the most instructive, attempted to 'transform the French class system along the lines of a meritocracy' (ibid). DeJean adds that 'many [aristocrats] were willing to accord the privileges of aristocracy to the artist' which allowed 'rebellious aristocrats to continue their politics of subversion in less visible ways' (ibid).

The salons' meritocratic subversion of dominant power occurred under the direction of women, 'the "author" is the woman who presided over the salon in which the novel developed, she who dictated the style of the salon, the style that lives on in each of these extended exercises in writing the politics of a salon' (DeJean 1991: 76–7). And, it was Scudéry's writing style in particular 'that early critics of the novel found so threatening' (ibid). Scudéry's major advance was that she provided a 'psychological' or 'affective' realism to interpersonal relations, 'especially of love:'

> Scudéry's illustrious women, however, pour out their passions not to win back a delinquent lover who would take pity on their suffering but in order to provide their side of tales already told by others, to supply that which has been left out of traditional historical accounts. (79)

DeJean clarifies that these testimonies of Scudéry's illustrious women were not characterised by the Ovidian model, instead arguing that:

> When they are given the opportunity to speak for themselves, Scudéry's heroines protest the slanders of history and attempt to vindicate themselves. Their collective testimonies demonstrate resoundingly that female autobiographical speech could be far removed from the pitiful cries of abandonment. (80)

In vindicating themselves, DeJean shows that the novelistic advances made by Scudéry's heroines also served to unseat the privilege usually accorded to the 'individual literary subject:' 'the dominant feature of Scudéry's vast novelistic enterprise is the erasure of the identity of the individual literary subject' (84). This effacement of the individual literary subject 'inevitably calls to mind the erasure of individual authorial identity in salon writing,' thereby strengthening DeJean's argument that Scudéry's contribution was to use the salon to democratise societal norms and bend them toward meritocracy. 'In *Clelia* conversation increasingly dominates action, indicating that the scene of aristocratic power has shifted from the battlefield to the salon' which allows 'her salon's members [to be] the generation that had made the transition from civil war to a life of civility' (85). The power that DeJean reads in *Clelia,* and Scudéry's salon, is deployed to show how *Clelia*'s chauvinistic reception was misguided, and, therefore, reading it as a subversive novel:

> [The Précieuses] were nevertheless widely perceived as a threat to what one eighteenth-century commentator on the novel termed "the laws most necessary to preserve society" [...] in particular, the legal and social code that governed women's status in marriage. [...] *Clelia* [is] a novel of social subversion. (86)

DeJean continues:

> It is easy to underestimate her project because her new subversiveness depends on an element in which the nonliterary implications are hardly evident, what early commentators saw as "her intimate knowledge of the human heart" [...]. From the beginning, even those critics who find fault with the "implausibility" of her narrative or with the "excessiveness" of her stylistic *préciosité* praise the "natural" quality of her portrayal of sentiments. (ibid)

DeJean makes a convincing case for salon writing as sites of proto-feminist resistance. However, the nature of this subversion seems ambiguous. Where DeJean reads subversion, we partly see, following Lacan, a kind of conformism; where France's meritocratic development is complying with *doxa*'s prevailing rule in exchange for selective freedoms accorded to a few, whereas the sheer 'excessiveness' and 'implausibility' of Scudéry's writings exposed the very fragmentation and disintegration of the language of *doxa* itself. It is for this reason that Scudéry's conservative critics reacted so vehemently to salon writing, since the upper-part of the *Map*, which includes The Dangerous Sea and the *Unknown lands*, is Scudéry's illustration of the Real and *jouissance*, and highlighting these was an implicit revolutionary gesture which threatened the upheaval of symbolic structures, and, therefore, language itself.

DeJean's underlying premise is to simultaneously maintain and propagate the ridiculous/sensible binary established by commentators; concluding that far from ridiculous these sensible salons precipitated France's meritocratic development. Similarly, Peters sees the *Map* as a site of relations of power (2004: 93). Instead, I show how Scudéry's additional proto-feminist move was to highlight the very contradictions and failures of *doxa* itself, thereby emphasising the vacuity of symbolic power. Scudéry demonstrated the incoherence of symbolic coordinates by highlighting their internal antagonisms, forcing them to disintegrate. Similarly, Lacan's psychoanalysis was, and continues to be, characterised as an equally silly, frivolous and superficial pastime. In "Hommage fait à Marguerite Duras," Lacan addresses this caricature and paradoxically deploys it to distinguish between the science of psychoanalysis and its opposite. For Lacan, the science of psychoanalysis is uncouth; by stressing its supposed calculable nature it is committing a boorish error ['*goujaterie*'] (*AÉ* 192). Instead, we should appreciate that psychoanalysis is not a scientific dogma but, rather, outplays ['*déjoue*'] scientific discourse itself (*SXXIII* 14/22), as we saw in chapter two.

Scudéry and Lacan's unorthodox approaches seem nonsensical from within a scientific worldview, because salon writing, the *Map*, the *Graph of Desire*, or psychoanalysis *are* ridiculous if we adopt the coordinates of prevailing doxa and negotiate their value from inside an incommensurable worldview (*AÉ* 192). Both salon writing and psychoanalysis are lucid when taken on their own terms; similarly, Schelling's highly speculative *Die Weltalter* [*Ages of the world*] needed to be appreciated from within an Abrahamic (Christian) theological paradigm, as we saw earlier. DeJean makes a similar point, stating that 'the strange format [of the *Map*] almost invites these criticisms' (1991: 87). We could say that Lacan's graphs also invite these criticisms. Therefore, *Clelia*'s 'ridiculous' reception was an unsurprising reaction; *doxa* will react with ridicule to highly original threats to its established power. For example, the medical sciences see the Lacanian clinic as a flippant social game, created for the shallow amusement of the idle rich.[19] We argue that we should assume that these modes of thinking *are* frivolous, and, in their frivolousness, pose a direct threat that seeks to outplay dominant paradigms and demand something more radical than subversion. It is for this reason that Lacan 'was on the side of the "Précieuses ridicules" [Ridiculous Précieuses] and the "Femmes Savantes" [Learned Women]' (Miller 2011: 336).

Scudéry's major stylistic innovation anguished commentators because her salon writings effectively outplay [*déjoue*] many of dominant *doxa*'s essential requirements of good writing, namely that of clarity and the singular male author. To decipher their anguish, we return to Lacan's method of *temporary misunderstanding*. For Lacan, as we saw in chapter two, one should not understand too well at first. If one understands too quickly, the subject has misapprehended the origin and locus of their speech, as well as their desires. This temporary incomprehensibility is necessary in order to elucidate any understanding of the Real (*SI* 271). It is for this reason that Lacan continuously refers to the instability of speech and language itself (*SIII* 239–40). As we saw, to get to the heart of the matter, the subject first needs to misrecognise themselves and others, and this is Lacan's method, to 'leave the reader no other way out than the way in, which I prefer to be difficult (*É* 493). In formal terms alone, Lacan shares this with Scudéry's salon writing. As DeJean points out:

> In *Clelia,* the situation is stranger still. Scudéry makes what may well be the major stylistic innovation in the early development of the novel when she introduces conversations on a larger scale. However, Scudéry's conversations seem almost to undermine the form's normal functioning. Since speaking styles are generally not differentiated, the demarcations among characters are rarely precise; the reader is confronted once again with a mass of referentially unbound, nearly free-floating pronouns, this time in the first person. (1991: 84)

Scudéry's writings are slippery and enigmatic, and, as Peters develops, 'in the opinion of Scudéry's critics, the spatial language of the map of *Tender* is another example of the apparently impenetrable jargon of the salons'

[19] See for example: Meyer (2005).

(2004: 91). DeJean highlights that commentators found fault with 'the "implausibility" of [Scudéry's] narrative [and] with the "excessiveness" of her stylistic *préciosité*' (1991: 86). We could say, paraphrasing Lacan, that Scudéry leaves her readers with only one exit; the one which doubled up as the entrance. As Peters argues, 'the members of Scudéry's *samedi* group communicated with each other through a gallant code of proverbs, riddles, and acrostic verses' (2004: 91), and, once again, the criticisms of these boorish commentators could apply just as much to Lacan as they supposedly had to Scudéry. Lacan also communicated with his salon through riddles and supposedly impenetrable jargon. It is for this reason that both *Clelia*, and the *Map*, need to be read on their terms, following Scudéry's precise path.

Scudéry, anticipating her critics, provides us with an apt illustration of Lacan's idea of *understanding through misunderstanding*. First, we are led to believe that Clelia thinks that the *Map* should only be disclosed to the already initiated, and not allow the public to learn about their highly original map:

> Aronces, Herminius, and I found this Map so exquisite, that we perfectly understood it before we departed; Clelia instantly prayed him for whom she had made it not to show it but to five or six persons whom the desired should see it, but as it was not but a simple delight of her spirit, she would not have it fall under the censure of those stupid persons, which neither know the beginning of it, nor are capable to understand the new gallantry. (*Clelia* 42)

However, Scudéry goes on to say: '[the *Map*] made such a noise in the world that there was nothing spoke of but this *Map of Tender*' (43). The *Map*'s instant popularity angered Clelia, 'Clelia was angry that there was so much spoken of it' (ibid). And, suddenly, she adopts a Lacanian approach:

> Said she one day to Herminius, do you think I imagined, this spective fancy had any thing pleasant, but for our *Cabala* in particular to become public, and that I made to be seen but five or six persons which have noble spirits, should be seen by two thousand who scarce have any, and who

> hardly understand the best things? [*Qui l'ont mal tourné et peu éclairé, et qui entendent fort mal les plus belles choses?*]. (*Clelia* 43/ *Clélie* 185)

Scudéry is situating *her* map within *her* language, customs, or 'cabal.' The *Map* is a personal object deriving from the salon's collective imagination, and Clelia almost admits that outside the salon the map becomes 'ridiculous' because it has been transplanted out of context and left to the stupidity of the indelicate to misunderstand, before turning this argument on its head:

> There are strange men in the world, I extremely fear that they will imagine I seriously considered of it, that I have trifled away many days to find it, and that I believe to have designed an admirable thing, but it is a momentary folly [*Cependant c'est une folie d'un moment*], that I look upon as a toy, which hath it may be either some gallantry or novelty for those whose spirits are well tuned to understand it. (*Clelia* 43/ *Clélie* 185)

Scudéry describes the *Map* as having been created in a *moment of madness* [*folie d'un moment*], seemingly agreeing with those indelicate and stupid readers she admonishes. Clelia states that, of course, she does not take the map seriously: 'that I look upon as a toy.' Except that she does—the map has the potential to create something new, 'some gallantry or novelty,' and it is only obtainable to those who are ready to hear it, 'for those whose spirits are well tuned to understand.' However, the *map's* radical originality forces *Clelia* herself to initially misunderstand, describing it as a moment of madness ('*folie d'un moment*'); a clear sign of the *Map*'s status in the Real. This passage in *Clelia* places the *Map* outside *doxa*'s prevailing symbolic coordinates. It is for this reason that the *Map* can strike the uninitiated as incomprehensible from without, and so it is only intelligible on its terms, inside the language of Scudéry's cabal. Scudéry's *Map* operates as an incomprehensible document, and, in its alleged incomprehensibility, it is a direct challenge to established *doxa*. The *Map* promises a temporary misunderstanding on the way to another (proto-feminist) understanding, and only once one has entered into her language can the *Map* make sense. Scudéry's move is not quite subversion but revolution; a demand to upend the very fabric of established language with a competing language and set of referents. Scudéry's argument concerning the '*moment of madness*' almost anticipates Lacan's argument about psychosis in *SXXIII, Le Sinthome*, where he will attempt to align psychosis with subjectivity.

Therefore, Scudéry's method mimics Lacan's, both call for a departure from existing symbolic coordinates, demanding that the reader enters into the language and customs of their creations.

> The word escapes me *[Le mot me manque]*—at what point in literature does such an expression come up? It is Saint Amand who uttered it for the first time—not even written, but said like that one day in the street, and it became part of the innovations introduced into the language by the *Précieux*. [...] As you see, there is a relation between the map of Tenderness [*la carte du Tendre*] and psychoanalytic psychology. *Le mot me manque*—you never would have said a thing like that in the sixteenth century. (*SI* 268)

It is for this reason that Lacan relies so heavily on homophones, to continually remind his audience of the audible instability of language and writing, including his own. Scudéry continues:

> Clelia had therefore no reason to disquiet herself, Madam, for' tis certain that all in general commended this new invention, which displayed the way how one might acquire tenderness from honest persons, except from some dull, stupid, malicious, wicked, *whose approbations were indifferent to Clelia, whether they praised it or no, yet it commonly drew some delight from the most stupid of those men*: for there was a man among the rest who demanded to see this Map with a strange obstinacy, and after he had heard many praises, he dully demanded for what use it served, and for what profit was this Map? I know not (replied he to whom he spoke, after he had diligently folded it up) if it will serve to everyone but I know it will never conduct you to *Tender*. (*Clelia* 43)

The strange men who question the *Map*'s utility and insist that it is but a frivolous game are much too stupid to understand its value, and, anticipating the commentators, Scudéry seems to suggest that: these men will mock us, and it will be their loss. The map will never lead these idiotic men to *Tendre*. Crucially, *Clelia* is indifferent to these men. We should follow Scudéry and adopt her attitude; Scudéry's *Map* exists on a different intellectual plane, one which is not understandable from the position of dominant intellectual discourse, and, therein lies the minor deviation I enact from DeJean's analysis. Which is not to say that I disagree with DeJean's overall goal, I agree that:

> The *Map of Tender* forces us to confront the central interpretative dilemma posed by *préciosité*: the conjunction it stages between a rhetoric that is by today's standards overblown virtually to the point of being no longer readable and the hard-hitting vindication of the rights of women that is couched in this rhetoric. (1991: 87)

The hard-hitting vindication of the rights of women couched in this rhetoric attests to the fact that Scudéry's work challenged the language *doxa* assigned to women, indeed, by bending the meaning of words Scudéry made visible the fabric of the Real. Scudéry ended up saying much more than *doxa* would have ever permitted if it were not for the subtlety of her sleight of hand, and it is for this reason that I place the *Map* in the category of the Real, focusing on the *Unknown lands*, as the site which causes the most anxiety. The inclusion of these lands is the proverbial "bone in the throat," which caused such anxiety to the masculine reception to Scudéry's work, and it was done in plain sight.

As we saw briefly, Lacan was similarly unfazed by how he was characterised as ridiculous. Echoing Scudéry, Lacan contended that: 'what is important is to understand what one is saying. And in order to understand what one is saying it's important to see its lining, its other side, its resonances, its significant superimpositions' (*SIII* 115). The double meanings, the resonances, the superimposed significations which Lacan highlights are the very distinctions Scudéry drew between the language inside and outside the salon. The *Map* plays with this dissonance. And we can now better understand Lacan's response to his critics, partially quoted earlier, when he offered a similar rebuke as Scudéry:

> They gave me their perspective as technicians—"we don't understand any of it," they tell me. Notice how it's already a lot. Something you don't understand offers all the hope in the world, it's a sign that you've been

> affected by it. Thankfully we haven't understood anything, because we can never understand what we already have in our heads. (*SXVIII* 105)

Lacan's argument mimics Scudéry's, which is to say that *doxa* cannot understand any original works because their biases are insurmountable, the paradigms are incommensurable, and their biased mode of thinking prevents them from understanding, so they simply proclaim that: 'we don't understand any of it.' Scudéry and Lacan's flair is to forgive and look beyond this imbecility, with Lacan stating that 'something you don't understand offers all the hope in the world, it's a sign that you've been affected by it;' coupled with Scudéry's, 'the Destiny of this Map, Madam, was likewise so happy, that those which were too stupid to understand it, used to divertise [*sic*] us in giving us subject to deride their follies' (*Clelia* 43).

Lacan's allegedly ridiculous persona was so prevalent that it was even picked up by Frantz Fanon, who was paraphrasing Henri Ey in his doctoral thesis:

> Few men are as contested as Jacques Lacan. Parodying the expression, it might be said that, among psychiatrists, Lacan has supporters and he has adversaries. It would be further necessary to add that the adversaries by far outweigh the supporters … The 'logician of madness' does not seem specially bothered by this. (2015: 262)

What Fanon saw was that being the 'logician of madness' was no slur.[20] As Fanon knew, Lacan directly provoked the medical establishment by daring to treat 'la folie' on its terms, and ultimately returning it within language itself—a democratising gesture which 'among psychiatrists' seemed ridiculous.[21] Which is why Lacan was firmly on the side of the ridiculous Précieuses, where Scudéry's *Map* equally emerged from a 'moment of madness,' and, as I have argued, Scudéry invites us to enter this madness, to initially misunderstand, precisely to outplay *doxa* and access the Real. Both Scudéry and Lacan were indifferent to the ridicule

[20] See my article Richards (2021).

[21] See: Lacan's doctoral thesis, *De la psychose* p. 345–348.

by others: 'those which were too stupid to understand it, used to divertise us in giving us subject to deride their follies' (*Clelia* 43).

The Mother's Trap

Scudéry's distinction between tenderness and sex is an artificial difference since, as we saw, there are no speech acts in psychoanalysis that can be isolated from their signifier—in our case, the *Mer(e) Dangereuse* [The Dangerous Mother/sea]. As I have argued, the prohibition expressed in this signifier is the very condition of possibility for Scudéry's *Map*, and this prohibition is deployed to regulate what Scudéry's cabal can and cannot say. Prohibitions are implemented using language, and these two are locked in a nexus whereby the excluded is never eliminable. Paradoxically, a strict prohibition has the effect of making all future discussions about the prohibition itself. The more the social order laboriously demands that we accept a prohibition, the more all subjects can do is discuss the prohibition. Lacan's psychoanalysis aims to recognise the centrality of language, the duplicitousness of words and speech, to tease out unconscious thoughts and desires. Language is trickery, and, for Lacan, this view of language as deceitful reads instability in all speech and communication, where everything becomes flexible and treacherous, as it was for Pascal and Montaigne earlier (*SIII* 131).

The idea that language is duplicitous develops our discussion which tried to read Scudéry's *Map* as a map which threatened language itself by highlighting the Real. By blending the treachery of language with its potential for expressing the unconscious, we open up the possibility of seeing the *Unknown lands* as depicting the *non-rapport* of the sexual relationship. As Laura Burch argues, echoing DeJean and Peters, Scudéry's language challenged dominant intellectual *doxa*, 'the anxiety produced by Scudéry's slippery use of language [was that] she used both text and her famous *Map of Tender* to provoke disruptions in dominant contemporary literary and epistemological discourse' (Burch 2014: 7). The disruption, Burch suggests, occurred because Scudéry cast the woman 'as friend,' and this was 'interpreted as a deceptive and dangerous fiction, a menace to the integrity of French literary and political territory, as well as to the masculinity of the "holy bond" (*sainte couture*) of male friendship through which that territory was organised' (ibid). Scudéry's disruption of dominant discourse was powerful because Scudéry also established a signifying chain based on the exclusion of the sex act, relegating sex beyond the *Mer dangereuse*. However, the power of Scudéry's disruption of *doxa*'s language is not predicated on the assumption that sex is somehow absent from the map; rather, the power of this move is that Scudéry even dared to prohibit, relegate, and, therefore, paradoxically, highlight bodily relations as central to the *précieuses*. The supposed prohibition provoked a disruption to the 'holy bond' of traditional male friendship.

Lacan argued that sex occurs *in* speech: 'In other words—for the moment, I am not fucking, I am talking to you. Well! I can have exactly the same satisfaction as if I were fucking' (*SXI* 151). Lacan's argument mirrors the argument I ascribe to Scudéry, which says that sex, entertained in speech, is much more dangerous to *doxa*, which is why the map was so powerful at disrupting it. The seemingly innocuous emotions of tenderness and the stressing of friendships are suffused with all sorts of drives: 'Yet they do have to come from somewhere, these elements which [Balint] calls tenderness, idealisation, which are these mirages of love with which the genital act is draped—the *Map of Tender*' (*SI* 238). And, as Taylor showed, Boileau's *Satire X* displays this classic example of knee-jerk masculine insecurity:

> To ridicule further the reign of the Précieuses, Boileau condemns the literary genre with which they were particularly associated: he accuses Scudéry's novel, *Clelia,* of immorality:
>
> > First you will see her, as in *Clelia*
> > Receiving her lovers under the gentle cover of friendship [...]
> > With crime it suffices that once we begin
> > A fall always attracts another fall. (Taylor 2017: 18, my translation)

Boileau's overwhelming fear was that *Clelia* would invite immorality by stealth, by hiding behind friendship. We partly agree with Boileau's fear. He absolutely should be afraid. Scudéry's language is treacherous, powerful, and threatening. The *Map* allegedly says so little about sex and so much about emotional relations because emotional relations are sexual in language, and, for Lacan, it is in this relationship that an impossible antagonism exists. The *Map* highlights this *non-rapport* as well as what is generally understood by the physical act. The insecurity engendered by exploring this aspect of sex produced much discontent within the masculine holy bond.

Scudéry's signifier *The Dangerous Sea* operates in the same way as Lacan's left-to-right arrow in the lower half of the Graph of Desire. For Lacan, meaning and truth are merely clipped together by signifiers, which are themselves only arbitrarily decided. *The Dangerous Sea* is chosen arbitrarily to create the space for discussions against it. We will recall that that is what Lacan called the quilting point, and this buttoning of meaning and truth in the arbitrary signifier inaugurates the master signifier which regulates all discussions in social life, yet: 'every real signifier is, as such, a signifier that signifies nothing' (*SIII* 185). The master signifier emerges as the vacuous deciding principle in our social life, and this is fixed by the choices and tacit consent of 'the collectivity' (Saussure 1995: 113). The graph's descriptive strength resides in its illustration of the arbitrariness of the marriage of truth and meaning for subject development, as expressed in the Symbolic. The *Mère dangereuse* [Dangerous Mother] is such a signifier which structures the social rules in the *Map*. We could say that the compelling challenge to dominant discourse evoked by DeJean, Peters, and Burch, resides in the threat Scudéry posed to the power of the signifier, the *Mère dangereuse* [Dangerous Mother].

DeJean argues that Scudéry's 'long term legacy' 'may well be' her concept of *inclination*. DeJean explains the political ramifications of Scudéry's concept:

> Scudéry's heroine turns to her mother, Sulpicie, for advice: she is torn between two suitors, her father's choice, the noble and Roman-born Horace, and Aronce, to whom she personally "inclines" even though he is of unknown birth and therefore expressly forbidden to her by her father's dictate that she can only marry a Roman. Sulpicie appears unmoved by either the paternal concern for pure lineage or the paternal definition of marriage as political alliance: she unhesitatingly encourages her daughter to "give over her heart to her inclination for Aronce" (I:424). [...] It is easy, for modern readers at least, to overlook the political implications of *Clelia*'s

> tender geography, but the mother's discourse reminds us that Scudéry is asserting such fundamental concepts as a woman's right to choose for herself. (DeJean 1991: 88)

However, as we saw, the *Mère dangereuse* as signifier is also an elaborate trap; mimicking the trap of all signifiers. For Lacan, we should not trust in these because they often describe sites of conservatism which, by my reading, is where DeJean's argument ends. The Mother's trap is that Sulpicie might appear a proto-feminist in her determination to overcome the Father's symbolic obstacles: as a result of the patriarchal command for a Roman-born husband, Sulpicie offers her daughter the space to love Aronce. However, the lesson of the signifier is that both those options reinforce the closed patriarchal circle of marriage, religion, and oppressive social norms. 'A woman's right to choose,' DeJean has argued, but what is the choice? Both paths lead to subjugation to the Father and the Mother's law, the symbolic structures serving to reinforce family relations. In this case, the right to choose does nothing but accommodate a fundamentally unperturbed structure. French society might have adopted modest meritocratic characteristics, though without really altering the core, heteronormative, symbolic coordinates of relations of power. The figure of the Mother is complicit with the Father, guaranteeing a form of enslavement which allows the daughter the freedom of a forced choice. Lacan does not offer any radicalism from within symbolic coordinates of the law. It is for this reason that I argue that any analysis within the remit of the Subject of Language only yields further subjugation. The lower part of the graph expresses desire in terms of language and symbolic structures, whereas the top expresses that which is beyond language: *jouissance.*

Beyond *The Dangerous Sea*

In *Clelia*, Scudéry hints at what could lie beyond the symbolic restraints of oppressive social norms. And, though Scudéry does write that 'beyond this Sea is that we call *Unknown lands,* because in effect we know not what they are' (*Clelia* 184), I contend that what is beyond the *Mer dangereuse* is: the no of the non-rapport.

The signifier, the *Mère dangereuse* [The Dangerous Mother], shelters the *Map*'s travellers from their desire for the *Unknown lands* (*jouissance*). Charles Sorel had understood that to pursue desire in this way would be to allow oneself to be 'carried away by the frenzies of Love' [emport(é) aux frénésies de l'Amour] (Sorel 1667: 185). However, what Sorel missed was that Scudéry's alleged *frenzy of love* is nothing other than the *fantasy of love,* and, highlighting the *Unknown lands,* exposed this fantasy. As Clelia clarified, no one knows what lies beyond tender friendship, confirming Lacan's insight that there is no sexual relationship, since both corroborate the failure of the beyond. It's not that nothing physically exists beyond, it's that whatever exists (*jouissance/ Unknown lands*) is necessarily a weak point which is prone to failure, forcing the *Map*'s travellers, or the Graph of Desire's subjects, to reintegrate the Mother's or the Father's law, respectively, and either accept the fantasy or risk psychic catastrophe. Therefore, the *non-rapport* has a dual meaning, on the one hand, it describes the incomplete physical act, which does not preoccupy Lacan (*TBW* 26–27), and on the other, it describes the frustrating inability to make a success of *jouissance.* Strikingly, Scudéry also suggested that the *Unknown lands* contain this dual meaning:

> I content myself to tell you two things, the first is, I absolutely forbid you ever to speak to me in particular, and the second is, that that *unknown of whom you speak, is not in these Unknown lands,* because no person is yet there; nor can never be there [*n'y peut jamais être*]. (*Clelia* 43)

Clelia firmly rebuffs Horace, yet, simultaneously acknowledges the possible double meaning of the *Unknown lands*; confirming Lacan's distinction between sex and *jouissance.* And, it is in *jouissance* that is the 'unknown of whom you speak [...] because no person is yet there; nor can never be there.' Moreover, 'nor can never be there' [*n'y peut jamais être*] can also be interpreted to mean never be/ become. The mere fact that *Clelia* deploys Horace's misunderstanding to point to the ontological status of the *Unknown lands,* as that which exists outside the symbolic limit of *doxa,* is a radical act mimicking the move in Lacan's upper-level of the graph. Therefore, the *Map* is both a radical feminist move, as well as being a despairing account of the failure of *jouissance*. By pointing to *jouissance* Scudéry revealed the insecurity and instability of seventeenth-century *doxa*, but this is simultaneously an act of subjective self-annihilation. The conclusion the subject must reach at the end of Lacan's Graph of Desire points to the failure of subjectivity itself, and the move from the *Mer dangereuse* to the *Unknown lands* is Scudéry's brush with the Real which offers the same conclusion.

Scudéry's *Map* opens a seventeenth-century social space for *jouissance*, and it is in crossing the *Mer(e) dangereuse* [The Dangerous Mother/Sea] that the consequences of rebelling against her law become overwhelming. Scudéry's inclusion of the *Mer dangereuse* [The Dangerous Sea] is an implicit invitation for her followers to violate this prohibition. However, those who reach the *Terres inconnues* substitute the fantasy for the thing-itself, the live-wire of the sexual relationship against which they were cautioned. In effect, the subjects which emerge in the *Unknown lands* know too much about the *Mère dangereuse* [The Dangerous Mother]: she was never really there; she was merely a fictive symbolic constraint—only the supposed guarantor of tender friendship. Therein lies the power of the *Unknown lands/jouissance*, once there, we realise they highlight the fragility of all signifiers—they are hollow, and yet we follow (or, *les non-dupes-errent* [the non-dupes-err]).

It is for this reason that Scudéry was ridiculed because she made visible in the *Unknown lands* the ultimate weakness of male power. The fantasy screen of a genuine tender friendship was the camouflage that the *Mère dangereuse* [The Dangerous Mother] employed to hide her inconsistency, and, in moving beyond her reach, the *Map*'s travellers realise the desolation of their new found freedom. This move is the Real, where the sheer fabric of symbolic meaning fragments, which is to say that the seventeenth-century aristocratic *monde* [world] of social exchange starts to unravel. Subjects can no longer pin the signifiers to the signified, and this instability is the beginning of *jouissance*. However, the desolate freedom found in *jouissance* or the *Unknown lands* is incoherent since it is outside the language of symbolic meaning, which is why 'no-one can ever be there' [personne n'y est et n'y peut jamais être].

As a result of making the *Unknown lands* visible, even as against the backdrop of a prohibition, Scudéry not only threatened the seventeenth-century social order's fantasy of coherence—thereby exposing the vacuity of the Symbolic—but also threatened the supposed 'laws most necessary to preserve society' (DeJean 1991: 86). Scudéry revealed, not just in writing but also by illustrating, *doxa*'s fragile power. However, as Scudéry knew, foreshadowing Lacan, in the end, both the *Dangerous Mother* and *Unknown lands* are frustratingly unsatisfying and incomplete:

> *Love is a pleasing Malady,*
> *For which my heart no cure can find:*
> *Yet if I could get Remedy,*
> *I'le rather dye than cure my mind.* (Clelia 43)
>
> [*L'amour est un mal agréable,*
> *Dont mon cœur ne saurait guérir:*
> *Mais quand il serait guérissable,*
> *Il est bien plus doux d'en mourir*]. (*Clélie* 188)

Scudéry's reinterpretation of this fragment from Sappho's poem suggests that when the fantasy disappears, *I'le rather dye than cure my mind* [*il est bien plus doux d'en mourir*] because *jouissance* (or the *Unknown lands*) is much too excessive and incomprehensible to bear. Instead, subjects will undoubtedly wish for the relative coherence of language and the signifiers (or, the *Dangerous Mother*)—the *pleasing Malady* that is the ultimate fantasy of love itself; '*for which my heart no cure can find* [*dont mon cœur ne saurait guérir*].

The process of subject formation, displayed in the graph of desire, demonstrates Lacan's commitment to the idea that the subject is left desolate. For Lacan, nothing is ever as it seems, since language is treachery, and the subject is never free of symbolic restrictions since this would mean to be outside of language. However, *jouissance* exists, for Lacan. It is the fictional (counterfactual) goal that subjects aim for in the pursuit of their own desires. As we have seen, the subject is necessarily expected to renounce *jouissance*, and re-enter into the symbolic coordinates of language, this means accepting the desires of the Other and installing them in one's subjective economy. The subject digests this process through the fantasy, as the upper level of the graph demonstrated. Scudéry's *Map of Tender* is a means of digesting this truth—it is the fantasy screen par excellence. The process of subject formation and the brush against *jouissance* in order to renounce it, is necessary, and the search for love (the *wish to be loved*) is always 'doomed to failure' (*BN* 502),' as Sartre had claimed, but, for Lacan, not without first feeling the desolation of one's subjective position.

To further sketch out this Lacanian fatalism, we turn to Sartre's concept of Loser Wins [*qui perd gagne*] which will show, through Lacan's discussions concerning the Name-of-the-Father [*Nom-du-Père*] in *SXXI*, *The Non-Dupes-Err* [*Les Non-dupes errent*], that although Loser Wins [*qui perd gagne*] there is always the '*but nevertheless*' [*oui mais quand même*] that once again shows the mechanism by which the duped subject restores the master signifier, for fear of falling foul of the Name-of-the-Father [*Nom-du-Père*], or master signifier (Φx).

Loser Wins (*I Know Very Well*)

Qui perd gagne [loser wins] is a convincing shorthand for the strategy that Sartre employs concerning subjectivity in *Being and Nothingness,* and, in many ways, Lacan re-articulates a version of the strategy of Loser wins in *SXXI, the Non-Dupes-Err*, under the guise of the homophony *le Nom-du-Père/ Les Non-Dupes Errent* [Name-of-the-Father/Non-Dupes-Err]. As I have suggested, Lacan's early work was indebted to Sartre's existential philosophy, and, while Lacan saw his later work as enacting a 'fatal deviation' [*déviation fatale*] away from Sartre (*AÉ* 179), I contend against Lacan's self-representation, that his later engagement with *les non-dupes errent* closely resembles Sartre's strategy of loser wins with a few fundamental revisions. To highlight the resemblance, I show how the 'recuperative transformation' of loser wins is a form of fetishistic disavowal if viewed in Lacanian terms (Howells 1988: 198). If we consider loser wins in this way, Lacan has effectively morphed loser wins into the non-dupes err [*les non-dupes errent*]. Sartre's loser wins effectively settles the impasse of subjectivity expressed in the symbolic triad: *le nom-du-père / le non du père /*

les non-dupes errent, and is also a shorthand for the dialectics of love as it is presented here: the necessary impossibility of love.

Although subjects originally encounter the Symbolic Order at the original level of naming, and so language, for Lacan, subjects are only correctly inculcated into the Symbolic Order from childhood onwards, and this inclusion occurs alongside the subjective journey expressed in the graph of desire. It is during this process that subjects are either properly oedipalized or not. As Howells puts it: 'entry into the Symbolic Order is conditional on the initial renunciation of *jouissance* in the castration complex; because the signifier creates and splits the subject' (Howells 2011: 137). Subjects are exposed to specific signifiers, for example, the Name-of-the-Father [*le Nom-du-Père*], and these are either recognised or misidentified, which results in a structuring or mis-structuring of a subject's relationship with the Symbolic Order. As we saw, this inculcation has serious consequences for subject development since, like language, the Symbolic Order is both beyond all comprehension, since it is founded on lies, and the mechanism by which all comprehension is apprehended because it contains communication in language. It is for this reason that Lacan refers to the big Other as something about which we know nothing: 'the Other,' Lacan says, 'in so far as it's not known' (*SIII* 40). The big Other belongs to the realm of the Symbolic, and, in simple terms, it is the mis-structuring of the subject's relationship to the big Other that might lead the subject to psychosis. Moreover, we argued that the Father was the signifier that structures the truth of the thing [*la vérité de la chose*], and we showed how Lacan separates the signifiers from the thing they supposedly signified, for example, one's father. The image of the signifier (a-Father [*Un-père*]), for Lacan, is more important than the empirical person who assumes the position of the signifier in the Symbolic Order. Therefore, the Father is founded on a lie, and, because the Symbolic Order is founded around the master signifier the Father, who need not exist, the Symbolic Order is also a fake. As Lacan puts it in *Seminar XIX*, 'this is what is called the Father, and this is why the Father exists at least as much as God does, that is to say, not much' (*SXIX* 25).

The master signifier (the name-of-the-father [*le nom-du-père*]) is the Symbolic Order's regulative principle, and it places restrictions on named subjects, hence the no/name [*non/nom*] homophony. In *SXXI, The*

Non-Dupes Err, Lacan further develops the homophony, transforming it into the non-dupes err [*les non-dupes errent*], and in so doing, Lacan suggests that we must be dupes to signifiers in the Symbolic Order. So, we argue that Lacan's necessary dupery is the 'recuperative transformation' of loser wins (Howells 1988: 198) in a slightly different form. Because, since the subject must accept the total power of the signifier in order to continue on the path of subject formation in language, the loss of the subject's desire becomes a Symbolic gain for the subject; the subject gains language and, therefore, the tools of expression and intersubjective communication. *The Non-Dupes Err* [*Les-non-dupes-errent*] codifies the argument that the subject necessarily required the "lie" in order to access some half-truths in the Symbolic Order. As we highlighted, for Lacan, the arbitrarily posited fiction retroactively [*après coup*] threw the truth into sharp relief, and, in short, this means that the subject needs certain untruths (the vacuous big Other, or God, for example) in the Symbolic for some truth itself to be half-expressible in language. As Lacan puts it, the truth can only ever be *mi-dit:*

> I know that there is *this sacred question of truth* [...]. But we are not going to stick to it like that, after what I have told you, and how many times... and coming back to it time and again, without knowing that *it is a choice,* since it can only be *half-said* [*c'est un choix*, puisqu'elle ne peut que se *mi-dire*]. (*SXXI* 19)

According to Lacan, the truth, if it exists at all, is only half-said, and, because we are unable to express the unconscious in speech, the truth is always a *choice* [*c'est un choix*]. The *non-dupes* are those subjects who refuse to recognize this Symbolic fact, and so, the Loser Wins because the subject must be a dupe to gain some half-truth in language, which is to say the gain of half-truth is mediated by a deceitful big Other.

However, what the subject gained in the form of linguistic dupery [*duperie*] also involves a necessary disavowal of something else, the full truth which is inaccessible for the subject and resides in the Real. For Lacan, the aspect of loss in loser wins needs to be disavowed in order for the subject to access their winnings. Octave Mannoni's formula for disavowal is: 'I know very well, but nevertheless' [*je sais bien, mais quand même!*], and, in his book, *Keys to the imagination or the other scene* [*Clefs pour l'imaginaire ou l'autre scène*] (1969), following Freud, Mannoni argues that disavowal is the moment the child recognises the feminine anatomy of his mother as the absence of the phallus (the 'I know very well' [*je sais bien*] moment). However, the child's immediate reaction is to repudiate this fact ('but, nevertheless!' [*mais quand même!*]). Following Freud, Mannoni reads this subjective experience as the paradigm for the fetishistic subject, arguing that the fetishist's original disavowal always leaves them marked with an 'indelible stigma' [*stigma indélébile*] from the original maternal disavowal (11). However, Mannoni is not suggesting that the fetishist *wishes* a phallus for the mother—they know she does not possess one. Thus, Mannoni states: 'the belief in the presence of the phallus in the mother is the first repudiated belief, and the model for all other repudiations' (17). For Lacan, the signifier *the-non-dupes-err* [*les-non-dupes-errent*] requires that the subject disavow the fact that the Symbolic is a closed circle, a prison (the subject's 'I know very well' [*je sais bien*] moment), yet this prison simultaneously offers the subject language and the comfort of the signifiers (the subject's '*but nevertheless!*' [*mais quand même!*] moment)—therefore, the loser wins [*qui perd gagne*].

But Nevertheless!

Nevertheless, there is also another aspect of disavowal at play in Lacan's re-conceptualisation of Sartre's strategy. For Lacan, as we saw, the subject is alone, irremediably lost to themselves, and unable to understand even the most basic features of their existence, and, as a result, the subject does not wish to abandon the safe confines of language, the seemingly coherent desires of the Other, or the comfort of the signifiers. As we said, as soon as the fantasy vanishes, *I'le rather dye* [*il est bien plus doux d'en mourir*] because the real of the unconscious is much too excessive and incomprehensible to bear directly. Therefore, subjects undoubtedly wish for some understanding in language, and the comfort of the signifiers. Moreover, despite the crucial differences that Lacan draws between the Symbolic and the Real, as we saw with Scudéry's *Clelia*, the desolate subject faces antagonisms in the Symbolic and incoherence in the Real, and it is this subjective inconsistency that the non-dupes err [*les non-dupes errent*] forces the subject to accept, under the guise of *le Nom-du-Père.* Lacan says:

> In these two terms put into words, of the Names of the Father [*Noms du Père*] and the non-dupes err [*non-dupes qui errent*], it is the same knowledge. In both. It is the same knowledge in the sense that the unconscious is a knowledge from which the subject can decipher themselves. This is the definition of the subject, that I give here, of the subject as the unconscious constitutes it. (*SXXI* 5)

Lacan is associating the Names-of-the-Father [*les noms-du-père*] and the non-dupes err [*les non-dupes errent*] in the same logic; they both contain the same knowledge [*savoir*]. However, the knowledge gained is akin to the knowledge the subject can decipher from the unconscious, which is a somewhat facetious point, since the subject is unable to learn much from the unconscious because it is an incoherent jumble. However, crucially, Lacan insists that the subject is only established in the relationship with the unconscious. Lacan explains:

> We should know that this unconscious, compared to what would normally couple so well, for example, the self and the world… or the body to what surrounds it, […] compared to these, the unconscious presents itself as essentially different from these harmonies—let's say the word—disharmonic [*dysharmonique*]. (*SXXI* 263)

For Lacan, although it is structured like a language, the unconscious is qualified as being *disharmonious*, and because a significant part of the subject is drawn from the unconscious, the subject must be formed from within the chaos of the Real. Therefore, for Lacan in *SXXI*, *The Non-Dupes Err*, we must not forget the impact of the Real and the knowledge of the Real [*savoir du Réel*] on the subject; which means that there will always be a minimum level of incoherence which cannot be subsumed by the subject in the winnings of loser wins [*qui perd gagne*], even though the subject's unconscious does sometimes emit incoherent bits of the Real in speech, which is why Lacan says, 'Say any old rubbish. It will always touch the truth [*dites n'importe quoi, ça touchera toujours au vrai*] (*SXXI* 178). However, when subjects are faced with these incoherent bits of speech that reflect the fundamental deadlock of human subjectivity, all these subjects can do is hide from the *disharmonious* impasse of the decentred subject by declaring: 'but nevertheless!' Therefore, disavowal is loser wins par excellence. The strategy of loser wins is a lie we tell ourselves to stave off the sickness [*maladie*] inscribed in our human condition, it is a form of self-deception. However, what the subject receives from such a lie is not a moralism, as though one should not lie. What one gets instead is the underlying positive value of the lie. The lie which, as Shakespeare's Sonnet 138 captures, is the sincerest demonstration of love itself:

> *When my love swears that she is made of truth,*
> *I do believe her, though I know she lies,*
> *That she might think me some untutored youth,*
> *Unlearnèd in the world's false subtleties.*
> *Thus vainly thinking that she thinks me young,*
> *Although she knows my days are past the best,*
> *Simply I credit her false-speaking tongue.*
> *On both sides thus is simple truth suppressed:*
> *But wherefore says she not she is unjust?*
> *And wherefore say not I that I am old?*
> *O, love's best habit is in seeming trust,*
> *And age in love loves not to have years told.*
> *Therefore I lie with her and she with me,*
> *And in our faults by lies we flattered be.* (Shakespeare 2002: 657)

'When my love swears that she is made of truth / I do believe her, though I know she lies': she lies because the truth is only ever *mi-dit* [half-said]. We are all 'untutored youth.' We are 'unlearnèd in the world's false subtleties' since we are privy only to conscious knowledge, not the knowledge of the Real in the unconscious. Therefore, all our tongues are 'false-speaking,' and it is the 'seeming trust' that is the key; we seemingly trust symbolic appearances. It would seem that it was the Bard who first theorised the non-dupes err [*les non-dupes errent*]: 'On both sides thus is simple truth suppressed / But wherefore says she not she is unjust?' The underlying value of the lie is finally redeemed 'Therefore I lie with her and she with me / And in our faults by lies we flattered be.' We can also draw a link with the *non-rapport sexuel* since, by the end of the sonnet, there seems to be a resignation that, although there will never be a true sexual relationship 'in our faults by lies,' nevertheless 'I lie with her and she with me.'

For Lacan, the fundamental ambivalence between the Symbolic and Real is the crucial tragedy that subjects have to confront in process of subject formation. For Lacan it is not quite Sartre's *loser wins*; we do not just win—*we win, but our gain is a loss* which has been repudiated or disavowed, and, according to Lacan, we simply persist incoherently (*homo alienatus*). Therefore, either we admit that we do not know, or we lie earnestly. However, we must be dupes to these lies, dupes to, for example, the *Nom-du-Père*. Gaining something from being duped is the reason why the non-dupes err [*les non-dupes errent*] is closely related to *loser wins*. Moreover, it is for this reason that I have been suggesting that attempting to "escape the Symbolic" is a fruitless task, the Subject's inculcation into the Symbolic Order is a necessary subjugation in order to for the subject to speak, and to enable subject formation. Any attempt to move beyond, or somehow escape, symbolic coordinates is incoherent from within the Lacanian conception of subject development: you would be a *non-dupe* babbling in incoherence. As I will show in the final chapter, the late Lacan makes one exception, *le sinthome*.

Although Lacan tried to distance himself from Sartre in his later work, the Sartrean concept of Loser wins, as articulated by Howells, returns in a different form. It remains, for Lacan, a manner of 'recuperative transformation,' however, the crucial difference concerns the (fictional) master signifier which governs the Symbolic Order. We might be aware of its deceit, but we must choose to be dupes to win (loser wins); yet, this is simultaneously a necessary choice, and ultimately a false choice. The false choice of the master signifier's deceit *is* the little bit of the real, the essential antagonism, included in 'but nevertheless!', the non-dupes err, which is missing from Sartre's strategy of loser wins. Regardless of the differences between loser wins and the non-dupes err, one thing is certain: 'On both sides thus is simple truth suppressed.'

The Subject of *Jouissance*

> At the level of the unconscious, the subject lies. And this lying is his way of telling the truth of the matter. (Lacan)

In *Donc*, Jacques-Alain Miller sought to qualify the differences between the Subject of the Signifier and the Subject of *Jouissance* in Lacan's work. Miller states: 'besides, we can ask ourselves, what is it that gives us food for thought on psychoanalysis. It is perhaps a certain antinomy between the signifier and what we call *jouissance*' (Miller 1994: unpublished, *seminar X, 9th March session*). The preceding discussions concerning the Graph of Desire and the *Map of Tender* will be helpful in elucidating the antinomy between these two subjects, and of course, it is worth clarifying that we are investigating the transformation of the same subject at two different moments in the process of subject formation.

As we have seen, the lower part of the graph expresses the Subject of the Signifier—a subject who uncritically obeys symbolic demands (a good dupe!). This subject has been ensnared by the battery of signifiers [*batterie signifiante*] where all possible societal restrictions apply. However, as we have noted, this subject experiences themselves as free of those restrictions: 'speaking beings are happy' [*les êtres parlants sont heureux*], Lacan had said (*AÉ* 556). The Subject of the Signifier does not know she/he/they are a symbolic prisoner; where the societal and familial restrictions applied onto the subject are the very conditions of possibility for the subject's development (*É* 682). It is my understanding that at this moment in *Écrits,* Lacan is building a rudimentary case for *les non-dupes errent.* On the other hand, the Subject of *Jouissance* describes no possible subject, yet Lacan nevertheless speculates on the nature of the Subject of *Jouissance.* According to Lacan, we are only able to grapple with the former of the two subjects in the facticity of everyday life. Therefore, the Subject of the Signifier *is* the "Subject of Science," Lacan says: 'the subject upon which we operate in psychoanalysis *can only be* the subject of science' (*É* 729: my emphasis). If this argument sounds familiar, it is because we find Lacan repeating this intellectual strategy throughout his work: the divided subject: *Maître* [Master] and *m'être* [be myself]; Man [*homme*] and Woman [*femme*]; *l'être parlant* [speaking being] and *parlêtre*; *langage* [language] and *lalangue* [lalanguage]; conscious and unconscious; and Subject of the Signifier vs. Subject of *Jouissance,* and S2. vs. S1. (among others), where the former is a subject for scientific analysis and the latter is merely a speculative fiction, the temporary detour or the theism at the core of atheism. In this section, we seek to develop the differences between the Subject of the Signifier and the Subject of *Jouissance,* and this distinction advances our discussion of *jouissance,* which is intimately linked to *das Ding, l'objet petit a,* and sublimation. In exploring these concepts, we demonstrate the necessity of subject formation and the castration complex. In turn, this establishes the necessary impossibility of love that we discussed at the outset of this book.

das Ding

In *SXVII, The Other Side of Psychoanalysis,* Lacan refers to the 'field of jouissance' [*champ de la jouissance*] (*SXVII* 81/93), and, though we have touched upon *jouissance* at various points, we have deliberately sought to minimise any direct discussions of it. In chapter two we investigated the non-rapport sexuel, a concept of the *Real,* and picked it up again it in the present chapter concerning Madeleine de Scudéry's *Unknown lands.* I have at various stages discussed the renunciation of *jouissance* as part of symbolic castration. However, what is *jouissance* for Lacan? And from where does it emerge?

Lacan employs an old French word '*jouir,*' whose modern usage mostly refers to orgasm. Geneviève Morel argues that *jouissance* is an uncommon word in contemporary French speech, '"*Jouir*" is an old word [...] that we find more in Racine and Corneille than in today's language' (2000: 25). Lacan employs the word *jouir* because of its wide gamut of meaning: *jouir* is also highly ambiguous and context is usually required to ascertain what is being described. *Jouissance* is Lacan's word for what Freud had placed beyond the pleasure principle:

> Because it implies a destruction of the homeostasis required by the pleasure principle; neither too much nor too little. "Jouissance" designates then as

> well the excess of pleasure, the satisfaction too intense for the subject, as the suffering which can result from a prolonged internal excitation which disturbs the balance required by the pleasure principle. (Morel 2000: 25)

Lacan begins to develop *jouissance* in earnest from around *SVII, The Ethics of Psychoanalysis,* where he identifies, clarifies, and substantiates what he calls: *das Ding* [*the thing*]. *Das Ding* sets the foundations for what will become The Other jouissance [*l'Autre jouissance*] from *SXX, Encore,* onwards. In *SVII, L'Éthique de la psychanalyse,* Lacan argues that 'what one finds in *das Ding* is the true secret [*secret veritable*]' (46). Lacan's ambiguity and equivocation in these pages illustrate that he is building something about which he is, at this stage, still uncertain.

For Freud, *das Ding* describes the relationship between the subject and their very first human contact or partner. Usually, this designates the mother or the maternal figure in the child's life. Lacan uses Freud's the *Nebenmensch* to highlight this primary maternal relation in his conceptualisation of *das Ding*. 'The *Nebenmensch* is the person who adequately hears the child's call (the mother, of course, but beyond her, any person exercising this function)' (Richard 2011: 1539). The mother is, usually, the first person who will be able to satisfy the infant's earliest needs and demands, eliciting in the infant either pleasure or displeasure. The infant will recognise in the mother her capacity to satisfy their needs, and so the child will conceptually divide the *Nebenmensch* into, on the one hand, the "satisfier" of their needs, and, on the other hand, the mother as the unassimilable *Ding* itself—that part of the *Nebenmensch* which is not for the child (Morel 2000: 26). Lacan's focus here is on the unassimilable thing from the *Nebenmensch.* Lacan says:

> The *Ding* is the element that is initially isolated by the subject in his experience of the *Nebenmensch* as being by its very nature alien, *Fremde.* The complex of the object is in two parts; there is a division, a difference in the approach to judgment. (*SVII* 64–65)

Lacan stresses that *das Ding* designates an aspect of the *Nebenmensch* that is foreign to the subject, and potentially even hostile to the subject. 'The whole progress of the subject is then oriented around the *Ding* as *Fremde,* strange and even hostile on occasion' (*SVII* 65). Lacan gives *das Ding* a central role in the entire structuring of the subject's path of desire:

> In any case as the first exterior, it is what the whole path of the subject is oriented around. It is undoubtedly a path of control, of reference, in relation to what?—to the world of its desires. It proves that something, after all, is there, which, to a certain degree, can be useful. Useful for what?—for nothing other than to serve as points of reference in relation to the world of wishes and expectations; it is turned toward that which helps on certain occasions to reach *das Ding*. That object will be there when in the end all conditions have been fulfilled—in the end—of course, it is clear what is found cannot be found again. It is of its nature that the object is lost as such. It will never be found again. Something is there waiting for better, or waiting for worse, but waiting [*quelque chose est là en attendant mieux, ou en attendant pire, mais en attendant*]. (*SVII* 52, translation modified)

In the context of satisfying the demands that lead to desire, and so the creation of *jouissance*, Lacan is implying that *das Ding* mediates and orients the subject, 'it is then in relation to the original *das Ding* that the first orientation, the first choice, the first seat of subjective orientation takes place' (*SVII* 54). However, *das Ding* is both elusive and always out of reach, and, therefore, the lack returns once again. *Das Ding* is the lost object that the subject cannot locate, forcing the subject to learn about patience. The subject, having split the *Nebenmensch,* is unable to acquire the missing aspect of *das Ding*; the object which serves no other function than to regulate their demands and needs. *Das Ding* is the absolute Other of the subject which the subject spends time trying to recover, 'the absolute Other of the subject that one is supposed to find again' (*SVII* 52). However, if the subject happens to find this *Ding*, they necessarily recover it in regret, and this reveals the coordinates of a former pleasure (*SVII* 52).

The structure of *jouissance* is closely related to the absence of *das Ding* and *jouissance* signals the subject's wish to recapture *the Thing*. However, Lacan argues that this desire to recover *das Ding* yields an excess of pleasure, which is why *jouissance* is situated beyond the pleasure principle because it is linked to this excess. 'Since the pleasure principle is presented to us as possessing a mode of operation which is precisely to avoid excess, the "too much" of pleasure' (*SVII* 54, translation modified). Moreover, as the upper level of the graph of desire demonstrates, *jouissance,* as well as the corollary 'leftover' demand arising from the desire elicited by *Che vuoi*, is situated beyond the remit of the signifier, leading Lacan to state:

> *Das Ding* is that which I will call the out-signified [*hors-signifié*]. It is as a function of this out-signified [*hors-signifié*], and of a pathetic relationship [*rapport pathétique*] to it that the subject maintains its distance and constitutes itself in a mode of relation characterized by primary affect, prior to any repression. *(SVII 54)*

The Thing is located outside signification, and its relationship with the subject is one of pathetic repression. Which is to say that *the Thing* necessarily belongs to the domain of *jouissance,* and apprehendable by the subject only as a result of the distance provided by the fantasy screen. Therefore, *das Ding* only appears to the subject in order to shut down their desire:

> The Thing only presents itself to the extent that it becomes word [*qu'elle fait mot*] [...] In Freud's text the way in which the stranger, the hostile figure, appears in the first experience of reality for the human subject is the cry [*c'est le cri*]. I suggest we do not need this cry. [...] "Mot" [word] is essentially "no reply." "Mot," La Fontaine says somewhere, is what remains silent; it is precisely that in response to which no word is spoken [*c'est justement ce à quoi aucun mot n'est prononcé*]. (*SVII* 55, translation modified)

The Thing reveals itself to the subject as a potentially promising route in their search for their true desire. However, the path through *das Ding* is a path that shuts down any discussions with the subject. The subject must unilaterally accept *the Thing* in order to continue on this path on the journey to subject formation, which is why, Lacan says, *the Thing* is accompanied by a transmuted 'cry,' but the cry is not something the subject needed or ever desired. *The Thing*'s cry is excessive, and the subject automatically wants to reject the excessive burden of *das Ding* howling at them. In *SVII*, Lacan is building a view of *jouissance* that is necessarily burdensome, he associates the wailing of the infant with the unattainable aspect of the *Nebenmensch* (the mother). The infant's cry is transubstantiated into its opposite; as the infant becomes a subject and searches for her/his/their desire, *das Ding* becomes the one who wails uncontrollably. It is for this reason that all subjects are forced to repudiate the unassimilable *Thing*. In more concrete terms, this is one aspect of symbolic castration; the subject rejects *das Ding*, and, in so doing, is simultaneously renouncing *jouissance*.

Instead of Being

Lacan's discussion in *SVII, The Ethics of Psychoanalysis*, of courtly love has less to do with the development of love within the scheme of R.S.I (Real, Symbolic, Imaginary), and more to do with elaborating the dual concepts of *das Ding* and sublimation which are the main objects of study in *SVII* (Allouch 2009: 122). Lacan insists on the elaborate rules of engagement in courtly love because, in this discussion, he is placing a greater emphasis on the "rules" rather than on the love that is generated, 'courtly love is mainly considered as a paradigmatic case of sublimation' (Allouch 2009: 122). Sublimation is the reinterpretation of sexual energies into non-sexual fields, for example in art. Lacan says, 'the sublimation [...] provides the *Trieb* with a satisfaction different from its aim' (*SVII* 111). Lacan interprets the complex rules of courtly love as a sublimation of the object:

> What Freud would call *Überschätzung* or overevaluation of the object—and that I will henceforth call object sublimation—under conditions in which the object of a loving passion takes on a certain significance (and, as you will see, it is in this direction that I intend to introduce the dialectic through which I propose to teach you how to identify what sublimation really is), under certain conditions of sublimation of the feminine object or, in other words, the exaltation we call love—a form of exaltation that is historically specific. (*SVII* 109)

Beyond the pleasure principle, in the field of jouissance, the subject is confronted with an excess of pleasure, and this provides the subject with the choice of two possible paths; either the subject integrates or rejects these drives. As Lacan puts it:

> I have outlined then two cases [...] two forms of transgression beyond the limits normally assigned to the pleasure principle in opposition to the reality principle given as a criterion, namely, excessive object sublimation and what is commonly known as perversion. (*SVII* 109)

Both sublimation and perversion belong to the realm of desire, 'sublimation and perversion are both a certain relationship of desire' (*SVII* 109). However, Lacan also argues that we need to account for a third dimension: the relationship the subject has with *das Ding*. *Das Ding* is important in the Lacanian schema because it describes, as we saw, a desire that is sacrificed in the process of symbolic castration:

> Well now, the step taken by Freud at the level of the pleasure principle is to show us that there is no Sovereign Good—that the Sovereign Good, which is *das Ding* which is the mother, is also the object of incest, is a forbidden good, and that there is no other good. Such is the foundation of the moral law as turned on its head by Freud. (*SVII* 70)

Lacan characterises *das Ding* as the 'object impossible to find again' [*objet irretrouvable*] (SVII 85), and, yet, we continually find it in reality. *Das Ding* destroys desire and is the figurative force behind *jouissance*. Additionally, according to Lacan, *das Ding* also founds the moral law:

> For there is another register of morality that takes its direction from that which is to be found on the level of *das Ding*; it is the register that makes the subject hesitate when he is on the point of bearing false witness against *das Ding*, that is to say, the place of desire, whether it be perverse or sublimated. (*SVII* 109–10)

Signalling that there is an aspect of *das Ding* which could be more important than its stated relation to subject development, Lacan is making a rudimentary case for the unassimilable *das Ding* as Other jouissance [*l'Autre jouissance*], which as we saw, he will develop more substantially in *Encore*. As we discussed in the previous chapter, this Other jouissance *is* the second qualification of the big Other as feminine *jouissance*, and Lacan is planting clues to this effect as early as *SVII*. The field of *the Thing* is the field beyond, 'this field onto which is projected something beyond, something at the point of origin of the signifying chain, this place in which doubt is cast on all that is the place of being, on the chosen place in which sublimation is produced' (*SVII* 214, translation modified). Confirming our reading, Lacan situates 'the woman' [*La femme*] on this transcendental field, at the origin of the signifying chain:

> It is also the place of the work that man, singularly, begins to court; that is why the first example I gave you was taken from courtly love. You have to admit that to place in this beyond a creature such as woman is a truly incredible idea. (*SVII* 214)

And Lacan says immediately after: 'Rest assured that I am in no way passing a derogatory judgment on these beings' (*SVII* 214). Lacan's point, his 'incredible idea' is to situate the psychoanalytic concept of woman 'in the place of being,' ontologically speaking, and this is 'nothing to do with her as a woman,' Lacan says, 'but as an object of desire' (*SVII* 214).

Lacan places *jouissance* beyond the function of desire, as it is illustrated in the graph of desire. However, desire is a necessary precursor to *jouissance*. *Jouissance* is characterised as obscure and opaque: 'the problem involved is that of *jouissance*, because *jouissance* presents itself as buried at the center of a field and has the characteristics of inaccessibility, obscurity and opacity; moreover, the field is surrounded by a barrier which makes access to it difficult for the subject to the point of inaccessibility maybe (*SVII* 209, translation modified). Lacan explains that the analytic value of *jouissance* is that it is a satisfaction of the drives and not just the satisfaction of leftover needs: '*jouissance* appears not purely and simply as the satisfaction of a need but as the satisfaction of a drive' (*SVII* 209). *Jouissance* is the subject's attempt to satisfy the drives, and that is why any analysis of *jouissance* is so difficult and inaccessible, because understanding the drives themselves, and what motivates them, is a singularly difficult task:

> The drive as such is something extremely complex [...] it refers back to something memorable because it was re-memorised. Re-memorising, "historicizing," is coextensive with the functioning of the drive in what we call the human psyche. It is there, too, that destruction is recorded, that it enters the register of experience [*c'est aussi là que s'enregistre, qu'entre dans le registre de l'expérience, la destruction*]. (*SVII* 209, translation modified)

Placing *La femme* at the point of *jouissance*, as beyond desire, is not designed to transform the woman into a scientific object of study but instead, it is attempting to do quite the opposite: how can we understand Being itself, which for Lacan *is* The woman. The central thesis to be gleaned from Lacan's focus on courtly love is not how it characterises love but how it captures desire. Desire is directly linked to *La femme* '*au lieu de l'être*,' which should be understood as 'in the place of being' as well as 'instead of being' because *La femme* is conceptualised by Lacan as an 'being as signifier' [*être de signifiant*] (*SVII* 254). We might already be able to see how *La femme*, as one of the names of God, is the reunification of *in itself* and *for itself*, 'au lieu de l'être,' [the place of being/ instead of being] as we detail in our final chapter.

Underneath Desire: Jouissance and Anxiety

Miller argued that anxiety underpins desire in the Lacanian psychoanalytic schema, 'what is there underneath desire? The answer is given here, repeated, hammered out, and I have left a summary diagram, even duplicated: underneath desire, there is *jouissance* and there is anxiety' (Miller 2005: 68). To better understand *jouissance*, we will first treat the concept of anxiety. Lacan's view of anxiety is heavily indebted to Sartre. However, Lacan claims that while Sartre focused on contrasting anxiety to both nothingness and liberty, he, instead, postulates a third relation to anxiety that Sartre had allegedly missed, namely, the relationship between anxiety and the desire of the Other (*SX* 5). Recalling the *Che vuoi* moment in the graph of desire, Lacan says:

> It justifies my having placed at the centre of the signifiers on the board the question […] *Che vuoi?*, *Que veux-tu?*, What do you want? Push the functioning, the insertion of the key, a little further and you have, *Que me veut-Il?* [what does he want from me?] with the ambiguity that the French permits with respect to the me between the direct or indirect object. It's not simply, *What does the Other want with me?* but also a suspended questioning that directly concerns the ego, not *How does He want me?* but, *What does He want concerning this place of the ego?* (*SX* 6)

As we saw briefly earlier, anxiety emerges for the subject as a result of the subject's exposure to *l'objet petit a*. Understanding anxiety in this way marks a pronounced shift in Lacan's thinking from *SX*, *Anxiety*, onwards. Prior to 1962, Lacan had believed that a subject's desire was aimed at a specific person or thing, making it object-orientated. However, desire can also aim at nothing, a lack of something, where desire becomes object-caused. In many ways, this move also marks a shift from the earlier to later Lacan, and it inaugurates Lacan's increasing concern with the Real.

For Lacan, anxiety unearths the insurmountable antagonisms which constitute the Real:

> Only the notion of the real, in the opaque function which is the function I set off from in order to contrast it with the function of the signifier, enables us to orient ourselves. We can already say that this *etwas*, faced with which anxiety operates as a signal, belongs to the realm of the real's irreducibility. It is in this sense that I dared to formulate for you that anxiety, of all signals, is the one that does not deceive. (*SX* 160)

Therefore, *SX* is an attempt to both outline the structure of anxiety and qualify a discussion about *jouissance* and the Real. Lacan says,

> On our path to anxiety, we find ourselves having to specify the status of what I designated at the outset with the letter *a* […]. The most striking manifestation of this object *a*, the signal that it is intervening, is anxiety. (*SX* 86)

For Lacan, the focus on anxiety is necessary because anxiety is not restricted to the signifiers, but, rather, as is evidenced in the graph of desire, anxiety is situated in the realm beyond the signifiers at the level of unregulated desire, and so 'the field of *jouissance*.' The subject's anxiety emerges from *objet petit a*, as we said, and this takes place, Lacan argues, after the subject confronts the question *Che vuoi?*. And, for Lacan, 'the problem is one of the signifier's entry in the Real and of seeing how the subject is born from this' [*de cela naît le sujet*] (*SX* 88). Lacan seeks to understand how the signifier can enter the Real and how this can create and split the subject; Lacan stresses that this process is one of complete foreignness, 'there's an *initium*, an aura, a dawning sense of uncanniness which leaves the door open to anxiety' (*SX* 88). Anxiety is provoked by a strange encounter with object *a,* it is the brush with *l'objet petit a* that generate feelings of anxiousness in the subject, and that is why Lacan is careful to insist that anxiety exists in a relationship with an object, '*it is not without an object*' (*SX* 89). However, the connection with the object is not a *rapport* 'this is the exact formula in which anxiety's relation to an object must be suspended' (*SX* 89). The loss of, or inability to fully grasp, the object small *a* causes the subject to feel anxious. Giving up the object *a* is synonymous with the renunciation of *jouissance* which results in symbolic castration, as we have seen. Therefore, subjects feel anxious when they realise that they will need to be symbolically castrated. Object *a* is also related to *jouissance* in this sense, since, in order to enter the world of signification, the subject needs to sacrifice the desire for object *a*. Earlier, we stated that the formula for fantasy was *$◇a,* which we can now better understand as: the barred subject's (*$*) desire for (◇) object *a* (*a*), which is a fantasy. Object *a* is also not qualified as intentional, it is not something which we desire intentionally, 'the object *a* [...] is not to be situated in [...] the intentionality of desire [...] is to be conceived of as the cause of desire' (*SX* 101).

Lacan's rhetorical strategy is 'what's underneath?' [*qu'y a-t-il en deçà*'], and this is evident from the way he develops the various elements of his theory, and how they converge in "Kant with Sade". In "Kant with Sade," Lacan shows how *das Ding* relates to the Real, as an early version of *jouissance*, or, I argue, *in itself for itself.* For Lacan, the Real in the Symbolic is not an *in itself,* the bits of the Real in the Symbolic describe the antagonisms found at the heart of the Symbolic Order. The Real in the Symbolic is the name Lacan gives for the disintegration of the Symbolic Order, where the metonymic structures begin to wear and tear. Analogously, in "Kant with Sade" Lacan uses the Marquis de Sade's writings to demonstrate the vulnerabilities of Kant's ethical system. Lacan investigates what might underpin Kant's ethical system. Our analysis of Lacan's argument illustrates how the various strands of Lacan's thought intersect, and enables us to ask: 'what is underneath love?'

Kant with Sade

Lacan's "Kant with Sade" is a highly original contribution to the history of philosophy, and he begins this chapter in *Écrits* by claiming that although the standard received view often sees Sade as a precursor to Freud: 'this is a stupidity repeated in the humanities' (*É* 645, translation modified). Instead, Lacan claims that it is, in fact, Kant and Sade who are much closer intellectual bedfellows. The move to disassociate Sade and Freud, and instead focus on the connection of Kant with Sade might seem paradoxical at first glance, on account of the rigid traditionalism of Kant's ethical philosophy and the Marquis de Sade's *libertinage*. Nevertheless, Lacan states: 'Sade represents here the first step of a subversion of which Kant, as piquant as this may seem in light of the coldness of the man himself, represents the turning point' (*É* 645). Moreover, Lacan, explicitly states that Sade's *La Philosophie dans le boudoir* strengthens the truth of Kant's *Critique*, 'I claim that [*La Philosophie dans le boudoir*] yields the truth of the *Critique*' (*É* 646). Lacan jokes that he is adding the grain of salt that Kant's ethical system is missing (*É* 648).

Kant's *Critique of Practical Reason,* and the categorical imperatives more specifically, describe an ethical position founded on a series of prohibitive laws. Lacan qualifies these as 'a voice in conscience,' and it ought to continually regulate the subject's actions. For Kant, the prohibitive law should offer universal maxims, 'it is necessary and sufficient that, being put to the test of such reason, the maxim may be considered universal as far as logic is concerned' (*É* 647). For Lacan, the prohibition, or 'Ethical Law,' is equal to desire, in the sense that the law is always a repressed desire. 'La loi et le désir refoulé sont une seule et même chose' (*É* 647). Lacan repeats this claim in *SX*, 'desire and law are the same thing in the sense that their object is common to both of them' (*SX* 106), and Lacan relates this to the Oedipus complex more generally by qualifying that:

> The Oedipus myth means nothing but the following—at the origin, desire, as the father's desire, and the law are one and the same thing. The relationship between the law and desire is so tight that only the function of the law traces out the path of desire. (*SX* 106)

Desire's relationship to the law is fundamental. Lacan says that the mother is not, in-and-of-herself, the most desirable: 'after all, in and of herself the mother is not the most desirable object there is' rather what makes her desirable, Lacan claims, is the prohibition itself, 'to spell it right out, one desires with a commandment' (*SX* 106). Subjects incline towards desires that are prohibited. Therefore, prohibitions mediate the desires subjects have for one another. Lacan summarises his argument in *SVII* in relation to Kantian ethics, 'that is the culminating point for both Kant and Sade with relation to the *Thing*; it is there that morality becomes, on the one hand, a pure and simple application of the universal maxim and, on the other, a pure and simple object' (*SVII* 70). For Lacan, *das Ding* is closely related to the moral law: 'because the reason is that *das Ding* is at the center only in the sense that it is excluded' (*SVII* 71). As we said, *das Ding* is the absence around which the subject is constituted, and this is also the case with the moral law, forerunning the concept of Other jouissance [*l'Autre jouissance*] which is precisely what the subject renounces in symbolic castration:

> This *das Ding*, this prehistoric Other that it is impossible to forget of which Freud affirms to us the necessity of the first position, in the form of something *entfremdet*, something strange to me, although it is at the heart of this me [*au coeur de ce moi*]. (*SVII* 87, translation modified)

Lacan argues that in the law there is always an unconscious relation to *das Ding*:

> The desire for the mother cannot be satisfied because it is the end, the terminal point, the abolition of the whole world of demand, which is the one

> that at its deepest level structures man's unconscious. It is to the extent that the function of the pleasure principle is to make man always search for what he has to find again, but which he never will attain, that one reaches the essence, namely, that sphere or relationship which is known as the law of the prohibition of incest. (*SVII* 68)

Therefore, *das Ding* refers to something which is outside permitted desire, and the paradigmatic example is the incest prohibition.

It is worth noting that Lacan is not laying down a challenge, suggesting that we ought to pursue all incestuous desires, whatever the cost. Instead, the point is quite the opposite, Lacan is merely recounting a system structure that explains the obstacles and conditions to desire. For Lacan, the subject is continually searching for what they think they want or are looking for, but they will never find it, and that desire is symbolically castrated, and this renunciation of incest is articulated in terms of *das Ding*. Lacan says that the essential desire is *the desire of the mother*, 'the maternal thing, of the mother, insofar as she occupies the place of that *thing*, of *das Ding*' (*SVII* 106). This desire-prohibition nexus is necessary (*SVII* 67) because it is the prohibition which structures desire:

> Is the Law the Thing? Certainly not. Yet I can only know of the Thing by means of the Law. In effect, I would not have had the idea to covet it if the Law hadn't said: "Thou shalt not covet it." But the Thing finds a way by producing in me all kinds of covetousness thanks to the commandment, for without the Law the Thing is dead. But even without the Law, I was once alive. But when the commandment appeared, the Thing flared up, returned once again, I met my death. And for me, the commandment that was supposed to lead to life turned out to lead to death, for the Thing found a way and thanks to the commandment seduced me; through it I came to desire death. (*SVII* 83)

Relating this discussion back to Kant's categorical imperatives, Lacan suggests that the commandment 'Thou shalt not covet' is what makes a subject covet, 'in effect, I would not have had the idea to covet it if the Law hadn't said: "Thou shalt not covet it."' Therefore, without the law, *das Ding* is dead for Lacan; they are connected; they go hand in glove.

Lacan is at pains to relate the concept of *das Ding* to a concept of the 'Good,' or employing Kant's language from the *Critique of Practical Reason*, the '*Wohl* that I propose in order to designate the good in question' (*SVII* 72). Indeed, for Lacan, *das Ding* ought not necessarily be considered a negative aspect of the unconscious, or a negative aspect of *jouissance*, 'although it must be said that at this level das Ding is not distinguished as bad' (*SVII* 73). However, the subject cannot cope with the extreme Good that *das Ding* could bring, which is why the subject pushes *das Ding* into the negative: 'he cannot stand the extreme good that *das Ding* may bring him, which is all the more reason why he cannot locate himself in relation to the bad' (ibid). The subject protects themselves from *das Ding* by creating a series of symptoms, Lacan calls these 'symptoms of defence' or we could say simply: defence mechanisms. This is an "organic" defence: 'here the ego defends itself by hurting itself as the crab gives up its leg' [*le moi se défend en se mutilant comme le crabe lâche sa patte*] (*SVII 73/*89, translation modified). However, there is another form of defence that is not the self-mutilation emulating the crab, which, for Lacan, is the lie: 'At the level of the unconscious, the subject lies. And this lying is his way of telling the truth of the matter' [*au niveau de l'inconscient, le sujet ment. Et ce mensonge est sa façon de dire là-dessus la vérité*] (*SVII* 73/90). So, it is at this point that the relationship between subject and *das Ding* is cast as either negative or pathologically mediated by the symptom (SVII 73). Lacan introduces *das Ding* and its relation to the moral law in order to develop his hypothesis that:

> My thesis is that the moral law is articulated with relation to the real as such, to the real insofar as it can be the guarantee of the Thing. That is why I invite you to take an interest in what I have called the high point of the crisis in ethics. (*SVII* 76)

The moral law is articulated in relation to the Real, Lacan states, to guarantee *das Ding,* and this is, for him, the crisis of ethics. Kantian ethics establishes a problematic ethic, which, instead of articulating a moral law that aims at the Real, offers morality without an object (*É* 647). Lacan caricatures the Kantian imperatives by employing 'the help of the language of electronics and automation: "Never act except in such a way that your action may be programmed"' (*SVII* 77). According to Lacan, Kant tried to implement rules of nature from the supposed universalism of the categorical imperatives, which is why Kantian ethics is unable to withstand criticism. Lacan says:

> But note that he affirms the laws of *nature*, not of *society*. It is only too clear that not only do societies live very well by reference to laws that are far from promoting their universal application, but even more remarkably, as I suggested last time, these societies prosper as a result of the transgression of these maxims. (*SVII* 77–8)

Paradoxically, transgressions of the law enable societies to prosper, whereas for Kant, there is no need for there to be a positive feeling or reason to act ethically, subjects must do their duty for the Good of all of mankind. If subjects pursue the Good by seeking pleasure they are acting pathologically, Lacan says: 'No *Wohl*, whether it be our own or that of our neighbour, must enter into the finality of moral action' (*SVII* 77). Lacan associates *Wohl* (the pathological, pleasure seeking, good), with *das Ding*, while he associates the Good (the dutiful, ethical Good) with the law. Lacan effectively splits Kantian ethics in two, on the one hand, the pleasure seeking *Wohl*, and the duty of obeying the rule of law on the other.

> We must obviously acknowledge this characteristic in the maxim for the simple reason that its sole proclamation (its *kerygma*) has the virtue of instating both the radical rejection of the pathological (that is, of every preoccupation with goods, passion, or even compassion—in other words, the rejection by which Kant cleared the field of moral law) and the form of this law, which is also its only substance, insofar as the will becomes bound to the law only by eliminating from its practice every reason that is not based on the maxim itself. (*É* 649)

Having established the dual nature of Kantian ethics and argued that Kant maintains his ethical system on one side of this dual system, Lacan says:

> The bipolarity upon which the moral law is founded is nothing but the split [*refente*] in the subject brought about by any and every intervention of

> the signifier: the split between the enunciating subject [*sujet de l'enonciation*] and the subject of the statement [*sujet de l'énoncé*]. (ibid)

In the Kantian categorical imperative, the law operates within the subject; the superego ethical imperative is installed inside the subject. According to Lacan, Kantian ethics is pursued symbolically. Bruce Fink argues that 'Kant is credited [by Lacan] with emphasising strictly symbolic relations: a relationship between the subject and the Other as Law' (Fink 2014: 114). Kant is attempting to universalise the symbolic function of his categorical imperative, and this is, Lacan says, congruous with the Sadian law. Sade's plea for *libertinage* is related to Kant's ethical plea. We are compelled by the big Other to act per the categorical imperatives and also by our own internal 'voice of conscience' (ibid).

> Of course, these two imperatives—between which moral life can be stretched, even if it snaps our very life—are imposed on us, according to the Sadian paradox, as if upon the Other, and not upon ourselves. (*É* 649)

This distinction, or split, is the difference between the subject as mediated by the signifier, the subject of the statement [*le sujet de l'énoncé*], and, the subject as negotiated outside language and signification, and so beyond meaning, the enunciating subject [*le sujet de l'énonciation*]. According to Lacan, the two subjects that are compelled by the ethical demand are considered separately by Sade but not by Kant. Kant collapses the two subjects into one, which is why, Lacan argues, Sade is Kant's necessary counterpart. The moral law, in emanating from the mouth of the Other, is more honest than Kant's singular appeal to the subject's internal voice. 'In coming out of the Other's mouth, Sade's maxim is more honest than Kant's appeal to the voice within, since it unmasks the split in the subject that is usually covered up' [*puisqu'elle démasque la refente, escamotée à l'ordinaire, du sujet*] (*É* 650). The moral law, as it is directed by the big Other, unmasks the split in the subject that ordinarily remains hidden in Kant's ethical paradigm. Therefore, Kant's system effectively ignores the object of ethics, the being-in-the-world, or *Dasein,* of the tormenting agent, 'is this not the very object we find in Sadian experience, which is no longer inaccessible and is instead revealed as the being-in-the-world, the *Dasein* of the tormenting agent' (651). This is an unnecessarily complicated (pseudo-Heideggerian) way of stating that the sadist ('the agent of torment') is an object-instrument of the Other's *jouissance*; a mere vector for the unchecked power of the big Other's unregulated *jouissance*. As Lacan puts it:

> What does the sadist seek out in the Other? It is very clear that, for him, the Other exists, and just because he takes him for an object, this doesn't mean we should say that we have some kind of immature or even pregenital relation here. The Other is absolutely essential and this is precisely what I wanted to spell out when I gave my Seminar on ethics by bringing Sade and Kant together and showing you that Sade's essential act of putting the Other to the question goes so far as to simulate, and this is not by chance, the exigencies of moral law, which are there to show us that the reference to the Other as such is part and parcel of his aim. (*SX* 164)

One of the central arguments of "Kant with Sade" is to affirm the implacable strength of the big Other in the structuring of the moral law. At Lacan's hand, Sade amounts to nothing more than the big Other's spokesperson. 'This is what becomes of the executioner in sadism when, in the most extreme case, his presence is reduced to being no more than the instrument' (*É* 652). What is the sadist's reward? Why does the sadist partake in these perversions, according to Lacan? Lacan postulates a series of reactions (symptoms) to symbolic structures.

One goal of psychoanalysis is to identify symbolic structures and determine how subjects react to these structures, in order to offer a partial remedy or 'cure.' Perversion expressed sadistically is one way that the subject learns to relate and engage with desire and pleasure. Sadism aims to embody the big Other, but as we have already seen the result is that the sadist becomes merely an instrument of the big Other. 'But the fact that the executioner's jouissance becomes fixated there does not spare his jouissance the humility of an act in which he cannot help but become a being of flesh and, to the very marrow, a slave to pleasure' (*É* 652). A mere slave to pleasure, the sadist operates an imagined power exercised on the split subject and obfuscates its own radical insecurity, 'This duplication neither reflects nor reciprocates (why wouldn't it "mutualize"?) the duplication that took place in the Other owing to the subject's two alterities' (ibid). The insight Lacan offers is that the sadist imagines themselves to be the embodiment of *objet petit a,* the sadist is an auto-object cause of desire. However, the sadist's view of themselves is not a structurally viable route to subject formation within the Lacanian schema, since the sadist is imagining themselves to be the cause of fantasy, which is a mere self-deception. Lacan denotes sadian desire (*a*◇*$*), which is the reversal of the inscription for fantasy (*$*◇*a*). Put simply, (*a*◇*$*) represents: 'the sadist as object *a* is the cause of the subject as split, is the cause of the split in the subject' (Fink 2014: 122). The crucial point about the sadist is that they do not only seek to inflict physical pain for the sake of making their partner suffer; the sadist's primary purpose is to elicit anxiety in their victim:

> The sadist's desire, with everything it entails by way of enigma, can only be formulated on the basis of the split, the dissociation, that he aims to introduce in the subject, the other party, by imposing upon him, up to a certain limit, what he is unable to tolerate up to the precise limit at which a division appears in this subject, a gap, between his existence as a subject and what he is undergoing, what he may be suffering from, in his body. [...] It is not so much the other party's suffering that is being sought in the sadistic intention as his anxiety [...] The anxiety of the other party, his essential existence as a subject in relation to this anxiety, is precisely the string that sadistic desire means to pluck [*s'entend à faire vibrer*]. (*SX* 104/123)

Lacan claims that Kant's categorical imperatives appeal to the same anguish, the same anxiety, which is elicited by the sadist. Effectively, Lacan has just labelled Kant a sadist, the Kantian imperatives are merely the instrument of the big Other, transforming them into vacuous ethical maxims. Lacan will later say in *SXX*, *Encore*, 'That is what I felt I needed to lay out in an article, "Kant with Sade"—morality admits that it is Sade' (*SXX* 87).

By flipping the schema below, Lacan is able to use the same schema to represent how, on the one hand, the sadist views themselves, and how, on the other, Lacan views the sadist. In the schema (Fig. 4.9), Lacan represents the sadist's (V) will [*volonté*]—to enjoy or engage in sadistic acts,

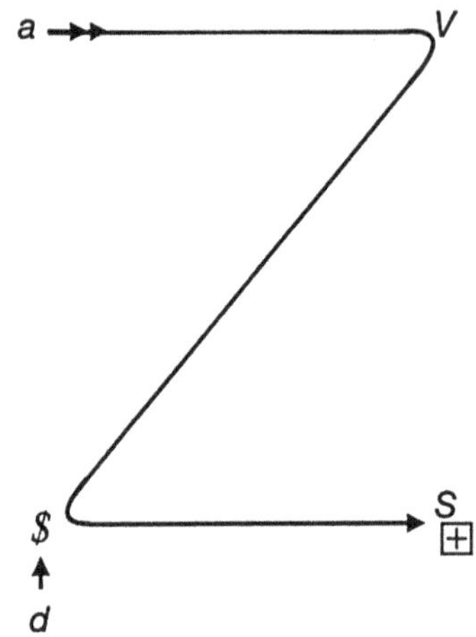

Fig. 4.9 Sadist's view

and (S) describes the sadist's victim. This first schema should be read from the top down, (V) to (S). The graph expresses the sadist's will to enjoy the victim's body unrestrictedly, which is the sadist's imaginary belief they hold of themselves. The victim, (S), that the sadist abuses is considered by the sadist to be a full 'S,' not characterised as barred or lacking subject ($) because the sadist wrongly believes in the fullness of being of his/her/their victim. This self-represented view is the Sadian fantasy since, in reality, Lacan states that the sadist's desire is actually: (*a*◇*$*), which is to say that the sadist is the mere instrument of the object small *a*. The sadist is her/himself a barred subject ($) just like everyone else, despite her/his impotent sadistic acts, and, therefore, the sadist is alienated. Lacan says, 'it is the subject reconstituted through alienation at the cost of being nothing but the instrument of jouissance' (*É* 654). To show this, Lacan flips the schema, and, in so doing, demonstrates why Kant must be understood *with* Sade. In this second schema, the sadist is more accurately, according to Lacan, represented as the barred subject ($) (Fig. 4.10). This time, the sadist ($) is a victim of the will (V) of the big Other. Lacan explains by appealing to the powerful will of Sade's mOther in law, *la Présidente de Montreuil* who successfully committed Sade to

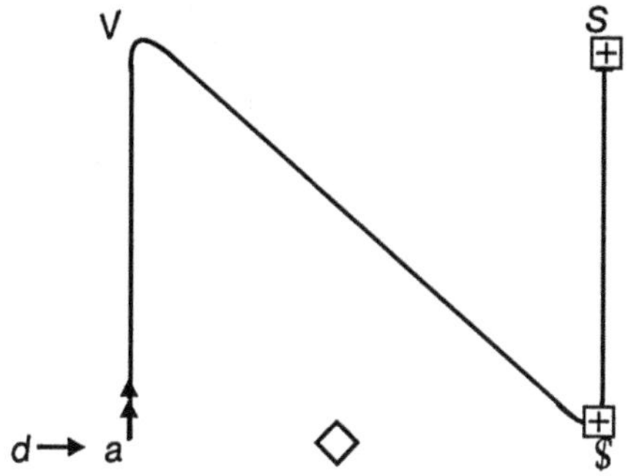

Fig. 4.10 Sadist as Barred Subject $

prison numerous times and was the one who exercised real power over Sade.

> V, the will to jouissance, leaves no further doubt as to its nature, because it appears in the moral force implacably exercised by the President of Montreuil [Sade's mother-in-law] on the subject; it can be seen that the subject's division does not have to be pinned together [*réunie*] in a single body. (*É* 657)

Therefore, the real sadistic *Volonté* [Will] always belongs to the big Other for the subject.

In a similar way, as we said earlier, "Kant with Sade" is controversial because Lacan is suggesting that Kant's categorical imperatives work in a sadistic way, 'and this is why I didn't hesitate in one of my previous Seminars to relate its structure to what is specially homologous in what Kant spelt out as the condition for practicing a pure practical reason, a moral will properly speaking, where he locates the sole point at which a relation with a pure moral good can emerge' (*SX* 104). For Lacan, following Freud, anxiety is a signal, a cue, alerting the subject to a specific and oncoming danger, 'the danger in question is bound to the characteristic of cession specific to the constitutive moment of the object *a*' (*SX* 324). Anxiety is related to the 'cessation of the object', the cessation of the objet petit a, and the cessation of objet petit a is the final aim of the Kantian moral imperatives. However, this does not happen, it cannot happen, according to Lacan, it must *persist*. Instead, *jouissance* empties the ethical act of all content, and that is *jouissance*'s aim. Paradoxically, Kant eliminates the pathological aspect of acting morally, which is to say, for Lacan, the enjoyable aspect of acting ethically, or the 'Good' as we said earlier. So that once the act of morality is restricted to its purely formal aspect, it becomes a purely sadistic endeavour. The sadistic aspect of the purely formal ethical act demonstrates that far from banishing *jouissance* (or, *objet petit a*) what the subject finds *under* the desire for a formal Law (Kantian imperatives) is surplus *jouissance*. Lacan argues that the supposed purity of the ethical act, in its formal structure, actually *produces* more of what it is trying to restrict, which is *jouissance*. This surplus enjoyment [*plus-de-jouir*] is object *a*.[22] The bubbling of *jouissance* always threatens to overspill and resurface, which is why the only real sadist is the Symbolic Law itself—personified by *la Présidente de Montreuil*, the mOther. In the next chapter, I will show how Lacan's relating of *das Ding* with *object petit a* as the basis of the big Other's total sadistic power, and the concomitant conclusion of surplus *jouissance*, informs his concept of surplus enjoyment [*plus-de-jouir*], which is central to his distinction between phallic *jouissance* and feminine *jouissance*. This distinction is crucial to elucidating the view that love is both necessary and impossible, since the big Other is both a necessary part of subject formation, as well as being the site of unfathomable excess and impossibility.

The Desolation of the Subject

Thus far, I have sought to highlight the necessary desolation facing all subjects who undergo the process of subject formation, as described by Lacan in the graph of desire. Whatever the chosen path, the subject will always be forced or coerced into making certain choices, and the subject will first be inculcated into an already existing Symbolic Order that had been merely clipped by certain lying signifiers, and only tacitly agreed by

[22] The translation of '*jouissance*' as 'enjoyment' is not an altogether appropriate one; however, we have used it since it continues to be translated in this way in the relevant scholarship.

the collective. The big Other will install its desires in the subject, as soon as the subject is named, and the subject might try to escape the big Other by pursuing their drives, as I suggested with Scudéry's *Map of Tender*—the traveller attempts to reach the *Unknown lands*. However, paradoxically, getting too close to the lying signifier dismantles the fantasy, which allows subjective instability to set in in the subject's psychic life. Language's grip is much too powerful for any subject to escape its clutches. One of the positive aspects of Lacan's psychoanalysis is his categorical refusal to consider psychotics as somehow outside symbolic coordinates. Lacan's stubbornness was that, rather than confine psychotics and label them 'mad,' he claimed that perhaps we were all psychotics (or what I have elsewhere termed *homo alienatus*)—trapped within symbolic coordinates—no better, only more numerous in our Symbolic Order (Richards, Forthcoming-b). Lacan saw that we could not merely point to madness; instead, he sought to identify madness within the symbolic structures of the 'typical' subject, as we grow up and face our inculcation into the Symbolic Order. The overarching theme in this chapter has been to demonstrate the necessity of this inculcation. Concerning the Law, I touched on some, I suggested, erroneous examples of those attempting to overcome symbolic obstacles. I contended that Lacan's psychoanalysis always already anticipated the strategies by which subjects would try and perturb its law, the non-dupes err [*les non-dupes-errent*]. The big Other, or master signifier, is much too powerful to be dethroned in this way. Instead, it is the subject who is dethroned, the inability to be one's own master, as Lacan puts it, the impossibility to be myself ['*m'être*'] (*SXVII* 178).

The desolation of the subject was further compounded with our analysis concerning the strategy of *loser wins*. In a way, *loser wins* still holds. However, the wish to abandon symbolic coordinates was the wrong demand because, for Lacan, the desire to exit language altogether would mean that subjects are not able to articulate themselves at all—the non-dupes err [*les non-dupes errent*]. Therefore, subjects do win, however, winning comes at a price, the subject's freedom to choose not to be in the Symbolic. Lacan describes a closed, almost claustrophobic, social field, and the result is a kind of social understanding that identifies few means of escape; for Lacan, a door ajar is simply another entrance into symbolic structures. The wish to love, and be loved, as well as the related impulse of reaching *in itself for itself* seems to be, for Lacan, just another impossibility. However, the difference with Sartre's position is that the path of subject formation, reaching desire and trying to access *jouissance*, though 'doomed to failure,' is always necessary. The subject is coerced and convinced to re-enter the fantasy, to accept the power of the big Other. And this is what we might call *living a human life*.

References

Allouch, Jean. 2009. *L'Amour Lacan*. Paris: EPEL.

Anzieu, Didier, and Gilbert Tarrab. 1990. *A Skin for Thought Interviews with Gilbert Tarrab on Psychology and Psychoanalysis*. London and New York: Routledge.

Beasley, Faith E. 2000. Altering the Fabric of History. In *A History of Women's Writing in France*, ed. Sonya Stephens. Cambridge: Cambridge Univerity Press.

Book XXIII, The Sinthome (1975–1976). (trans: Price, A.R.) Cambrige: Polity.

Burch, Laura. 2014. New Pleasure in Life Unfolding: Madeleine de Scudéry's Friendship Fan. *Seventeenth-Century French Studies* 36 (1): 4–17.

Chaplin, Charlie. 1940. *The Great Dictator*. DVD.

de Saussure, Ferdinand. 1995. *Cours de linguistique générale*. Paris: Payot. English edition: Saussure, Ferdinand, de. 2011. Course in General Linguistics (trans: Baskin, W.). New York: Columbia University Press.

de Scudéry, Madeleine, 2001. *Clélie, histoire romaine, Première partie 1654*. Ed. Chantal Morlet-Chantalat. Paris: Honoré Champion. English edition: Scudéry, M.d. 1678. Clelia, An Excellent New Romance: The Whole Work in Five Parts. London: H. Herringman, D, Newman, T. Cockerel, S. Heyrick, E. Cadman, S Loundes, G. Marriot, W. Crook, and C Smith.

DeJean, Joan. 1991. *Tender Geographies: Women and the Origins of the Novel in France*. New York: Columbia University Press.

Fanon, Frantz. 2015. *Écrits sur l'aliénation et la liberté*. Paris: La découverte. English edition: Frantz Fanon, Alienation and Freedom, 2018. Eds. Jean Khalfa and Robert J. C. Young. Trans. Steven Corcoran. London: Bloomsbury Academic.

Feyerabend, Paul. 1993. *Against Method*. London and New York: Verso.

Filteau, Claude. 1979. *Le Pays de Tendre: l'enjeu d'une carte*. Littérature No.36.

Fink, Bruce. 2004. *Lacan to the Letter: Reading Écrits Closely*. Minneapolis and London: University of Minnesota Press.

Fink, Bruce. 2014. *Against Understanding Volume 2: Cases and Commentary in a Lacanian Key*. New York/London: Routledge.

Freud, Sigmund. 1960. *The Standard Edition of the Complete Psychological Works of Sigmund Freud, Jokes and their Relation to the Unconscious*, Vol. VIII. Trans. James Strachey, Anna Freud, Alix Strachey and Alan Tyson. London: Hogarth Press.

Greisch, Jean. 1994. *Ontologie et temporalité*. Paris: PUF.

Howells, Christina. 1988. *Sartre: The Necessity of Freedom*. Cambridge: Cambridge University Press.

———. 2011. *Mortal Subjects: Passions of the Soul in Late Twentieth-Century French Thought*. Cambridge: Polity.

Ibbett, Katherine. 2008. Productive Perfection: The Trope of the River in Early Modern Political Writing. In *EMF: Studies in Early Modern France 12*, ed. Anne L. Birberic. Charlottesville: Rookwood Press.

Kuhn, Thomas. 1996. *The Structure of Scientific Revolutions*. London and Chicago: University of Chicago Press.

Lacan, Jacques. 1960. *Le Séminaire de Jacques Lacan, VIIa, L'Éthique de la psychanalyse, (1959–1960) Patrick Valas*, unpublished transcript. http://www.valas.fr/IMG/pdf/S7_L_ETHIQUE.pdf. Accessed 30 July 2019.

———. 1966. *Écrits*. Paris: Seuil. English edition: Lacan, J. 2006. Écrits. (trans: Fink, B.) London: W.W. Norton & Company.

———. 1973. *Le Séminaire: Livre XI, Les Quatre concepts fondamentaux de la psychanalyse (1963–1964)*. Paris: Seuil. English edition: Lacan, Jacques. 1981. The Seminar of Jacques Lacan, Book XI, The Four Fundamental Concepts of Psychoanalysis (1963–1964) (trans: Sheridan, A.). London and New York: W.W. Norton & Company.

———. 1974. *Le Séminaire de Jacques Lacan, XXI, Les Non-dupes errent (1973–1974)*, Patrick Valas, unpublished transcript. http://www.valas.fr/IMG/pdf/S21_NON-DUPES%2D%2D-.pdf. Accessed 30 July 2019.

———. 1975a. *Le Séminaire de Jacques Lacan, Livre XX, Encore (1972–1973)*. Paris: Seuil.. English edition: Lacan, J. 1998. The Seminar of Jacques Lacan, Book XX, Encore, (1972-1973). (trans: Fink, B.). London and NY: W.W. Norton & Company.

———. 1975b. *Le Séminaire de Jacques Lacan, Livre I, Les Écrits techniques de Freud (1953–1954)*. Paris: Seuil. English edition: Lacan, J. 1991. The Seminar of Jacques Lacan Book I, Freud's Papers on Technique (1953–1954). (trans: Forrester, J.). London and New York: W.W. Norton & Company.

———. 1981. *Le Séminaire de Jacques Lacan, Livre III, Les Psychoses (1955–1956).* Paris: Seuil. English edition: Lacan, J. 1993. The Seminar of Jacques Lacan Book III, The Psychoses, (1955–1956). (trans: Grigg, R.). London and New York: W.W. Norton & Company.

———. 1986. *Le Séminaire de Jacques Lacan, Livre VII, L'Éthique de la psychanalyse (1959–1960).* Paris: Seuil. English edition: Lacan, J. 1992. The Seminar of Jacques Lacan, Book VII, The Ethics of Psychoanalysis, (1959-1960). (trans: Porter, RD.). London and NY: W.W. Norton & Company.

———. 1991. *Le Séminaire: Livre XVII, L'Envers de la psychanalyse (1969–1970).* Paris: Seuil. English edition: Lacan, Jacques. 2007. The Seminar of Jacques Lacan, Book XVII, The Other Side of Psychoanalysis (1969–1970). (trans: Grigg, R.). London and New York: W.W. Norton & Company.

———. 1998. *Le Séminaire de Jacques Lacan, Livre V, Les formations de l'inconscient (1957–1958).* Paris: Seuil. English edition: Lacan, J. 2017. The Seminar of Jacques Lacan, Book V, The Formations of the Unconscious, (1959–1960). (trans: Grigg, R.). Cambridge: Polity.

———. 2001a. *Le Séminaire de Jacques Lacan, Livre VIII, Le Transfert (1960–1961).* Paris: Seuil. English edition: Lacan, J. 2015. The Seminar of Jacques Lacan, Book VIII, Transference, (1960–1961). (trans: Fink, B.). Cambridge: Polity

———. 2001b. *Autres Écrits.* Paris: Seuil.

———. 2004. *Le Séminaire de Jacques Lacan, Livre X, L'Angoisse (1962–1963).* Paris: Seuil: Paris. Lacan, Jacques. 2014. The Seminar of Jacques Lacan, Book X, Anxiety (1962–1963). (trans: Price, A.R.) Cambrige: Polity.

———. 2005. *Le Séminaire de Jacques Lacan, Livre XXIII, Le Sinthome (1975–1976).* Paris: Seuil. English edition: Lacan, J. 2016. The Seminar of Jacques Lacan,

———. 2007. *Le Séminaire de Jacques Lacan, Livre XVIII, D'un discours qui ne serait pas du semblant (1970–1971).* Paris: Seuil.

———. 2011. *Le Séminaire de Jacques Lacan, Livre XIX, … Ou pire (1971–1972).* Paris: Seuil. English edition: Lacan, Jacques. 2018. The Seminar of Jacques Lacan, Book XIX, …Or Worse, (1971–1972). (trans: Price, A.R.). Cambridge: Polity.

Lakatos, Imre. 1998. Science and Pseudoscience. In *Philosophy of Science: The Central Issues*, ed. Martin Curd and J.A. Cover. New York and London: W. W. Norton & Company.

Malle, Louis. 1958. *Les Amants*. DVD.

Mannoni, Octave. 1969. *Clefs pour l'imaginaire ou l'autre scène*. Paris: Seuil.
Meyer, Catherine. 2005. *Le Livre noir de la psychanalyse: Vivre, penser et aller mieux sans Freud*. Paris: Éditions des Arènes.
Miller, Jacques-Alain. 2005. Introduction à la lecture du Séminaire *L'Angoisse* de Jacques Lacan. *La Cause freudienne* 59 (1): 65–103.
———. 2011. Vie de Lacan. *La Cause freudienne* 79 (3): 305–343.
———, *Séminaire X, Donc: La Logique de la cure, (1993-1994)*, cours du 9 mars, (unpublished). http://jonathanleroy.be/wp-content/uploads/2016/01/1993-1994-Donc.-La-logique-de-la-cure-JA-Miller.pdf. Accessed 15 April 2023.
Milner, Jean-Claude. 1995. *L'Œuvre claire*. Paris: Éditions du Seuil.
———. 2009. *L'Amour de la langue*. Paris: Verdier. English edition: Milner, J-C. 1990. For the Love of Language (trans: Banfield, A.). New York: The Macmillan Press.
Morel, Geneviève. 2000. *Ambiguïtés sexuelles*. Paris: Anthropos.
Peters, Jeffery. 2004. *Mapping Discord: Allegorical Cartography in Early Modern French Writing*. Newark: University of Delaware Press.
Popper, Karl. 1998. Science: Conjectures and Refutations. In ed Martin Curd and J.A. Cover, *Philosophy of Science: The Central Issues*. New York and London: W. W. Norton & Company.
Richard, François. 2011. Le Paradigme du Nebenmensch et la fonction maternelle. *Revue française de psychanalyse* 75 (5): 1539–1544.
Richards, Sinan. 2021. The Logician of Madness: Fanon's Lacan. *Paragraph* 44 (2): 214–237.
Sartre, Jean-Paul. 1943. *L'Être et le néant*. Paris: Gallimard. English edition: Sartre, J-P. 2021. Being and Nothingness (trans: Richmond, S.). London and New York: Routledge.
Shakespeare, William. 2002. *The Oxford Shakespeare: Complete Sonnets and Poems*. Ed. Colin Burrow. Oxford: Oxford University Press.
Sorel, Charles. 1667. *La Bibliothèque françoise, de M. C. Sorel premier historiographe de France*. Paris: Compagnie des Libraires du Palais.
Steigerwald, Jörn. 2008. L'Oiconomie des Plaisirs. La Praxéologie de l'amour galant: à propos de la *Clelia*. Zeitschrift für französische Sprache und Literatur, Bd. 118, H. 3.
Taylor, Helena. 2017. Ancients, Moderns, Gender: Marie-Jeanne l'Héritier's 'le Parnasse Reconnoissant, ou, le Triomphe de Madame Des-Houlières. *French Studies* LXXI (I): 15–30.
X, Malcolm. 2003. In ed Marcus D. Pohlmann. *African American Political Thought, Volume 2, Confrontation Vs. Compromise: 1945 to the Present*. New York and London: Routledge.

5

Sent Home—Lacan's Final Heresy

The R.S.I [*l'hérésie*]

> And then I realized that what constituted my course was a sort of "*I don't want to know anything about it*" (Lacan, *Encore*).

The three psychoanalytic realms, the Real, the Symbolic, and the Imaginary (R.S.I), foreground most of Lacan's various teachings, and these three registers are never too far from Lacan's considerations at any given time.[1] As Malcolm Bowie noted in *Lacan* (1991), these three registers seek 'to extend psychoanalytic discussion into a fully intersubjective dimension' (91). After a long break from straightforwardly advancing the three registers individually, the late Lacan, around seminars *SXXII, R.S.I,* and *SXXIII, The Sinthome,* explicitly returns to R.S.I to join them in the Borromean knot. We can better understand why Lacan refashions the Real, the Symbolic, and the Imaginary into R.S.I by reconstructing

[1] In French, RSI is pronounced *hérésie* (Rabaté 2001: 155) which is a neat Lacanian formula for the heretic nature of the signifier in relation to the three registers, or, put another way, *les-non-dupes-errent*. See also: *SXXII.*

S. Richards, *Dialectics of Love in Sartre and Lacan*, The Palgrave Lacan Series,
https://doi.org/10.1007/978-3-031-45798-2_5

Lacan's Borromean knot which preoccupied him in the final years of his life.

The Borromean knot not only shows the three different registers (R.S.I) interlinking, but the schema also demonstrates the interdependence of each realm upon the others, while maintaining each register's relative autonomy. A central feature of the Borromean knot is that if any of the rings are ruptured, the whole knot is undone, thereby stressing the interdependence of the three registers (*SXXIII* 11–2). If we isolate the Symbolic ring, we notice that the Real and the Imaginary registers cleave through the Symbolic Order at four different points (Figs. 5.1 and 5.2):

If we maintain our focus on the Real (the dark ring), we notice that this section of the Real is *within the Symbolic* from the perspective of the subject. The same insight also applies to the Imaginary ring (the light grey ring). Lacan chooses to focus on the Symbolic, and this is neither an arbitrary nor an accidental choice since the symbolic *is* the means by which subjects comprehend the world. This ring, the Symbolic Order, is the only bit of the world subjects have a handle on, since it is the only ring that contains language, and is the only means by which subjects can intelligibly make sense of the world. Therefore, Lacan sees the 'middle' ring, the symbolic, as worthy of special notice for the subject. The entire Lacanian formulation of subject development that I have thus far

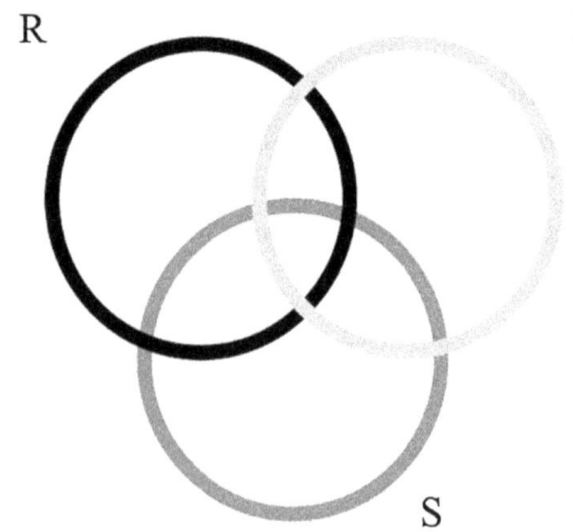

Fig. 5.1 Borromean Knot (inexact for illustrative purposes)

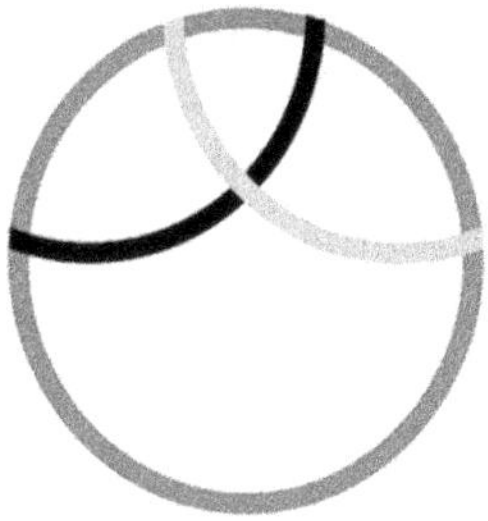

Fig. 5.2 Isolated Symbolic Ring (Borromean Knot)

described: the second mirror stage, the process of identification, symbolic castration, the partial renunciation of *jouissance*, the subject's desire and leftover desire, the articulation expressed in the graph of desire, the master signifier, all take place *within* the Symbolic Order for the subject of language. As Miller put it:

> Symbolic, imaginary, real, it is psychoanalysis thought from the symbolic. Lacan introduced, haphazardly, his stage of the mirror already by giving the image symbolic virtues. This primacy of the Other is marked at the deepest level of the identity of the subject, it constitutes it (Miller 2007: 134).

In other words, the subject's relationship with the big Other is the foundation for all three realms.

Lacan spends an inordinate amount of time speculating on the relationship between the Symbolic and the Real using a series of respective pairs: conscious/unconscious, language [*le langage*]/lalanguage [*lalangue*], speaking being [*être parlant*]/*parlêtre*, signifier/*jouissance*, *phallic jouissance*/*feminine jouissance*, (*a*)*mur*/*amour*, *symptom*/*sinthome*, where the former is symbolically recognisable, and the latter is speculative. In previous chapters, I suggested that subjects had an inkling about the unconscious and argued that subjects could learn about the concept but not much about its content.[2] Through the Borromean knot, we can now better appreciate how subjects interact with the unconscious; the address

[2] See also Lacan's discussion of syntax in (*SXXIII* 117). Furthermore, there is a strong link between Lacan's contention that we can know the form of the unconscious but not its content and the concept of the "unfathomable" we discussed in our first chapter in relation to Schelling. We had said that for Schelling man was privy to a glimpse of the origins of the world. Schelling had called this 'the unfathomable' (*Weltalter*, 14). See discussion in chapter one.

black and white image ring carries the knowledge of the unconscious, which cleaves through the symbolic field. However, a large section of the Real is not in the Symbolic Order and is, therefore, unintelligible for the subject, which is why the Real's uncanny manifestations in the subject's daily life can make us feel uneasy. Lacan confirms this by stating: 'it is necessary to *demonstrate* it, not only to show it! Demonstrating it is a matter of the *Symbolic*' [encore faut-il le *démontrer*, pas seulement le *montrer*! Le démontrer relève du *Symbolique*] (*SXXII* 207). Therefore, the Symbolic is the only medium through which subjects can have any knowledge of the Real, or the Imaginary, since all discussions about R. and I. are necessarily mediated by language and, so, necessarily from the perspective of S. The only clue subjects have of what might exist on the other side of the Real: *Amour* [Love], *unconscious, parlêtre, jouissance,* and *lalangue,* rest with the limits of language itself. It is for this reason that Lacan dialectically relates 'necessity' with 'impossibility,' characterising them as antagonistic partners.

Some interpretations of Lacanian psychoanalysis have suggested that Lacan located the Real outside the Symbolic. For example, Bowie argued that 'the Real is that which lies outside the symbolic' (1991: 94). However, this is not, strictly speaking, true since as Lacan's Borromean knot has clearly shown, the Symbolic mediates a significant part of the Real (*SXXIII* 12).[3] Lacan deliberately placed a vital component of the Real within the Symbolic, and he substantiated this aspect of the Real by associating it with non-rapport sexuel [*il n'y a pas de rapport sexuel*]. As we will see, this connection to the *non-rapport sexuel* qualifies the Real as impossible. The Real's role for the subject is partly to reveal the difference between the conscious/unconscious, *le langage*/*lalangue*, and signifier/*jouissance*. Which is to say that the Real is one of the words that Lacan employs to describe the differences between the two opposing concepts that we can sum up thus: 'knowledge' [*savoir*] and 'truth' (*É* 672–3), where knowledge is *necessarily* mediated through language for the subject, and where truth is always only half-said [*mi-dit*], and, therefore, *impossible*. For Lacan, this dualism

[3] Of course, this light critique is unfair because Lacan's later seminars were not as widely available in the late 1980s and early 1990s as they are today.

between knowledge and truth expresses the difference between the Symbolic and the Real (Barnard and Fink 2002: 4).

More precisely, the Real in the Symbolic (as observable in the isolated Borromean knot) describes the tasselling of the symbolic fabric at the limit of the Symbolic, which is to say that it represents the beginning of the disintegration of symbolic meaning, and this is strictly correlative to the beginning of *jouissance*. Although it might still seem odd that Lacan had placed a significant aspect of the Real in the Symbolic, as Lacan had explained in *Écrits*, the Real reveals itself in the Symbolic as the 'noise in which one can hear anything and everything' [*bruit où l'on peut tout entendre*] (324). This noise means that the Real is audible from inside the Symbolic, which is why Lacan represents the Real as slicing through the Symbolic field in the Borromean knot. Therefore, the Real describes the moment symbolic coordinates begin to disintegrate, or, in other words, the Real is the name Lacan gives to the limits of the Symbolic from the subject's perspective.

Moreover, this disintegration of symbolic meaning, which the Real describes, is, *stricto sensu*, an impossible process (*AÉ* 573), since, from the subject's perspective, this disintegration is an attempt to surpass language, and language is a crucial pillar of the Symbolic. Therefore, transcending the Symbolic is incomprehensible from the standpoint of language, which is to say from the perspective of the Symbolic itself. Bowie correctly identified this impossible paradox when he stated: 'language has powers over the Real' (1991: 94), which is why it is odd for him to have argued, as quoted above, that the Real is outside the symbolic process. However, Bowie got tantalisingly close when he wrote: 'for Lacan, the Real thus comes close to meaning "the ineffable" or "the impossible"' (95). Close but inexact, because, for Lacan, the Real *does* refer to an impossibility of signification. And, therein lies the fundamental research problem of Lacanian psychoanalysis: how can we understand the unstable relationship between the Symbolic and the Real? As hinted at above, this is a problem otherwise known as the *non-rapport sexuel*, or, put differently, how can we understand the relationship between knowledge and truth? (Barnard and Fink 2002: 4). Lacan says, 'So here we are at the palpable border between truth and knowledge; and it might be said, after all, that at first sight our science certainly seems to have readopted the solution of closing the border' (*É* 674–5).

The Real is impossible to support because it points to what might exist beyond language; it highlights the absolute limit of linguistic comprehension, and it is this supposition that is expressed in the formula: *there is no sexual relationship* [*il n'y a pas de rapport sexuel*]. A sexual relationship between subjects is impossible to pronounce or enunciate in language, and, for Lacan, that is why it is impossible: because it cannot be symbolised:

> Impossibility is the real, quite simply, the pure real. The definition of the possible always requires a first symbolisation. If you exclude this symbolisation, this formula will appear much more natural: "*the impossible is the real*" (*SXIV* 443).

Therefore, the Real in the Symbolic highlights the impossible task of resolving the structural antagonisms that are present in the Symbolic. Put differently, the Real describes the structural failure of symbolisation itself, which is why an aspect of the Real is symbolically oriented. The Real describes that moment when things seem "off" in our daily lives, and, to deal with this instability, subjects raise a fantasy screen in their subjective economy to overcome this structural failure of the Symbolic. Without the fantasy, the Real of the *non-rapport* prompts the total disintegration of symbolic markers in the subject's psyche.

L'(a)mur/L'Amour

Earlier, I showed how the subject's inability to develop a successful sexual relationship in Lacan's sense [the *non-rapport sexuel*] presented subjects with an impossible ontological problem. According to Lacan, this impasse describes the sex act's inability to fuse two subjects into one, in language. In Plato's *Symposium*, Aristophanes infamously articulated Plato's philosophical position by arguing that love accomplished the final reunification of two partial subjects:

> The two parts longed for each other and tried to come together again [...]. Love [*eros*] of one person for another has been inborn in human beings, and its role is to restore us to our ancient state by trying to make unity out of duality and to heal our human condition [...] we are continually searching for our other half (2008: 24 [191a; 191d]).

Plato characterises the human condition as something that requires healing ['restore us to our ancient state ... to heal our human condition'], which is a philosophical position that both Schelling's 'contraction of being,' and Sartre's '*une maladie*' inherit and develop. Lacan, too, imagines an ailing subject who is irredeemably marked by various pathologies and symptoms. However, for Lacan, the afflictions that impress upon our human condition do not require a cure. The Lacanian position is to accept the subject's terminal state and demonstrate to the subject that *loving* necessitates that we acquiesce to our *maladie.* Lacan's psychoanalysis only offers the subject a palliative remedy which invites them to confront their desolation by *holding it together*—Lacan's *le sinthome.*

Plato's dialogues are clearly in the background to Lacan's considerations in the introductory lesson of *SXX, Encore,* when he asks: 'is love about making one? [*l'amour, est-ce de faire un*?]' (*SXX* 5).[4] And, in contrast to Aristophanes, Lacan's ambition in *Encore* is to insist against the alleged unification of two subjects in love, instead emphasising the disharmonious quality of all intersubjective relationships in language. When Lacan advances the *non-rapport sexuel,* he does not suggest that sex is physically impossible. Rather, Lacan proposes that it is impossible for subjects to relate to each other in language through sex, which is to say that it is impossible to enunciate or inscribe the sexual relationship, and concomitantly this impossible relationship prevents two subjects from ever forming a "One." 'it is strictly impossible to consider the copulation of two bodies as becoming One alone' Lacan says (*SXIX* 108–9). At this early stage in *Encore,* Lacan is advancing the argument he made in *SXVI, D'un Autre à l'autre* [*From an Other to the other*], where he had asserted:

[4] NB: Lacan often discusses Plato's *Symposium,* notably in *SIX, L'Identification,* and *SXIX, ...Or Worse.* We know Lacan is referring to Aristophanes in this section of *SXX* since he says in *SXIX, ...Or Worse*: 'Aristophanes is the one who comes up with the famous bipartition of being' [*c'est Aristophane qui invente la fameuse bipartition de l'être*] (*SXIX* 109/127).

'in the field which is apparently ours, no harmony, in any way that we have to designate it, is in order/required/admitted' [*dans le champ qui est apparemment le nôtre, nulle harmonie, de quelque façon que nous ayons à la désigner, n'est de mise*] (*SXVI* 12). Thus, the ontological rupture which the *non-rapport sexuel* describes is a cornerstone of the psychoanalytic understanding of intersubjective relationships, and these relations are necessarily qualified as antagonistic and disharmonious, which is why Lacan picks up this conflict again in *SXXI*, *The Non-Dupes Err* [*Les Non-dupes errent*], where he will rebrand it: 'disharmony.'

The subject's necessary exposure to the *non-rapport sexuel* emerges at some point in their life and triggers the subject's awareness of their 'disharmonious' psychic state. However, the subject's experience of this ontological deadlock (which is linguistic [*langagière*]) is not easily noticeable because, for Lacan, the *non-rapport sexuel* does not necessarily involve the physical, sexual act, since the *non-rapport sexuel* primarily refers to a linguistic problem. And, if that is so, what does Lacan mean by the sexual relationship in language? And moreover, what is it about the sexual relationship that is impossible? Why should it prevent two subjects becoming One, as it had for Aristophanes? To clarify these questions, Lacan distinguishes *(a)mur* [(a)wall] from *amour* [love], and *jouissance* from sex. The distinction he draws between *(a)mur* and *amour* partially clarifies the differences between sex and *jouissance* as they relate to the Symbolic Order, further developing the impasse at stake in the *non-rapport sexuel.* Foregrounding Lacan's discussion of the *non-rapport sexuel* is a sustained treatment of the various modes of *jouissance*, and, in his characteristically spasmodic style, Lacan examines *jouissance* in order to establish the differences between *(a)mur* and *amour.*

The most fruitful way to enter into Lacan's discussion of love in *SXX* is through Lacan's treatment of *jouissance.* Lacan attempted to clearly define *jouissance* in "La place de la psychanalyse dans la médecine," published in 1967 in *Lettres de l'École freudienne de Paris.* In this text, Lacan describes *jouissance* as a kind of corporeal 'tension,' a bodily 'forcing,' that is inextricably linked to a 'spending,' or it would be better to say 'costing,' for the subject. Lacan goes so far as to claim that *jouissance* is both exploitative and unbearable for the subject:

What are we told about pleasure? That it is the least excitation, that it is what makes tension disappear, that it tempers it the most, therefore what necessarily stops us at a point of distance, of very respectful distance from *jouissance*. For what I call *jouissance* in the sense that the body experiences itself, is always of the order of tension, of forcing, of expenditure, of even exploit. *There is unquestionably jouissance at the level where pain begins to appear*, and we know that it is only at this level of pain that a whole dimension of the organism can be experienced that otherwise remains veiled (1967: 46: my emphasis).

Therefore, pain is a central feature of *jouissance*, and not only is this pain embodied [*en-corps*] but the subject always demands more [*encore*] (*SXX* 11), and it is in this precise sense that Lacan connects *jouissance* to (*a*)*mur*. In Lacanian psychoanalysis, the '*encore*' [again/more] quality is a central aspect of what Lacan calls "doesn't stop being written" [*ne cesse pas de s'écrire*] (*SXX* 94), which is the lover's demand par excellence. Love, then, is an always unfinished task. It is for this reason that some children apoplectically rail against their parents, for there will never be enough love conveyed, transferred, or shared by the parent—it will never be enough to satisfy their demands to be loved. Therefore, a necessary absence will always mark love, and the fact that this lack cannot be readily filled is why a lover might continuously ask their lover: *do you (still) love me*?

The *encore, encore, … encore* is a key feature of *jouissance*, the subject's necessary thirst for love is never satisfied, and, for Lacan, the relationship between *impossibility* and *necessity* finds its locus here in our discussion of the subject's demand for more love from the Other. Lacan says, 'the necessary is the "doesn't stop being written" (*ne cesse pas de s'écrire*). Analysis of the reference to the phallus apparently leads us to this necessity' (*SXX* 94). For Lacan, the necessary aspect of the subject's articulation in relation to the phallic function is identical to the structure of *jouissance* and love, and Lacan characterises it as a continuous demand, or '… *encore*.' Whereas its obverse is the impossible aspect of the subject's development (outside the phallic function) which is identical to the *non-rapport sexuel*:

The "doesn't stop not being written" [*ne cesse pas de ne pas s'écrire*] on the contrary, is the impossible, as I define it on the basis of the fact that it

> cannot in any case be written, and it is with this that I characterize the sexual relationship—the sexual relationship doesn't stop not being written [*le rapport sexuel ne cesse pas de ne pas s'écrire*] (*SXX* 94).

Therefore, the subject is trapped between over-articulating their demands for love ["doesn't stop being written"—*ne cesse pas de s'écrire*], and not being able to articulate them at all ["doesn't stop not being written"—*ne cesse pas de ne pas s'écrire*].[5] Which is why a subject will necessarily want to ask the person they love: *do you (still) love me*? because it is impossible in both speech and writing to eloquently articulate love in measured terms, it is either excessive or inexpressible.

Lacan captures, in an uncharacteristically clear passage from *Encore*, the relationship between necessity and impossibility:

> You can write *Sade* however you like: either with a capital S, to render homage to the poor idiot who gave us interminable writings [...] or, still better, you can write it as *çade*, since one must, after all, say that morality ends at the level of the id (*ça*), which doesn't go very far. Stated differently, *the point is that love is impossible, and the sexual relationship drops into the abyss of nonsense, which doesn't in any way diminish the interest we must have in the Other* [*c'est que l'amour soit impossible, et que le rapport sexuel s'abîme dans le non-sens, ce qui ne diminue en rien l'intérêt que nous devons avoir pour l'Autre*] (*SXX* 87/80–1: my final emphasis).

Sade, Lacan believed, demonstrated the paradox inherent to articulating our love. Lacan, the master of homophony that he was, explained that he preferred to denote the core of Sade's contribution to philosophy and psychoanalysis as '*çade*' which succinctly captures the role of the id [*ça*] in the loving relationship. The final three lines of the extract, quoted above, explain the complex relationship between necessity and impossibility. It is also worth noting that the insight expressed here, in relation to love, is almost identical to the argument I unearthed in the discussion of *loser*

[5] In many ways, Lacan's description of love's bipolarity between insufficiency and excess resembles Schelling's discussion of time that we developed earlier. We had said: 'Schelling argues that to understand the Absolute Past we need to appreciate that time itself is constituted by two motions. One which propels time forwards, the other a slowing mechanism that attempts to prevent it from going too fast.'

wins. Lacan says that love is impossible as it relates to the ontological impasse in the *non-rapport sexuel,* which does not placate [*ne diminue en rien*] the necessary interest the subject owes the big Other [*l'intérêt que nous devons avoir pour l'Autre*]. Lacan is arguing that even though love is impossible, it is a necessary impossibility, which is the same Lacanian argument I developed earlier as *loser wins, But Nevertheless!* The subject's demand for infinite *Love* ('*Encore*') always refers the subject to (a)wall [(*a*)*mur*] since this demand is impossible.

One of Lacan's major contributions to the history of philosophy rests in this dialectic he highlights between necessity and impossibility, which is, in turn, related to the psychoanalytic task of elucidating the relationship between knowledge and truth. Indeed, in *SXIX*, …*Or Worse*, Lacan says, not in relation to love but concerning the relationship between phallic *jouissance* and feminine *jouissance* that: 'on one side, we have the universal founded on a necessary relation to the phallic function, and, on the other, a contingent relation, because woman is *pas toute*, not all' (*SXIX* 89), further demonstrating the connection between the two sides of the duality he develops. To borrow Sartre's language, the task of reuniting the two sides is 'doomed to failure' (*BN* 502) but that does not mean that subjects do not try to love, 'doesn't in any way diminish' […] 'that we chase after it' [*qu'on coure après*] Lacan had said (*SXX* 81; *AÉ* 571). This fundamental Lacanian insight is crucial to understanding the concept of the *sinthome*, introduced in *SXXIII*, which I have formulated as *holding it together*, and to which we will return.

Surplus Enjoyment on the Cusp of (a)mur

In *SXVI*, *D'un Autre à l'autre* [*From an Other to the other*], Lacan introduced the concept of *plus-de-jouir* which he connects to object small *a* (object cause of desire), and later will rename *phallic jouissance* in *SXX*, *Encore*. Lacan culls the concept of *plus-de-jouir* [surplus enjoyment] from Marx's notion of *plus-value* [surplus value] (*SXVI* 17). It is worth noting that Lacan's discussions of *jouissance* in *Encore* are heavily indebted to his many preparatory comments from *The Ethics of Psychoanalysis* to *Or… Worse*. However, Lacan confused matters in *Encore* by referring to *jouissance* without qualifying which of the various modes of *jouissance* he was developing at any one time (Tricot 2006: 152). It is for this reason that *Encore* is a notoriously difficult work to understand because it presumes a large amount of familiarity with Lacan's previous teachings. In order to clarify the discussion of *jouissance* as it relates to *(a)mur*/*Amour*, I have arranged the many formulations of *jouissance* into two main modes which Lacan deploys most frequently—*phallic jouissance* and *feminine jouissance*. Nothing prevents the interplay between the two sides of this table so that desiring the impossible does not preclude it from showing up as necessary for the subject.

Phallic Jouissance	*Feminine Jouissance*
Necessary	**Impossible**
Jouissance [said to be] phallic	*Jouissance of the woman*
Phallus	~~*The*~~ *woman*
Doesn't stop being written"	*Doesn't stop not being written"*
Dupe	*Non-dupe*
(a)mur	*Amour*
Castrated	*Psychosis*

We know from previous chapters that *jouissance* plays a crucial role in negotiating the subject's exposure to the *non-rapport sexuel*, and if, as I have suggested, the physical act is not necessarily the aim of the statement *il n'y a pas de rapport sexuel*, then why does Lacan deliberately use a phrase suffused with overtly sexual connotations? Moreover, why does Lacan choose a slogan which is so prone to misinterpretation? Following his longstanding method of wilful misunderstanding, misdirection, and dislocated meaning,[6] Lacan believed that psychoanalysis should differentiate between sex as it appears in 'genital plane' (*SI* 67) where 'what appears on the bodies under these enigmatic forms that are the sexual characteristics—*which are only secondary*—makes the sexed being (*SXX* 5, translation modified), and sex as it relates to *lalangue*. Indeed, *lalangue* plays a role in Lacan's schema. He says:

[6] 'In other words, there is a kind of confusion. This is not unusual because we live in confusion, and it would be wrong to believe that we live *on* it.' (*SXIX* 102).

> The question, in the end which is *very interesting*, is to know how something that we can—momentarily—say is correlative of this disjunction of the sexual jouissance, something that I call "*lalangue*," obviously it has a relationship with something of the real, but whether it can lead to mathemes that allow us to build science, that then is obviously the question (*SXIXa* 53).[7]

This latter view of sex as related to *lalangue* is crucial to understanding the late Lacan's philosophical project since this difference resembles the many distinctions that Lacan developed throughout his teaching; as evidenced by the distinctions drawn between, for example, the *conscious* and the *unconscious.* Once again, it is worth noting that Lacan's focus is neither on biology nor empirical reality, '*which are only secondary.*' And so, we can begin to understand why the sex act differs from both *l'(a)mur* and *l'amour.*

According to Allouch's *L'Amour Lacan*, we can trace Lacan's (*a*)*mur* to his early work "Écrits inspirés" [Inspired Writings] published in 1931 in the *Annales médico-psychologiques* [*Annals of Medical-Psychology*], around the time he was working on his doctoral thesis *De la psychose paranoïaque dans ses rapports avec la personnalité suivi de Premiers écrits sur la paranoïa* (Allouch 2009: 251). In the 1931 "Écrits inspirés," Lacan quotes the letters of a patient where she writes: 'it is ripe in the love of the other world, you will make, I believe Jesus in the other world still, provided that one floods the poor of the habit of the monk who made it' [*il est mûr dans l'amur de l'autre monde, tu feras, je crois Jésus dans l'autre monde encore, pourvu qu'on inonde le pauvre de l'habit du moine qui l'a fait*] (Allouch 2009: 252). This is a remarkable passage because, although it is almost meaningless, it foreshadows many of the notions Lacan will pick up again in the later seminars. Notice Lacan's patient's use of '*amur*,' '*l'autre monde*,' '*l'habit du moine*,' and '*encore*.' If we did not understand this excerpt, we are in good company since it is equally incomprehensible for Allouch,

[7] During the 1971–1972 academic year, Lacan held his main seminars (*…Ou pire*) as usual. However, that year, he also gave parallel lectures at *La chapelle de l'hôpital Sainte-Anne* under the title *Le Savoir du psychanalyste.* It is during the 6th January 1972 session of this parallel seminar series that Lacan re-introduces the concept of (*a*)*mur*. This context is important because the official *Seuil* edition of *SXIX*, *…Ou pire,* does not include this 6th January session of *Le savoir du psychanalyste*, therefore, I will quote from the unofficial stenograph transcript (*SXIXa*) when discussing this particular session.

who says 'one remains largely unable to read this sentence.' Allouch argues that this is simply a draft, an incoherent series of codes for Lacan to pick up and formalise later on (251).

In the 1930s, Lacan related *(a)mur* to 'a world' [*un monde*], and in "The Function and Field of Speech and Language in Psychoanalysis" from *Écrits* (1966) Lacan again picks up this theme, and develops it by reproducing a fragment of a poem from Antoine Tudal's *Paris en l'An 2000* [Paris in the year 2000]:

> Between man and love
>   There is woman.
> Between man and woman
>   There is a world.
> Between man and the world
>   There is a wall (Tudal in *É* 239, translation modified).

Allouch explains that Lacan had chosen to selectively quote Tudal's poem since Lacan omits the final verses: *To the walled-in everything is a wall/Even an open door* [*Aux emmurés tout est mur/Même une porte ouverte*], and these lines seem to contradict Lacan's intention for *(a)mur* in "Function and Field." Whereas Tudal ends his poem with an open door, Lacan elects to end his Tudal quotation on a closed wall [*il y a un mur*] (Allouch 2009: 253). Moreover, Lacan does not comment further on the poem in "Function and Field," leaving the poem's inclusion in this chapter ambiguous and open to interpretation (253). Allouch states:

> By reading to the end the following pages, where there is no question of love, nor of the woman, nor of the world, one is led to conclude that their presence can only be due to their fall, to their last word, to the "wall" (253).

Years later, in *...Or Worse, the knowledge of the psychoanalyst*[8] Lacan seemingly remembers Tudal and his *Écrits*, picks up on this poem fragment again, and flips the order of the poem to make his point about *(a)mur*:

> *Between man and woman, there is love...*

[8] *cf. ...Ou pire, le savoir du psychanalyste* refers to the unpublished edition (*SXIXa*).

> -But of course! There is only that, even!
> *Between the man and the love, there is a world, ...*
> It's always what we say: *"there is a world,"* just like that *"there is a world."* It means: *You! you will never make it*! Water off a duck's back, in the beginning, *"Between man and woman, there is love,"* it means that [Lacan claps his hands] it sticks, a world floats, eh! But with *"there is a wall"* well then, here you understand that "*between*" [*entre*] means "*interposition.*" Because it's very ambiguous, the "*between*" (*SXIXa* 37).

Lacan comments that '*entre*' can mean both 'between' and 'interposing,' which suggests that there might be something blocking, or preventing, a connection between the two sides: 'there is a wall' [il y a un mur], Lacan says. Lacan then appeals to an image of Melanie Klein's bottle drawn on the blackboard behind him to illustrate the relationship between man, woman, and love (which is needlessly complicated to reproduce here), and finally, Lacan reaches his conclusion:

> What allows us to see topologically—what it's all about, as it were—is that afterwards when we are told: "*between man and the world*" this world substituted to the volatilization of the sexual partner—how did it happen?—we'll soon find afterwards—well, "*there's a wall*," that is to say the place where this *rebounding* occurs, this *rebound* that I introduced one day as signifying the cusp between *truth* and *knowledge*: *I* didn't say that it was cut, it's a *poète de Papouasie* [untranslatable] who says that it's a wall.
>
> It is not *a wall*: it is simply *the place of castration*. So that *knowledge* [*le savoir*] leaves the field of *truth* intact, and vice versa. Only what we have to see is that *this wall is everywhere* (*SXIXa* 38).

Lacan's philosophical programme is an attempt to show the incongruity between knowledge and truth; to put it in Lacanian terms: how are we to understand the unstable relationship between the Symbolic and the Real? For example, in the *non-rapport sexuel* (Barnard 2002: 4). In *Écrits*, Lacan says: 'so here we are at the palpable border between truth and knowledge; and it might be said, after all, that at first sight our science certainly seems to have readopted the solution of closing the border' (*É* 674–5). Lacan is picking up this thread once again in advancing the concept of (*a*)*mur*, and he suggests that between Man and Woman is Love, yet, between

Man and Love is the World, and, worse, between Man and the World is a Wall. Put another way we could say, love blocks the relationship between man and woman because love is the world itself, and the world is just a wall. Lacan calls this mode of love *l'(a)mur.*

The 'wall' that Lacan is talking about *is* the process of symbolic castration [*c'est pas un mur: c'est simplement le lieu de la castration*], which is, as we know, the renunciation of *jouissance* and the installation of the power of the master signifier in the subject's psychic life. Therefore, the wall which separates knowledge from truth is nothing other than the same wall which separates Man from Love, Man from Woman, Man from the World. Moreover, Lacan qualifies the features of this mode of love in the process of castration, he says 'the place where this *rebounding* occurs, this *rebound* that I introduced one day as signifying the cusp between *truth* and *knowledge* [l'endroit où se produit ce *rebroussement*, ce *rebroussement* que j'ai introduit un jour comme signifiant la jonction entre *vérité* et *savoir*]. This *rebounding* [*rebroussement*], a concept Lacan has borrowed from mathematics, is a point at which a line hits a wall and rebounds forming a *cusp*. Therefore, *(a)mur* is a dead-end, sending subjects who hit its wall flying in the opposite direction, to demand more love: *encore, encore, …encore*, and *'this wall is everywhere.'*

When Lacan picks up *(a)mur* again in *SXX* we can now better follow what he means; love is Janus-faced, as the dialectical table above had anticipated. On the one hand there is a mode of love, *(a)mur*, which is characterised as necessary because it follows the process of symbolic castration [*it is simply the place of castration/c'est simplement le lieu de la castration*], and the proper development of the subject within societal norms. This is the form of love that is constantly demanding more, *encore*, because in this mode of love the subject faces a wall, and is never satisfied, and the subject keeps hurtling themselves against this wall, it is something which "doesn't stop being written" [*ne cesse pas de s'écrire*]. However, the subject can sense that *(a)mur* is merely a placebo for the real thing: *Amour* [Love]—*(a)mur* merely placating the subject's desolation in the face of the failed sexual relationship. On the other hand, Lacan suggests that there is *Love* [*Amour*] which is characterised as impossible, unsayable, and related to feminine *jouissance*. Lacan states:

> It is even for this reason that *the unconscious* was invented, it is to realize that "*the desire of man is the desire of the Other*," and that *love* is a passion that can be *the ignorance* of this *desire*, but that does not leave it any *less of its scope* [*toute sa portée*]. When we look at it more closely, we see its devastation [*ravage*].
>
> So, of course, this explains why the jouissance of the other's body—it [*elle*]—is not a necessary response. It goes even further, it's not a sufficient answer either because love—it [*lui*]—asks for love, it doesn't stop asking for it [*il ne cesse pas de le demander*], it asks for it *encore*. *Encore* is the proper name of this fault [*cette faille*] from which the demand for love starts in the Other. So, from where does it leave, from where does *that* [*ça*] leave which is capable, certainly… but in a way that is not necessary, not sufficient… of responding by jouissance, jouissance of the body, of the body of the other?
>
> It is indeed what last year, inspired in a certain way by the chapel of Saint-Anne, which got on my nerves, I allowed myself to call the *(a)wall* (*SXXa* 8–9: my underlining).[9]

Confirming my reading of *SXIXa*, *The Knowledge of the Psychoanalyst* [*Le Savoir du psychanalyste*], Lacan is suggesting that *l'(a)mur* describes a necessary mode of love which is adopted by the subject in the process of symbolic castration, where jouissance is mostly renounced. However, Lacan qualifies *(a)mur* as something specifically related to the form of jouissance which is connected to the superego injunction: *Jouis*!, shorthand for phallic jouissance, that emerges from the body of the other [*corps de l'autre*]. Therefore, *Amour* and *(a)mur* are circular and work in tandem. *Amour* only exists outside the process of symbolic castration, whereby the subject continuously misrecognises Love [*Amour*] in the Other as a never-ceasing reservoir of infinite love, and the Other merely refers the subject back to the dead end of *(a)mur*. Lacan had said, 'Encore is the proper name of this fault [*cette faille*] from which in the Other the demand for love starts.' Therefore, Encore is the proper name for the

---

[9] The published version *SXX* (1975) is highly misleading and problematic; therefore, I have chosen to cite the stenographed version, (*SXXa*). As my underlining shows in the above quote, the context implies that Lacan is referring to 'le corps de l'autre' with small 'a' instead of 'A'—which the stenographed version, *SXXa*, captures accurately. Whereas the 1975 Seuil version has it as: 'le corps de l'Autre' (*SXX* 11), and by changing the meaning to 'big Other,' the official version fundamentally altered what Lacan meant.

place where the demand for love comes from, and, as I will show later, this place resembles the object a in the impossible *in itself for itself*.

Phallic Jouissance/Jouissance of the Other

In *D'un Autre à l'autre* [*From one Other to another*], ...*Or Worse*, and *Encore*, Lacan elaborates at considerable length the distinctions between *phallic jouissance* and *jouissance of the Other*, and particularly in *Encore*, Lacan develops this notion alongside the French legal concept of usufruct [*usufruit*]. In French Civil Law, usufruct [*usufruit*] is the right to use a property or a good, codifying a process where a freeholder might let an individual *use* a property in question (beneficial ownership). As the French Civil Code puts it: 'Usufruct is the right to enjoy things of which another has ownership in the same manner as the owner himself, *but on condition that their substance be preserved*' [l'usufruit est le droit de *jouir des choses* dont un autre a la propriété, comme le propriétaire lui-même, *mais à la charge d'en conserver la substance*] (Code Civil, Article 578, Crée par Loi 1804-01-30: my emphasis). Lacan's 1972–73 seminar, *Encore*, was held at Paris 2 (Sorbonne Panthéon-Assas), part of the Law faculty, and Lacan is half-jokingly applying this legal concept to *jouissance*:

> "Usufruct" [...] brings together in one word what I already mentioned in my seminar on ethics, namely, the difference between what's useful and jouissance. [...] "Usufruct" means that you can enjoy [*jouir de*] your means, but must not waste them. When you have the usufruct of an inheritance, you can enjoy the inheritance [*en jouir*] as long as you don't use up too much of it (*SXX* 3).

For Lacan, the value of *usufruit* for psychoanalysis rests in its capacity to regulate, modulate, and moderate the subject's enjoyment, where the law [*droit*] enters to apportion *jouissance* (*SXX* 3). For Lacan, the importance of the *right-to-jouissance* [*droit-à-la-jouissance*] is to stress the role of the superego in distributing any leftover [surplus] *jouissance* to further cajole the subject to remain within the bounds of the master signifier. *Jouissance* belongs to the master signifier, and, as the Code Civil had put it is 'the right to enjoy things of which another has ownership.' Which is why Lacan says: 'what is jouissance? Here it amounts to no more than a negative instance [*Elle se réduit ici à n'être qu'une instance négative*]. Jouissance is what serves no purpose [*ne sert à rien*] (*SXX* 3). Notably, Lacan states that *jouissance* is reduced to being only a negative instance; which means that *jouissance*'s role in the subject's psychic life is to frighten the subject into controlling their subjective economy. However, Lacan also means that *jouissance*, in its specific form here [note that Lacan says: '*ici*'—which is to say as '*droit-à-la-jouissance*' (*SXX* 10)], is the birth [implied by '*n'être*'] of the negative aspect of *jouissance* in the subject's psyche, which is that aspect of the law which keeps the subject within the realm of the signifier. Therefore, Lacan's concept of *jouissance* evinces multiple meanings and functions: on the one hand it is a regulative function, and on the other, feminine *jouissance* offers something highly ambiguous [*équivoque* (*SXXIII* 117)].

In order to develop the various meanings of *jouissance*, Lacan splits love in two [*l'(a)mur* and *l'Amour*], and this division also resemble the two modes of *jouissance* [*phallic* and *feminine]*. Clearly, the mode of *jouissance* that Lacan cast as a 'negative instance' which seeks to regulate the partial pleasure of unregulated *jouissance*, founding the symbolic law in the eye of the Subject, refers to *jouissance* in its phallic variety [*plus-de-jouir*]. This seems like a very complicated idea, but it is neither complicated nor counterintuitive. For example, in the previous chapter, I had argued that the paradigmatic form of unregulated *jouissance* was incest. I demonstrated that, in the process of subject formation, the subject was expected to renounce incest (thereby installing the incest prohibition), which necessarily implied that the subject accepted the symbolic law. The incest prohibition states that subjects must not partake in acts of incest. However, what the subject mostly forewent in accepting the incest prohibition did not amount to a total proscription of the concept of incest itself; the subject *is* able to continue "enjoying" incest as a *partial* pleasure in language, should they so wish. In fact, Lacan seems to be arguing that "incest" (which I am using here as a shorthand for unregulated enjoyment) is actually solicited by the superego injunction: *Jouis!* [enjoy!], but with the usual caveat that the line between fantasy and reality should not be crossed. This logic of surplus enjoyment [*plus-de-jouir*] of phallic *jouissance* is not exclusive to the incest prohibition, incest is merely one example which demonstrates the logic of this form of *jouissance*. Nonetheless, our Western cultural obsession with incest, as evidenced by incest's continued relevance in the arts, attests to the continued relevance of Lacan's idea of phallic *jouissance*, for, although acts of incest are prohibited, they nonetheless continue to found the superego injunction *Jouis*!.[10] Incest, as a sexual perversion, is solicited so long as it is libidinally *regulated;* which is to say, prohibited physically and empirically, but partially solicited linguistically or intellectually.

The renunciation of *jouissance* in the process of symbolic castration is, for Lacan, a kind of bet with the big Other, homologous to a Pascalian wager, where some of the subject's *jouissance* is staked in exchange for the 'surplus value' inherent in the big Other's command to *Jouis!.* Lacan says, 'Pascal's wager [...] illustrates excellently the relation between the renunciation of jouissance and the dimension of the wager' (*SXVI* 18). Earlier, I inadvertently demonstrated this logic of the *plus-de-jouir* in my analysis of "Kant with Sade," where I argued that Kant's ethical demand (or, the categorical imperatives) produced the very result it had sought to restrict, producing what I had called a kind of 'surplus enjoyment' inherent to violating the categorical imperatives. About ten years after having developed that argument, Lacan says in *D'un Autre à l'autre* [*From an Other to the other*]:

> But this is not so new to your ears if you've read me before, because it is the object of my writing "Kant with Sade." There, I demonstrated the total reduction of the *plus-de-jouir* to the act of applying to the subject what is the term *a* of the fantasy, by which the subject can be posited as cause-of-self in desire (*SXVI* 18).

Therefore, *plus-de-jouir* [surplus *jouissance*] is linked to phallic *jouissance;* the unregulated desire which subjects renounce in the process of symbolic castration is merely transformed into an acceptable, even solicited, form of desire, one which is *regulated*, and whose establishment enables the subject to articulate a form of subjectivity which is acceptable to society's symbolic formations.

[10] For example: Sophocles's *Oedipus Rex*, Marquis de Sade's *Juliette*, Michele Haneke's *La Pianiste* (not exhaustive).

For Lacan, surplus *jouissance* in the subject's libidinal economy is all that is left after the majority of *jouissance* is renounced in the process of the subject's symbolic castration. The leftover *jouissance* grants the subject 'the usufruct of an inheritance' [*l'usufruit d'un heritage*] that acts to regulate the subject's drives when they re-integrate the coordinates of symbolic regulations. Which is why Lacan says: 'nothing forces anyone to enjoy [*jouir*] except the superego. The superego is the imperative of jouissance—Enjoy!' (*SXX* 10). Lacan's concept of *jouissance*, as I have stated, evinces multiple meanings. The phallic *jouissance* that Lacan is talking about here in the opening pages of *Encore* is the form of *jouissance* that all subjects who have been symbolically castrated can access, and it is related to (*a*)*mur*. Lacan clarifies:

> Phallic jouissance is the obstacle by which man is unable [*n'arrive pas*] to 'enjoy' [*jouir*] the body of the woman, precisely because what he enjoys [*ce dont il jouit*] is the jouissance of the organ. That is why the superego, which I qualified earlier as based on the (imperative) "Enjoy!", is the correlate of castration (*SXX* 7, translation modified).

All human beings fall prey to the *phallic jouissance* that describes only a partial enjoyment of the organs of others, or one's organ, which leads to (*a*)*mur*. Therefore, (*a*)*mur* is a form of masturbatory enjoyment; the other side of *jouissance* (*feminine jouissance*) is inaccessible to all subjects, it is both impossible and unsayable:

> That everything revolves around phallic jouissance, that is precisely what the psychoanalytic experience bears witness to, and bears witness in that woman is defined by a position that I have indicated as "not-all" (*pas-tout*) with respect to phallic jouissance (*SXX* 7, translation modified).

For Lacan, all subjects (all human beings regardless of gender) find themselves on the side of *jouissance phallique*. The other side of *jouissance* is inaccessible, it is not-all [*pas-tout*].

> Here then is the statement [*le dit*] of what is said about jouissance insofar as it is sexual. For one pole, jouissance is marked by the hole that leaves it

> no other path than that of phallic jouissance. For the other pole, can something be attained that would tell us how that which up until now has only been a fault [*faille*] or gap in jouissance could be realized? (*SXX* 8).

The entire discussion of feminine *jouissance, pas-toute* [*not-all*], and *non-rapport sexuel* takes place in the context of a discussion of the Symbolic Order's relationship with the Real. Lacan, quite earnestly, sets himself the speculative task of trying to identify and elucidate what might be 'on the other side' [*de l'autre côté*] of phallic *jouissance.* Phallic *jouissance* is total [*tout*] in the process of subject formation, there is no mystery, it is structured around the lack (or, object *a*), it has a defined role and function in regulating the subject's libidinal economy, yielding the *plus-de-jouir* [surplus enjoyment] and *(a)mur.* Beyond this form of *jouissance* is the not-all and *Amour* [Love] itself. However, *pas-toute* in relation to what? Lacan says:

> What becomes for the woman this second bar that I have only been able to write by defining it as *pas toute*, not all? She is not contained within the phallic function, without being its negation either. Her mode of presence is between centre and absence (*SXIX* 104, translation modified).

Without phallic *jouissance, feminine jouissance* cannot exist, and concomitantly, there can be no all without the not-all—no Man without Woman, and *vice versa.* For Lacan, *the woman* is not-all [*pas-toute*] in relation to the big Other. It is also notable that the structure of the feminine *jouissance* is the opposite of the *non-rapport sexuel*; in which sexual relations are possible, but a linguistic relationship is impossible (*SXX* 8), which is why the *non-rapport* signals to the subject the possibility of another form of *jouissance*, the Other's jouissance which Lacan calls the *jouissance of the Other* [*de l'Autre*], or the feminine *jouissance.*

As I showed in chapter three, the difference between Scudéry's the *Dangerous Sea* [*Mer dangereuse*] and the *Unknown lands* [*Terres inconnues*] (I can now more accurately say) mirrors the difference between phallic *jouissance* and feminine *jouissance* respectively. However, these two realms work to support each other, and the phallic *jouissance* inaugurates the superego injunction: *Jouis!*; it is the regulative power that guarantees the power of the master signifier, and pushes the subject to accept the norms and terms of social life—which are undoubtedly patriarchal for Lacan (hence: phallic). As I mentioned a bit earlier, we should never forget that Lacan's discussions are always suffused with irony, and I believe it is incontestable that Lacan's entire psychoanalytic project is an ironic critique of patriarchal social relations. It is for this reason that I believe Darian Leader is unfair in his reading of *Encore* when he states:

> Lacan's discussion of female sexuality in *Encore* is taken to be the next big development around the idea of jouissance, but what really does it tell us? Women experience a powerful jouissance yet they are unable to say anything about it. The thesis is appealing because everyone loves a bit of negative theology—the opaque core of femininity—yet doesn't this just replicate the familiar trope of the woman as enigma, while at the same time managing to ignore the very rich and precise formulations about arousal and sexuality that women have made and continue to make? It is just bizarre to say that women have not managed to articulate anything about their experience of the Other jouissance, as if to cancel not only their speech but so much of their literary, poetic and artistic productions (Leader: 2021: 117–18).

The empiricism of Leader's argument is wholly absent from Lacan's psycho-philosophical schema, as I have been at pains to show throughout this book, up to and including stressing that women are on the side of phallic *jouissance*, since feminine *jouissance* does not, strictly speaking, exist. Lacan does clearly say the mad and some mystics can dwell on the side of Other *jouissance*, for example, Lacan himself (the dupes who have erred). However, it is clearly not an empirically gendered distinction in the way Leader seems to suggest. The power of Lacan's argument is that since we live in a patriarchal society—as evidenced by the ironically named master signifier: "Phallus"—women (*qua* empirical beings) are governed by the same phallic power as men (*qua* empirical beings), which is the very patriarchal power that actually silences women, that it would seem Leader misattributes to Other *jouissance*.

It is important to restate that, for Lacan, master signifiers are always ironic, and that is the point since they are bloated castrators who wield obscene power against subjects, madmen, and madwomen. The way I read this Lacanian philosophy is an ontological discussion of subjectivity as attempting to include sexuality into speech and ideas—which Lacan wishes to discuss by including both men and women, a hitherto ignored philosophical reality, which is precisely designed to respond to the philosophical ascendency of feminism in French intellectual circles at the time. It is for this reason that ~~the~~ woman (or, God *par excellence* for Lacan) is impossible since she is but a line of flight out of the symbolic prison within which we (as unfree dupes) dwell. Labelling God "woman" in this way is the exact opposite of Leader's argument since Other *jouissance* is on the side of non-dupery, *lalangue*, the unconscious, the Real, and the infinite.

In the same vein as Leader's argument, would it be at all interesting or relevant to empirically interpret Bernini's focus on women in, for example, the *Ecstasy of Saint Teresa* (1647) or the *Blessed Ludovica Albertoni* (1671–4) by claiming 'doesn't this just replicate the familiar trope of the woman as enigma?' Would not such a statement have missed the vital importance of Bernini's baroque project? Up to and including the 'mystical jaculations' [*jaculations mystiques*] that Lacan ironically imbues Bernini's Teresa of Ávila with in *Encore*. Remember that Lacan says: '*qu'elle jouit*, ça fait pas de doute!' [to immediately understand that she's coming. There's no doubt about it!], before adding: 'at the bottom of the page, drop a footnote, "Add to that list Jacques Lacan's *Écrits*," because it's of the same order' (*SXX* 76), which tells the reader or auditor all they need to know: that this is Lacanian irony against the Church and received doxa in general, a hallmark of his mysticism. It is Bernini's statue of *Ecstasy of Saint Teresa* that is coming, not the historical person of Teresa of Ávila. Analogously, it is the mystics, not women *qua* empirical women, who 'know nothing about it' (*SXX* 76).

This interplay between phallic *jouissance* and feminine *jouissance* is part of Lacan's focus in *Encore*. The discussions from this period are foregrounded in the earlier discussions on the graph of desire, which help explain the formation of the subject. In order to acquiesce to the desires of the Other, the subject accepts the fantasy of (*a*)*mur*, and accepting *l'(a)mur* reinforces the symbolic wall which surrounds the subject.[11] The subject demands love, and this insatiable demand is *corporeal*: 'that's where the body comes from' [*c'est de là que vient l'en-corps*] because *l'(a)mur* is a dead end encountered in 'the body of the other' [*le corps de l'autre*] (*SXXa* 8–9: my underlining).

Moreover, for Lacan, it is this aspect of sex which is pacified by the illusion of love. 'L'amur is what appears in the form of bizarre signs on the body.'[12] Therefore, love [*l'Amour*] is not bodily, rather, it is ontological, which aligns love closely with the *non-rapport sexuel*, 'stated differently, the point is that love is impossible and the sexual relationship drops into the abyss of nonsense, which doesn't in any way diminish the interest we must have in the Other' (*SXX* 87). Lacan's formulas of sexuation, the *non-rapport sexuel*, the subject as it relates to *jouissance* are ontological problems as they affect beings in our world, which is why it is not surprising that Lacan claims so forcefully that we need to abandon the sexed body as only a secondary consideration. The primary question concerns the status of sex and love at an ontological level. For Lacan, *l'Amour* [Love] eludes the subject's reach, it escapes the subject's grasp with the not-all [*pas-toute*] of the *jouissance of the woman* [*jouissance de la femme*], qualified as both impossible and unsayable. Therefore, Lacan's concept of love falls squarely on the side of the impossible Real, and his concept of *l'(a)mur* falls on the side of the Symbolic necessity.

Object a, Love, and the One

The impossibility expressed in the *non-rapport* is primarily related to language, and it describes how the speaking subject [*l'être parlant*] is unable to formulate sex in speech or enunciate the sexual relationship, as such. For Lacan, when the subject is confronted with this insurmountable

[11] Additionally, in French, 'mur' also describes fruits that are ripe [*mûr*]. We could say that subjects that are confronted by *(a)mur* are ripe for inculcation into the Symbolic Order.

[12] Lacan is clear that the subject he is describing is not tied to gender in an essentialist sense: 'what appears on the bodies under these enigmatic forms that are the sexual characteristics—which are only secondary—makes the sexed being' (SXX 5, translation modified), [*l'être du corps, certes, est sexué, mais c'est secondaire, comme on dit*] (*SXX* 11).

deadlock, the subject's first wish is to try and transform their relationship into One, in order to attempt to resolve the problem of the un-enunciable sexual act. These subjects might be tempted by Aristophanes's allegory, explored earlier. However, in a striking echo to the question Schelling asked himself in *Die Weltalter* [*Ages of the World*] explored earlier concerning the beginning of the beginning, Lacan says in *SXX*:

> People have been talking about nothing but the One for a long time. "There's such a thing as One" [*Y a d' l'Un*]. I based my discourse last year on that statement, certainly not in order to contribute to this earliest of confusions, because desire merely leads us to aim at the gap [*faille*] where it can be demonstrated that the One is based only on [*tenir de*] the essence of the signifier. I investigated Frege at the beginning [of last year's seminar] in the attempt to demonstrate the gap [*béance*] there is between this One and something that is related to being [*tient a l'être*] and, behind being, to jouissance (*SXX* 5–6).

For Lacan, the idea of the One belongs to the realm of the Signifier (or, the big Other), whereas outside symbolic structures, in the realm of the *jouissance de la femme*, the One multiplies (incidentally, just like the 'truth' multiplied earlier). What does this mean? If we contrast Lacan with Schelling, this becomes clearer. For the middle Schelling, the philosophical quest was to identify the 'beginning of the beginning,' which in simple terms is how did God himself come to be? For Schelling, the position of the world was irrevocably tied to the central tenets of the Abrahamic religions, namely Christianity, so that inside this worldview no other truth exists. Therefore, for Schelling, if we adopt an Abrahamic perspective on the world, it is evident that the human story begins with Adam and Eve. Schelling's deceptively naïve question was to ask: how would God have told his version of the human story?[13] This prelapsarian credulity is Schelling's heresy; Schelling wished to imagine God's world from the perspective of God himself, and this logical reasoning forced

[13] Schelling's question echoes Lacan's naïve question posed in …*Ou pire, le savoir du psychanalyste,* 6 January 1972, 'Because it's sort of curious, it's a question that has never been asked to my knowledge "Does God believe in himself? [*parce que c'est assez curieux, c'est une question qui n'a jamais été posée à ma connaissance "Est-ce que Dieu croit en lui?"*] (*SXIXa* 33).

Schelling to dream up a split in God himself—forcing God to divide into two distinct thoughts.

Similarly, we could say that for Lacan, the Abrahamic perspective resembles the perspective of the Symbolic Order where the "One" is tied up with the master signifier. The phallic *jouissance* mostly remains within the Symbolic from the subject's standpoint, whereas Lacan's suggestion with feminine *jouissance* is to think about the world without symbolic coordinates; which is to say, God's perspective of the world. It is in this "outside" the Symbolic Order that the One multiplies to become not-One [*pas-toute*], for precisely the same reason that it did for Schelling two centuries earlier. Schelling forced God to break up—one half of God had to fall to earth, and as I suggested earlier, this half of God washed up on the beach, hidden and afraid, as a decorator crab, imperceptible and ambiguous.

In *Encore*, Lacan aligns phallic *jouissance* with the Symbolic and explains how the subject's insatiable demand for love stems from having tied their demand for love to the essence of the One. This identification is impossible, as we have seen, and that is why it forces the subject towards *l'(a)mur*. For example, earlier, I stated that a child might always demand more love from their parents, and in that case, the child is mistaking their mother or father for an infinite well of love. Whereas the parent is not the material embodiment of the Other, they merely represent it for the child (*SXXa* 8). Therefore, while the child might think that the parent is "One" in the sense that all meaning and signification stems from the parent, this is not the case. Therefore, the demand for infinite love (or, '*Encore*') just refers the child back to the wall of *(a)mur*. Lacan explains by referring to a parakeet:

> I can tell you a little tale, that of a parakeet that was in love with Picasso. How could one tell? From the way the parakeet nibbled the collar of his shirt and the flaps of his jacket. Indeed, the parakeet was in love with what is essential to man, namely, his attire [*accoutrement*]. The parakeet was like Descartes, to whom men were merely clothes [habits] … walking about [*en…pro-ménade*]. Clothes promise debauchery [*ça promet la ménade*], when one takes them off. But this is only a myth, a myth that converges with the bed I mentioned earlier. To enjoy a body [*jouir d'un corps*] when

> there are no more clothes leaves intact the question of what makes the One, that is, the question of identification. The parakeet identified with Picasso clothed [*habillé*] (*SXX* 6).

According to Lacan, Picasso's parakeet loved his owner, but clearly, the parakeet loved him dressed as Picasso ['namely, his attire']. The signifier's essence lies in its regalia, which is to say its external appearance makes recognising the signifier possible as such—as 'One' Picasso. 'Because desire merely leads us to aim at the gap [*faille*] where it can be demonstrated that the One is based only on (tenir de) the essence of the signifier' (5–6). The clothes Picasso wore identified him as the "One" for the parakeet in the realm of signification, which is to say Picasso's dress describes the place from where the parakeet's demand for infinite love stems. Whereas under his clothes, Picasso is simply one in a series of other human bodies (or, *not-one*), and the parakeet would no longer be able to identify with Picasso's desire. Lacan develops this idea further by returning to the incomprehensible phrase from the "Écrits inspirés" we saw earlier; Lacan says about monks: 'The habit loves the monk, since it's through this that they are but one' [*l'habit aime le moine, parce que c'est par là qu'ils ne sont qu'un*] (*SXX* 6/12), which is to say that, in their case, their habits and dress make them a "One." The One is the essence of the signifier, and the subject attempts to locate in them their demand for infinite love. The subject believes that there is a mythical place in the One, which is the source of their love. This mistaken view of the location of infinite love in the One is nothing other than the *object a* (the object cause of desire):

> In other words, what lies under the habit, what we call the body, is perhaps but the remainder (*reste*) I call object a. What holds the image together is a remainder. Analysis demonstrates that love, in its essence, is narcissistic, and reveals that the substance of what is supposedly object-like (*objectal*)—what a bunch of bull—is in fact that which constitutes a remainder in desire, namely, its cause, and sustains desire through its lack of satisfaction (*insatisfaction*), and even its impossibility. (SXX 6).

For the subject, love is tied to castration—(*a*)*mur*. The One only exists as an essential component of the signifier, and outside this nexus, in the realm of the Other's *jouissance*, the One is two, or three, or four, or, simply uncountable. 'Love is impotent, though mutual, because it is not aware that it is but the desire to be One, which leads us to the impossibility of establishing the relationship between "them-two" [*la relation d'eux*]. The relationship between them-two what?—them-two sexes' (*SXX* 6). Lacan is seeking to develop a model of love which moves subjectivity beyond the entrapment by the signifier One to the impossible relationship between *d'eux* (that is to say: "of them," which is at least more than one. *D'eux* [of them] is homophonous with *deux* [two]). The fact that the *d'eux* [of them] exists means that there is a certain ambiguity at the heart of the "One," which Lacan will further develop in *Le Sinthome* (117). Therefore, the opposite of (*a*)*mur* is the *Amour* that is connected to the other side of object *a*, which is ~~The~~ *woman.* Lacan says 'for ~~The~~ *woman*, something other than object *a* is at stake in what comes to make up for [*suppléer*] the sexual relationship that does not exist' [*suppléer ce rapport sexuel qui n'est pas*] (*SXX* 63).

Many of Lacan's slogans from around this period (phallic *jouissance*, feminine *jouissance*, *there is no sexual rapport, non-rapport sexuel,* ~~The~~ *woman does not exist*) concern and describe the subject's ontological difficulties in language, and do not describe empirical relations between people. Throughout the present work, I have often alluded to the conviction, wrongly held in my judgment, that Lacan was a prescriptive patriarch.[14] Lacan, some allege, was a heterosexist theoretician of human oppression.[15] The problem with such a view is that it fails both to understand the intricacies of Lacan's particular brand of psychoanalysis, nor does it account for Lacan's irony in his written statements, style, and presentation.[16] Moreover, Lacan's detractors almost exclusively miss the auto-critique that Lacanian psychoanalysis carries. For example, Jane Gallop states in *Reading Lacan* that:

---

[14] For example, see Irigaray's misleading argument in "Cosi fan tutti" in *Ce sexe qui n'en est pas un* (1977).

[15] For example, Merrill Cole states: 'it is crucial to critique Lacan's lapses into sexism and heterosexism, as well as his tendency to make all meaning depend on the phallus' (2018: 85).

[16] (St. Pierre 2017) discusses this Lacanian particularity pp. 93–94.

> This is, I believe, what Lacan means by the phallus. The phallus "designates as a whole the effects of signification" [...]. If I had the phallus, then I would know what all my signifiers meant, I would command the play of signification (Gallop 1985: 112).

All human beings, no matter their allegedly empirical, desired, or incorrectly assigned gender, sexuality or race are subject to the same psychoanalytic investigations applied to *$*, which is to say a subject entrapped by the signifier and whose *jouissance* is said to be '*phallic*.' It is meant to be comical. Gallop recognises this, saying: 'for women, Lacan's message that everyone, regardless of his or her organs, is "castrated," represents not a loss but a gain,' and later Gallop argues again that 'Lacan says that everyone is castrated, I understand that to mean not only do men no more have the phallus than women, but psychoanalysts have it no more than literature professors' (Gallop 1985: 20 & 112). This view of the subject is not heterosexist since 'phallic' is meant to be taken ironically. The centrality of the phallus in Lacan's system is a comical self-critical notion, a reminder designed by Lacan to provoke in his audience the heteronormative symbolic limits of a patriarchal society. Gallop states: 'if I had the phallus,' but for Lacan, no human being possesses 'the phallus.' As I showed earlier, the phallus is a fraud, a lie, an absent organising principle, and yet, it symbolically functions to regulate, oppress, and contain subjects.

Moreover, when Michael Warner writes, for example, 'my point, however, is not simply that we should depathologize the homosexual' (Warner 1990: 195), what Warner misses is that, for Lacan, all subjects are characterised by their numerous pathologies, and to move beyond one's pathologies is to seek to be unhuman. Lacanian psychoanalysis's default position is to presume we are all sick. No one subject is more especially pathological than anyone else. Moreover, Lacan's psychoanalysis does not offer any solutions to these pathologies:

> This is the only genuinely decisive function of the father. I've already marked out how it was not the Oedipus complex, how it was fucked [*que c'était foutu*], how if the father was a legislator, the child this would produce is President Schreber. No more no less (*SXIX* 208).

The Oedipus complex necessarily *creates* psychotic subjects, and a necessary characteristic of the father is that they are legislators, they lay down the symbolic law, which Lacan admits 'the child this would produce is President Schreber. No more no less.' *Therefore, the signifier Phallus only creates psychotic subjects.* This statement Lacan makes is not extolling the values of the signifier Phallus. For Lacan, that is why all subjects share psychotic tendencies, as defined in *The Psychoses* as the foreclosure of central elements of the signifier (in symbolic castration), and this is also why Lacan had a difficult time within the medical establishment.[17] For Lacan, the psychotic element exists in us all as subjects of an oedipal structure. As Lacan will further develop in *SXXIII, The Sinthome*, the latent psychotic tendency of subjectivity is not something he prescribes but merely describes.

All human beings are subject to the same process of inculcation by the big Other into the Symbolic Order, unless, of course, they seek to babble outside grammar or any system of language, cultivating their animal voice in an attempt to suppress the coordinates of human language. Lacan's conclusion, which could be caricatured as a kind of fatalism inherent in the-non-dupes-err [*les non-dupes-errent*], is a final claim which suggests that a subject cannot live outside of language, symbolic rules and norms, and without a Master. Any attempt to found a life outside a form of symbolic mediation, is not a human life; in short, it is impossible, and in merely seeking to express itself will necessarily found its own symbolic. Lacan is not seeking to privilege one system over another; he is only pointing out the structural limits of life and language.

We might hesitate to accept this view since it is hopeless and asphyxiating if misunderstood. Yet, for Lacan, the subject is a being who only exists insofar as they are symbolisable, which is why ~~the~~ woman doesn't exist because ~~the~~ woman resists any symbolisation, or inculcation into the Symbolic Order. In other words, Lacan is contrasting the barred subject (*$*) with an impossible subjective image that opposes this form of subjectivity: ~~*La*~~ *femme*. Concomitantly, the *non-rapport* works in the same way; it is something which is outside symbolisation.

[17] See for example: Meyer 2005.

Jouissance is mostly inaccessible for the subject, which is why the minimal access to the enjoyment that subjects possess is the 'jouissance of the body as such' and this has nothing to do with sex, it is an ontological point about the limits of being. Lacan's discussions about the different forms of *jouissance* which exist beyond the asexual limits of being are, strictly speaking, merely speculative—as was God's failure for Schelling earlier. The real of the *non-rapport sexuel* states that 'sexual jouissance is marked and dominated by the impossibility of establishing as such, […] this only One' (*SXX* 7, translation modified). For Lacan, there is only the concept of being—the subject—and evidently, Lacan is not suggesting that women do not exist empirically. Lacan sets the coordinates for an exact ontological problem, which he summarises in the final section of the first lesson from *Encore*:

> Everything that has been said about being assumes that one can refuse the predicate and say "*man is*," for example, without saying what. The status of being is closely related to this lopping off of the predicate. From now on, nothing can be said of it except through dead-end detours and demonstrations of logical impossibility, whereby no predicate suffices. As for being [*Ce qui est de l'être*], a being that would be posited as absolute, it is never anything but the fracture, break, or interruption of the formulation "sexed being," insofar as sexed being is involved [*intéressé*] in *jouissance* (*SXX* 11).

What can we say about being? For Lacan, we can only say something through detours and through impasses and dead ends; what appears to us as a fullness of being [*comme absolu*] is only ever a fractured being, a subject marked by a rupture at the core of its being. To understand this division, Lacan uses *jouissance* and an elaborate scheme to show how subjects believe themselves to be whole, or One. The Lacanian challenge is to question this perceived wholeness in the first place.

The *Sinthome*, or how to Be *Sent Home*

Though it is not as explicit, in many ways *SXXIII*, *The Sinthome*, revisits the central theme of *SIII*—psychosis. *The Sinthome* marries two of Lacan's longest running interests: psychosis and James Joyce,[18] and, to put it in simple terms, Lacan argues in *Le Sinthome* that Joyce's writings exude psychotic features. However, Joyce, unlike Schreber, for example, *was* able to hold his symptoms together, 'Joyce embodied the "symptoms" as such' (Rabaté 2014: 165). Lacan, transfixed by Joyce's remarkable capacity to *hold it together* despite foreclosing key elements of the Symbolic Order, elevates this Joycean capacity for subjective survival into the final insight of his entire psychoanalytic practice—the subject's identification with the *sinthome* itself. In so doing, Lacan sanctifies Joyce as the *saint homme* (*sinthome*) of literature (*SXXIII* 167). Allowing the patient to recognise and identify with their *sinthome* is the moment the patient is, finally, *sent home*.

In an echo to Schelling and Sartre, Lacan begins his analysis of the *sinthome* by relating it to the Fall, arguing that *le sinthome* has a connection with the word sin in English.

> This is the fault, the *sin*, which my *sinthome* has the advantage to start with. In English, *sin* refers to the trespass of original sin, hence the necessity of the fact that the fault-line that is always growing doesn't stop [*ne cesse pas la faille qui s'agrandit toujours*], unless it should undergo the stop of castration as possible (*SXXIII* 5).

We can extract the gist of Lacan's *SXXIII* argument from this short excerpt. In psychosis, the subject forecloses the signifier, a crucial part of the process of symbolic castration. Which is to say that the psychotic subject does not undergo the process of symbolic castration, and ends up misidentifying the big Other. This misidentification is the psychotic subject's original error [*première faute*] in their process of typical subject

[18] Rabaté explains Lacan's long running fascination with Joyce which began with Lacan's chance encounter with Joyce at the age of 20 in Adrienne Monnier's bookshop in Paris (2003: 158).

development, and this original error, then, only festers as the subject gets older [*la faille qui s'agrandit toujours*]. The misidentification grows until such a time as a certain life-event triggers the psychotic's decompensation, as we saw with Schreber, where his election to the position of a Judge precipitated his mental collapse. Except, Lacan says, 'the fault-line that is always growing doesn't stop, unless it should undergo the stop of castration as possible [*la faille qui s'agrandit toujours sauf à subir le cesse de la castration comme possible*]' (*SXIII* 5). In effect, Lacan is putting forward the possibility of surviving a life outside the nexus of identification with the big Other.

According to Lacan, Joyce identified with his *sinthome* and outplayed or cheated the master signifier; he lived between the Symbolic Order and the Real, bridging the gap between necessity and impossibility, or knowledge and truth, and, for Lacan, *that* is the Joycean lesson, and that is why Joyce is central to the elucidation of the concept of *le sinthome*.

> The sole import of all this is that it brings us closer to the fact that saying *Joyce the sinthome* and saying *Joyce the symbol* are not the same thing. If I say *Joyce the Symptom* it's because the symptom, with respect to the symbol, a-*bol*-ishes it, if I may continue in this same vein. It is not simply *Joyce the Symptom*, it is Joyce in so far as he has, as it were, cancelled his subscription to the unconscious [*c'est Joyce en tant que, si je puis dire, désabonné à l'inconscient]* (*SXXIII* 144).

Lacan believed that Joyce's writing abolished symbolic constraints [*il l'abolit*], or we could say Joyce's writing outplays ['*déjoue*' (*SXXIII* 14/22)] the Phallic function, or master signifier. Lacan highlights the game-like quality of the *sinthome* when he says that language could at some stage 'consist in playing on the *equivoque* that might free up something of the sinthome' [*consiste à jouer de cette* équivoque *qui pourrait libérer du sinthome*] (*SXXIII* 9/17: my emphasis). Joyce's radical move was to revoke his relationship to the unconscious, effectively uncoupling himself from the restrictive forces which clip the subject to the Symbolic Order.

So far, I have only highlighted Lacan's radical statements on the *sinthome*; however, *how* is Joyce's writing an example of the *sinthome*? What is it about Joyce's writings that abolish, or outplay symbolic constraints?

As we might have expected, Lacan explains that Joyce's power rests in his ability to manipulate language, to bend words, phrases, and expressions into an almost coherent translingualism [*translinguistique*] which manages to outplay the rigid and permanent structure of the Symbolic. 'Read Finnegans Wake. You will notice that this is something that is played out not at the level of each line but at the level of every single word. It plays on the *pun*, a highly particular *punning*' (*SXXIII* 144). It is no surprise that Lacan chooses to focus on *Finnegans Wake* in his attempt at elucidating the *sinthome*, since, as Rabaté notes, *Finnegans Wake* is 'a book that Joyce declared to be founded on one main mythical paradigm: original sin' (Rabaté 2014: 153). Moreover, in *Finnegans Wake*, Lacan finds a convincing example of how Joyce realised the *sinthome*:

> The most extreme case, I can tell you [...] is—*Who ails tongue coddeau, aspace of dumbillsilly?* Had I come across this piece of writing on my own, would I have perceived or not—*Où est ton cadeau, espèce d'imbecile?* [Where's your present, you imbecile?] (*SXXIII* 145).

Joyce's '*who ails tongue coddeau aspace of dumbillsilly?*,' pronounced in almost the same way in French, gives: '*où es ton cadeau, espèce d'imbécile*' [Where's your present, you imbecile], which, for Lacan, shatters the entire relationship between signifier and signified. 'The signifier stuffs the signified' [*c'est le signifiant qui vient truffer le signifié*] (*SXX* 37/37), Lacan says. The sheer fabric of language, grammar, systems of communication, collapse under the inventiveness of Joyce's translinguistic art, 'to the point that he ends up imposing on language itself a sort of fracturing, a sort of decomposition, which makes it so that there is no longer any phonatory identity' (*SXXIII* 79), and for a brief moment the artist (Joyce) has stumbled on the truth.

> I've said that the unconscious is structured like a language. It's odd that I'm also able to speak in terms of a *cancellation of subscription to the unconscious* [*désabonné de l'inconscient*] for someone who plays strictly on language, though he did use one particular tongue among others, one that is not his own—for his own is precisely a tongue that had been wiped off the map, to wit, Gaelic, of which he had a smattering, enough to get by, but hardly

> much more not his own, then, but the tongue of the invaders, the oppressors (146).

Lacan ties the *sinthome* to his infamous statement 'the unconscious is structured like a language,' and, although acknowledging the potential conflict between his early theory and later theory, Lacan claims there is no disunity between them. For Lacan, the uncoupling from the restrictive power of the unconscious *is* possible through punning and homophony, and, in an echo to Deleuze's *minor language*, there is a sense by which subjects can bifurcate language, and make language vibrate in the way Joyce did (*Critical* 109). Furthermore, in an obvious allusion to the bits of the real ['As I said earlier, we can only reach small bits of the real' (*SXXIII* 104, translation modified)] that we discussed earlier, Lacan says that the 'small bits' of Gaelic that Joyce possessed could be used to outplay the master signifier (which Lacan aligns with colonial oppressors and invaders) (*SXXIII* 146). In a way, language is the subject's tool of resistance to the power of the big Other, which, if masterfully deployed, can sow confusion in the enemy and allow the subject to break free. However, this masterful use of language is also a feature of psychosis, and Lacan purposefully casts the *sinthome* in ambiguous terms.

We would be hard-pressed to describe the *sinthome* in only positive terms. For example, Žižek argues in *Looking Awry* that the *sinthome* is a 'psychotic kernel that can neither be interpreted (as symptom) nor "traversed" (as fantasy)' (1991a: 137), as being characterised as a 'fragment of the signifier permeated with idiotic enjoyment' (128–9). However, Žižek also clarifies, *le sinthome* 'is the leftover of enjoyment, beyond meaning, resisting symbolization, which is why, as Lacan put it, woman is "the sinthome of man"' (137). The *sinthome* is the process of identifying with the impossible real we discussed at the outset of this chapter, those bits of the real [*bouts du reel*], which resist any symbolisation. *Le sinthome* describes the same deadlock that Sartre identified in *Being and Nothingness* when he stated that 'desire is itself doomed to failure' (*BN* 522). Which is why, Lacan says, 'a woman is a sinthome for all man' [*une femme est un sinthome pour tout homme*] (*SXXIII* 84/101) because ~~The~~ *woman* represents the *jouissance of the Other* that is both impossible and unsayable.

> The whole necessity of the human species is that there should be an Other of the Other. This is what is generally called God, but which analysis unveils as being quite simply *La* femme, *The* woman (*SXXIII* 108).

Lacan stresses that human beings necessarily wish for the existence of an Other of the Other, some higher power which could guarantee the guarantee, and as Lacan had been insisting for some time: 'the big Other is barred because there is no Other of the Other' [*le grand A est barré, (A̸), parce qu'il n'y a pas d'Autre de l'Autre*] (*SXXIII* 108). For Lacan, that desire for 'Other of the Other' is the wish for God to exist, or we could say in Sartre's language, to actualise *in itself for itself*, and Lacan's branch of psychoanalysis reads *La* femme as God herself, which is why she does not exist. Lacan asks rhetorically: 'and why not interpret one face of the Other, the God face, as based on feminine jouissance?' (*SXX* 77). So, 'in the last Lacan, in contrast, the analysis is over when we take a certain distance toward the fantasy and identify with the pathological singularity on which the consistency of our enjoyment depends' (Žižek 1991a: 138) which is to say the inexistent God herself.

Earlier I explained that Lacan believed that *jouissance* should not be wasted [*gaspiller*], and in another echo to *Encore*, Lacan says in *Le Sinthome*:

> Both spellings concern him, but it's a fact that Joyce makes a choice, and in this regard he is, like me, a heretic. For *haeresis* is precisely what specifies the heretic. *One has to choose the path by which to capture the truth* [*il faut choisir la voie par où prendre la vérité*]—especially since, once the choice has been made, no one is prevented from subjecting it to confirmation, that is, from being a heretic in the right way [*c'est-à-dire d'être hérétique de la bonne façon*]. The right way [*La bonne façon*] is the one that, when the nature of the sinthome has been recognized, doesn't shrink from using it logically, that is, from using it to the point of reaching its real, at the end of which he is no longer thirsty [*c'est-à-dire d'en user jusqu'à atteindre son réel, au bout de quoi il n'a plus soif*] (*SXXIII* 7, translation modified).

We will remember that the mode of *jouissance* that Lacan aligned with *usufruit* was the *phallic jouissance*, the *jouissance* that I suggested was necessary for the process of symbolic castration whose by-product was the *plus-de-jouir*. In this excerpt, Lacan is seemingly imbuing *le sinthome*, that *stricto sensu* ought to be impossible, with the characteristics of *jouissance* (*phallic*) which is necessary. Lacan is endowing the *sinthome* with a contingent structure [one has to choose the path by which to capture the truth/*il faut choisir la voie par où prendre la vérité*] even though it describes something which ought to be necessary. Which is to say, Lacan is arguing that the subject is able to cheat the big Other [which means being a heretic in the right way/*c'est-à-dire d'être hérétique de la bonne façon*] in order to reach one's real [using it to the point of reaching its real/*d'en user jusqu'à atteindre son réel*], to drink from *le sinthome* until we are no longer thirsty. This radical move runs counter to almost everything Lacan had built up to this point, and he says 'he is, like me, a heretic' [*il est, comme moi, un hérétique*].

Previously, Lacan had been adamant that no subject was able to exist outside the process of symbolic castration, and now Lacan is seemingly arguing that Joyce was a *non-dupe* who did not err. The *non-dupe* argument required the subject to accept the total power of the *Nom-du-Père* [Name-of-the-Father] which, even as a mere *semblant*, had to be protected and respected by the subject. Lacan seemingly suggests that although the symbolic coordinates are deceptive and insubstantial, we accept them in order to prevent social and psychic chaos within the patriarchal social that is our reality. However, with the *sinthome* a different *non-dupe* arises, and Lacan is seemingly amending the concept of *les non-dupes-errent* (Žižek 2012: 971). Joyce's writings demonstrate that it is the impossible Real of *jouissance* that is deceptive and insubstantial, that we do not need to believe in its impossibility to sustain our deceptive *semblant* of symbolic reality (971). Identifying with the *sinthome* demonstrates to the subject the power they possess is in the Symbolic Order, through language, which might give them the tools to tear down the wall of (*a*)*mur*. Effectively, the real *dupes* are those who believed the Symbolic was but an unchangeable rigid total power, and instead sought the impossible Other *jouissance*. Žižek summarises thus:

> In other words, those who err are precisely those cynics who dismiss the symbolic texture as a mere semblance and are blind to its efficacy, to the

way the symbolic affects the Real, to the way we can intervene into the Real through the symbolic (971).

For Lacan, Joyce duped the master signifier by intervening in the Real through the Symbolic. Joyce demonstrated the power of the Symbolic on the Real, and we can now better understand Bowie's earlier statement: 'language has powers over the Real' (1991: 94). In *SXXIII*, Lacan accomplishes his final heresy; Lacan is a heretic to his own earlier doctrine.

Lacan's *sinthome* strikes a highly personal note, and Lacan deliberately aligned it with Joyce's person [*son réel*]; Lacan has moved so far away from the prescriptive clinical blueprinting that characterised aspects of his middle period, and is instead arguing in the most speculative, philosophical, terms the result of a subject's analysis.[19] For Lacan, the heresy (*R.S.I*) explored at the outset of this chapter is the only way of potentially reuniting knowledge and truth, or necessity and impossibility. Heresy is cast as a positive quality of truth, if the truth is expressible it is a heresy, since truth is only ever half-said, *mi-dit* (*SXXIII* 14). 'There is no truth that, in passing through attention, does not lie. This does not prevent us from chasing after it' [*il n'y a pas de vérité qui, à passer par l'attention, ne mente. Ce qui n'empêche pas qu'on coure après*] (*AÉ* 571). The key, for the subject, is to choose the most appropriate path to truth [one has to choose the path by which to capture the truth/*il faut choisir la voie par où prendre la vérité*], and, for Lacan, the right way is by having recognised and identified with the *sinthome.*

The *sinthome* is perhaps the most hopeful of Lacan's many theoretical positions which he develops in his refashioning of Freudian psychoanalysis. The subject's identification with the *sinthome* allows the subject to live on the margins between the Real, the Symbolic, and the Imaginary (see Lacan's updated Borromean knot, below, which encircles the *sinthome*, the fourth ring). The *sinthome* allows the subject to drink until their thirst is satisfied. But what does Lacan mean?

Traditionally, the symptom was thought to be something which necessitated a cure, and in many ways Lacan's early psychoanalytic task was to

[19] Of course, Lacan was always somewhat speculative: in a review of his doctoral thesis, the *Journal of the American Medical Association* stated 'the third and final part of the book discusses, in a manner that is admittedly speculative, the significance of the paranoid states.' (JAMA 1934: 285).

develop a psychoanalytic cure. However, the late Lacanian gambit is to ask: what if after analysis the subject still clings to their symptom? The moment after the subject has concluded the process of subject formation, when a psychotic subject has gone through the process described by Lacan, recognised their symptom, and the parts of the signifier that have been foreclosed, what if they are still not any better? In *SXXIII*, *The Sinthome*, Lacan seems to argue that all subjects are pathological, marked in one way or another by psychosis. In a sense, Lacan is universalising the psychotic experience, he says:

> There was a time, before I came to the path of analysis, when I was moving down another path, that of my thesis, *De la psychose paranoiaque dans ses rapports*, that's how I put it, *avec la personnalité* [*On paranoid psychosis in its relationships with personality*]. If I resisted the republication of my thesis for so long, it was quite simply because paranoid psychosis and personality as such do not have any relationship, for the simple reason that they are one and the same thing [*c'est parce que c'est la même chose*] (*SXXIII* 41).

Lacan finally makes the argument that has lurked in the background to so much of his work: *homo alienatus*. It was clear but not explicit in *SIII*, *The Psychoses*, that all subjects are psychotics, those the medical establishment label "psychotics" have merely misrecognised a slightly different form of generalised psychosis. Moreover, Lacan's wish to totalise madness across subjectivity follows the impulse already present in his doctoral thesis, where he intimated that madness is not somehow outside humanity and language but a vital part of it, saying: 'before the psychosis, these tendencies are latent' [*avant la psychose, ces tendances sont latentes*] (*De la psychose* 348). Lacan's theoretical impulse had always been to read madness *in* reason, as we saw in our discussion with "Kant with Sade." Lacan dedicates substantial intellectual space to diagnosing what Deleuze and Guattari in *l'Anti-Œdipe* call the '*socius*' (18), and it was only much later that Lacan began thinking, not of a cure, the quest for which he abandoned quite early,[20] but how to offer patients a palliative response to their subjectivity, or how to *send home* patients, the *sinthome*. For Lacan, Joyce

[20] Lacan says: 'to be rid of a symptom, I promise them nothing' [*être débarrassé d'un symptôme, je ne leur promets rien*] (*Scilicet* 32).

seemed to offer the closest approximation of a subject whose work clearly demonstrated the subject's ability to *hold it together.*

The subject is characterised by *une maladie* as Sartre had said, marked by a 'contraction of Being' as Schelling had put it, and the Lacanian mode of life, in the end, is simply a process of *keeping it together* in the face of our madness. And, *stricto sensu*, *that* is the nature of the *sinthome.* This conclusion is striking in its reverberating echo to Sartre and Schelling. We are all ontologically sick but somehow, we *hold it together.* The subject's original sin is that we are all guilty, characterised by a *maladie* at the heart of our being. We 'necessarily' wish for *in itself for itself*, or *~~La~~ femme* (*~~The~~ woman*), to exist, attempting to reunite with God, but this 'impossible' desire to unite *in itself* with *for itself*, to marry permanence and contingency, impossibility and necessity, or simply to love, always seems impossible unless we identify with our madness. Love is simply another word for this madness; it denotes the psychotic subject's *modus operandi*, how to try and fail to identify with the impossible object cause of desire found in *in itself for itself.* To put it in Lacanian terms: we drink until we are no longer thirsty, and although drinking will never quench our thirst, we keep drinking. *Encore, encore, …encore.*

References

Allouch, Jean. 2009. *L'Amour Lacan*. Paris: EPEL.

Bowie, Malcolm. 1991. *Lacan*. Cambridge, MA: Harvard University Press.

Code Civil (*Français*). version consolidée au 21 juillet 2019, (LegiFrance) https://www.legifrance.gouv.fr/affichCode.do?cidTexte=LEGITEXT000006070721. Accessed 15 Apr 2023. English edition: French Civil Code. https://vdocuments.mx/french-civil-code.html?page=1.

Cole, Merrill. 2018. The Queer Repression of Jacques Lacan. In *After Lacan: Literature, Theory, and Psychoanalysis in the Twenty-First Century*, ed. Ankhi Mukherjee. Cambridge: Cambridge University Press.

Gallop, Jane. 1985. *Reading Lacan*. Ithaca: Cornell University Press.

Irigaray, Luce. 1977. *Ce sexe qui n'en est pas un*. Paris: Minuit.

JAMA. 1934. De la Psychose paranoïaque dans ses rapports avec la personnalité. *Journal of the American Medical Association* 103 (04): 285–285.

Lacan, Jacques. 1966. *Écrits*. Paris: Seuil. English edition: Lacan, J. 2006. Écrits. (trans: Fink, B.) London: W.W. Norton & Company.

———. 1973. *Le Séminaire de Jacques Lacan, XXa, Encore (1972–1973)*. Patrick Valas, unpublished transcript. http://www.valas.fr/IMG/pdf/s19.ou_pire.pdf. Accessed 30 July 2022.

———. 1974. *Le Séminaire de Jacques Lacan, XXI, Les Non-dupes errent (1973–1974)*. Patrick Valas, unpublished transcript. http://www.valas.fr/IMG/pdf/S21_NON-DUPES%2D%2D-.pdf. Accessed 30 July 2019.

———. 1975a. *Le Séminaire de Jacques Lacan, Livre XX, Encore (1972–1973)*. Paris: Seuil. English edition: Lacan, J. 1998. The Seminar of Jacques Lacan, Book XX, Encore, (1972–1973). (trans: Fink, B.). London and NY: W.W. Norton & Company.

———. 1975b. *Le Séminaire de Jacques Lacan, Livre I, Les Écrits techniques de Freud (1953–1954)*. Paris: Seuil. English edition: Lacan, J. 1991. The Seminar of Jacques Lacan Book I, Freud's Papers on Technique (1953–1954). (trans: Forrester, J.). London and NY: W.W. Norton & Company.

———. 1975c. Conférences et entretiens dans des universités nord-américaines. In *Scilicet n° 6/7*, 32–37. Paris: Seuil.

———. 1975d. *Le Séminaire de Jacques Lacan, XXII, R.S.I. (1974–1975)*. Patrick Valas, unpublished transcript. http://www.valas.fr/IMG/pdf/s22_r.s.i.pdf. Accessed 30 July 2019.

———. 1975e. *De la psychose paranoïaque dans ses rapports avec la personnalité suivi de Premiers écrits sur la paranoïa*. Paris: Seuil.

———. 2005. *Le Séminaire de Jacques Lacan, Livre XXIII, Le Sinthome (1975–1976)*. Paris: Seuil. English edition: Lacan, J. 2016. The Seminar of Jacques Lacan, Book XXIII, The Sinthome (1975-1976). (trans: Price, A.R.) Cambrige: Polity.

———. 2006. *Le Séminaire: Livre XVI, D'un Autre à l'autre (1968–1969)*. Paris: Seuil.

———. 2011a. *Le Séminaire de Jacques Lacan, Livre XIX, …Ou pire (1971–1972)*. Paris: Seuil. English edition: Lacan, Jacques. 2018. The Seminar of Jacques Lacan, Book XIX, …Or Worse, (1971–1972). (trans: Price, A.R.). Cambridge: Polity.

———. 2011b. *Je Parle Aux Murs*. Paris: Seuil. English edition: Lacan, Jacques. 2017. Talking to Brick Walls. Cambridge: Polity.

———. *Le Séminaire de Jacques Lacan, XIXa, …Ou pire, le savoir du psychanalyste (1971–1972)*. Patrick Valas, unpublished transcript. http://www.valas.fr/IMG/pdf/s19.ou_pire.pdf. Accessed 30 July 2019.

———. *Le Séminaire de Jacques Lacan, XIV, La Logique du fantasme (1966–1967).* Patrick Valas, unpublished transcript. http://www.valas.fr/IMG/pdf/S14_LOGIQUE.pdf. Accessed 14 Apr 2023.

Leader, Darian. 2021. *Jouissance: Sexuality, Suffering, and Satisfaction.* Cambridge: Polity.

Meyer, Catherine. 2005. *Le Livre noir de la psychanalyse: Vivre, penser et aller mieux sans Freud.* Paris: Éditions des Arènes.

Miller, Jacques-Alain. 2007. L'envers de Lacan. *La Cause freudienne* 67 (3): 133–140.

Plato. 2008. *The Symposium,* ed. M.C Howatson, tr. Frisbee C. C. Sheffield. Cambridge: Cambridge University Press.

Rabaté, Jean-Michel. 2001. *Psychoanalysis and the Subject of Literature.* Basingstoke: Palgrave Macmillan.

———. 2014. *The Cambridge Introduction to Literature and Psychoanalysis.* Cambridge: Cambridge University Press.

Sartre, Jean-Paul. 1943. *L'Être et le néant.* Paris: Gallimard. English edition: Sartre, J-P. 2021. Being and Nothingness (trans: Richmond, S.). London and NY: Routledge.

———. 1983. *Cahiers pour une morale.* Paris: Gallimard. English edition: Sartre, J-P. 1992. Notebooks for an Ethics (trans: Pellauer, D.). Chicago: The University of Chicago Press.

Schelling, Friedrich Wilhelm Joseph von. 1997. *Ages of the World: Die Weltalter/ The Abyss of Freedom (second draft, 1813).* Trans: J. Norman. Ann Harbour: University of Michigan Press.

Sophocles. 1982. *Oedipus Rex.* Ed. R.D. Dawe. Cambridge: Cambridge University Press.

St. Pierre, Scott. 2017. Psychoanalytic Thinking and the Sexual Politics of Style. *Criticism* 59 (1): 75–98.

Tricot, Monique. 2006. Jouissance(s) et loi du surmoi. *Che Vuoi?* 25: 143–155.

Warner, Michael. 1990. Homo-narcissism, or Heterosexuality. In *Engendering Men, The Question of Male Feminist,* ed. Joseph A. Boone and Micheal Cadden. London/New York: Routledge.

Žižek, Slavoj. 2002. The Real of Sexual Difference. In *Reading Seminar XX: Lacan's Major Work on Love Knowledge, and Feminine Sexuality,* ed. Susanne Barnard and Bruce Fink. New York: State University of New York Press.

———. 2012. *Less than Nothing, Hegel and the Shadow of Dialectical Materialism.* London/New York: Verso.

6

Conclusion—Hold Me Tight [*Serre-moi fort*]

> [Love is], in essence, an illusion and an infinite referral (Sartre).

> This jouissance of the Other, everyone knows how impossible it is, and contrary even to the myth evoked by Freud, namely that *Eros* is to make one. Yet, that's precisely what kills us, since two bodies can never make one, no matter how tightly they squeeze each other. I didn't go so far as to include it in my text, but the best thing to do in these famous embraces is to say "hold me tight" [*serre-moi fort*] (Lacan).

At the outset of this work, I remarked on the centrality of the French language to Lacan's psychoanalysis. I implied that Lacan's practice was difficult to understand because it was predominantly designed for a French audience, and I am now in a better position to expand on those remarks. Lacan's manipulation of the French language was creative; for example, as many as seven hundred and eighty-nine of his neologisms have been identified and catalogued in *789 néologismes de Jacques Lacan* (2002). However, more than the many neologisms are Lacan's numerous homophonies, many of which I have touched upon, and these suggest much more than I had initially appreciated. For Lacan, homophony

S. Richards, *Dialectics of Love in Sartre and Lacan*, The Palgrave Lacan Series,
https://doi.org/10.1007/978-3-031-45798-2_6

highlights the deep connection *le langage* shares with *lalangue*, since contained in each homophone is its speculative extra, the Real fiction which creates the Symbolic truth (*Troisième* 63–64). For Lacan, the audible speculative extra contained in homophonies signals to the subject that something must exist beyond the confines of language, and, according to Lacan, this is not a coincidence. Instead, it is a structural fact of language itself, giving subjects a clue about the Real. For example, when Lacan says the subject is unable to articulate their subjectivity, '*m'être sujet*' [be myself as subject] (*AÉ* 473), it is because the subject is a prisoner of the desires of the Other—otherwise known as the *signifiant Maître* [Master signifier], where *m'être* is homophonous with *Maître*. When Lacan says the master signifier is *le-Nom-du-Père* [The-Name-of-the-Father], he means not only the name [*nom*] but also the No! [*non*, a homophone of *nom*] of the Father. The formulation in turn becomes "les non-dupes errent" by way of other homophones, and thereby comes to suggest that the subject stood outside of the nexus of signification errs—*les non-dupes-errent.* Lacan explains:

> Lalangue is the concept that enables us to see that it is not by chance that the word 'wish' in French [*vœu* (*souhait*)], is considered to include the want [*veut*] of wanting [*vouloir*], third person indicative, that the 'not' [*non*] in its function of denial and the [*nom*] 'name' in its naming function [*non niant et le nom nommant*], is not by chance either. It is also not by chance that 'of them' [*d'eux*] (where the apostrophe before this "them" is what designates those whom we speak of) is written in the same way as the number: two [*deux/d'eux*], it is not there by pure chance, nor is it arbitrary, as Saussure says. What's necessary to conceive in these moments in language is that it is the deposit, the alluvium, the petrification that is marked by the handling by a group of its unconscious experience.
>
> [Lalangue, c'est ce qui permet que le vœu (souhait), on considère que ce n'est pas par hasard que ce soit aussi le veut de vouloir, troisième personne de l'indicatif, que le non niant et le nom nommant, ce n'est pas non plus par hasard; ni que d'eux (d'apostrophe avant ce "eux" qui désigne ceux dont on parle) ce soit fait de la même façon que le chiffre deux, ce n'est pas là pur hasard ni non plus arbitraire, comme dit Saussure. Ce qu'il faut y concevoir, c'est le dépôt, l'alluvion, la pétrification qui s'en marque du maniement par un groupe de son expérience inconsciente] (*Troisième* 63–64).

For Lacan, it is no accident that *d'eux* [of them] implies at least *deux* [two] in French; that *nom* [name] signals *non* [no!], and, in another possible figurative connection to the visual aspect of Scudéry's *Map of Tender*, Lacan says that homophony is the deposit [*dépôt*], or the alluvium [*alluvion*], of the unconscious. Through an organic force that is a feature of language itself, homophony amasses and deposits signification (for example: *Mer/Mère* in Dangerous Sea/Mother), and—like the movements of a river whose continual motion dislodges and sediments bits of earth forming a new riverbank that finally settles and stabilizes [*pétrification*]—language, as brute matter, becomes ripe for excavation and gentle unearthing only once the homophony signals to the subject that they may begin panning for gold *here* [*/hear*], to discover and learn more about what *lies* beneath.

In "Back and Forth from Letter to Homophony," Milner comments on this 'remarkable' passage in *La Troisième* and reflects on its centrality to Lacan's view of language:

> Homophony is not an addition to the various dimensions of language; it is not an ornamental superstructure that does not modify the foundations of the building. On the contrary, it transforms radically everything that can be theorized about the Unconscious and its relationship to the fact of *lalangue* (2017: 84–5).

Recognising the value of homophones is, for Milner, recognising the subject's radical power in the Symbolic. Moreover, as I said much earlier, in *Écrits*, when Lacan speaks about the *audibility* of the Real, we can now see that Lacan partly meant *homophony*. Homophony offers that speculative extra which might give the subject a clue of what might lie beneath conscious speech—'*Who ails tongue coddeau aspace of dumbillsilly?*

In the third chapter, I discussed what I had called Lacan's *temporary detours*, and I suggested that his intellectual strategy was to posit a fiction that, *retroactively*, threw his central object of study into sharp relief. Lacan's metaphysical method, I believe, resembles the onto-theological method that Schelling pursued in *Die Weltalter*, and, evidently, Lacan's heavy emphasis on God as ~~La~~ *femme* makes his later philosophy similarly onto-theological. I suggested that Lacan posited the fictitious feminine *jouissance* to make clearer the concept of phallic *jouissance*. Indeed, I suggested with *Clelia* that Scudéry opted for a similar strategy, creating the *Terres inconnues* to clarify the prohibition contained in the *Mère dangereuse*. For Lacan, we can never directly access the truth since the truth is only ever *mi-dit* [half-said], because language itself is an imperfect tool for the truth. Therefore, 'Read!' Lacan had said about Aristotle's *Nicomachean Ethics* and Joyce's *Finnegans Wake*, by which he meant that we should not give up trying to reach *lalangue* in language. The odds are stacked against the subject because there is no clear technique for accessing the impossible *lalangue*, but in trying to reach for the impossible, the subject fulfils a necessary aspect of their always already desolate subjectivity.

The subject's dialectical strategy of necessarily reaching for the impossible recurs throughout Lacan's work; for example, in chapter four, I showed how the subject journeys along the path to subject formation, trying to achieve their ideal-ego; however, this process was simply an operation of coming to terms with society's many restrictions, discovering how the big Other creates one's Ego-Ideal. I suggested that symbolic injunctions (or, the desires of the Other) weigh heavily on subjects as they make their way through the process of identification: symbolic castration; the renunciation of *jouissance*; accepting the fantasy; and finally, learning to comply with those desires of the Other. I also suggested that, for Lacan, the subject cannot work outside of this symbolic articulation, the-name-of-the-father [*le Nom-du-Père*], that any attempt to supersede the *Father* was always already accounted for in the subject's articulation within the symbolic frame. There is no doubt that Lacan describes an asphyxiating social theory, leaving the subject no escape, since the subject is necessarily a subject in language, and the Symbolic contains all language. However, I also noted that the speaking being [*l'être parlant*] is happy [*heureux*], because, for Lacan, the subject is ignorant about their imprisonment (*AÉ* 556). The subject is not a subject at all without the necessary deceit [*tromperie*] of the language they deploy, which imprisons them. The deceit is necessary for the subject to survive in the world, and subjects are not supposed to know that they are symbolic prisoners, because, as Lacan puts it: the-non-dupes-err [*les non dupes errent*]. Which is why Lacan's version of loser wins [*qui perd gagne*] is slightly different to

Sartre's version since, for Sartre, the subject needs to experience the loss as a real loss even though they ultimately win, whereas, for Lacan, the loss is not experienced as loss by the happy speaking subject, rather they choose to be ignorant of their loss [*dupes*], and so they suffer peacefully, which is a (linguistic) gain that is finally a necessary loss for the subject: loser wins, but nevertheless! [*qui perd gagne, oui mais quand même!*]

Crucially, however, traumas and anxieties arise, for Lacan, when subjects are exposed to the Real; for example, in the *il n'y a pas de rapport sexuel*, anxiety is engendered by the subject's desire for the impossible *objet petit a* immanent to feminine *jouissance*. Therefore, according to Lacan, from the subject's perspective, the impossible truth [*vérité*] is deeply interlinked with the necessity of knowledge [*savoir*] because we are continually forced to confront those 'bits of the real' [*bouts de réel*] in, for example: homophonies, the *non-rapport sexuel*, and the cry of *das Ding*. Therefore, the subject is qualified as a continually searching subject, and they become less content as they encounter those 'bits of the real' [*bouts de réel*]. As I showed with Lacan's *le sinthome*, the gain that is still a loss is, at the bitter end, a gain once again, should subjects be able to recognise it as such; because the power the subjects had in the Symbolic was a form of power after all. As James Joyce's pre-psychotic trans-linguistry showed, the entire relationship between signifier and signified was shattered, and the sheer fabric of language, grammar, systems of communication, collapsed under the inventiveness of Joyce's translinguistic art. Joyce unearthed those bits of [*bouts de*] *lalangue* that I suggested the subject exhumed from the deposited [*dépôt*] material of language that had been fossilised [*pétrifié*].

As the Borromean knot emphasises, the Real and the Symbolic interlink, and, although the subject can only access the bits of the real [*bouts de réel*] in the Symbolic, it is enough to make the subject nervous and anxious, revealing something beyond the fences encircling our subjectivity. The subject, I suggested, could hear the cry of the Real from inside the Symbolic. I say cry because, as we saw with *das Ding*, the subject perceives the unassimilable *Thing* as the infant's desperate cry transmuted onto the mOther. More often than not, the subject's overwhelming reaction is to castrate the desire for this *Thing*—to get rid of it, to not deal with it, and so, the subject makes the wager, as Lacan put it, they are coerced by the big Other into gambling their bits of *jouissance* in order to suffer peacefully. However, the ominous howling follows the subject in the Symbolic, which is why all subjects are necessarily pre-psychotic, because the mental collapse that could befall a clinical psychotic is identical to the mental collapse which threatens all subjects at all times. Because, by its very structure, the Oedipal complex produces subjects who could decompensate in this way, and Lacan's psychoanalysis aims to show that all subjects are vulnerable to such a collapse—that we could all be affected by the structural failures of the Symbolic itself.[1]

Therefore, for Lacan, the subject is always hanging in the balance, aiming for the impossible but doing so necessarily since there are too many clues for the subject to ignore. One such clue is the *non rapport sexuel*, which is why Lacan qualifies it as a feature of the Real, since the genital act (*SI* 238) is something most subjects will engage in at some stage in their lives, and the subject's bodily awareness of the *non rapport sexuel* resonates with the ontological *disconnection* that Lacan is describing. In their lives, subjects will seek to uncover the object that causes their desires, which the subject necessarily locates in the Other. The Other is the site of their pleasure, the site of all potential answers to all their questions, but nothing guarantees the big Other for the subject, there is no Other of the Other, and when the subject realises this, they are left petrified and alone. Therefore, this Other is a lie, a temporary detour, a fiction, the lie that qualifies the subject as both scared and alone, rather than saying anything substantial about what is (noumenally) beyond—the Other *jouissance*. Therefore, as subjects keep nudging ever closer, hoping to reach the

[1] Lacan's criticism of the Oedipus complex, as outlined here, is one of the reasons that *Anti-Oedipus* is not, as the title might suggest, hostile to Lacanian psychoanalysis, but instead, the works of Deleuze, Guattari, and Lacan may share philosophical connections. As Daniel Smith explained in "The Inverse Side of the Structure," Lacan recognised this connection when he summoned Deleuze to his office shortly after the publication of *AO* in 1972, and, recounting their meeting shortly before his death, Deleuze stated that the purpose of Lacan's invitation was to try and recruit Deleuze as one of his disciples. Lacan found *AO* to be a genuinely original breakthrough to his psychoanalytic project; Smith explaining that what Lacan found in Deleuze was a teachable and 'highly original fellow traveller' (2004: 636), and I believe *AO's* impact on Lacanian psychoanalysis merits further investigation. Indeed, there are numerous such 'impacts' on Lacan's philosophy, and it is worth noting another example, otherwise altogether missing from this work, Philippe Lacoue-Labarthe and Jean-Luc Nancy's *Le Titre de la lettre.* It would be interesting to analyse the ways in which Lacan adapted his ideas in the later seminars in light of seminal criticisms of his practice, as Lacoue-Labarthe and Nancy imply in the preface to the third edition (1990: 9).

Other, they will never find her, and it is for this reason that love is a demand that is never fulfilled—love is continually cast as *Encore*, and instead, the subject finds *(a)mur* [(a)wall] in the Symbolic. However, the subject necessarily continues to seek Love [*Amour*] in the fiction that is God herself—the Other. The subject should not stop searching simply because it is a futile task since, if she/he/they did, she/he/they would be faced with the truly unbearable reality: that there is no God's God, no Other of the Other, which is why, as Scudéry put it, 'Yet if I could get Remedy, I'le rather dye than cure my mind' [*quand il serait guérissable/il est bien plus doux d'en mourir*].

For Lacan, the subject searches for Love [*Amour*], and this continual search is a symptom for a kind of madness, it expresses the psychotic subject's *modus operandi*, how to try and fail to identify with the impossible object cause of desire which lies at the heart of *in itself for itself*, to borrow Sartre's language, and it is here that I am able to connect the argument back to the beginning. Sartre said in *Being and Nothingness*: '[love] is, in essence, an illusion and an infinite referral' [*(l'amour) est, par essence une duperie et un renvoi à l'infini*] (*BN* 499/*EN* 445), which, we can now see, mirrors Lacan's double definition of love. Lacan's psychoanalytic wager was to speculatively imagine *in itself for itself* as ~~The~~ *woman*, since, as Lacan had said, ~~The~~ *woman* is another one of the names of God. ~~The~~ *woman* is the *sinthome* of Man because ~~The~~ *woman* is the impossible and unsayable herself, she is the fictitious marriage of *in itself* with *for itself* as *in itself for itself*, and we can now see—*retroactively*, as it were—that that is why Sartre was unable to erase this Woman-God as *in itself for itself*, because we need to reconcile with her, and identify with her. In a sentence that almost summarises the entire Lacanian paradigm, Sartre says, in *Notebooks for an Ethics*, under different circumstances, 'the spontaneous movement of the For-itself as a lack (on the plane of the unreflective) is to seek the In-itself-For-itself' [*le mouvement spontané du Pour Soi comme manque (sur le plan irréfléchi) est de chercher l'En Soi Pour Soi*] (*NFE* 11/*CPM* 17–8), because, although she might not exist, she necessarily persists, and she is forever impossible to erase.

For Lacan, then, that mystic and baroque philosopher of desolation, the necessity of impossibility is the dialectic inherent in the concept of love. We could say that love (that *pleasing malady*) forces subjects to hold it together in the face of an impossible circumstance. We so desperately want to make two into one, but we cannot, so instead, Lacan says: 'hold me tight' [*serre-moi fort*] (*La troisième* 86).

References

Deleuze, Gilles, and Felix Guattari. 1972. *Anti-Œdipe*. Paris: Minuit.

Lacan, Jacques. 1975b. *Le Séminaire de Jacques Lacan, Livre I, Les Écrits techniques de Freud (1953–1954)*. Paris: Seuil. English edition: Lacan, J. 1991. The Seminar of Jacques Lacan Book I, Freud's Papers on Technique (1953–1954). (trans: Forrester, J.). London/New York: W.W. Norton & Company.

———. *La Troisième, VIIème congrès de l'École freudienne de Paris, Rome 31 Octobre–3 Novembre 1974*. Patrick Valas, (unpublished). http://www.valas.fr/IMG/pdf/la_troisieme_integrale.pdf. Accessed 15 Apr 2023.

———. 2001. *Autres Écrits*. Paris: Seuil.

Lacoue-Labarthe, Philippe, and Jean-Luc Nancy. 1990. *Le Titre de la lettre*. Paris: Galilée.

Milner, Jean-Claude. 2017. Back and Forth from Letter to Homophony. *Problemi International* 1 (1): 81–98.

Pélissier, Yan, Marcel Bénabou, Dominique de Liège, Laurent Cornaz, et al. 2002. *789 néologismes de Jacques Lacan*. Paris: EPEL.

Sartre, Jean-Paul. 1943. *L'Être et le néant*. Paris: Gallimard. English edition: Sartre, J-P. 2021. Being and Nothingness (trans: Richmond, S.). London/New York: Routledge.

———. 1983. *Cahiers pour une morale*. Paris: Gallimard. English edition: Sartre, J-P. 1992. Notebooks for an Ethics (trans: Pellauer, D.). Chicago: The University of Chicago Press.

Smith, Daniel. 2004. The Inverse Side of the Structure, Žižek on Deleuze and Lacan. *Criticism* 46 (4): 635–650.

Bibliography

Allouch, Jean. 2009. *L'Amour Lacan*. Paris: EPEL.

Anzieu, Didier, and Gilbert Tarrab. 1990. *A Skin for Thought Interviews with Gilbert Tarrab on Psychology and Psychoanalysis*. London/New York: Routledge.

Aronson, Nicole. 1986. *Mademoiselle de Scudéry, ou le voyage au pays de Tendre*. Paris: Fayard.

Balmès, François. 2007. *Dieu, le sexe, et la vérité*. Ramonville: Érès.

Barnard, Susanne, and Bruce Fink. 2002. *Reading Seminar XX: Lacan's Major Work on Love Knowledge, and Feminine Sexuality*. New York: State University of New York Press.

Baudelaire, Charles. 1868. *Œuvres complètes de Charles Baudelaire, Tome I, Les Fleurs du mal*. Paris: Michel Lévy Frères, Librairies Éditeurs.

———. 1993. *The Flowers of Evil*. Trans: J. McGowan. Oxford: Oxford University Press.

Baugh, Bruce. 2003. *French Hegel: From Surrealism to Postmodernism*. London/New York: Routledge.

Beasley, Faith E. 2000. Altering the fabric of history. In *A History of Women's Writing in France*, ed. Sonya Stephens. Cambridge: Cambridge University Press.

S. Richards, *Dialectics of Love in Sartre and Lacan*, The Palgrave Lacan Series,
https://doi.org/10.1007/978-3-031-45798-2

Bell, Matthew. 2005. *The German Tradition of Psychology in Literature and Thought, 1700–840*. Cambridge: Cambridge University Press.
Benjamin, Walter. 1999. *Illuminations*. Trans: Harry Zorn. London: Pimlico.
Berlant, Lauren. 2011. *Cruel Optimism*. Durham: Duke University Press.
Borch-Jacobsen, Mikkel. 1990. *Lacan: Le Maître absolu*. Paris: Flammarion.
Bowie, Malcolm. 1991. *Lacan*. Cambridge, MA: Harvard University Press.
Burch, Laura. 2014. New Pleasure in Life Unfolding: Madeleine de Scudéry's Friendship Fan. *Seventeenth-Century French Studies* 36 (1): 4–17.
Butler, Judith. 1987. *Subjects of Desire: Hegelian Reflections in Twentieth Century France*. New York: Columbia University Press.
Chaplin, Charlie. 1940. *The Great Dictator*, DVD.
Chiesa, Lorenzo. 2016. *The Not-Two: Logic and God in Lacan*. Cambridge, MA: MIT Press.
Cole, Merrill. 2018. The Queer Repression of Jacques Lacan. In *After Lacan: Literature, Theory, and Psychoanalysis in the Twenty-First Century*, ed. Ankhi Mukherjee. Cambridge: Cambridge University Press.
Copjec, Joan. 1994. *Supposing the Subject*. London: Verso.
David-Ménard, Monique. 1997. *Les Constructions de l'universel*. Paris: Presses Universitaires de France.
DeJean, Joan. 1991. *Tender Geographies: Women and the Origins of the Novel in France*. New York: Columbia University Press.
Deleuze. 1993. *Critique et clinique*. Paris: Minuit. English edition: Deleuze, Gilles. 1998. *Essays Critical and Clinical*. (trans: Smith, D.W. and Greco, M.A.). London: Verso.
Deleuze, Gilles. 2002. *L'Île déserte et autres textes: Textes et entretiens (1953–1974)*. Paris: Minuit. English edition: Deleuze, G. 2004. Desert Islands and Other Texts (1953–1974). (trans: Taormina, M.). Los Angeles: Semiotext(e).
Deleuze, Gilles, and Felix Guattari. 1972. *Anti-Œdipe*. Paris: Minuit.
Derrida, Jacques. 1990. *Heidegger et la question de l'esprit et autres essais*. Paris: Flammarion.
———. 1998. *Geschlecht III: Sexe, race, nation, humanité*. Paris: Seuil.
Descartes, René. 1996. *Descartes Meditations on First Philosophy, with Selections from the Objections and Replies*. Trans. John Cottingham. Cambridge: Cambridge University Press.
Fanon, Frantz. 2015. *Écrits sur l'aliénation et la liberté*. Paris: La découverte. English edition: Frantz Fanon, Alienation and Freedom, 2018. Eds. Jean Khalfa and Robert J. C. Young. Trans: Steven Corcoran. London: Bloomsbury Academic.

Feyerabend, Paul. 1993. *Against Method.* London/New York: Verso.
Filteau, Claude. 1979. *Le Pays de Tendre: l'enjeu d'une carte.* Littérature No.36.
Fink, Bruce. 1995. *The Lacanian Subject.* Princeton: Princeton University Press.
———. 2004. *Lacan to the Letter: Reading Écrits Closely.* Minneapolis/London: University of Minnesota Press.
———. 2013. *Against Understanding Volume 1: Cases and Commentary in a Lacanian Key.* New York/London: Routledge.
———. 2014. *Against Understanding Volume 2: Cases and Commentary in a Lacanian Key.* New York/London: Routledge.
Frank, Manfred. 1992. *Der Unendliche Mangel an Sein: Schellings Hegelkritik Und Die Anfänge Der Marxschen Dialektik.* Munich: Wilhelm Fink Verlag.
———. 2004a. *The Philosophical Foundations of Early German Romanticism.* Trans. E. Millàn-Zaibert. New York: State University of New York Press.
———. 2004b. Schelling and Sartre on Being and Nothingness. In *The New Schelling,* ed. Judith Norman and Alistair Welchman. London/New York, Continuum.
Freud, Sigmund. 1960. *The Standard Edition of the Complete Psychological Works of Sigmund Freud, Jokes and their Relation to the Unconscious.* Vol. VIII. Trans. James Strachey, Anna Freud, Alix Strachey and Alan Tyson. London: Hogarth Press.
Gallop, Jane. 1985. *Reading Lacan.* Ithaca: Cornell University Press.
Gardner, Sebastian. 2005. Sartre, Intersubjectivity, and German idealism. *Journal of the History of Philosophy* 43 (03): 325–335.
———. 2006. Sartre, Schelling, and Onto-Theology. *Religious Studies* 42 (03): 247–271.
———. 2009. *Reading Being and Nothingness.* London: Continuum.
———. 2011. The Transcendental Dimension of Sartre's Philosophy. In *Reading Sartre on Phenomenology and Existentialism,* ed. Jonathan Webber. New York/ London, Routledge.
Gherovici, Patricia. 2017. *Transgender Psychoanalysis.* London/New York: Routledge.
Goodrich, Peter. 2018. *Schreber's Law: Jurisprudence and Judgment in Transition.* Edinburgh: Edinburgh University Press.
Greisch, Jean. 1994. *Ontologie et temporalité.* Paris: PUF.
Grigg, Russell. 2008. *Lacan, Language, and Philosophy.* Albany: State University of New York.
Hartmann, Klaus. 1966. *Sartre's Ontology: A study of Being and Nothingness in the light Hegel's Logic.* Illinois: Northwestern University Press.

Hayman, Ronald. 1986. *Writing Against: A Biography of Sartre*. London: Weidenfeld and Nicolson.

Hegel, G.W.F. 2010. *The Science of Logic*. Trans. George Di Giovanni. Cambridge: Cambridge University Press.

Heidegger, Martin. 1985. *Schelling's Treatise on the Essence of Human Freedom*. Trans. J. Stambaugh. Ohio/London: Ohio University Press.

———. 2002. *On Being and Time*. Trans. Joan Stambaugh. Chicago: University of Chicago Press.

Henry, Michel. 1993. *The Genealogy of Psychoanalysis*. Stanford: Stanford University Press.

Howells, Christina. 1988. *Sartre: The Necessity of Freedom*. Cambridge: Cambridge University Press.

———. 2011. *Mortal Subjects: Passions of the Soul in Late Twentieth-Century French Thought*. Cambridge: Polity.

Ibbett, Katherine. 2008. Productive Perfection: The Trope of the River in Early Modern Political Writing. In *EMF: Studies in Early Modern France 12*, ed. Anne L. Birberic. Charlottesville: Rookwood Press.

Irigaray, Luce. 1977. *Ce sexe qui n'en est pas un*. Paris: Minuit.

JAMA. 1934. Journal of the American Medical Association's Review: *De la Psychose paranoïaque dans ses rapports avec la personnalité. Journal of the American Medical Association* 103 (04): 285–285.

Kristeva, Julia. 2013. *Pulsions du temps*. Paris: Fayard. English edition: Kristeva, J. 2018. *Passions of Our Time* (trans: Borde, C and Malovany-Chevallier, S.) New York: Columbia University Press.

Krutzen, Henry. 2009. *Jacques Lacan, séminaire 1952–1980, index référentiel*. Paris: Economica.

Kuhn, Thomas. 1996. *The Structure of Scientific Revolutions*. London/Chicago: University of Chicago Press.

Lacan, Jacques. 1960. *Le Séminaire de Jacques Lacan, VIIa, L'Éthique de la psychanalyse, (1959–1960)*. Patrick Valas, unpublished transcript. http://www.valas.fr/IMG/pdf/S7_L_ETHIQUE.pdf. Accessed 30 July 2019.

———. 1966. *Écrits*. Paris: Seuil. English edition: Lacan, J. 2006. Écrits. (trans: Fink, B.) London: W.W. Norton & Company.

———. 1973a. *Le Séminaire: Livre XI, Les Quatre concepts fondamentaux de la psychanalyse (1963–1964)*. Paris: Seuil. English edition: Lacan, Jacques. 1981. The Seminar of Jacques Lacan, Book XI, The Four Fundamental Concepts of Psychoanalysis (1963–1964) (trans: Sheridan, A.). London/New York: W.W. Norton & Company.

———. 1973b. *Le Séminaire de Jacques Lacan, XXa, Encore (1972–1973)*. Patrick Valas, unpublished transcript. http://www.valas.fr/IMG/pdf/s19.ou_pire.pdf. Accessed 30 July 2022.

———. 1974. *Le Séminaire de Jacques Lacan, XXI, Les Non-dupes errent (1973–1974)*. Patrick Valas, unpublished transcript. http://www.valas.fr/IMG/pdf/S21_NON-DUPES%2D%2D-.pdf. Accessed 30 July 2019.

———. 1975a. *Le Séminaire de Jacques Lacan, Livre XX, Encore (1972–1973)*. Paris: Seuil. English edition: Lacan, J. 1998. The Seminar of Jacques Lacan, Book XX, Encore, (1972–1973). (trans: Fink, B.). London/New York: W.W. Norton & Company.

———. 1975b. *Le Séminaire de Jacques Lacan, Livre I, Les Écrits techniques de Freud (1953–1954)*. Paris: Seuil. English edition: Lacan, J. 1991. The Seminar of Jacques Lacan Book I, Freud's Papers on Technique (1953–1954). (trans: Forrester, J.). London/New York: W.W. Norton & Company.

———. 1975c. Conférences et entretiens dans des universités nord-américaines. In *Scilicet n° 6/7*, 32–37. Paris: Seuil.

———. 1975d. *Le Séminaire de Jacques Lacan, XXII, R.S.I. (1974–975)*. Patrick Valas, unpublished transcript. http://www.valas.fr/IMG/pdf/s22_r.s.i.pdf. Accessed 30 July 2019.

———. 1975e. *De la psychose paranoïaque dans ses rapports avec la personnalité suivi de Premiers écrits sur la paranoïa*. Paris: Seuil.

———. 1978a. *Le Séminaire de Jacques Lacan, XV, L'Acte psychanalytique (1967–1968)*. Patrick Valas, unpublished transcript. http://staferla.free.fr/S15/S15%20L%27ACTE.pdf. Accessed 4 Apr 2023.

———. 1978b. *Le Séminaire de Jacques Lacan, XXV, Le Moment de Conclure (1977–1978)*. Patrick Valas, unpublished transcript. http://www.valas.fr/IMG/pdf/s25.pdf. Accessed 4 Apr 2023.

———. 1980. *Le Séminaire de Jacques Lacan, XXVII, La Dissolution, Caracas (12/7/1980)*. Patrick Valas, unpublished transcript. http://www.valas.fr/IMG/pdf/lacan_caracas_12_7_1980_bis_.pdf. Accessed 4 Apr 2023.

———. 1981. *Le Séminaire de Jacques Lacan, Livre III, Les Psychoses (1955–1956)*. Paris: Seuil. English edition: Lacan, J. 1993. The Seminar of Jacques Lacan Book III, The Psychoses, (1955–1956). (trans: Grigg, R.). London/New York: W.W. Norton & Company.

———. 1986. *Le Séminaire de Jacques Lacan, Livre VII, L'Éthique de la psychanalyse (1959–1960)*. Paris: Seuil. English edition: Lacan, J. 1992. The Seminar of Jacques Lacan, Book VII, The Ethics of Psychoanalysis,

(1959–1960). (trans: Porter, RD.). London/New York: W.W. Norton & Company.

———. 1991. *Le Séminaire: Livre XVII, L'Envers de la psychanalyse (1969–1970)*. Paris: Seuil. English edition: Lacan, Jacques. 2007. The Seminar of Jacques Lacan, Book XVII, The Other Side of Psychoanalysis (1969–1970). (trans: Grigg, R.). London/New York: W.W. Norton & Company.

———. 1998. *Le Séminaire de Jacques Lacan, Livre V, Les formations de l'inconscient (1957–1958)*. Paris: Seuil. English edition: Lacan, J. 2017. The Seminar of Jacques Lacan, Book V, The Formations of the Unconscious, (1959–1960). (trans: Grigg, R.). Cambridge: Polity.

———. 2001a. *Le Séminaire de Jacques Lacan, Livre VIII, Le Transfert (1960–1961)*. Paris: Seuil. English edition: Lacan, J. 2015. The Seminar of Jacques Lacan, Book VIII, Transference, (1960–1961). (trans: Fink, B.). Cambridge: Polity.

———. 2001b. *Autres Écrits*. Paris: Seuil.

———. 2004. *Le Séminaire de Jacques Lacan, Livre X, L'Angoisse (1962–1963)*. Paris: Seuil. Lacan, Jacques. 2014. The Seminar of Jacques Lacan, Book X, Anxiety (1962–1963). (trans: Price, A.R.) Cambridge: Polity.

———. 2005. *Le Séminaire de Jacques Lacan, Livre XXIII, Le Sinthome (1975–1976)*. Paris: Seuil. English edition: Lacan, J. 2016. The Seminar of Jacques Lacan, Book XXIII, The Sinthome (1975–1976). (trans: Price, A.R.) Cambrige: Polity.

———. 2006. *Le Séminaire: Livre XVI, D'un Autre à l'autre (1968–1969)*. Paris: Seuil.

———. 2007. *Le Séminaire de Jacques Lacan, Livre XVIII, D'un discours qui ne serait pas du semblant (1970–1971)*. Paris: Seuil.

———. 2011a. *Le Séminaire de Jacques Lacan, Livre XIX, …Ou pire (1971–1972)*. Paris: Seuil. English edition: Lacan, Jacques. 2018. The Seminar of Jacques Lacan, Book XIX, …Or Worse, (1971–972). (trans: Price, A.R.). Cambridge: Polity.

———. 2011b. *Je Parle Aux Murs*. Paris: Seuil. English edition: Lacan, Jacques. 2017. Talking to Brick Walls. Cambridge: Polity.

———. *Le Séminaire de Jacques Lacan, XIXa, …Ou pire, le savoir du psychanalyste* (*1971–1972*). Patrick Valas, unpublished transcript. http://www.valas.fr/IMG/pdf/s19.ou_pire.pdf. Accessed 30 July 2019.

Lacan, Jacques. *Le Séminaire de Jacques Lacan, XIV, La Logique du fantasme (1966–1967)*. Patrick Valas, unpublished transcript http://www.valas.fr/IMG/pdf/S14_LOGIQUE.pdf. Accessed 14 Apr 2023.

Lacan, Jacques. *La Troisième, VIIème congrès de l'École freudienne de Paris, Rome 31 Octobre–3 Novembre 1974*. Patrick Valas, (unpublished). http://www.valas.fr/IMG/pdf/la_troisieme_integrale.pdf. Accessed 15 Apr 2023.

Lacoue-Labarthe, Philippe, and Jean-Luc Nancy. 1990. *Le Titre de la lettre*. Paris: Galilée.

Lakatos, Imre. 1998. Science and Pseudoscience. In *Philosophy of Science: The Central Issues*, ed. Martin Curd and J.A. Cover. New York/London: W. W. Norton & Company.

Laplanche, Jean, and J.-B. Pontalis. 2014. *Vocabulaire de la psychanalyse*. Paris: PUF.

Leader, Darian. 2021. *Jouissance: Sexuality, Suffering, and Satisfaction*. Cambridge: Polity.

Leguil, Clotilde. 2012. *Sartre avec Lacan: Corrélation antinomique, liaison dangereuse*. Paris: Navarin.

Longuenesse, Béatrice. 2012. Kant's 'I' in 'I Ought To' and Freud's Superego: Freud and Philosophy. *Proceedings of the Aristotelian Society* IXXXVI: 19–39.

Malle, Louis. 1958. *Les Amants*, DVD.

Mannoni, Octave. 1969. *Clefs pour l'imaginaire ou l'autre scène*. Paris: Seuil.

Mansfield, Nick. 2000. *Subjectivity: Theories of the Self from Freud to Haraway*. New York: New York University Press.

Marquet, Jean-François. 1973. *Liberté et existence, études sur la formation de la philosophie de Schelling*. Paris: Galimard.

Meyer, Catherine. 2005. *Le Livre noir de la psychanalyse: Vivre, penser et aller mieux sans Freud*. Paris: Éditions des Arènes.

Miller, Jacques-Alain. 2005. Introduction à la lecture du Séminaire *L'Angoisse* de Jacques Lacan. *La Cause freudienne* 59 (1): 65–103.

———. 2007. L'envers de Lacan. *La Cause freudienne* 67 (3): 133–140.

———. 2011. Vie de Lacan. *La Cause freudienne* 79 (3): 305–343.

———. 2012. Préface. In *Sartre avec Lacan: Corrélation antinomique, liaison dangereuse*, ed. Clotilde Leguil, 7–10. Paris: Navarin.

———, *Séminaire X, Donc: La Logique de la cure, (1993–1994)*, cours du 9 mars, (unpublished). http://jonathanleroy.be/wp-content/uploads/2016/01/1993-1994-Donc.-La-logique-de-la-cure-JA-Miller.pdf. Accessed 15 Apr 2023.

Milner, Jean-Claude. 1995. *L'Œuvre claire*. Paris: Éditions du Seuil.

———. 2009. *L'Amour de la langue*. Paris: Verdier. English edition: Milner, J-C. 1990. For the Love of Language (trans: Banfield, A.). New York: The Macmillan Press.

———. 2017. Back and Forth from Letter to Homophony. *Problemi International* 1 (1): 81–98.

Monnier, David. 2011. *Le Réel de l'amour, trois modèles lacaniens*. Rennes: Presses Universitaires de Rennes.

Morel, Geneviève. 2000. *Ambiguïtés sexuelles*. Paris: Anthropos.

Nancy, Jean-Luc. 2001. *L'"Il y a" du rapport sexuel*. Paris: Galilée.

Nicholls, Angus, and Martin Liebscher. 2010. *Thinking the Unconscious: Nineteenth Century German Thought*. Cambridge: Cambridge University Press.

Norman, Judith, and Alistair Welchman. 2004. *The New Schelling*. London/New York: Continuum.

Pélissier, Yan, Marcel Bénabou, Dominique de Liège, Laurent Cornaz, et al. 2002. *789 néologismes de Jacques Lacan*. Paris: EPEL.

Peters, Jeffery. 2004. *Mapping Discord: Allegorical Cartography in Early Modern French Writing*. Newark: University of Delaware Press.

Plato. 2008. *The Symposium*, ed. M.C Howatson, tr. Frisbee C. C. Sheffield. Cambridge: Cambridge University Press.

Popper, Karl. 1998. Science: Conjectures and Refutations. In *Philosophy of Science: The Central Issues*, ed. Martin Curd and J.A. Cover. New York/London: W. W. Norton & Company.

Rabaté, Jean-Michel. 2001. *Psychoanalysis and the Subject of Literature*. Basingstoke: Palgrave Macmillan.

———. 2014. *The Cambridge Introduction to Literature and Psychoanalysis*. Cambridge: Cambridge University Press.

———. 2020. Jacques Lacan's Evanescent Affects. In *Affects and Literature*, ed. Alex Houen. Cambridge: Cambridge University Press.

———. 2021. *Rires prodiges: Rire et jouissance chez Marx, Freud et Kafka*. Paris: Stilus.

Richard, François. 2011. Le Paradigme du Nebenmensch et la fonction maternelle. *Revue française de psychanalyse* 75 (5): 1539–1544.

Richards, Sinan. 2018. Rühre nicht, Bock! denn es brennt. In *Slavoj Žižek and Christianity*, ed. Sotiris Mitralexis and Dionysios Skliris. London: Routledge.

———. 2019. Sartre and Lacan: Reading *Qui Perd Gagne* alongside *Les Non-Dupes Errent*. In *Freedom and the Subject of Theory: Essays in Honour of Christina Howells*, ed. Oliver Davis and Colin Davis. Oxford: Legenda.

———. 2021a. The Logician of Madness: Fanon's Lacan. *Paragraph* 44 (2): 214–237.

———. 2021b. *La Mère dangereuse* Reimagining Scudéry's *Carte de Tendre* with Lacan's *Graph of Desire*. *French Studies* 75 (2): 163–183.

———. A lesson for the world: Solange Faladé's anti-colonial multiracialism, Modern & Contemporary France, 31(4), 435-450.

———. Forthcoming-a. 'I am a clown': Lacan's Difficult Literary Dandyism. *Paragraph*.

———. Forthcoming-b. *Homo Alienatus: Freedom and Psychosis in Lacan and Fanon*. British Academy Monographs. Oxford: Oxford University Press, Forthcoming.

Rose, Jacqueline. 1982. Introduction – II. In *Feminine Sexuality: Jacques Lacan and the École Freudienne*, ed. Jacqueline Rose and Juliet Mitchell. London: The Macmillan Press.

Roudinesco, Élisabeth. 1993. *Jacques Lacan: Esquisse d'une vie, histoire d'un système de pensée*. Paris: Fayard. English edition: Roudinesco, Élisabeth. 1997. Jacques Lacan (trans: Bray, B.). New York: Columbia University Press.

Sartre, Jean-Paul. 1934. *La Transcendance de l'ego*. Paris: Vrin. English edition: Sartre, J-P. 1960. Transcendence of the Ego (trans: Williams, F. and Kirkpatrick, R.). New York: Hill and Wang.

———. 1943. *L'Être et le néant*. Paris: Gallimard. English edition: Sartre, J-P. 2021. Being and Nothingness (trans: Richmond, S.). London/New York: Routledge.

———. 2007 [1946]. *L'Existentialisme est un humanisme*. Paris: Folio Gallimard. English edition: Sartre, J-P. 2007. Existentialism is a Humanism (trans: Macomber, C.). New Haven: Yale University Press.

———. 1947 [1975]. *Baudelaire*. Paris: Folio Gallimard. English edition: Sartre, J-P. 1967. Baudelaire (trans: Turnell, M.). New York: New Directions Paperbook.

———. 1983. *Cahiers pour une morale*. Paris: Gallimard. English edition: Sartre, J-P. 1992. Notebooks for an Ethics (trans: Pellauer, D.). Chicago: The University of Chicago Press.

Saussure, Ferdinand de. 1995. *Cours de linguistique générale*. Paris: Payot. English edition: Saussure, Ferdinand, de. 2011. Course in General Linguistics (trans: Baskin, W.). New York: Columbia University Press.

Schelling, Friedrich Wilhelm Joseph von. 1997. *Ages of the World: Die Weltalter/ The Abyss of Freedom (second draft, 1813)*. Trans. J. Norman. Ann Harbour: University of Michigan Press.

———. 2010. *Philosophy and Religion (1804)*. Trans. Kaus Ottmann. Connecticut: Spring Publications Inc.

Schilpp, Paul Arthur. 1981. *The Philosophy of Jean-Paul Sartre*. Illinois: Open Court Publishing Co.

Schreber, Daniel Paul. 2000. *Memoirs of my Nervous Illness*. Trans. Ida Macalpine and Richard A. Hunter. New York: NYRB.

Scudéry, Madeleine, de. 2001. *Clélie, histoire romaine, Première partie 1654*. Ed. Chantal Morlet-Chantalat. Paris: Honoré Champion. English edition: Scudéry, M.d. 1678. Clelia, An Excellent New Romance: The Whole Work in Five Parts. London: H. Herringman, D. Newman, T. Cockerel, S. Heyrick, E. Cadman, S. Loundes, G. Marriot, W. Crook, and C. Smith.

Seel, Gerhard. 1995. In *La dialectique de Sartre*, ed. Trans E. Müller, Ph. Muller, and M. Reinhardt. Lausanne: L'Age de l'Homme.

Shakespeare, William. 2002. In *The Oxford Shakespeare: Complete Sonnets and Poems*, ed. Colin Burrow. Oxford: Oxford University Press.

Smith, Daniel. 2004. The Inverse Side of the Structure, Žižek on Deleuze and Lacan. *Criticism* 46 (4): 635–650.

Snow, Laurence, and D. 1996. *Schelling And The End of Idealism*. Albany: State University of New York Press.

Soler, Colette. 2003. *Ce que Lacan disait des femmes*. Paris: Éditions du Champ Lacanien.

———. 2006. Lacan en antiphilosophe. *Filozofski vestnik* XXVII (2): 121–144.

———. 2008. Du Parlêtre. *L'En-Je Lacanien* 2: 11.

Sophocles. 1982. *Oedipus Rex*. Ed. R.D. Dawe. Cambridge: Cambridge University Press.

Sorel, Charles. 1667. *La Bibliothèque françoise, de M. C. Sorel premier historiographe de France*. Paris: Compagnie des Libraires du Palais.

St. Pierre, Scott. 2017. Psychoanalytic Thinking and the Sexual Politics of Style. *Criticism* 59 (1): 75–98.

Steigerwald, Jörn. 2008. L'Oiconomie des Plaisirs. La Praxéologie de l'amour galant: à propos de la *Clelia*. *Zeitschrift für französische Sprache und Literatur*, Bd. 118, H. 3.

Tauber, Alfred I. 2010. *Freud, the Reluctant Philosopher*. Princeton/Oxford: Princeton University Press.

Taylor, Helena. 2017. Ancients, Moderns, Gender: Marie-Jeanne l'Héritier's 'le Parnasse Reconnoissant, ou, le Triomphe de Madame Des-Houlières. *French Studies* LXXI (I): 15–30.

Tillich, Paul. 1972. *A History of Christian Thought, from Its Judaic and Hellenistic Origins to Existentialism*. ed. Carl E. Braaten. New York: Simon and Schuster.

Tricot, Monique. 2006. Jouissance(s) et loi du surmoi. *Che Vuoi?* 25: 143–155.

Code Civil (*Français*). version consolidée au 21 juillet 2019, (LegiFrance) https://www.legifrance.gouv.fr/affichCode.do?cidTexte=LEGIT

EXT000006070721. Accessed 15 Apr 2023. English edition: French Civil Code. https://vdocuments.mx/french-civil-code.html?page=1.

Verstraeten, Pierre. 1992. Appendix: Hegel and Sartre. In *The Cambridge Companion to Jean-Paul Sartre*, ed. Christina Howells. Cambridge: Cambridge University Press.

Warner, Michael. 1990. Homo-narcissism, or Heterosexuality. In *Engendering Men, The Question of Male Feminist*, ed. Joseph A. Boone and Micheal Cadden. London/New York: Routledge.

Whyte, Lancelot Law. 1960. *The Unconscious Before Freud*. London: Tavistock Publications.

X, Malcolm. 2003. In ed Marcus D. Pohlmann. *African American Political Thought, Volume 2, Confrontation Vs. Compromise: 1945 to the Present.* New York/London: Routledge.

Zatkin, Emily. 2011. Psychoanalytic Feminism. https://plato.stanford.edu/Archives/Win2012/entries/feminism-psychoanalysis/. Accessed 14 Apr 2023.

Žižek, Slavoj. 1994. *Metastases of Enjoyment: On Women and Causality*. London/New York: Verso.

———. 1997. *The Abyss of Freedom/Ages of the World: Die Weltalter (second draft, 1813)*. Trans. Judith Norman. Ann Harbour: the University of Michigan Press.

———. 2002. The Real of Sexual Difference. In *Reading Seminar XX: Lacan's Major Work on Love Knowledge, and Feminine Sexuality*, ed. Susanne Barnard and Bruce Fink. New York: State University of New York Press.

———. 2012. *Less Than Nothing, Hegel and the Shadow of Dialectical Materialism*. London/New York: Verso.

———. 2016. *Disparities*. London: Bloomsbury.

Zupančič, Alenka. 2017. *What is Sex?* Cambridge, MA: MIT Press.

Index[1]

A

A̸, 146, 148, 150–153, 158, 162, 251
The Absolute, 41n14, 43, 44, 47, 57, 64, 111, 224n5
Algebra, 146
Allouch, Jean, 6n2, 62, 227, 228
Althusser, Louis, 7n3
(A)mur, 217, 220–233, 227n7, 235, 236, 238, 239, 239n11, 241, 242, 252, 265
Anxiety, xvi, 195–198
Anzieu, Didier, 127n5
Aristophanes, 31n3, 86, 220–222, 221n4, 240
Aristotle, 67, 262
Autres Écrits, xv, 7, 64n4, 93, 157, 166, 180, 187, 219, 225, 253, 260, 262

B

Baudelaire, Charles, xvi, 26, 30
Being and Nothingness, 2–4, 3n1, 11, 16, 17, 21–23, 25, 34, 37–39, 40n13, 41, 44, 45, 47, 48, 54, 55, 58, 74, 112, 180, 250, 265
    Pierre, 21, 22, 25, 26, 30–32, 34, 36, 112, 112n25, 243n16
Being-for-itself, 22, 33
Berlant, Lauren, 38n7
Bernini, Gian Lorenzo, 238
Bits of the real, 107, 109, 250, 263
Borromean knot, 43, 215–219, 253, 263
Bowie, Malcolm, 215, 218, 219, 253
Butler, Judith, 36, 39n8

[1] Note: Page numbers followed by 'n' refer to notes.

S. Richards, *Dialectics of Love in Sartre and Lacan*, The Palgrave Lacan Series,
https://doi.org/10.1007/978-3-031-45798-2

C

Castration, 79, 80, 83, 84, 87, 88, 94, 95, 97, 101, 136, 144, 148, 150, 151, 181, 188, 192, 193, 197, 199, 217, 229–231, 234, 235, 242, 245, 247, 251, 252, 262
Che Vuoi, 124, 138, 148, 151, 191, 195, 197
Chiesa, Lorenzo, 101, 105
Copernicus, Nicolaus, 125, 134
Courtly love, 192, 194, 195

D

D'un Autre à l'autre, xvi, 120n3, 221, 222, 225, 234
D'un discours qui ne serait pas du semblant, xvi, 68, 99–101, 172
Das Ding, 118, 188–193, 197, 199–202, 208, 263
Dasein, 139n9, 203
de Scudéry, Madeleine, ix, 11, 110n24, 118, 153–161, 163–180, 183, 188, 209, 236, 261, 262, 265
DeJean, Joan, 162–168, 162n17, 171, 173, 175, 176
Deleuze, Gilles, xv, 5, 15, 16, 21, 22, 250, 254, 264n1
Derrida, Jacques, 102n20
Descartes, René, 64, 107–109, 241
Desire, 6, 10, 11, 16, 17, 22–26, 29, 30, 34–39, 38n7, 44, 47, 48, 58, 63, 64, 71n9, 72–75, 79, 82, 83, 88, 96, 97, 101, 110, 117, 120, 120n3, 122–124, 128, 130, 132, 133, 135–137, 141–153, 156, 158, 161, 162, 176, 177, 179, 181, 182, 190–200, 204–206, 208–210, 217, 225, 231, 234, 238, 240, 242, 243, 250, 251, 255, 263, 265
Desire and Its Interpretation, xv, 120n3
Die Weltalter, 4, 17, 39, 42, 166, 240, 261
Doxa, 155, 169

E

École normale supérieure de Paris, 40n13, 120
Écrits, 4, 66, 70, 71, 73, 77, 80, 83, 91, 92, 123–129, 125n4, 131–137, 140–147, 150–152, 155n11, 161, 167, 187, 198, 201–204, 206, 207, 218, 220, 228, 229
  Presentation on Psychical Causality, 3
Encore, 1, 39, 64n4, 87, 89, 95–100, 97n19, 102–107, 110, 119n1, 120, 120n3, 145, 189, 194, 205, 215, 221–226, 221n4, 230–233, 231n9, 235–243, 239n12, 246, 249, 251, 255, 265
The Ethics of Psychoanalysis
  SVII, 62, 63, 67, 69, 149, 155n11, 156, 162–163, 189–195, 199–202, 225

F

Faladé, Solange, 95n14
The Fall of Man, 11, 24, 39–47, 50, 57, 102, 111, 247

Fanon, Frantz, xv, 47n15, 172
Fantasy, 84, 117, 118, 146–148, 150, 151, 157, 158, 177–180, 183, 191, 197, 205, 206, 209, 210, 220, 233, 234, 238, 250, 251, 262
Fear-of-God, 80, 85
Feminism, 162, 163, 165, 166, 169, 176, 178
Fink, Bruce, 145, 203, 219
Finnegans Wake, 249, 262
Foreclosure, 64, 77–79, 82, 84, 95, 96, 99, 105, 121, 245, 254
For itself, 5, 10, 11, 16, 17, 22–29, 31, 35, 36, 38, 40, 43–45, 47–49, 53–55, 57, 58, 64, 65, 110–112, 151, 195, 255, 265
The Formations of the Unconscious, xv, 120–123, 120n3
The Four Fundamental Concepts of Psychoanalysis, xvi, 62, 120, 174
Frank, Manfred, 39, 39n9, 41
Freedom, 1, 2, 4–6, 15, 17, 24–27, 30, 31, 33, 35–37, 40–45, 47–50, 54, 57, 58n18, 106, 110–112, 176, 178, 209
Freud, Sigmund, xv, 2, 7, 7n3, 16, 63, 63n3, 66, 68, 69, 69n8, 78, 83n12, 89, 101, 119, 125n4, 134n6, 144, 183, 188, 189, 191–193, 198, 199, 207, 259
Freud's Papers on Technique, 16, 63, 70, 119, 135, 155n11, 158, 167, 170, 174, 226, 264

G

Gallop, Jane, 243, 244
Gardner, Sebastian, 39–41, 39n9, 40n11, 40n13, 45, 47, 48, 54, 56–58, 58n18
Gegenbild, 43, 44, 47, 54, 111, 112
Gherovici, Patricia, 83n12
God, x, 4, 6, 10, 23, 25, 29, 39, 40n11, 41n14, 42–50, 53, 57, 58n18, 64, 65, 77, 79, 82, 83n12, 87–89, 99, 102–112, 108n22, 108n23, 151, 152, 161n16, 181, 182, 195, 238, 240, 240n13, 241, 246, 251, 255, 261, 265
  Man-God, 10, 44
  Woman-God, 10
God hypothesis, the, 102, 106
Graph of Desire, 153, 155, 161, 166, 175, 177, 178, 187
Greisch, Jean, 139n9
Guattari, Felix, xv, 254, 264n1

H

Hegel, Georg Wilhelm Friedrich, 24, 26, 32, 37, 38, 39n8, 40, 40n12, 40n13, 43, 45, 51, 63n3, 74, 102, 124, 133, 141
Heidegger, Martin, 27n2, 34, 37, 40n13, 42, 43, 55, 63n3, 102n20, 139, 139n9
Heresy, 215n1, 251–253
Heterosexism, 243, 244
Homo alienatus, 186, 209, 254
Homosexuality, 83n12
Howells, Christina, xi, 4–6, 34–36, 40n12, 67, 70, 180–182, 186

I

Ibbett, Katherine, xi, 161n16
Imaginary, 7, 63, 66, 71–76, 79, 108, 121, 192, 215, 216, 218, 253
In itself, x, 1, 5, 10, 16, 17, 23–25, 27–29, 31, 33, 37, 40, 43–45, 47–49, 51, 53–55, 57, 58, 64, 65, 89, 100, 110–112, 131, 150–152, 195, 197, 210, 232, 251, 255, 265
In itself for itself, x, 10, 16, 17, 23–25, 27, 29, 31, 33, 37, 44, 45, 48, 49, 64, 65, 89, 110–112, 150–152, 197, 210, 232, 251, 255, 265
Irigaray, Luce, 243n14
Ironic, 86, 237
  irony, 80n10, 150, 237, 243

J

Jouissance
  feminine jouissance, 99, 103, 105, 107, 110, 155, 194, 208, 217, 225, 226, 230, 233, 235–238, 241, 243, 251, 263
  phallic jouissance, 97, 102, 235, 236
Joyce, James, 9, 119, 247–254, 247n18, 262, 263

K

Kant, Immanuel, 7n3, 50, 69n8, 102, 197–208, 234, 254
Kant with Sade, 7n3, 50, 197, 198, 204, 205, 207, 234, 254

L

L'Acte psychanalytique, xvi, 64n4, 67
L'être parlant, 157, 160, 160n14, 188, 239, 262
L'Identification, xvi, 221n4
La Dissolution, xvi, 66
La Logique du fantasme, xvi, 93, 99, 220
La Troisième, xvi, 260, 261
Lacan's doctoral thesis
  De la psychoses, 172n21, 227, 254
Lalangue, 8, 9, 188, 217, 218, 226, 227, 260–263
Law, 76, 77, 85, 102, 119, 131–133, 150, 160, 162, 176–178, 193, 198–204, 206, 207, 209, 232, 233, 245
Leader, Darian, 237
Leguil, Clotilde, 2, 6, 8, 63n3
Le Moment de conclure, xvi, 7n3
Les Non-dupes errent, xvi, 178, 180–182, 184, 185, 209, 222, 245, 252, 260
Les Temps Modernes, 3
Loser Wins, 180–184, 186, 209, 224–225, 262
Love, ix, x, 1, 4, 9, 10, 16, 27, 30–33, 48–58, 177, 179, 218, 221, 223, 225, 229–231, 236, 239, 243, 255, 265

M

Madness, vii, 1, 3, 4, 82, 169, 170, 172, 209, 254, 255, 265
Malcolm X, 136, 136n8
Malle, Louis, 145
Mannoni, Octave, 182, 183

Map of Tender, 110n24, 153, 156, 159, 163n18, 168, 171, 174, 180, 187, 209, 261
Marquet, Jean-François, 41, 42, 46
Master signifier, 64, 76, 77, 85–89, 95, 97, 98, 102, 107, 117, 121, 122, 128, 133, 135, 139, 144, 151, 152, 160, 175, 180, 181, 186, 209, 217, 230, 232, 236, 237, 241, 248, 250, 253, 260
  A-father, 80, 81
M'être, 63, 187, 209, 260
Miller, Jacques-Alain, 2, 3, 3n1, 104n21, 153, 156, 187, 195, 217
Milner, Jean-Claude, 9, 120n2, 160n14, 261
Mirror stage, 72–74, 137, 140, 217
  mirror stage part II, 137
Molière, 86, 156, 163
Morel, Geneviève, 102, 188

N

Name-of-the-Father, 76, 77, 79, 80, 82, 95, 95n15, 96, 144, 159, 160, 180, 181, 252
  Nom-du-Père, 76, 79, 82, 83, 95, 96, 144, 152, 159, 160, 180, 181, 184, 186, 252, 260, 262
Nancy, Jean-Luc, 107, 264n1
Necessary, necessity, ix, x, 10, 11, 24, 30, 37, 38, 45, 46, 49, 52, 54, 56, 58, 64, 69, 71, 103, 105, 109, 112, 113, 118, 122, 127, 132, 133, 137, 150, 151, 153, 155, 161, 165, 167, 172, 179–182, 186, 188, 194, 196, 198–200, 203, 208–210, 218, 222–226, 230, 231, 239, 245, 247, 248, 251–253, 255, 260, 262, 263, 265
Non-rapport sexuel, 99, 127, 155, 157, 158, 162, 173, 175, 177, 186, 188, 218–223, 225, 226, 229, 236, 239, 243, 245, 246, 263, 264

O

Objet petit a, 197, 208, 239–246
  object small *a*, 197, 206, 225
Oedipus complex, 76, 77, 82, 95, 150, 151, 199, 244, 245, 264n1
Ontologically sick, 47n15, 255
  maladie, 46, 47, 120, 185, 221, 255
. . . or Worse, xvi, 156, 160, 181, 221, 221n4, 225, 226n6, 227n7, 236, 244
The Other Side of Psychoanalysis, xvi, 63, 64, 97, 188, 209
...Ou pire, le savoir du psychanalyste (conférences à Saint-Anne), xvi, 227, 227n7, 228n8, 229, 231, 240n13

P

Parlêtre, 157, 188, 217
Phallic Φx, 77, 80, 83, 85, 88, 95–98, 100–105, 107, 155, 208, 217, 223, 225, 226, 231–238, 241, 243, 244, 251, 252, 262

Phallus, 79, 85, 85n13, 86, 98, 99, 105, 183, 223, 243n15, 244
Plato, 31n3, 220, 221, 221n4
The Psychoses, xv, 63, 65, 66, 68–83, 69n8, 85, 87, 88, 91, 102, 107–111, 119n1, 121, 127, 141, 149, 155, 156, 167, 171, 173, 175, 181, 247, 254

Q

Quilting point, 69, 86–89, 91, 105, 117, 119, 120, 122, 128, 175

R

Rabaté, Jean-Michel, xi, 2, 3, 5–7, 16n1, 86, 91, 215n1, 247, 247n18, 249
Racine, Jean, 16n1, 87, 88, 188
Real, 7–9, 9n4, 66, 68, 71, 73, 79, 107, 108, 126, 151, 153, 155, 158, 162, 166, 167, 169, 171–173, 178, 182–186, 188, 192, 196, 197, 201, 215–220, 229, 236, 238, 239, 248, 252, 253, 260, 261, 263, 264
Recul néantisant, 27, 40
Rose, Jacqueline, 85n13
R.S.I., xvi, 7, 129, 215, 215n1, 218

S

Saussure, Ferdinand de, 2, 3, 8, 63n3, 89–91, 122, 126, 260
Schelling, Friedrich Wilhelm Joseph, vii, xvi, 4, 6, 7n3, 10, 11, 17, 24, 29, 38–54, 39n9, 41n14, 56–58, 58n18, 64, 69n8, 99, 102, 105, 106, 110–112, 120, 139n9, 166, 217–218n2, 221, 224n5, 240, 240n13, 241, 246, 247, 255, 261
Schreber, Daniel Paul, 78, 79, 82–84, 83n12, 155, 244, 245, 247, 248
Sexuality, 8, 85, 85n13, 86, 94, 95, 100, 102, 107, 237, 244
Shakespeare, William, 119, 185
Sinthome, x, 8, 62, 106, 119, 170, 186, 215, 217, 221, 225, 243, 245, 247–255, 263, 265
Soler, Colette, 7n3
Soul, 35, 50, 155
Subjectivity, x, 4, 7, 17, 27, 31, 34–36, 38, 40n11, 50, 54, 56, 63, 64, 66, 69, 70, 84, 85n13, 109, 149, 152, 170, 178, 180, 185, 234, 238, 243, 245, 254, 260, 262, 263
Surplus enjoyment, 208, 225, 233–236
Symbolic, 7–9, 11, 63, 66, 70–74, 76–82, 84–86, 88, 89, 92, 95, 96, 98, 107, 108, 110, 119, 121, 133, 140, 142, 144, 146, 148, 150, 152, 153, 155, 175, 179, 181–183, 186, 192, 197, 208, 209, 215–220, 222, 229, 236, 239, 239n11, 241, 245, 247–249, 252, 253, 260–263, 265

T

Talking to Brick Walls, xvi
Temporary detours, 11, 103, 261

There is no sexual relationship, 62, 64, 77, 93, 95, 99, 107, 153, 158, 177, 220
Transference, xv, 137–140, 163n18
Truth, vii, 8–10, 42, 51, 69, 80, 81, 93, 94, 99, 106, 107, 111, 112, 121–128, 144, 152, 159, 175, 180–182, 185–187, 198, 201, 218, 219, 225, 229, 230, 240, 248, 249, 251–253, 260, 262, 263

U

The Unconscious, 9, 10, 52, 52n17, 53, 62, 66, 68–70, 69n8, 74, 76, 78, 89, 91, 93, 100, 103, 126, 127, 127n5, 146, 173, 182–185, 187, 188, 199–201, 217, 217n2, 218, 227, 231, 238, 248–250, 260, 261
structured like a language, 62, 68, 70, 127, 184, 249, 250

V

Verwerfung, 78, 79

Z

Žižek, Slavoj, 46, 53, 84, 87, 102, 106, 107, 250–252
Zupančič, Alenka, 90–92, 96n17

GPSR Compliance
The European Union's (EU) General Product Safety Regulation (GPSR) is a set of rules that requires consumer products to be safe and our obligations to ensure this.

If you have any concerns about our products, you can contact us on

ProductSafety@springernature.com

In case Publisher is established outside the EU, the EU authorized representative is:

Springer Nature Customer Service Center GmbH
Europaplatz 3
69115 Heidelberg, Germany

www.ingramcontent.com/pod-product-compliance
Lightning Source LLC
Chambersburg PA
CBHW071924011225
36163CB00005B/339
* 9 7 8 3 0 3 1 4 5 7 9 7 5 *